Mozambique and Brazil

Mozambique and Brazil

Forging New Partnerships or Developing Dependency?

Edited by Chris Alden, Sérgio Chichava
and Ana Cristina Alves

First published by Fanele, an imprint of
Jacana Media (Pty) Ltd in 2017

10 Orange Street
Sunnyside
Auckland Park 2092
South Africa
+27 (0)11 628 3200
www.jacana.co.za

© Individual contributors, 2017

All rights reserved.

ISBN 978-1-928232-37-7

Cover design publicide
Set in Bembo 10.9/14pt
Printed and bound by Shumani Mills Communications,
Parow, Cape Town
Job no. 003046

See a complete list of Jacana titles at www.jacana.co.za

Contents

List of acronyms and abbreviations vii

List of contributors xii

Introduction Mozambique and Brazil (Sérgio Chichava, Ana Cristina Alves and Chris Alden) 1

Chapter 1 Brazil–Mozambique relations: From the geopolitics of the Cold War to South–South cooperation (Analúcia Danilevicz Pereira and João Marcos Tatim) 9

Chapter 2 Brazil, Mozambique and the PALOP: An analysis of high-level relations and policy stances (Kamilla Raquel Rizzi and Nathaly Xavier Schutz) 26

Chapter 3 What Brazil–Mozambique relations tell us about South–South cooperation (Robert Myles McDonnell) 46

Chapter 4 The role of Brazil in the consolidation of an extractive model of development in Mozambique (Carolina Milhorance) 65

Chapter 5 Brazilian interventions in the Nacala Corridor development programme: From rhetoric to practice in South–South development cooperation (Isabela Nogueira de Morais and Ossi I Ollinaho) 87

Chapter 6 Brazil in international cooperation: A study of the ProAlimentos project in Mozambique (Natalia N Fingermann) 107

Chapter 7 Civil society and the opposition to ProSavana in Mozambique: End of the line? (Sérgio Chichava and Chris Alden) 130

Chapter 8 Foreign direct investment inflows and transfer of tacit knowledge: The case of the Brazilian company Cine Group in Mozambique (Roberto Gonzalez Duarte, José Márcio de Castro and Renata Borges Guimarães) 144

Chapter 9 Mediascapes of Brazil's investments in Mozambique: Reporting on the Tete-Nacala Development Hub in the Brazilian press (Potyguara Alencar dos Santos)..........................160

Chapter 10 Brazilian South–South cooperation in public health: Dilemmas of the ARV factory initiative (Adriana Abdenur and Danilo Marcondes) 173

Chapter 11 Resettled by Coal: Vale in Mozambique (Joana Pedro)..194

Chapter 12 Cultural exchange between Brazil and Mozambique: The positive impact of the activities of the Maputo Theatre of the Oppressed Group (Elizabete Sanches Rocha)..................214

Chapter 13 The culture politics of Brazilian Christianity in Mozambique (Linda van de Kamp) 235

Conclusion Beyond partnership and dependency? (Sérgio Chichava, Ana Cristina Alves and Chris Alden)...............261

Index 268

Acronyms and abbreviations

AAJC	Association of Support and Legal Assistance to Communities (Mozambique)
AAPAS	Solidary Literacy Programme Support Association (Mozambique)
ABC	Brazilian Cooperation Agency (*Agência Brasileira de Cooperação*)
ACFI	Investment Cooperation and Facilitation Agreement
Adecru	Academic Action for the Development of Rural Communities
AIC	African Independent Church
AJF	Africa–Japan Forum
AMETRAMO	National Association of Traditional Healers (Mozambique)
ANVISA	Brazil's National Health Surveillance Agency
ARVs	antiretroviral drugs
BNDES	Brazilian Development Bank
BRICS	Brazil, Russia, India, China and South Africa
BRT Maputo	Maputo Bus Rapid Transport
CAADP	Comprehensive African Agriculture Development Programme
CajuPaNa	Justice and Peace Commission of the Nampula Archdiocese
CCDM	Citizens Concerned with the Development of Mozambique
CDJPN	Nacala Diocesan Justice and Peace Commission
CIP	Centre for Public Integrity (Mozambique)
CNCS	National HIV/AIDS Council (Mozambique)
CPLP	Community of Portuguese Language Countries (*Comunidade dos Países de Língua Portuguesa*)
CRIS	Centre for International Relations in Health (Brazil)
CSOs	civil society organisations
DAC-OECD	Development Assistance Committee of the Organisation for Economic Cooperation and Development
DFID	Department for International Development (United Kingdom)

DNTF	Directorate of Forestry and Land (Mozambique)
ECOSOC	United Nations Economic and Social Council
Embrapa	Brazilian Agricultural Research Corporation
ENDE	National Development Strategy, 2015–2035 (Mozambique)
FAO	Food Agricultural Organization (United Nations)
FDA	Agricultural Development Fund (Mozambique)
FDI	foreign direct investment
FGV	Getúlio Vargas Foundation
Fiocruz	Oswald Cruz Foundation (*Fundação Oswaldo Cruz*)
Fonagni	Niassa Forum of Non-governmental Organisations
Fongza	Forum of Zambézia Non-governmental Organisations
FRELIMO	Mozambique Liberation Front
GIZ	German Cooperation Agency (*Deutsche Gesellschaft für Internationale Zusammenarbeit*)
GTO-Maputo	The Maputo Theatre of the Oppressed Group
GPZ	Zambezi Valley Development Planning Office
HPG	Health Partners Group (Mozambique)
IBSA	India–Brazil–South Africa (Dialogue Forum, also called the G-3)
ICTC	International Centre for Technical Cooperation
IDC	international development cooperation
IFAD	International Fund for Agricultural Development
IIAM	Mozambican Agricultural Research Institute
IILP	International Portuguese Language Institute (*Instituto Internacional da Língua Portuguesa*)
ILC	International Land Coalition
IMF	International Monetary Fund
INEFP	Mozambique's National Employment and Professional Training Institute
IPE	international political economy
IR	international relations
IURD	Universal Church of the Kingdom of God
JA	Environmental Justice (*Justiça Ambiental*, Mozambique)
JBPP	Japan–Brazil Partnership Programme
JICA	Japanese International Cooperation Agency
JIRCAS	International Agricultural Science Research Centre of Japan
JVC	Japan International Volunteer Centre
LDH	Human Rights League
MANU	Mozambique African National Union
MASA	Ministry of Agriculture (Mozambique)

MCSC	Civil Society Mechanism for the Development of the Nacala Corridor
MCSO	Mozambican civil society organisations
MDA	Ministry of Agrarian Development (Brazil)
MDGs	Millennium Development Goals
MDM	Mozambique Democratic Movement
MIC	Ministry of Trade (Mozambique)
MINAG	Mozambique Ministry of Agriculture
MINED	Mozambican Ministry of Education
MIREM	Ministry of Mines (Mozambique)
MISAU	Mozambican Ministry of Health
MMM	World March of Women
MNC	multinational company
MONASCO	Mozambican Aids Organisation
MPLA	People's Movement for the Liberation of Angola
MRE	Ministry of Foreign Affairs (Brazil)
NSC	North–South cooperation
OAU	Organisation of African Unity
ODA	Official Development Assistance
OECD	Organisation for Economic Development
OMR	Countryside (Rural) Observatory
ONUMOZ	United Nations Operation in Mozambique
ORAM	Rural Mutual Aid Association (Mozambique)
OSCM	Mozambican civil society organisations
PAE	Economic Recovery Programme, Mozambique (*Programa de Reabilitação Econômica*)
PALOP	Portuguese-speaking African countries (*Países Africanos de Língua Oficial Portuguesa*)
PASMO	Solidary Literacy Programme (Mozambique)
PCT	Cooperation Technical Project (*Projeto Técnico de Cooperação*)
PEC	Student Agreement Programme (*Programa Estudantes Convênio*)
PEDSA	Agricultural Sector Development Strategic Plan (Mozambique)
PEI	Independent Foreign Policy, Brazil (*Política Externa Independente*)
Piait	Agricultural Research and Technological Innovation Platform
Pnisa	National Agricultural Sector Investment Plan (Mozambique)
PPOSC-N	Nampula Provincial Platform of Civil Society Organisations
PRAI	Principle of Responsible Agricultural Investment (ProSavana)

PRE	Economic Reconstruction Programme, Mozambique (*Programa de Reabilitação Econômica*)
PRN	Party of National Reconstruction, Brazil
PSDB	Brazilian Social Democracy Party
Producer	Brazilian Programme for the Development of the Cerrado
ProSavana	Programme of Triangulated Cooperation for Agricultural Development of the Tropical Savannahs of Mozambique
QIP	Quick Impact Projects
Radeza	Network of Organisations for the Environment and Sustainable Development of Zambézia
RAP	Resettlement Action Plan
RENAMO	Mozambique National Resistance Movement
SADC	Southern African Development Community
SENAI	National Service for Industrial Training, Brazil (*Serviço Nacional de Aprendizagem Industrial*)
SENAC	National Commercial Apprenticeship Service, Brazil (*Serviço Nacional de Aprendizagem Comercial*)
SICAR	Investment Company Risk Capital
SMM	Mozambican Pharmaceutical Association (*Sociedade Moçambicana de Medicamentos*)
SSC	South–South cooperation
SSDC	South–South development cooperation
SWAp	sector-wide approach (to health, Mozambique)
TCDC	Technical Cooperation between Developing Countries
TCTP	Third Countries Training Programme
TRIPS	Agreement on Trade-Related Aspects of Intellectual Property Rights
UAB	Open University of Brazil
UDENAMO	National Democratic Union of Mozambique
UEM	Eduardo Mondlane University
UN	United Nations
Unac	National Union of Peasants (Mozambique)
UNAMI	National African Union for Independent Mozambique
UNAVEM	United Nations Angola Verification Mission
UNCTAD	United Nations Conference on Trade and Development
UNDP	United Nations Development Programme
UNESCO	United Nations Educational, Scientific and Cultural Organization
UNGA	United Nations General Assembly
UNICEF	United Nations Children's Fund

ACRONYMS AND ABBREVIATIONS

UNUMOZ	United Nations Operation in Mozambique
USAID	US Agency for International Development
WHO	World Health Organization
WTO	World Trade Organization
WWF	World Wide Fund for Nature
ZEE	Special Economic Zones
ZOPACAS	South Atlantic Peace and Cooperation Zone

Contributors

PROFESSOR CHRIS ALDEN teaches International Relations at the London School of Economics and Political Science (LSE), a senior research associate with the South African Institute of International Affairs (SAIIA) and a research associate of the Department of Political Sciences, University of Pretoria. Professor Alden taught International Relations at the University of the Witwatersrand from 1990 to 2000 where he conducted research into emerging powers and Africa, South African foreign policy and post-conflict peace building. His most recent publications are 'South Africa's Symbolic Hegemony in Africa' (with Maxi Schoeman), *International Politics* 52, 2015, pp. 239–254; *China and Mozambique: From comrades to capitalists* (Jacana 2014) co-edited with Sergio Chichava; *Emerging Powers in Africa*, editor and contributor (London: LSE IDEAS 2013), and *Mozambique and the Construction of the New Africa State* (Palgrave 2001). j.c.alden@lse.ac.uk

DR SERGIO CHICHAVA is a senior researcher at the Institute of Social and Economic Studies (IESE) in Mozambique, where he leads a new research programme on rising powers and development. Chichava has lectured in the Sociology of Politics and Mozambican Politics at Eduardo Mondlane University, Maputo and has held fellowships at Oxford University and the London School of Economics and Political Science (LSE). His recent work focuses on the role of China and Brazil in Mozambique's agriculture sector. His most recent publications are: *China and Mozambique: From comrades to capitalists* (Jacana 2014) co-edited with Chris Alden; Mozambican elite in a Chinese rice 'friendship': an ethnographic study of the Xai-Xai irrigation scheme, *Future Agriculture Consortium Working Paper* 111 (2015); 'Chinese and Brazilian Agricultural Models in Mozambique: the case of the Chinese Agricultural Technology Demonstration Centre and of the Brazilian ProALIMENTOS Programme', *Future Agriculture Consortium Working Paper* 111 (with Natália Fingermann). chichava@gmail.com

CONTRIBUTORS

DR ANA CRISTINA ALVES is Assistant Professor at Nanyang Technological University (School of Humanities and Social Sciences – Public Policy and Global Affairs Programme) Singapore. She was a Senior Research Fellow at the South African Institute of International Affairs (SAIIA, Johannesburg) from 2010 until 2014 and has published extensively on emerging powers in Africa. Her latest publications include 'China and Brazil in Sub-Saharan African Fossil Fuels: A Comparative Analysis', in S. Scholvin (ed.), *A New Scramble for Africa: The Rush for Energy Resources in Sub-Saharan Africa* (Farnham: Ashgate, 2015); 'China's Economic Statecraft in Africa: continuity and change' (2015) *Harvard Asia Quarterly*, 8(1), pp. 4–12; 'Chinese Economic Statecraft: A Comparative Study of China's Oil-backed Loans in Angola and Brazil' (2013) *Journal of Current Chinese Affairs*, 42 (1) pp. 99–130; *Brazil–Africa Technical Cooperation: Structure, achievements and challenges*, Policy Briefing, SAIIA (August 2013).
anacristina@ntu.ed.sg

DR ADRIANA ERTHAL ABDENUR (PhD Princeton, AB Harvard) is a Fellow at Instituto Igarapé and Collaborating Researcher at the Brazilian Naval War College. She is also a consultant for the UN Department of Economic and Social Affairs and sits on the Advisory Board of the Department of Political Affairs' internal reviews for field-based conflict prevention and resolution. Her work focuses on the role of rising powers in development cooperation, international security, and global governance, especially within the UN and the BRICS.
adriabdenur@gmail.com

DR KAMILLA RAQUEL RIZZI is an assistant professor of International Relations at the Federal University of Pampa (UNIPAMPA. She has a PhD in Political Science, a master's in International Relations and graduated in History from the Federal University of Rio Grande do Sul (UFRGS). She is a research associate of the Brazilian Center for African Studies (CEBRAFRICA / UFRGS and GeAFRIA / UNIPAMPA. Her research involves the Brazilian Foreign Policy for Portuguese Africa.
kamillarizzi@unipampa.edu.br

DR NATHALY XAVIER SCHÜTZ is an assistant professor of International Relations at the Federal University of Pampa (UNIPAMPA). She has degree in International Relations from the Federal University of Rio Grande do Sul (2008), a master's degree (2011) and a PhD in Political Science (2014) from the Federal University of Rio Grande do Sul and is a research associate of CEBRAFICA. Her interests are in the areas of Africa, Integration, and International Relations Theory.
nathalyschutz@unipampa.edu.br

Dr Natalia N. Fingermann holds a PhD in Public Administration and Government at the FGV-SP and a master's of Social Development from the University of Sussex. She currently serves as coordinator, researcher and professor of the Bachelor of International Relations at Senac University Center, as well as an independent consultant in international relations. Her research areas include: relationships between the emerging economies in sub-Saharan Africa, South–South Cooperation, Brazil's foreign policy and international public policy.
nataliafinger@yahoo.com.br

Dr Analúcia Danilevicz Pereira has a PhD in History and is Professor of International Relations and Graduate in International Strategic Studies Program at the Federal University of Rio Grande do Sul, Brazil. Pereira is also a Researcher at the Brazilian Center for Strategy and International Relations – NERINT/UFRGS and a coordinator of the Brazilian Center of African studies CEBRAFRICA/UFRGS.
ana.danilevicz@ufrgs.br

Dr Roberto Gonzalez Duarte is a Professor of the Department of Administrative Sciences, Federal University of Minas Gerais. He holds a doctorate in Business Administration from the University of Cambridge (UK). His research interests include international transfer of knowledge, technology and organizational practices, mergers and acquisitions, foreign investment, and Mozambique.
rgonzalezduarte@gmail.com

Dr José Márcio de Castro is a professor of the Graduate Program in Business Administration at the Catholic University of Minas Gerais, Brazil. He holds a doctorate in Business Administration from USP / SP, University of São Paulo. His research interests include Innovation and inter-firm knowledge transfer, Organizational networks and knowledge transfer, absorptive capacity of organisations, and knowledge management.
josemarcio@pucminas.br

Dr Renata Simões Guimarães e Borges is a professor in the Department of Administrative Sciences, Federal University of Minas Gerais. She has a PhD in Business Administration from Southern Illinois University. Her research interests include tacit knowledge transfer, innovation, organisational culture, social networking and motivation at work.
renatasg@face.ufmg.br

Contributors

Dr Isabela Nogueira de Morais is a professor of Economic Development at the Economics Institute (EI) and of the Graduate Program in International Political Economy (PEPI) of the Federal University of Rio de Janeiro (UFRJ). She conducts research in the areas of economic and social development, wealth distribution and income, and international development cooperation.
isabela.nogueira@ie.ufrj.br

Joao Marcos Tatim holds a degree in International Relations at EPSM-RS and is currently researching South–South Cooperation and Brazilian foreign policy at the Federal do Rio Grande do Sul (UFRGS).

Dr Ossi Ollinaho had a PhD from Aalto University and is a lecturer in the Department of Sociology at the Institute of Philosophy and Social Sciences (IFCS) of the Federal University of Rio de Janeiro (UFRJ). He conducts research in the area of sociology of knowledge, social theory, environmental sociology and agricultural development.
ossi.ollinaho@gmail.com

Elga Lessa is a professor at the Reconcavo Federal University of Bahia / Brazil and researcher at the Laboratório de Análise Política Mundial – LABMUNDO/UFBA. Her research is focused on recognition policies and social movements, South-South cooperation and relations between Brazil and African countries in the contemporary context.
elgalessa@yahoo.com.br

Dr Elsa Sousa is a professor at the Federal University of Bahia, Brazil where she teaches International Relations in administration graduate programmes. Her research focuses on interdisciplinary character in the social sciences, emphasising the theme of development, especially in the International Cooperation Analysis for Development and International Organizations Studies.
ekraychete@hotmail.com

Dr Linda van de Kamp is an assistant professor at the Department of Sociology, University of Amsterdam, the Netherlands. Her research activities concentrate on religion, South–South transnational connections, gender and reproductive issues, cities, violence and insecurity. She has done in-depth research on the emergence of Brazilian Pentecostalism in Mozambique. Various Pentecostal churches, preachers of Brazilian origin and elements of Brazilian cultural styles have become influential, and provide Pentecostalism in Mozambique with a transnational dimension that is oriented on South–South relations.
lvandekamp@ascleiden.nl

Dr Danilo Marcondes de Souza Neto received his PhD from the University of Cambridge and is a fellow of the CAPES – Cambridge Trust. He served as Professor at the Institute of International Relations at the Catholic University of Rio de Janeiro (PUC-Rio) between 2010 and 2012. His areas of research include Brazilian foreign policy, South–South Cooperation and international relations within the South Atlantic.
dm595@cam.ac.uk

Potyguara Alencar dos Santos is a PhD candidate in Social Anthropology from the University of Brasilia (PPGAS / UNB), and researcher of the Study of Globalization and Development Laboratory (LEG /UNB) and Labour Studies Group and Capitalist Transformation (GET / UFC). He conducts ethnographic research focused on social movements, the right to territoriality, knowledge and state interests.
potyguara.alencar@gmail.com

Joana Pedro is an environmental engineer and has developed her professional career in the private sector in the field of Environmental Impact Assessment (EIA) and Action Plans for Resettlement (PAR). Joana has a master's degree in Environmental Engineering, from the New University of Lisbon and a master's in International Development from the University Institute of Lisbon. During the latter Joana developed her research thesis on forced resettlement in Tete province, Mozambique. Joana currently lives in South Africa and has been involved in projects in Portugal, Angola, Mozambique (where she lived for about four years) and Malawi.
joanajcpedro@gmail.com

Dr Carolina Milhorance de Castro is a researcher at the Center for Sustainable Development, University of Brasìlia. She has published on South–South Cooperation and development issues with a special focus on Brazil and Mozambique in numerous international journals.
cmilhorance@gmail.com

Robert Myles McDonnell is a doctoral candidate in International Relations at the International Relations Institute of the University of São Paulo (USP) and researcher of the International Negotiations Studies Center (CAENI). His research interests include foreign policy, the link between domestic sectors and international politics, roll calls and Bayesian methods for social sciences.
robertmcdonnell@usp.br

ELIZABETE SANCHES ROCHA is a lecturer and researcher at the Universidade Estadual Paulista (UNESP), working in the Department of International Relations Faculty of Humanities and in the Graduate Program in Literary Studies , Faculty of Science and Letters of Araraquara. She is the head of the Center for Language and Cultural Studies (NELC). Her areas of research include theatrical theories and analysis, theatre of the oppressed, cultural studies, discourse analysis, relations between culture and power in the contemporary international system.
elizabete.sanches@gmail.com

Introduction
Mozambique and Brazil

Sérgio Chichava, Ana Cristina Alves and Chris Alden

The intimate relationship between Brazil and Africa has its roots in the early colonial area, under the yoke of the Portuguese crown. Brazil was built with the sweat and blood of successive waves of slaves brought from West Africa, and their presence over the centuries imprinted strong African nuances onto the identity of the modern Brazilian nation, namely, through their genes, their culture and their linguistic heritage.

Although this is an intrinsic element of the history of Brazil, its actual link with the African continent declined significantly after the abolition of slavery in 1888 under Imperial Law No. 3.353, known as the *Lei Áurea* (Golden Law). As a result, by the first half of the 20th century, Africa had practically disappeared from the agenda of Brazilian foreign policy because the Ministry of Foreign Affairs (known colloquially as 'Itamaraty') gave preference to its special relationship with the United States.[1] This distancing from Africa increased with the launching of the United Nations (UN) in 1945, and Brazil's foreign policy alignment with the leading colonialist countries – namely France, Britain and Portugal – who supported their claim that the colonies were, in fact, 'overseas territories' and, therefore, not open to scrutiny, given the UN Charter's statute on non-interference in domestic affairs (a legal fiction that was necessitated by pressures from the UN General Assembly).

By the 1950s, as the pressure for independence began to stir in Africa, and in the 1960s, when Jânio Quadros and João Goulart occupied the Brazilian Presidency, the strategy began to shift towards a foreign policy of 'autonomy' (founded by the diplomats Afonso Arinos de Melo Franco and San Tiago Dantas), which supported the self-determination and independence of the African colonies. At the time, Brazil forged diplomatic relationships with eight African countries and established an Africa Division within Itamaraty. This approach was, however, interrupted by the military dictatorship in Brazil in 1964. The dictatorship's African policy was guided initially by its loyalty to Portugal (which wanted to maintain its colonial yoke over the so-called

---

1 This is the term used by Soares de Lima (2005:9) who argues that there were two international strategies followed by the country in the 20th century: that of 'bandwagoning' and that of equilibrium (or autonomy).

'overseas provinces', thus, swimming against the tide that had already seen other European metropoles grant independence to most of their African colonies) and its loyalty to the apartheid regime in South Africa, which was responsible for the bulk of Brazil's trade with the continent.

The independence of the African countries that used Portuguese as their official language in the 1970s, the growing economic appeal of decolonised Africa and the economic consequences of the oil crisis, led to a gradual change, with Itamaraty adopting a strategy of diversifying international alliances, taking up an anti-colonial and anti-apartheid stance. This approach bore good commercial fruit: exports and imports grew, and Brazilian companies, such as Petrobrás[2] and the building company Noberto Odebrecht,[3] entered the African market (Ribeiro, 2007; Saraiva, 2012).

The democratisation of Brazil in the 1980s led to the gradual liberalisation and stabilisation of its domestic economy over the subsequent decade. However, the strategy of nurturing a special relationship with the United States prevailed, further postponing the revival of relations with Africa in the light of limited resources. The improvement of the macroeconomic situation of Brazil in the early 2000s coincided with the economic recovery of Africa and this convergent framework prepared the stage for the gradual resurgence of the continent in Brazil's foreign policy in the early 21st century. The impetus in this direction resulted largely from the vision of President Lula da Silva (2003–2010) and Foreign Minister Celso Amorim.

Indeed, during the period when Lula da Silva was president, the economic, political and diplomatic relations between Brazil and Africa underwent unprecedented growth. During his two terms of office, apart from opening 19 embassies, Lula da Silva made 33 visits to Africa (Lula Institute, 2013). Because of this expansion in foreign relations, trade between Brazil and the African countries increased from US$4 billion to US$20 billion in the same period (MDIC, 2015). The main areas of economic cooperation during the presidency of Lula da Silva were agriculture, health and education, with a stress on the transfer of technology (Chichava and Duran, 2016). However, it should be noted that at the end of Lula da Silva's second term of office 55 per cent of the Brazilian technical cooperation in Africa was in the Portuguese-speaking countries. This was undoubtedly due to their cultural and linguistic proximity.

---

2   Petrobrás began its operations on the Angolan coast in 1979, when it acquired 27.5 per cent of the exploration rights in the shallow waters of Block 2, in the Lower Congo Basin. In addition to Petrobrás, Chevron, Sonangol (the Angolan state company) and Total participated in the project with 20 per cent, 25 per cent and 27.5 per cent shares, respectively (Ribeiro, 2009).

3   Odebrecht entered Angola in 1982, with the purpose of building the Capanda hydroelectric dam, in partnership with the then USSR (Ribeiro, 2009).

INTRODUCTION

Brazil legitimised its presence in Mozambique, and in Africa more generally, through recourse to arguments which included demand, the pursuit of non-profit-making goals that were not tied to commercial interests, that were exempt from political impositions or conditions, and inspired by solidarity and participative diplomacy, 'moral debt' and 'cultural proximity', because of slavery and a similar type of tropical climate. Fundamentally, Brazilians believe that their experience and development model could be exported to Africa, if adapted to the local context. From this perspective, the Brazilian concept of development cannot be distinguished from that of other 'emerging powers', such as China, and more 'traditional donors', who postulate the same vision, arguing that their development model can be replicated on the African continent (Chichava *et al*, 2013; Chichava and Fingermann, 2015). Despite its limited financial resources, Brazil's great advantage, compared with its southern and northern competitors, lies in the technical solutions the country has developed in critical areas, namely agriculture, health and social programmes to fight poverty. These have the greatest potential for applicabilty in Africa due to sociocultural and geoclimatic similarities.

In all these respects, Mozambique is an emblematic case for understanding the involvement of Brazil in Africa. Having established relations in 1975, Mozambique is the main technical cooperation partner of Brazil on the continent, with 21 active projects, and nine others under negotiation. Agriculture, health and education were the most important sectors (Chichava *et al*, 2013:8).[4] In fact, Mozambique hosts the largest agricultural cooperation project, ProSavana,[5] involving Brazilian technical cooperation in Africa. This is a trilateral project which, apart from Brazil, brings together Japan and Mozambique, and is inspired by the Brazilian experience of the 'cerrado' (the dry savannah characteristic of northeast Brazil), which transformed the country into one of the world's most important agricultural producers. ProSavana is being implemented along the Nacala Corridor, covering several districts in the northern provinces of Nampula, Zambézia and Niassa. Mozambique is also one of only two African countries, along with Ghana, that hosts offices of the Brazilian Agricultural Research Corporation (Embrapa). In addition, Mozambique hosts the only factory manufacturing antiretroviral (ARV) drugs on the African continent that is financed and built by Brazil. And, apart from

---

4   According to the current Brazilian ambassador to Mozambique, the level of Brazil's involvement remains the same in 2016, with 40 technical cooperation projects under way. For more details, see Notícias (2016).
5   ProSavana is the Programme of Triangulated Cooperation for Agricultural Development of the Tropical Savannahs of Mozambique, backed by the cooperation agencies of Brazil (ABC) and Japan (JICA).

being Brazil's main development cooperation partner, during the presidency of Lula da Silva, Mozambique received the highest proportion of Brazilian debt relief in Africa; moreover, 95 per cent of this debt to Brazil was pardoned in 2004 (Moura, 2013).

Beyond technical cooperation, Mozambique is a significant destination for Brazilian investment. According to the Brazilian foreign ministry (MRE), Brazilian investments in Mozambique are concentrated in mining, energy and construction, and up to 2015, they were estimated at US$9.5 billion (Itamaraty Blog, 2015). Mozambique was also the first African country to sign, in March 2015, an Investment Cooperation and Facilitation Agreement (ACFI), which seeks to promote flexible investments between the two countries. Mozambique hosts signature Brazilian multinationals such as Vale, the second largest mining company in the world, which operates a coal-mining concession in Moatize in Tete Province, one of the largest investments in the country.

Some of the most globalised Brazilian construction companies also operate in Mozambique, namely, Camargo Corrêa, Andrade Gutierrez and Odebrecht. These are involved in building major infrastructures, such as the Nacala International Airport, the Moamba-Major Dam and the Maputo Bus Rapid Transit (BRT Maputo), respectively. At the same time, the long arm of the scandals, which have plagued Brazil in recent years, bringing down senior Brazilian politicians, including President Dilma Rouseff in 2016, have reached into Brazilian–Mozambican relations. Odebrecht, for instance, was accused of paying nearly US$1 million in bribes to Mozambican officials between 2011 and 2014, as were other companies.[6]

To understand the dynamic relationship between Brazil (an emerging power despite the domestic turmoil it is currently experiencing) and Mozambique (a country once plagued by civil war and, thereafter, one of Africa's fastest growing economies) is to open a window, which we believe sheds light on the general nature of Brazilian–African relations. Mozambique's singular position as the largest recipient of Brazilian technical assistance, a key destination for Brazilian investment, a willing consumer of Brazilian culture and a target for Brazilian civil society, offers a more detailed framework for the Brazilian presence in Africa and its countless nuances. The chapters in this publication discuss not only the main areas of Brazilian technical cooperation and investment, but also the other networks that connect the two countries, such as the presence of Pentecostal churches and Brazilian theatre groups.

---

6   'Brazilian Odebrechts to have paid US$900 000 in bribes in Mozambique', Club of Mozambique, 23 December 2016. Available at: www.clubofmozambique.com/news/brazilian-odebrechts-paid-us900000-bribes-mozambique.htm.

INTRODUCTION

Chapter 1 undertakes a historical analysis of the relations between Mozambique and Brazil since Mozambican independence in 1975. It presents the process through which these relations, which started out as insignificant and confined to merely the political sphere, have become more prominent, transforming Mozambique into Brazil's most important partner in Africa.

Broadening the focus, Chapter 2 provides a comparative study of ties between Brazil and Mozambique from independence in 1975 to the end of the presidency of Lula da Silva in 2010. It examines the degree to which these relations complement or diverge from Brazil's interactions with the other Lusophone African countries. It argues that, although influenced by the context and conjuncture of each country, these interactions have followed the same logic and trends, and in general slot into the Brazilian conception of South–South cooperation (SSC).

Chapter 3 examines the relations between Mozambique and Brazil to analyse the meaning and characteristics of South–South cooperation and in particular to assess how it differs from North–South cooperation. It argues that Brazilian aid is not altruistic and lacking in self-interest, but is governed by logic which is not unlike that used by the traditional aid donors; although South–South cooperation is generally governed by equality and is horizontal in nature, the relationship between Mozambique and Brazil is *not* exactly horizontal, neither is it one between equal partners.

Chapter 4 looks at the role of Brazil in facilitating a distinctively 'southern' form of extractive development in Mozambique and the degree to which this offers a more developmentalist alternative to the historical dependency model found in Mozambique.

Chapters 5 and 6 discuss the Brazilian involvement in Mozambican agriculture and how this fits into the context of Brazilian South–South cooperation. Chapter 5 takes this discussion further through an analysis of the ProSavana project; it argues that the design and implementation of the ProSavana project contradicts the principles of Brazilian South–South cooperation, which is why the programme is strongly opposed in Mozambique, particularly by Mozambican civil society organisations (CSOs).

Chapter 6 uses the example of the Technical Support Project for the Nutrition and Food Security Programme, better known as ProAlimentos, to examine how trilateral Brazilian cooperation works on the ground; how relations develop between those implementing the programme, in this case the Americans and the Brazilians, who come from different paradigms and practices, that is, North–South and South–South cooperation, respectively, and between these and the Mozambican beneficiaries of the programme. The author argues that Brazilian trilateral cooperation is not linear and continual, that there are constant negotiations and tensions between the various actors involved, and that this dynamic establishes a new model of cooperation.

Chapter 7 analyses the opposition of Mozambican CSOs to ProSavana, and argues that, for reasons linked to the struggle for external financial resources and the search for protagonism, these organisations, which at the start of their fight displayed a certain consensus on the need to stop the programme and reformulate it, are today deeply divided. Some are calling for the definitive suspension of the programme, while others are in favour of developing it, if the conditions they defend are met.

Chapter 8 discusses the social mechanisms used to share technology, as well as the mechanisms for its appropriation, based on the case of the Brazilian multinational audio-visual company, Cine Group, which has been operating in Mozambique since 2008. It shows how the local institutional context and management, social practices and cultural challenges influence the transfer of knowledge between Brazilian multinational companies and their Mozambican subsidiaries, and what can be done to solve the challenges raised by this dynamic.

Chapter 9 discusses how the Brazilian media has portrayed Brazilian investment and development cooperation with Mozambique from the final years of the government of Lula da Silva up to Dilma Rousseff's initial term in office. Based on a close examination of two of Brazil's leading newspapers, namely *Folha de São Paulo* and *O Estado de São Paulo*, the author demonstrates how, through speculation and media sensationalism, the Brazilian press reinvented northern Mozambique: they presented it as not only favourable for development, but also as an unoccupied and underutilised area, which was, therefore, appropriate for large-scale investments such as ProSavana.

Health cooperation is the focus of Chapter 10, taking as an example the factory that produces antiretroviral drugs, which was established in Maputo with Brazilian financing in 2012. This chapter investigates how the Brazilian model of preventing and treating HIV/AIDS is being transferred to Mozambique and the challenges associated with this. Furthermore, it analyses how the Brazilian bureaucracy delays implementation of its development cooperation programmes and how this affects the image of the country among its cooperation partners.

Chapter 11 discusses the social, economic and cultural impacts of the activities of the mining company Vale in Moatize, in Tete Province. It highlights how Brazilian technicians resettled local people to facilitate the implementation of the Vale project, without the involvement of its Mozambican counterpart or consultation with the local population, resulted in transforming these people into new 'development refugees'.

The next two chapters in the book discuss the Brazilian presence in

Mozambique through cultural and religious interchange. Chapter 12 looks at the cultural interchange between Mozambique and Brazil through the medium of theatre. Taking as an example the Maputo Theatre of the Oppressed Group (GTO-Maputo), set up in Maputo in 2001 with the support and in the image of its Brazilian counterpart, the Theatre of the Oppressed Centre of Rio de Janeiro (CTO-Rio de Janeiro), the author examines how, beyond the official interchange between the two countries, culture plays an important role in bringing culturally different peoples together and helping vulnerable groups to cope with crucial social problems such as HIV/AIDS.

Chapter 13 analyses the presence of Brazil in Mozambique through the Pentecostal churches. Based on an empirical investigation, the author argues that the penetration of the Brazilian Pentecostal churches is legitimised through the historical and cultural proximity between Africa and Brazil, dating from the days of slavery. This conversion to Brazilian Pentecostalism has contributed to a growing critical awareness among Mozambicans, encouraging them to break with some local cultural practices such as witchcraft, which are regarded as archaic and as a source of countless social problems and conflicts. However, the author warns that, although Brazilian Pentecostalism leads to some positive changes in the lives of Mozambicans, it also creates new obstacles and problems because it destabilises the dominant local cultural order and generates tensions between Pentecostalists and their relatives, who do not see themselves reflected in its practices.

Chapter 14 provides a provocative look at the future of the relationship, especially in the light of the dramatic political changes within Brazil and the equally disruptive economic challenges it faces, alongside the problems experienced recently in Mozambique.

The key question, cutting across all these chapters, is whether Brazil has the capacity to articulate, defend and implement its principles of South–South solidarity at the same time as it expands its economic footprint on the continent. As Brazil's involvement with Africa deepens, it is likely that more frictions will arise between the various agents and actors of this multifaceted interaction, as well as alterations in the norms and practices that guide this relationship. The chapters in this volume condense many years of field research undertaken by Mozambican, Brazilian and foreign researchers. It thus constitutes a privileged window for anyone who wants to understand the dynamics that govern Brazil's relations, not only with Mozambique but also with the rest of the continent.

References

Chichava, S, Duran, J, Cabral, L, Shankland, A, Buckley, L, Lixia; Tang, L and Zhang, Y (2013) *Chinese and Brazilian Cooperation with African Agriculture: The case of Mozambique*, FAC

Working Paper CBAA 49, Brighton.

Fael, B and Cortez, R (2016) Os Exemplos das Operações 'Lava Jato' e 'Marquês' e a Inacção do Nosso Ministério Público, *CIP Newsletter*, 51/2016, Maputo.

Instituto Lula (2013) *Com nova embaixada no Malauí, presença diplomática do Brasil na África estende-se para 38 países*. Available at: http://www.institutolula.org/com-nova-embaixada-no-malawi-presenca-diplomatica-do-brasil-na-africa-estende-se-para-38-paises (accessed 27 June 2016).

Itamaraty Blog (2015) *Brasil e Moçambique assinam acordo de cooperação e facilitação de inveentos*. Available at: http://blog.itamaraty.gov.br/22-assuntos-economicos-e-financeiros/124-brasil-e-mocambique-assinam-acordo-de-cooperacao-e-facilitacao-de-investimentos (accessed 28 June 2016).

Moura, R (2013) Perdão às dívidas de países africanos atinge US$ 717 mi, *Estadão*. Available at: http://economia.estadao.com.br/noticias/geral,perdao-as-dividas-de-paises-africanos-soma-us-717-mi-imp-,1055694 (accessed 31 March 2016).

Notícias (2016) *Brasil alinha investimentos para o agro-processamento*. Available at: http://www.jornalnoticias.co.mz/index.php/main/52164-brasil-alinha-investimentos-para-o-agro-processamento, 10 de Março (accessed 10 April 2016).

Ribeiro, CO (2009) As relações Brasil-África entre os governos Collor e Itamar Franco', *Revista Brasileira de Ciência Política*, 1, pp 289–329.

Soares de Lima, MR (2005) A política externa brasileira e os desafios da cooperação Sul-Sul. *Revista Brasileira de Política Internacional*, 48 (1), pp 24–59. Available at: https://dx.doi.org/10.1590/S0034-73292005000100002 (accessed 31 March 2016).

Chapter 1

Brazil–Mozambique relations: From the geopolitics of the Cold War to South–South cooperation

Analúcia Danilevicz Pereira and João Marcos Tatim

Brazil's policy for Africa gained fresh impulse from 2003 under the Luiz Inácio Lula da Silva government. The special priority given to relations with Africa, together with the establishment of the South–South axis of cooperation, reflect a longstanding Brazilian aspiration. However, this had not been pursued with much determination earlier, because Africa had been of secondary importance to Brazilian diplomats at the end of the Cold War. Lula's election as president inaugurated a new chapter in Brazilian diplomacy, a moment when various African nations were identified as strategic partners within the broader context of South–South relations. This chapter reflects on this change and analyses the trajectory taken by the relations between Brazil and Mozambique, highlighting the ebbs and flows in Brazil's Africa policy. To gain a better grasp of the topic, we provide a historical overview of Brazilian foreign policy up to the adoption of the so-called Independent Foreign Policy (*Política Externa Independente:* PEI) in the 1960s.

Thereafter, we provide an account of how Brazil's Africa policy was established, covering the period from 1961 to 2010. In the following section, we analyse the trajectory of the relations between Brazil and Mozambique following the latter's independence in 1975. Special attention is paid to the bilateral relations between the two countries as they developed at the end of the Cold War. One must appreciate the strategic importance of the closer ties between the two countries, despite their different levels of development, and the impacts of this approximation on the consolidation of a new political geography.

The ebb and flow of relations between Brazil and Africa

Brazil's relations with the African continent, especially the Portuguese-speaking countries, are old and deep, and were stronger than its links with Portugal. This is not just a reflection of the Africanisation of Brazil, which started with the arrival of the first slaves and created a socio-economic structure that lasted throughout Brazil's colonial and imperial periods. It also traces back to the emergence of a strategic axis of political and economic–commercial cooperation which acquired its own dynamic by gradually reducing Portugal's capacity to interfere since the 17th century.

With the advent of the Pax Britannica in the 19th century, the South Atlantic, Brazil and Africa acquired a new meaning in the global strategy of hegemonic power, which stifled the potential of the Brazil–Africa axis. However, this fails to explain precisely why Brazil was so slow to re-establish an African policy. At the start of the 20th century, some Brazilian authorities[7] began to manifest an interest in Africa, no longer just as a source of labour and commodities as in previous centuries, but also as a space for commercial transactions. This trade was not constant or large in volume. Without doubt, European domination controlled or curbed this relation until the period of African decolonisation. Even so, because of a foreign policy vision geared to the United States–Western Europe axis, Brazil took a long time to realise the potential of the African continent as a space for cooperation. Brazil therefore closed the doors not only to its own internationalisation but also to the possibility of moving beyond its agro-export economic model.

During the Second World War, Brazilian interest in Africa was revived, principally in the north of the continent. The foreign minister at the time, Osvaldo Aranha, decided to send a diplomatic officer to the continent, which was becoming increasingly important in the overall context of the war. Vasco Leitão da Cunha was appointed to this position, which included assessing the creation of a consulate in Algiers. Military missions were sent to establish military cooperation with the Allies prior to the dispatch of the Brazilian Expeditionary Force (Rodrigues, 1964).

At the end of the war, between 1945 and 1955, there was further discontinuity when Brazil largely ignored Africa's evolution. The Brazilian position was limited to lukewarm, formal declarations in favour of Africa's first steps towards emancipation, announcing its support for the 'reconciliation' between the new states and their former colonial powers. Brazil's main concern was continental policy and the links with Western Europe, despite the rhetoric backing a 'union of all the peoples in working towards international reconciliation' (Café Filho, 1955).

The curious aspect of this position is that, even when faced with the isolation

---

7   After the 1930 revolution in Brazil, the foreign minister, Afrânio de Melo Franco, looked to stimulate a new overseas commercial policy, resulting in the 1931 and 1932 trade agreements with Great Britain, which extended to the colonies, protectorates and territories under British rule, reciprocal treatment no less favourable than that granted to any other country. See Rodrigues (1964).

caused by the strength of US capitalism and Europe's exhaustion (when the United States and Europe saw Africa as the stimulus or last chance to be reborn as a pole of power), Brazil dismissed the possibility of commercial expansion with the Soviet Union, China and the so-called People's Democracies of Eastern Europe, which combined amounted to about a billion potential customers.

Notably, the policy of the Juscelino Kubitschek government made this reality very clear. Concentrating on the Pan American Operation, or on the idea of valorising Latin America, the government showed little enthusiasm when African independence erupted in 1956 with eight independent countries; in 1960, another 20 new countries gained their freedom. Brazilian activity was limited to the formalities of diplomatic recognition. Despite the Brazilian government efforts to establish an American policy, its disregard for what was happening in Africa could have had harmful consequences in the future. In fact, Brazil was slow to identify itself as a 'historic and strategic partner' of the new African nations, revealing the absence of any strategic vision for the international system. As José Honório Rodrigues wrote at the time (1964:218):

> The lack of attention to Africa, whose most westerly point is just a few hours flight time from our Northeastern coast, and the importance of the South Atlantic, the base of our economic cooperation and strategic defence plans, set new courses for our foreign policy. Neither the lesson of the Great War … nor our connections with Africa has taught us that a top-level intercontinental policy, which improves our possibilities for protection and security and develops our foreign policy is probably our manifest destiny, which emerged from the past, collides in the present and will advance in the future.

The implementation of the Independent Foreign Policy from 1961 to 1964 included a more substantial attempt to forge closer ties, but this was followed by a phase of distancing during the first two military governments (1964–1969). From the Médici government to the end of the Sarney government (1969–1990), there was a qualitative leap in Brazil–Africa relations, especially with Portuguese-speaking countries, and intense cooperation in various areas. However, between 1990 and 2002, under a series of neoliberal governments from Fernando Collor de Mello to Fernando Henrique Cardoso, in the framework of globalisation, the distances grew once more.[8] At the turn of the century, though, especially when the Lula da Silva government came to power,

---

8   For an analysis of foreign policy during the Cardoso (FHC) period, see Vigevani, Oliveira and Cintra (2003).

the African continent finally became a priority for Brazil.

Relations between Brazil and Mozambique, first established in 1975, were initially more political than economic–commercial. The difficulties in establishing a development model in Mozambique and the civil war, which broke out in 1977, were key factors that influenced Brazil's retraction of its intentions to expand economic cooperation with the country. Despite the 1980s seeing profound political (and thus economic) changes in Mozambique, the expectation of an intensification in cooperation with Brazil was frustrated by Brazil's lack of diplomatic foresight. In a global and regional context defined by the end of the Cold War and the creation of Mercosul in 1991, Africa was pushed into the background by the frameworks of a diplomacy based around a 'First World' and neoliberal vision of globalisation.

Lula da Silva's presidency began a new chapter in Brazil–Africa relations, though, combining an innovative view of the international system with social transformation at a domestic level. This shift towards South–South cooperation created huge expectations for the expansion of bilateral cooperation with Africa, especially considering Brazil's increasingly prominent international profile and partners like Mozambique, who were keen to expand cooperation through activities that were compatible with its own development priorities.

It is worth emphasising that South–South cooperation emerged as an alternative to the previous practices adopted by Brazilian foreign policy. Soares de Lima (2008) argues that the analysis of South–South relations can be approached via two frameworks. The first is defined by the 'Third World' coalition of developing countries and the establishment of a forum for discussing issues concerning North–South relations. Criticising the liberal principles that had regulated economic relations, and based on the proposition that it was unjust to treat 'unequals' as 'equals', the coalition created the Group of 77 (G77),[9] of which Brazil assumed the leadership in the 1960s. The G77 began to demand a new approach to challenge the unequal competition existing in the international economic order.

The second framework for analysing South–South relations considers contemporary changes to the international order. Here we can identify the emergence of a new meaning to South–South relations. For the author, 'territorial expansion and the configuration of a truly global capitalism, along with the incorporation of the periphery into the system of States, have removed the last political obstacles to capitalism's globalization' (Soares de Lima, 2008).

---

9   The Group of 77 was created on 15 June 1964 when 77 developing countries issued a joint declaration at the conclusion of the First United Nations Conference on Trade and Development. Available at: http://www.g77.org/40/commemoration.htm (accessed 4 December 2013).

As a result, peripheral countries started to become more closely integrated into the global economy, leading to a new category of emerging countries in the international system. As part of these new relations, Brazil began to show a greater interest in reactivating or establishing stronger links with southern countries, reorganising its international agenda without, though, ceasing its dialogue with its traditional partners. The renewed interest in developing ties with the African continent, especially with southern Africa, became a reality through joint actions with the region's countries.

Brazil's African policy (1961–2010)

The diplomatic relations between Brazil and the African continent began to be developed in a more effective form through the Independent Foreign Policy (*Política Externa Independente*: PEI) of San Tiago Dantas[10] and Araújo Castro.[11] This policy was based on principles such as autonomy and universalisation. In fact, the PEI introduced substantial changes to the country's foreign policy, altering the bases of its diplomatic work and marking a turning point in Brazil's international policy over the period. Through the PEI, Brazil strengthened its diplomatic activities with African and socialist countries, sounding out an increased involvement in international affairs. According to Vilalva and Gala (2001:39):

> With the PEI, Brazil–Africa relations acquired a new dimension. The attempt to achieve closer relations with the African continent, like the new Brazilian foreign policy initiatives as a whole, reflected the search for greater autonomy, as well as new markets, in Africa, in Asia and also in socialist countries, in order to guarantee capitalist expansion coordinated by the state and the developmentalist project. During the years of the PEI, Brazilian diplomacy was inspired by new values, such as the right to self-determination, but also by Brazil's legitimate aspiration for development and complete economic emancipation... During the short period of the Quadros Government, the idea was officially inaugurated that the South Atlantic would be the ideal area for Brazil to expand its interests.

Hence, the PEI raised the prospect of a change in the primary axis of the international system, amounting to a critique of bipolarity. Through these principles, Brazil adopted an independent stance, prioritising the country's interests without ideological preconceptions. However, although the 1964 military

---

10 Minister of Foreign Affairs (from 1961 to 1962) during the João Goulart government.
11 Minister of Foreign Affairs (from 1963 to 1964) during the João Goulart government.

coup had characterised itself as an intervention against the economic, social and national project represented by the PEI, this autonomous foreign policy, in the words of Visentini (1994:34), 'revealed itself to be much more ahead of its time than mistaken, since many of its postulates were later resumed by the diplomacy of the military government in the mid-1970s with the so-called Responsible Pragmatism', which implicitly contained the idea of Brazil as a world power.

Therefore, in terms of Brazil–Africa relations under the military regime, and in contrast to the concept defined by the PEI of supporting the recently independent nations, Brazil's African policy looked to strengthen relations with former Portuguese colonies, envisioning, along with Portugal, an alliance of Portuguese-speaking countries, including Mozambique, which would improve economic and commercial relations over the long term.

Brazil's Africa policy subsequently experienced various advances and setbacks. Understanding the Brazilian position concerning the prospects of a new relationship with the African continent, however, requires a brief examination of the final years of the country's military regime. The strategic importance of the west coast of Africa (where Dakar forms an axis of aerial connection with the Brazilian northeast) is not purely military: it defines the conditions for coordinating cooperation initiatives and friendship. During the Geisel government (1974–1979), renewed efforts were made to forge closer ties with Africa by opening new embassies and expanding pre-existing ones on the continent – the case in Angola, Mozambique and Equatorial Guinea – and by promoting the activities of Brazilian companies in numerous African countries. These companies included Braspetro, a subsidiary of Petrobrás, Companhia Vale do Rio Doce (today Vale) and the Odebrecht and Mendes Jr construction and engineering firms, which began looking for business on African soil.

The Figueiredo government (1979–1985) continued the same policy, resized during Brazil's return to democracy. Under the Sarney government (1985–1990), Brazilian diplomacy recognised the need to deepen ties with new African and Asian partners. This decision was linked to the transformations in the international system, which would eventually lead to the end of the Cold War, following the strategic lines of action first established by the Itamaraty (Foreign Ministry) during the military regimes. Although a specific policy for the African continent had yet to be presented, it was during this period that important topics started to be discussed. For example, the South Atlantic Peace and Cooperation Zone (ZOPACAS), approved by the United Nations in 1986, served as an embryo for the creation of the Community of Portuguese Language Countries (CPLP) with a meeting held in 1989 in São Luís[12] involving the

---

12   Capital of Maranhão state, situated in Brazil's northeast region.

Heads of State from some of the countries that would later become members of the group.

Under the subsequent government of Fernando Collor (1990–1992), however, influenced by market globalisation and the adoption of neo-liberal policies, relations with Africa were once again pushed into the background. Although his government negotiated with Near and Far East countries such as China, Israel and the Arab Emirates regarding technological training, demonstrating the resilience of the universalist dimension of Brazilian foreign policy (at a time of international crisis and the blocking of a national project), trade between Brazil and Africa was clearly and notably of little significance.

Collor's premises, reflected in his administration's foreign policy, reveal that Africa was not considered relevant to Brazilian diplomatic efforts. Considering the interests pursued by the country internationally, which led it to adopt a position of subservience to the traditional centres of power (the United States and Europe), Africa was relegated to a secondary plane of Brazil's policy agenda, despite the reaffirmation of the country's historical links with the continent at a discursive level. In Ribeiro's analysis (2009:20):

> The redesign of Brazilian foreign policy, taken as an essential factor in boosting the country's international standing, makes it transparently clear that Africa is taken to be a less relevant space geopolitically. Observing the changes occurring at international level, it is deemed essential to promote actions to ensure that the country is not left on the side-lines of the new international order… The idea sustaining this position is that the African continent would be unable to respond positively to Brazilian demands. Aside from the fact that they were also, like Brazil, in profound economic collapse, African countries – particularly the Portuguese-speaking nations – were governed by political regimes unfavourable to increased dialogue or closer ties.

However, Collor's impeachment and the promotion of Itamar Franco (1992–1995) to the presidency led to a renewed politicisation of the diplomatic agenda. It was during the brief period of the Itamar Franco government that African policy acquired a new impetus, including the reactivation of ZOPACAS in 1993. As a result, Brazilian foreign policy, despite failing to advance substantially due to international difficulties and internal tensions, introduced some important initiatives at the level of regional integration with a greater emphasis on closer ties with neighbouring countries and the South Atlantic axis.

Thus, the diplomatic efforts of the Franco government were aimed at reestablishing and complementing initiatives taking place at multilateral level, a historical characteristic of Brazilian diplomacy. Concerning the resumption of this foreign policy trait during the period, Pereira (2007:107) states that:

> In line with its traditional universalist vocation, Brazil sought to establish relations with all areas of the world. However, some initiatives had a special significance for Brazilian diplomacy, such as relations with Asia and Africa. Relations with the United States and Europe were an immediate necessity. Brazil's relations with the United States were once again marked by a series of legal confrontations principally involving the commercial sphere and intellectual property... Brazil oscillated between accepting negotiations with developed countries, incorporating the new issues of the global agenda, especially human rights, the environment and non-proliferation, and establishing discursive strategies capable of accommodating national interests.

In terms of Africa, an important move towards closer relations occurred due to the multidimensional approach[13] once more assumed by Brazilian foreign policy. During this period, there was a return to coordinating policies designed, above all, to attract the support of African countries for Brazilian positions in international forums. According to Ribeiro (2009:34), 'the closer dialogue with African countries on multilateral issues, such as the environmental domain signify the attempt to build bridges over the Atlantic not solely through trade'. In this sense, the policies introduced also looked to consolidate ZOPACAS as a cooperation strategy in the South Atlantic, as well as promote the negotiations over the creation of the CPLP and closer ties with South Africa.[14]

In terms of foreign policy, the Fernando Henrique Cardoso (FHC) government (1995–2002) was marked by the search for spaces of integration. With the goal of enhancing Brazil's credibility at international level, new policies were defined for South America and for the African continent, even though, in the latter case, they remained at the level of rhetoric. Indeed, Cardoso's foreign policy for Africa proved somewhat modest, save for a few standout initiatives, and failed to alter the relations with African states in any effective way. However, the grounds were laid for policies that would be better designed and executed in the following government.

---

13   In the sense of diplomatic action and coordination at various levels (bilateral, multilateral and regional).
14   For an analysis of foreign policy during the Collor and Itamar Franco periods, see Ribeiro (2009).

During the period, Brazil sought a more important role in the CPLP. In looking to establish greater dialogue with Portuguese-speaking African countries, Brazil achieved an important position within the CPLP, emerging as an indispensable member of the organisation.[15] Furthermore, in addition to its overall relations with Portuguese-speaking African countries, an important step was taken, especially in relation to Angola. Essential in terms of its political and symbolic impact, the dispatch of Brazil's largest ever overseas force, as part of the United Nation's pacification programme in Angola,[16] stimulated the interest of Brazil's business sectors in the country – a fact that later became consolidated with the implantation of Brazilian companies in Angola.

Commercial interests in Nigeria also grew. With the participation of Petrobrás, Brazil began to see the country as an important space for oil drilling, a relationship that would also be improved later. Oil imports from Nigeria can also be considered significant during the Cardoso period.[17] Another country that emerged as an important partner was South Africa. The end of apartheid enabled closer relations between Brazil and South Africa, resulting in the official visit of President Fernando Cardoso to the country in 1996, when several cooperation agreements were signed. Two years later, in 1998, it was Brazil's turn to receive Nelson Mandela, which showed the interest in deepening the bilateral agreements between the two nations.

The public-health question was similarly an important factor in achieving closer Brazil–Africa relations. According to Vigevani (2003), during Cardoso's second mandate, 'the relative success of the Brazilian AIDS prevention policy allowed the development of horizontal international cooperation projects in the area through the Brazilian Cooperation Agency'. This event marked the beginning of increased cooperation in public policies between Brazil and the

---

15 In a speech given on the day of the creation of the CPLP, the Brazilian president at the time, Fernando Henrique Cardoso, referred to Brazil's role in giving birth to the project: 'Brazil had the original idea ... which is a source of pride for us. President Itamar Franco interpreted the Brazilian sentiment by giving full support to the initiative, while the former ambassador, José Aparecido de Oliveira, was tireless in pushing and promoting the idea.' Available at: http://www.biblioteca.presidencia.gov.br/ex-presidentes/fernando-henrique-cardoso/discursos-1/1o-mandato/copy_of_1996/10.pdf (accessed 4 December 2013).

16 From August 1995 to July 1997, Brazil contributed an infantry battalion (800 men), a company of engineers (200 men), two advanced health posts (40 health officers, including medics, dentists, pharmacists and health-care assistants) and approximately 40 general staff officers to the United Nations Angola Verification Mission III (UNAVEM III). During the entire mission period, Brazil also contributed an average of 14 military observers and 11 police observers. Brazil became the largest contributor of troops to UNAVEM, which, for almost two years, was the United Nations' largest peace operation. Brazilian participation in UNAVEM III meant that at the start of 1996, Brazil was the fourth largest contributor of troops to United Nations peace operations. Source: Brazilian Army. Available at: http://www.eb.mil.br/unavem (accessed 4 December 2013).

17 For more information on Petrobrás's activities in Nigeria, see: http://fatosedados.blogspetrobras.com.br/wp-content/uploads/2011/04/RevistaNig%C3%A9ria.jpg.

African continent, demonstrated by specific initiatives in combatting AIDS,[18] the training of public-health professionals in Africa and Brazil's willingness to breach patent rights on drugs used to fight the disease, which had spread across the entire continent with devastating impacts, particularly in southern Africa.

Thus, Brazil's activities vis-à-vis cooperation with African countries, despite being modest in the Cardoso period, were important in terms of establishing connections, which were subsequently deepened during the Lula da Silva government. The position adopted by Brazil in relation to Africa, especially during Cordoso's second mandate, was cautious and began to acquire greater importance only when the president criticised 'asymmetric globalisation' and promoted Brazil's attempts to be recognised as a strategic country at the international level.

Hence, the foundations for multidimensional diplomacy, which developed and improved over the eight years of the Da Silva presidency (2003–2010), were in fact planned during the preceding government. However, Lula da Silva developed much closer relations with Africa with a clear attempt to define real cooperation along the South–South axis. He managed to combine progress in domestic social issues with a multilateral international agenda, placing relations with Africa as a central theme of Brazil's foreign policy, defined as 'proud and affirmative' by the Minister of Foreign Affairs, Ricardo Amorim.

The Da Silva government introduced concrete and significant changes to Brazil's domestic and international agenda. Although Da Silva's election in 2003 had aroused some concern both domestically and internationally – many sectors of society considered him to be unprepared and anticipated an ideologically driven foreign policy – the policies he adopted over the course of his two mandates projected a multidimensional approach at international level and combined continuity in economic spheres with the application of social policies.

Lula da Silva declared his interest in developing multidimensional cooperation programmes with a wide variety of partners, including African countries, during his inauguration speech in 2003.[19] On this occasion, he argued that achieving closer relations with Africa was a political, moral and historical obligation for Brazil, and he placed South Africa among the major developing powers (with China, Russia and India). In this sense, his government went beyond rhetoric by defining foreign policy for the African continent as one of the main issues on Brazil's diplomatic agenda.

---

18 For details on cooperation in health and fighting AIDS, see: http://www.itamaraty.gov.br/temas/balanco-de-politica-externa-2003-2010/2.2.4-africa-saude.

19 The full version can be found at: http://www.biblioteca.presidencia.gov.br/ex-presidentes/luiz-inacio-lula-da-silva/discursos-de-posse/discurso-de-posse-1o-mandato/view.

Having taken the decision that Brazilian foreign policy needed to set more emphasis on Africa, his government introduced significant changes to the organisational framework of the Itamaraty (Foreign Ministry) and created the *Africa Division III* (DAF-III) from the breakup of the Department of Africa and the Middle East. This new division would join the existing *Africa Division I* and *II* in a clear demonstration of the importance that Africa attained during his mandate.

From the other side of the South Atlantic, clear signs of a new relationship began to emerge with a South African initiative for South–South cooperation: the creation of the India, Brazil and South Africa (IBSA) Dialogue Forum, also called the G-3. The IBSA initiative confirmed an increased alignment between the three countries on a variety of issues. Another priority for the government was the opening and reactivation of stations and embassies, closed during the previous Cardoso government. According to Ribeiro (2009), this activation of embassies, stations and consulates general increased the intensity of relations between Brazil and Africa and generated cooperation, because diverse African countries such as Benin, Equatorial Guinea, Namibia, Kenya, Sudan and others then opened diplomatic stations in Brazil.

With the aim of expanding agreements and markets in Africa, the Lula da Silva government also undertook diverse official trips to the continent, which resulted in strengthening bilateral relations, reflecting the long-term strategic dimension of these missions. Brazil also collaborated with debt-relief initiatives for African countries as part of the United Nations Development Programme's (UNDP's) Millennium Development Goals (MDGs), designed to establish global coordination to develop countries with structural problems. In addition to debt relief,[20] Brazil contributed technical support to these states, with the transfer of technologies, knowledge and staff training to assist development. Among the beneficiaries were Nigeria and Mozambique,[21] where the cancelled debts were significant, and these began to be important trading partners for Brazil.

The flow of commercial exchanges between Brazil and African countries increased substantially under the Da Silva government, especially with Angola, South Africa and Nigeria. Important educational initiatives were also implemented. According to Visentini and Pereira (2008), 'the Student Agreement Programme (*Programa Estudantes Convênio*: PEC) was expanded and extended to postgraduate studies with Brazilian scholarships and cooperation

---

20 According to data from the UNDP, the amount cancelled was over US$1 billion.
21 Nigeria: debt relief of 67 per cent, corresponding to US$162 million; Mozambique: debt relief of 95 per cent, estimated at US$351 million.

fostered in the field of scientific research and academic staff exchange'. This transformed Africa into an important laboratory for South–South cooperation, fomenting reciprocal knowledge on both sides of the Atlantic beyond the increase in bilateral trade.

Another new element introduced by the Da Silva government involved measures to combat some of the problems afflicting the African continent, such as poverty and epidemic diseases (especially HIV/AIDS). Using knowledge gained from programmes to eradicate famine and HIV that had been relatively successful in Brazil, the country collaborates with African countries to introduce and develop technologies adapted 'to Third World problems and the active alliance in multilateral forums in defence of common interests in the search to develop and build a multipolar and peaceful world system' (Visentini and Pereira, 2008:5).

It is clear, therefore, that in terms of the Lula da Silva government's foreign policy, Africa was much more than a commercial partner: it was a fundamental space in the context of South–South cooperation. In this sense, it could be said that the role played by Brazil in Africa – both through its diplomacy and through the interests of non-state agents like companies and other organisations – has been crucial in strengthening multilateral relations between partners facing similar adversities and possessing substantial historical links.

Hence, over the trajectory of the relations between Brazil and Africa, we can observe periods of closer proximity and greater distance. Brazil began to see Africa as an important space in the international community, an approach developed through the PEI with its premises of autonomy and universalisation. Africa has subsequently been a part of Brazil's foreign policy during most periods, although there have been alternating moments of growing strategic importance, connected to the perception of the international system, and moments of uncertain foreign policy commitment, on the part of the governing elite.

Relations between Brazil and Mozambique

The independence of Mozambique, which occurred on 15 November 1975, marked the beginning of diplomatic relations between the new African state and Brazil. These relations began to concretise with the signing of a General Cooperation Agreement in 1981, followed by a period of relative distancing in the 1990s, when intense political and economic changes were unfolding in both countries. This was also a period when Brazilian diplomacy 'disregarded' not only Mozambique, but also the whole African continent, as discussed earlier.

However, the signing of this General Cooperation Agreement between Brazil and Mozambique clearly announced the intention to establish closer ties between the two countries and the desire to promote cooperation for development based on mutual benefit and reciprocity.

Nonetheless, it is worth considering several factors that preceded this agreement and ended up delaying the pursuit of closer relations. First, in Mozambique there was resentment in some quarters about Brazil's stance during the fight for liberation. For leaders of the Mozambique Liberation Front (FRELIMO), this had revealed Brazil's passive response to Portuguese colonialism (CAU, 2011:70). Consequently, the development model adopted by Mozambique was socialist in inspiration, which brought the country closer to the Soviet bloc and distanced it from those countries, like Brazil, that were influenced by Western models. It should also be noted that these recently independent African countries faced considerable economic difficulties in the first years after liberation; Mozambique specifically had developed a 'war economy', guided by the actions of the Mozambique National Resistance Movement (RENAMO).

Furthermore, the conflict in Mozambique did not cease, even after independence. The challenge of establishing a development model, as well as the problems posed by the war of intervention, which began in 1976 and spiralled into civil war, hindered any approach by Brazilian diplomacy. Even so, Brazil still played an important role in the pacification of the conflict.

The civil war in Mozambique escalated into a general crisis, raising the question of which social forces would be able to assume the role of leading and representing the country. Writing about the conflict, Visentini (2013:365) tells us that:

> The Mozambique civil war, begun shortly after the war of independence, would lead the country to the verge of collapse through the destruction it unleashed. It was the outcome of a mixture of internal and external factors, stimulated mainly by the reaction to the government's policies and by the situation that had taken shape in southern Africa at the end of the 1970s.

Mozambique changed tack in 1987 and moved from a socialist-inspired development model to a market economy. This involved deep structural adjustment through the Economic Reconstruction Programme (*Programa de Reabilitação Econômica:* PRE), which was the result of an agreement with the IMF and the World Bank. Mozambique's affiliation to international financial institutions initiated a change in both domestic and foreign policy: it began to direct its attention to the West, away from the Eastern bloc. Following these structural adjustments, the country began to benefit from outside investments and the influx of funds, which empowered its capitalist economy. These foreign investments strengthened its strategic role in the south of the African continent and its importance in the Southern African Development Community (SADC).

The spread of war across almost the entire territory, the crisis in the socialist bloc and the growth in Mozambique's external debt had large-scale political and economic impacts. Finally, in 1992 a General Peace Agreement was established, which pacified of the conflict. Between independence and this peace agreement, it was almost impossible to consolidate a development project in the country and closer links with Brazil, which was itself still recovering from the crisis of the 1980s and an even more critical period during the neoliberal governments of Collor and Cardoso.

In response to the global instability and crises produced by the end of bipolarity, the United Nations began to develop 'peacekeeping' initiatives. This approach was reinforced by the establishment of the United Nations Operation in Mozambique (ONUMOZ) in 1993. Discussing this operation, Visentini (2013:377) writes:

> The UN was committed to ensuring that the Agreement be put into practice and ended up having a much more influential role in the rebuilding of the country than foreseen during the negotiations. Fearing that low-level participation would allow Mozambique to slip back into civil war, as had occurred in Angola, the UN decided to introduce a stronger presence in the country.

Because of its historical relations with the African continent and its search for a higher-profile international standing, Brazil sought to perform an important role in ONUMOZ. According to information from the Brazilian Army (2013), 'from January 1993 to December 1994, Brazil contributed to the mission with a total of 26 military observers, 67 police observers, a medical unit and a company of infantry comprising 170 soldiers and officers'. In addition, the Division General, Lélio Gonçalves Rodrigues da Silva, headed the command of ONUMOZ from February 1993 to February 1994.

Following the demobilisation of the Mozambican combatants, finally achieved in September 1994, Mozambique held its first multiparty elections. During the run-up, RENAMO received financial backing from the United Nations administered Trust Fund to put together its electoral campaign, as well as other financial resources from abroad. However, FRELIMO won the elections with slightly more than half the votes. This resulted in what could be regarded as a two-party system but with clear leadership from FRELIMO, which secured a larger quantity of votes than RENAMO and the other parties.

While the 1990s saw important political changes in Mozambique, Brazil's diplomatic efforts in relation to Africa were mostly ineffective. With the end of the Cold War and the creation of Mercosul in 1991, Brazilian foreign policy was focused on the regional level and adopted a 'developed world' vision, guided by neoliberal globalisation. In terms of Brazil's initiatives for Africa in the 1990s, the most relevant was the creation of the Community of Portuguese Language Countries (CPLP). This revealed Mozambique, the second largest Portuguese-speaking African country, to be of considerable interest to Brazil, which later intensified its cooperation.

Following Lula da Silva's election, Africa became a priority for Brazilian diplomatic work, opening a new and important chapter in Brazil–Africa relations. Because of this, Mozambique's expectation for a strategic partnership with Brazil also grew. Brazil became one of the leading forces in South–South relations by stimulating dialogue with countries from the axis. In the case of Africa, this also involved generating closer ties and joint projects for the development of all the parties involved. These actions highlight the fundamental characteristic of the Lula da Silva government's foreign policy, namely, the desire to boost multilateral relations beyond cooperation with developing countries, and an emphatic defence of sovereignty and the principle of self-determination and equality between peoples. This stance looked to produce a consensus in the international agenda on the need for action and involvement based on pacifism, on the respect for international law, on the defence of the principles of self-determination and non-intervention and, finally, on pragmatism, as necessary and effective instruments for legitimising the country's interests at a global level (Oliveira 2003:15). Through this approach, the Lula da Silva government excelled in achieving closer ties with medium-income countries and in developing formal alliances for technological and economic cooperation with emerging countries, thereby helping to strengthen South–South relations.

In Mozambique, there was a significant increase in commercial trade, which included a rise in Brazilian imports – essentially machinery, cars, household appliances and tinned food. Brazilian businesses perceived the potential of the Mozambican market, while Mozambique saw in the Brazilian partnership a chance to make its projects possible without the political costs traditionally imposed by Western powers. During his two mandates, President Lula da Silva signalled the strong Brazilian interest in consolidating bilateral relations on the African continent by opening new embassies and through a series of official visits (19 African countries, with three visits to Mozambique).

Among the key areas, we can cite the efforts made by Embrapa (the Brazilian Agricultural Research Corporation) to establish cooperation in technology transfer through the implementation of joint projects in agriculture, livestock farming and natural resources. In education, diverse institutional exchange and long-distance teaching programmes were developed between the universities from the two countries to teach professional qualification and train new managers. Important advances were also made in health with the development of a pharmaceutical plant to produce antiretroviral drugs in Mozambique; this generated considerable enthusiasm because the Mozambican population suffers from a high rate of HIV infection. Moreover, Mozambique was one of the main beneficiaries of the Brazilian AIDS-treatment partnership: Brazil began to supply therapeutic drugs at cheaper prices; it also established a Fiocruz office in Maputo to manage the supply and production of the foundation's vaccines and the installation of the pharmaceutical plant mentioned earlier.[22]

Research agreements on natural resources were also signed, followed by the involvement of the Brazilian company Vale do Rio Doce in coal prospecting and surveying, and the cooperation of Brazil's National Petroleum Agency in the hydrocarbon area. Cooperation projects were also developed in the biofuels sector through the promotion of joint partnerships, technical exchanges and professional training, at private, government and academic levels. In the security area, technical cooperation agreements were also signed through 'mixed commissions' to discuss actions to combat drug trafficking. Similarly, in the defence sphere, the two countries signed a technical-military cooperation agreement, which enabled Brazilian support for peace missions and the provision of military training to Mozambicans.

In adopting this approach, Brazil was transformed into one of the leading actors in the construction of a new international order, based on multilateralism and open and opportune dialogue with all nations. Africa, and particularly Mozambique, occupies a strategic position in the new scenario that is unfolding.

Conclusion

Brazil's renewal of close ties with the African continent shows a clear willingness to consolidate the South–South cooperation axis, building on their common historical and developmental experiences. The promotion of more heterogenic and inclusive international relations, in which partners mutually benefit, also signals the most substantial change of the 21st century: the shift in the political geography towards the South. Defining an international system to replace the world order led by the North has become the demand of many other nations. This has the potential to contribute to a more balanced global system without the dominators and the dominated. Nonetheless, effective transformations will

---

22 On Fiocruz's cooperation in installing the pharmaceutical plant, see: http://www.fiocruz.br/fiocruzbrasilia/cgi/cgilua.exe/sys/start.htm?infoid=585&sid=6 (accessed 4 December 2013).

depend on the political will and international agenda of these states. Brazil and Mozambique, in this case, need to continue to develop and strengthen their multidimensional cooperation to ensure the developtent of both countries and construct a fairer and more egalitarian international order.

References

Café Filho (1955) Mensagem do Presidente Café Filho, de 15 de março de 1955 (Diário Oficial, 16 March 1955).
Cau, HS (2011) A construção do Estado em Moçambique e as relações com o Brasil. PhD thesis, Postgraduate Programme in Political Science, Federal University of Rio Grande do Sul.
Exército Brasileiro (n.d.) Onumoz. Available at: http://www.exercito.gov.br/web/guest/onumoz. (accessed 4 May 2013).
Oliveira, MF (2003) Breve ensaiosobre a política externa brasileira, *Revista Autor*, **III** (24), June.
Penha, EA (2011) *Relações Brasil–África e a geopolítica do Atlântico Sul*. Salvador: EDUFBA.
Pereira, AD (2007) África do Sul e Brasil: Doiscaminhos para a transiçãoaopós-Guerra Fria. Porto Alegre.
Ribeiro, CO (2009) As relações Brasil-África entre os Governos Collor e Itamar Franco, *Revista Brasileira de Ciência Política*, **1**, Jan–Jun. Available at: http://seer.bce.unb.br/index.php/rbcp/article/view/6600 (accessed 4 December 2013).
Rodrigues, JH (1964) *Brasil e África. Outro horizonte*. Rio de Janeiro: Civilização Brasileira (2 volumes).
Soares de Lima, MR (2008) O Brasil e as Relações Sul-Sul. Trabalho publicado no Dossiê Cebri, *Desafios da Política Externa Brasileira,* Edição Especial, Cebri, **1**, Year 7.
Vigevani, T, Oliveira, MF de and Cintra, R (2003) Política externa no período FHC: A busca de autonomia pela integração, *Tempo Social*, **15** (2), Nov. Available at: http://www.scielo.br/scielo.php?pid=S0103-20702003000200003&script=sci_arttext (accessed 4 December 2013).
Vilalva, M and Gala, IV (2001) Relações Brasil–África do Sul: Quatro décadas rumo à afirmação de umaparceria democrática (1948–1998), *Cena Internacional*, **III** (2), pp 33–54.
Visentini, PF (1994) O Nacionalismo desenvolvimentista e a Política Externa Independente (1951–1964), *Revista Brasileira de Política Internacional*, **37**, pp 24–36.
Visentini, PF and Pereira, AD (2008) *A Política Africana do Governo Lula*. Porto Alegre: Núcleo de Estratégia e Relações Internacionais, UFRGS.
Visentini, PF, Teixeira, LD and Pereira, AD (2007) *Breve História da África*. Porto Alegre: Leitura XXI.
Visentini, PF, Teixeira, LD and Pereira, AD (2013) *História da África e dos Africanos*. Petrópolis: Vozes.
Visentini, PF, Pereira, AD, Martins, JM, Ribeiro, LD and Gröhmann, LG (2013) *Revoluções e Regimes Marxistas: Rupturas, experiências e impacto internacional*. Porto Alegre: Leitura XXI, Nerint, UFRGS.

Chapter 2

Brazil, Mozambique and the PALOP: An analysis of high-level relations and policy stances

Kamilla Raquel Rizzi and Nathaly Xavier Schutz

Diplomacy without policy is just empty behaviour, aimless movement, international action without a strategy for achieving national or even collective interests. It is the role of foreign policy to combine the interests, values and intended rules for global order, integration or bilateral relations; that is, to provide the content for diplomacy from an internal perspective, whether national and regional or universal (Cervo, 2008: 9).

Mozambique's history has been shaped by the European presence in Africa, as well as the deep problems left by the process of decolonisation. According to Bauer and Taylor (2005), one of the first commercial trading posts in southern Africa was established by the Portuguese in Mozambique in 1534. Like its other Portuguese colony, Angola, this served as a base for slave trafficking. Portugal's presence in the Mozambican territory persisted for centuries, evolving from trading hub to effective occupation at the start of the 20th century.

Following the Carnation Revolution and the fall of Salazar in Portugal in 1974, Portuguese decolonisation in Africa – one of the few colonial powers that remained after the long process of decolonisation in Africa began at the end of the 1950s – acquired fresh momentum. The path to Mozambican independence, as occurred in Angola, was also conflict-ridden. In August 1974, negotiations were initiated between the leaders of the Mozambique Liberation Front (FRELIMO) and the government of Portugal. The position of Mozambique's nationalists prevailed over Portuguese wishes and, with the Lusaka Agreement signed in September 1974, a direct transition to independence was established without prior elections. In June 1975, despite the divergences, the Republic of Mozambique became officially independent.

As we shall see over the course of this chapter, the Brazilian government's recognition of Mozambique's independence marked the beginning of diplomatic relations between the two countries (although Brazilian diplomatic representation had existed in Lourenço Marques since 1974). This initiated the first phase of Brazil–Mozambique relations, therefore, which, albeit varying in intensity over the last four decades, have remained extremely relevant and influential up to the present.

The objective of this analysis is to identify Mozambique's position within the wider context of Brazilian foreign policy for Portuguese-speaking African countries (PALOP countries).[23] Hence it is worth formulating a clearer idea of what is understood by foreign policy and the relation between a country's domestic factors and the determination of its foreign policy. Here we can turn to the survey of the topic by Christopher Hill (2003:3) who argues that foreign policy is 'the sum of official external relations conducted by an independent actor (usually a state) in international relations'. Though succinct, this definition has several theoretical implications: first, the use of the term 'actor' rather than just country allows the encompassment of other agents in the analysis and, second, the idea of relations as a whole; in other words, foreign policy is not composed of isolated facts but a set of actions.

The formulation of foreign policy is a complex process involving the relation between actors and structures. Exploring along these lines, we can identify several conditioning factors and constraints to the establishment of foreign policy. One of the influencing factors (Hill, 2003) is that historical events, to a greater or lesser extent, affect the decisions taken in the present, commonly called lessons of history. Hence three kinds of historical constraints exist: 1) questions deeply embedded in the country's institutions and culture, which are almost impossible to counter; 2) perceptions rooted in society, which may be altered over the course of a generation; and 3) more recent conceptions, which may be changed easily without much resistance.

In terms of Brazil–Mozambique relations, the African axis of Brazilian foreign policy was launched with the recognition of the independence of Portugal's other African colony in southern Africa, Angola. As Soares de Lima points out (2009:28), this marked 'the beginning of autonomous and active diplomacy on the African continent', ultimately shaping the pattern of relationships pursued by Brazil with the other PALOP countries.

It should, nonetheless, be recognised that Brazil's foreign policy is based primarily on achieving various predetermined objectives; these set the conditions of its policies and shape the choice of instruments used by policy-makers to attain the country's aims. Rather than the more common concept of national interest, Hill (2003) uses the idea of a continuum within which certain actors need to differentiate their objectives. The first continuum is the temporal notion of the negotiation period and the time span of the established objective: short, medium and long term. The second continuum is the spectrum

---

23 From the Portuguese term, *Países Africanos de Língua Oficial Portuguesa*.

of variation between the implicit and the explicit; the difference between the declared objective and those pursued, which may or may not overlap. The third continuum refers to individual and collective values, and when the core issues concern the country itself or when they more strongly reflect the rest of the international system. Finally, there are the actual targets of foreign policy, which vary enormously, ranging from domestic issues to transnational actors, as well as the influences on third parties not initially targeted by the foreign policy in question, but who end up being affected in some way.

Very often the literature treats the domestic environment and foreign policy as two separate spheres. In practice, though, there is a very close relation between the internal and external questions, and the domestic situation strongly influences how the country's foreign policy is directed. Internal considerations thus constitute another important conditioning factor in the formulation of foreign policy. Hill (2003) suggests that the domestic context is unlikely to be homogenous: on the contrary, it comprises diverse forces that sometimes work in opposite directions.

The main factor in the numerous domestic constraints to foreign policy is the constitutional structure.[24] In terms of foreign policy, Hill (2003) identifies the principal aspect of the constitutional structure as the relationship between the executive and the legislature, together with the relationship between subnational entities and the central government in the case of federal systems. In this sense, as a presidential federal republic, Brazil's political formulations in terms of foreign policy are centred on the executive. As Soares de Lima (2009) stresses, the legislature's delegation of greater autonomy over foreign policy to the executive is an outcome of the elites' view that foreign policy is an instrument for development. This fact is compounded by the constitutional legitimacy conferred to the executive in this sphere and the general public's disinterest in the topic.

We can note a strong relationship between domestic factors and the elaboration and implementation of foreign policy. Although the internal and external spheres are autonomous, they cannot be investigated independently since their structures, actions and actors are interconnected and affect one another. It becomes apparent that Brazil's relations with Mozambique form part of a foreign policy interest in generating a space for Brazilian diplomacy to have a direct influence on the African Portuguese-speaking world. Given the difficulties faced by Brazilian foreign policy in consolidating economic ties, this action was based on development as a vector, concretised through *cooperative action* – the guiding thread of Brazilian foreign policy for PALOP countries (Rizzi, 2012).

---

24   Hill (2003) emphasises that although some countries see themselves as non-constitutionalist, in the sense of not adhering to the supremacy of the law, they are still subject to a formal structure.

This cooperation, present in Brazil's international affairs ever since the Independent Foreign Policy (*Política Externa Independente*: PEI), went through various redefinitions of its key concept, with three changes identifiable during the period studied here: 1) from 1974 to 1990, Brazil's cooperation with the PALOP countries was based on identifying bilateral demands and combined horizontality (South–South relations) with a political dimension, seeking to prevent the leftward drift of these countries in the Cold War context; 2) in the period between 1990 and 2002, when changes at a global level had a negative impact on Brazilian foreign policy towards small PALOP countries, cooperation remained as a minimum point of contact between the two sides of the South Atlantic, limited during this time to a technical dimension; and 3) from 2003 to 2010, cooperation once again assumed a political dimension, in defence of democratic institutions and values, based on South–South cooperation. Considering the theoretical concepts and approaches outlined earlier, this chapter investigates the main aspects of the relations between Brazil and Mozambique, identifying the maintenance of a common thread to Brazil's foreign policy: cooperative action based on an 'active development policy'.

Horizontality in the establishment of bilateral diplomatic relations (1975–1990)

In recognising the independence of the Republic of Mozambique on 12 July 1975, Brazil was reiterating a diplomatic stance that would become firmly established under the government of President Ernesto Geisel (1974–1979) and set the pattern for Brazil's policy towards Africa, with an emphasis on the expansion of multilateralism and political horizontality. With its support for the independence of the PALOP countries and other African nations, Brazilian diplomacy in the 1970s saw the African continent as a concrete possibility for enhancing Brazil's own autonomy in the world system through horizontality, prioritising this approach in its international initiatives (Rizzi, 2012).

Brazilian foreign policy under military rule (1964–1985) was not a single block of actions and approaches to the international system. In relation to Africa, the first two military governments set a more geopolitical tone to relations with the continent, reverting to a pro-Portugal stance. The later military governments, especially after 1970, reformulated the role of Africa in Brazil's foreign policy, clearing up its ambiguity concerning the Portuguese colonies on the continent and shaping the future of Brazil's presence in the recently independent states.

The government of Marshal Humberto Castelo Branco (1964–1967) was based on the idea of the 'redeeming revolution' and promulgation of 'order and social peace … fighting corruption and a return to growth by stimulating private capitalism' (Visentini, 2003:40). The renewal of closer ties to the United States meant that Brazilian foreign policy lost its multipolar dimension in favour of bipolarity, linked to the National Security Doctrine. With the sharp retreat in Brazilian anti-colonialism, the ambiguity in the country's policy toward Africa returned and there was official support once again for Portuguese colonialism.

Under General Arthur da Costa e Silva's government (1967–1969), the development theme gradually returned to the foreign policy agenda and relations with other regions of the world were resumed (Africa, Asia and Eastern Europe), previously emphasised in the PEI. The Diplomacy of Prosperity promoted relations with the 'Third World' within the sphere of South–South relations, particularly with the African continent.[25] At the same time, the special relationship with Portugal continued to sustain the ambiguity of Brazilian foreign policy in relation to Portuguese colonies.

Based on these elements, the 'golden era' of Brazil's African policy occurred between 1969 and 1985, at the end of the Figueiredo government. The fresh attempt to increase Brazil's international influence, enabled by economic development and by the specific foreign policy pursued by the military regime and its promotion of the nationalist–developmentalist project, amplified the geostrategic vision of the Atlantic Ocean. Consequently, this made evident the growing Brazilian interest in the African continent as a political partner (after the end of the ambiguities with Portugal) and as a potential consumer market in the wake of the independence of African countries – which, indeed, occurred under later governments. We can clearly recognise, therefore, the strong relationship between domestic conditions and the formulation and implementation of Brazilian foreign policy, as explored by Hill (2003).

The foreign policy of the government of General Emílio Garrastazu Médici (1969–1974) consolidated the qualitative change in Brazil's attitude towards Africa, marked by new trading partnerships resulting from its direct relations with the continent. 'National Interest Diplomacy' proposed a long-term diplomatic approach designed to achieve a new form of international insertion by expanding the country's relations with the African continent (30 trade agreements were signed with African countries during the period).

Relations with Portugal continued to be privileged, with Médici visiting Portugal between 13 and 20 May 1973. However, in the multilateral forums, Brazil gradually revealed its position on the end of colonialism and fighting racism. One of the key moments occurred in the 26th United Nations General Assembly (UNGA, 1972) when Brazil voted in favour of adopting

---

25   In 1968, the Brazil–Africa Chamber of Commerce was created and special missions were also sent to Angola, Mozambique and South Africa.

the Resolution recognising the authenticity of the liberation movements of Angola, Mozambique and Cape Verde/Guinea-Bissau.

Brazilian policy towards Africa became consolidated under the government of General Ernesto Geisel (1974–1979). The 'Responsible and Ecumenical Pragmatism' of Foreign Minister Antônio Azeredo da Silveira prioritised the African continent, as well as Arab and socialist countries. A key moment in this policy and the end of the earlier ambiguity occurred in 1974. The fall of Marcello Caetano in Portugal in April of the same year encouraged the definitive return of the anti-colonialist and anti-racist tone to Brazilian foreign policy. The emblematic moment in terms of Brazil's stance – already announced at UNGA 1972 – occurred in June 1974, when the Foreign Ministry (Itamaraty) received an official communication from the Organisation of African Unity (OAU) on 4 June, asking Brazil 'as a friend of Portugal, to exert its influence on the new Portuguese government in favour of granting the independence of Mozambique and Angola, and the recognition of the Republic of Guinea-Bissau' (OAU, 1974:67).

On 8 June, Itamaraty issued an official statement finally setting out Brazil's position unquestionably in favour of the independence of the former Portuguese colonies in Africa, as well as anticipating its recognition of the Republic of Guinea-Bissau, already declared independent from Portugal. Highlighting the 'special ties of friendship' between Brazil and Portugal, and between Brazil and all African nations, the Brazilian position also emphasised the need for a peaceful solution to the independence of the countries in question, 'which assures respect for the legitimate aspirations of the peoples concerned', reiterating its condemnation of 'any policy of a colonialist or racist nature' (*Problema Português*, 1974:67). The ambiguous stance that for more than 20 years had left Brazil and Africa alternately closer and further apart was over.

Foreign Minister Azeredo da Silveira personally made explicit Brazil's support for the elimination of forms of colonial domination, specifying the independence of Portuguese territories in Africa and stressing Brazil's

> historical responsibility for the future of these African communities, communities to which we are not only connected by blood and culture, but that, just like Brazil, emerged from the same irrepressibly creative movement of Portuguese overseas expansion. *Brazil's historical responsibility requires that we are ready to collaborate with our voice and our actions* in pursuit of fair and urgent solutions (Da Silveira, 1974b:43; our emphasis).

In sum, having defined the official Brazilian position in relation to 'the

Portuguese problem', effective actions soon followed. On 14 July, Brazil recognised the Republic of Guinea-Bissau as the first African country to gain independence from Portugal. Next, at the 29th United Nations General Assembly, Foreign Minister Azeredo da Silveira again questioned the problem of decolonisation, where he argued that

> Brazil believes unreservedly that procrastinations or subterfuges in implementing the process of decolonization are unjustified… What matters is not to vilify the colonial past, but to help build the future of the free nations… Thus, when we celebrate the emergence of newly independent Portuguese-speaking nations, we are not advocating any kind of cultural supremacy but simply congratulating the opportunities that these language communities open up for better fraternal understanding (Da Silveira, 1974c:40–1).

Events in Portuguese Africa continued to evolve in 1975. In March, Brazil installed a Special Representation in Luanda, Angola, headed by Ambassador Ovídio de Melo and in April, another Special Representation was opened in Lourenço Marques (present-day Maputo) in Mozambique. On 25 June, Mozambique proclaimed its independence; on 5 July, Cape Verde and on 12 July, São Tomé and Príncipe became independent. On 11 November 1975, Brazil was the first country to recognise the independence of the People's Republic of Angola, governed by the People's Movement for the Liberation of Angola (MPLA).[26] The recognition shown to the independence of all the PALOP countries should be interpreted as part of the Brazilian strategy to situate itself as a country capable of bridging the interests of the First and Third Worlds, and, according to Dombe, 'thereby assuring, through the gaps emerging in the world economy, its own space for reproducing its capital' (1997:69).

In Mozambique, the movement for national liberation became more prominent from 1964 with the growing influence of the Mozambique Liberation Front (FRELIMO), which emerged from the unification of the National Democratic Union of Mozambique (UDENAMO), the and the National African Union for Independent Mozambique (UNAMI). The armed struggle for National Liberation lasted almost 10 years and ended with the Lusaka Agreements, signed in September 1974 between

---

26 Following Angola's independence, Brazil's Special Representation in Luanda was transformed into an embassy, the first head of which was Ambassador Rodolpho Godoy de Souza Dantas, officially welcomed by President Neto in May 1976.

the Portuguese government and FRELIMO. These led to the formation of a transitional government headed by Joaquim Chissano, which included ministers nominated by the Portuguese government and others nominated by FRELIMO. Mozambique became independent on 25 June 1975.

Brazil–Mozambique diplomatic relations were officially established on 15 November 1975 through an Official Communiqué released by the Brazilian government. On 31 December, the Brazilian Embassy was opened in Lourenço Marques, also providing representation to the Kingdom of Lesotho. High-level relations between Brazil and Mozambique then gradually increased until the start of the 1990s. From 1976, Brazil began to export commodities to Africa in a more constant form, along with technology and capital, principally in the areas of civil construction and technical, industrial and agricultural consultancies.

Hence the Brazilian presence on the African continent in general, and particularly in the PALOP countries, was based on what would later be called South–South cooperation; in other words, its initiatives sought to avoid suggesting any ambition to take the place of the former imperialist powers on the continent, explaining the 'strong determination to highlight affinities, the complementary nature of the exchanges and the *horizontality* of relations' (Santana, 2003:163; our emphasis). This pursuit of horizontal relationships from 1974 to 1990 – which diplomatic texts from the period called 'mutual cooperation', 'joint interests', 'political coordination' and 'mutually satisfactory advantages' – underwent mutations in response to the domestic and international contexts of the 1990s, becoming referred to simply as technical cooperation, before returning strongly to the country's foreign-policy agenda from 2003 to 2010 under the broader concept of South–South cooperation.

The foreign policy of the João Baptista Figueiredo government (1979–1985) vis-à-vis Africa sought to maintain the cooperation begun earlier through horizontal cooperation, despite the economic crisis affecting Brazil and the African continent.[27] In 1981 the General Cooperation Agreement was signed between Brazil and Mozambique, a kind of umbrella agreement anticipating bilateral cooperation in economic, scientific, technical and cultural areas.

It is worth emphasising that the 3rd FRELIMO Congress, held in February 1977, instituted socialism as the form of government in Mozambique, the same

---

27 In 1980, correspondence between the Brazilian ambassador in Mozambique, Ítalo Zappa (Memorandum41/1980), and President Chissano established the start of talks on the agreement to create the Centre for Professional Training for Offices and Administrations in the country, to be run through a partnership between Brazil's National Commercial Apprenticeship Service (*Serviço Nacional de Aprendizagem Comercial*: SENAC) and the Mozambican Ministry of Work.

year that the civil war broke out. The combination of the devastating effects of the conflict and the major economic difficulties already faced by the country led the government to apply for funding from the International Monetary Fund (IMF) in 1982 (which was granted from 1984, after a devastating drought worsened the food shortages in the region).

The signing of the Nkomati Agreement (1984) between South Africa and Mozambique highlighted the respect for national sovereignty and committed to non-interference in each other's domestic affairs (agreeing to the use of peaceful means to resolve divergences). According to Pavia (n.d.), the agreement was simultaneously an arrival point and a departure point in the process of political transformation in Mozambique: at the same time as FRELIMO began to adopt a more pragmatic attitude in the postcolonial period, the country saw a political and economic opening and the start of greater dependency on the West. In October 1986, the Mozambican President, Samora Machel, died in an air accident and his Minister of Foreign Affairs, Joaquim Chissano, assumed the presidency, beginning the process of political opening and the peace dialogues with RENAMO. In 1987, after the country's economic collapse was recognised and an agreement was reached with the IMF and World Bank, Mozambique implemented its Economic Recovery Programme (*Programa de Reabilitação Econômica*: PAE) without, however, attaining the proposed objectives.

In Brazil, indirect elections saw Tancredo Neves become President of Brazil, but his vice-president, José Sarney, assumed the post after the former became seriously ill in 1985. Sarney tried to maintain the multilateralism of his predecessor at an international level and it was his government that took an important step towards the formation of what later became consolidated as the Community of Portuguese Language Countries (*Comunidade dos Países de Língua Portuguesa*: CPLP). In 1986, two conventions were held on technical cooperation between the customs administrations and on joint administrative assistance to combat the illegal traffic in narcotics and psychotropics among Portuguese-speaking countries. In 1989, the first meeting was held between the heads of staff and government of Portuguese-speaking countries (Angola, Brazil, Cape Verde, Guinea-Bissau, Mozambique, Portugal and São Tomé and Príncipe) in São Luis, Maranhão, at the invitation of President José Sarney. At the meeting, it was decided to create the International Portuguese Language Institute (*Instituto Internacional da Língua Portuguesa*: IILP). The possibility of creating a community uniting Portuguese-speaking countries was also discussed.

In 1987, the Complementary Adjustment to the 1981 General Cooperation Agreement in the Area of Communications was signed by Brazil and

Mozambique. On 8 and 9 April 1988, Joaquim Alberto Chissano, President of the People's Republic of Mozambique, accompanied by a delegation, made the first ever official visit of a Mozambican head of state to Brazil. In the Joint Communiqué released later, President Sarney's desire to maintain closer diplomatic relations with his colleague, Chissano, became clear, with the visit highlighted as 'clear proof of the solid ties existing between the two nations, and the desire of both governments to make these closer still, respecting the principles of equality, non-interference, cooperation and solidarity between the States' (*Communiqué*, 1988:1).

The visit was important for promoting bilateral relations, since it foregrounded the advances made in technical cooperation – specifically in the coal sector and in the close working relationship established between the ministries of Labour, Cooperation and State Administration to set up staff capacity-building programmes. Also in 1988, the 2nd Meeting of the Joint Committee was held in Brasília. The main themes discussed were new areas for cooperation and new mechanisms or schemes capable of identifying and speeding up solutions for existing problems.

In 1989, the Cultural Cooperation Agreement was signed between the two countries, as well as the Complementary Adjustment to the 1981 General Cooperation Agreement (in the Area of Irrigated Agriculture). The Brazil–Mozambique José Aparecido de Oliveira Cultural Centre (previously the Brazilian Studies Centre) was also inaugurated, having originated from the General Cooperation Agreement between Brazil and Mozambique signed in 1981.[28]

Liberal reforms, distancing and the Portuguese language (1990–2002)

Although the period from 1990 to 2002 involved political and economic changes on both sides of the Atlantic Ocean, with negative repercussions on Brazil–Mozambique relations (such as the decline in high-level contacts and trade), the period is important because of the socio-cultural dimension and the high-level encounters and meetings that took place to promote the Portuguese language.

Responding to the new international configuration, Brazil partially embarked on a neoliberal cycle. In other words, a new period began mixing diverse and contradictory factors, which also resulted in the dubious approach taken by Brazilian foreign policy in the 1990s, in the face of changes to the world system. Save for the Itamar Franco Government, the 1990s saw the

---

28 Also in 1989 the Scientific, Technical and Technology Cooperation Agreement was signed, along with its complementary protocol, as well as the Film Coproduction Agreement and the complementary protocol to the General Cooperation Agreement in the Area of Meteorology, all still active.

incomplete introduction of neoliberalism in Brazil under the governments of Fernando Collor de Mello (from the Party of National Reconstruction: PRN) and Fernando Henrique Cardoso (from the Brazilian Social Democracy Party: PSDB).

In 1990, the first direct elections held after the military dictatorship ended led to Fernando Collor de Mello becoming president. This was the start of the liberalisation of the Brazilian economy through the adoption of prescriptions recommended by the Washington Consensus, abandoning the national development project in the process. During this period, Brazilian diplomacy prioritised relations with central developed countries (in Western Europe and the United States) and nations in the Southern Cone, shifting its attention away from the African continent. It is worth adding that this diminution in relations with Africa was also conditioned by the international crisis, which affected both Brazil and the African countries in the 1980s.

On 30 November 1990, Mozambique adopted a new constitution, which introduced the Democratic Constitutional State, based on the separation and interdependence of powers and on pluralism. This contributed decisively to establishing a democratic climate, which allowed the country to hold the first multiparty elections. In October 1992, the Mozambique General Peace Agreement was signed in Rome between the leader of FRELIMO (Joaquim Chissano) and the president of RENAMO (Afonso Dhlakama). This agreement established United Nations monitoring of the agreement's implementation and contained clauses linked to the maintenance of the ceasefire, elections and humanitarian aid.

Then in December 1992, UN Security Council Resolution 792 established a peace mission: the United Nations Operation in Mozambique (ONUMOZ). Its mandate included monitoring the ceasefire, the withdrawal of foreign troops, securing the transport corridors and supervising the electoral process. From January 1983 until the end of the mission (December 1994), Brazil sent 26 military observers, 67 police observers, a medical unit and a company of infantry, comprising 170 soldiers, to Mozambique.

In Brazil, after a series of denunciations of corruption and irregularities in his government, Fernando Collor was impeached in 1992 and, in December of the same year, his vice-president, Itamar Franco, assumed the presidency of the country. Foreign policy during this period was based on continued integration with South America and proactive involvement in multilateral forums.

As a result, Brazil's relations with Mozambique – as with the other PALOP countries – diminished appreciably, suggesting that the reduction seen in the number of diplomats working on the African continent matched the downward trend in politico-commercial relations. High-level contacts remained limited to the signing of several agreements and a few state visits, including a visit by President Collor to Mozambique in 1991 (President Collor was awarded the Order of Friendship and Peace of the Republic of Mozambique). We can note, however, a new impetus to Brazil–Africa relations in the multilateral sphere through the relaunching of the South Atlantic Peace and Cooperation Zone (ZOPACAS) (1994) and the creation of the Community of Portuguese Language Countries (CPLP) from 1996. Despite a shrinking in Brazil–Africa relations, therefore, in part a reflection of domestic changes in Brazil, this clearly indicates a desire to retain Mozambique as an important partner, continuing the relations with countries from southern Africa, as explored by Soares de Lima (2009), first initiated with the establishment of diplomatic relations with Angola.

In October 1994, democratic elections were held in Mozambique under UN supervision. Joaquim Chissano was elected with 53 per cent of the votes and, with a degree of stability established in the country, the ONUMOZ mission came to an end in December. In January 1995, Fernando Henrique Cardoso became President of Brazil and maintained a policy of aligning with the central countries, based on the diversification of bilateral relations and multilateralism through international bodies. He prioritised Mercosur and shut down diplomatic offices and embassies in Africa. Despite this policy, on 17 July 1996, the CPLP was created with the goal of deepening friendship and cooperation between its members. In 1997, two decades after the opening of the Brazilian Embassy in Maputo, the Embassy of Mozambique was opened in Brasília (and started operating the following year).

Also in 1997, the Complementary Adjustment to the General Cooperation Agreement in the Area of Mining was signed, along with an agreement through an exchange of diplomatic notes between Brazil and the United Nations, regulating the assignment of a company of infantry from the Brazilian Army to ONUMOZ. In 1998, Mozambique's General Inspector of Finance, Jorge Marcelino, and the Home Minister, Almerino Manhenje, visited Brasília. This period – during which Fernando Henrique Cardoso was re-elected to a second term of office lasting until 2002 – was marked by various meetings and agreements signed in the context of the CPLP, including the cooperation agreement between higher education institutions. In 1999, during Cordoso's second term, elections were held in Mozambique and Chissano was re-elected to the presidency.

In March 2000, Brazil sent a Brazilian Air Force plane carrying a donation of 10 tonnes of medications to Mozambique in response to floods in that country. In addition, an agreement was signed in April between the Brazilian

Cooperation Agency (*Agência Brasileira de Cooperação*: ABC) and the German Cooperation Agency (*Deutsche Gesellschaft für Internationale Zusammenarbeit*: GIZ) to develop programmes for Technical Cooperation between Developing Countries (TCDC), prioritising the PALOP countries.[29]

South–South cooperation and the deepening of relations (2003–2010)

The foreign policy of the government of Luiz Inácio Lula da Silva (two mandates from 2003–2006 and 2007–2010) marked a shift in the country's international stance, combined with an appreciation of the changing world system, with a clear emphasis on multipolarity, which required capacity to adapt and respond. A founding member of the Workers' Party (PT), President Lula da Silva looked to project this foreign policy as 'personal', 'charismatic' and 'nationalist' (Ricupero, 2010). During both his mandates, Brazil's foreign-policy initiatives aimed to restimulate alliances at the South–South level and challenge the hegemony of developed central countries. This 'democratisation of international relations', advocated by President Lula da Silva, involved an understanding of the new international context and its transformation into a multipolar order in which developing states like Brazil would play a decisive role. This creative foreign policy (high-minded and active in the words of the president himself) also revised Brazil's policy for Africa, adopting a proactive, optimistic and pragmatic approach, which had been pushed into the background between 1990 and 2002. In this new setting, the African continent was revalued as part of the legitimisation of South–South cooperation – that is, the pursuit of an active development policy. For Foreign Minister Amorim, this cooperation comprised part of 'a diplomatic strategy stemming from an authentic desire to show solidarity to poor countries', but also one that 'helps expand Brazilian involvement' in the world system where cooperation,

> in matters of trade, investment, science and technology and other fields

---

[29] In November 2000, the Mission of Centres of Excellence in Public Administration was held in Maputo (including representatives from the ABC, FUNDAP/IPEA, SEBRAE/SENAI and representation from the CPLP). In 2001, the Mozambican Minister of Agriculture and Rural Development, Hélder dos Santos FM Muteia, the Minister of Women and Social Coordination, Virgília Matabele, and President Joaquim Chissano visited Brazil. Numerous agreements were signed, principally technical cooperation agreements in the areas of health, education and security. It is worth pointing out that, during this period, Brazil began its support for the National STD/AIDS Prevention Programme. The latter is of extreme importance to the Mozambican population, since it is one of the countries with the highest rates of HIV infection, while Brazil is one of the few countries with the resources to produce the pharmaceutical drugs needed to control the virus. Another cooperation project started in 2001 (through a Complementary Adjustment signed between the two countries) was the Solidary Literacy Programme (PASMO). Also in 2001, two academic missions involving partner universities from the Solidary Literacy Programme Support Association (AAPAS) took place in Maputo.

reinforces our stature and strengthens our position in trade, finance and climate negotiations. Last, but not least, building coalitions with developing countries is also a way of engaging in the reform of global governance in order to make international institutions fairer and more democratic (Amorim, 2010:230).

As a complement to this political advance of South–South cooperation, the theme of development also returned to the Brazilian agenda. Here Foreign Minister Amorim similarly founded his argument on the African Renaissance and the opportunities for Brazil: 'Coming back [from the tour of Africa], I can affirm that Africa is following what is happening in Brazil with huge interest and expectation. Moreover, it seems that there is a real heartland of Brazil on the other side of the Atlantic' (Amorim, 2003:239).

The pragmatism revived by Lula da Silva's foreign policy was discussed by the president himself in an interview given to the Algerian press in 2006 on the relations with PALOP countries as a 'reality of political diplomacy and cooperation'. Foreign Minister Amorim, in a general analysis of his eight years in office, claimed that the PALOP countries 'are, quite understandably, the ones with whom Brazil has the most enduring, solid and diversified relationships' (Amorim, 2010:233).

The number of high-level contacts increased significantly over this period, with no other government in Brazil's history investing so much, in both quantitative and qualitative terms, in its foreign policy for Africa. Through visits, agreements, meetings and actions in multilateral bodies, Brazil's presence on the continent returned to the levels seen prior to 1990, increasing the volume and content of contacts. In 2003, President Lula da Silva visited Maputo, when 11 technical cooperation agreements were signed.[30] President Joaquim Chissano returned the gesture with an official visit to Brazil in August 2004, an event dominated by the signing of an agreement to write off 95 per cent of Mozambique's public debt

---

30 The following agreements were signed: 1) Memoranda of Understanding in the Areas of (a) Geology, Mining and Mineral Transformation, and (b) the Environment; 2) Complementary Adjustments to the General Cooperation Agreement for: (a) Education for the Implementation of the 'School Allowance' Project, (b) Support for Development of the National Pilot Literacy Programme for Mozambique, (c) Implementation of the PCI-NTWANANO Project as part of the International Cooperation Programme for Brazil's Ministry of Health, (d) cooperation in the field of sports, and (e) implementation of the Support Project for the Development and Strengthening of the Agricultural Research Sector of the Republic of Mozambique; 3) Agreement on Technical Cooperation and Procedures in Sanitation and Phytosanitation, 4) Memorandum of Understanding in the context of the International Cooperation Programme of Brazil's Ministry of Health (HIV and AIDS); 5) Work Programme in Scientific and Technological Cooperation; 6) Protocol of Intentions on Technical Cooperation in the Area of Lands and Mapping; 7) Protocol of Intentions on Scientific and Technological Cooperation in the Area of Health; and 8) Protocol of Intentions on Technical Cooperation in the Area of Public Administration.

with Brazil, amounting to around US$280 million in commercial loans granted within the context of PROEX. Other Acts were also signed.[31] Chissano showed Mozambique's interest in reactivating relations with Brazil at a more pragmatic level, reflecting a demand on both sides of the Atlantic:

> Recent experiences in Africa show that the impact of natural calamities, like floods and cyclones, can be just the same as or worse than armed conflicts. In this context, Africa would benefit from Brazilian technology in controlling natural resources through the use of satellites. Brazil could equally help promote a partnership between Africa and Mercosur, which would amplify economic and political relations between the two regions (Chissano, 2004:30).

In February 2005, the Brazilian delegation, headed by Vice-President José Alencar, attended the inauguration of President Armando Guebuza. In March of the same year, Foreign Minister Amorim visited Maputo, where he met the Head of State and other recently appointed Mozambican authorities, including the Prime Minister, Luísa Diogo, and the Minister of Foreign Affairs and Cooperation, Alcinda Abreu. In July, the Overseas Office of the Armed Forces was established at the embassy in Maputo and, in September, the fourth meeting of the bilateral Joint Commission was held. In 2006, a visit to Brazil by the Minister of Youth and Sports, David Simago, including the signing of the Protocol of Intentions for Exchange and Technical Cooperation in the Area of Social Inclusion and the Promotion of Youth Rights, and the First Amendment to the Protocol of Intentions in the Area of Fighting Discrimination and Promoting Racial Equality (of 2004).

In September 2007, the Mozambican President Armando Guebuza made an official visit to Brazil as guest of honour at the Seventh of September parade (Brazilian Independence Day). Various new agreements were signed, especially

---

31 Protocols of Intentions on (a) Technical Cooperation in the Area of Training Specialised Prison Staff, and (b) in the Area of Fighting Discrimination and Promoting Racial Equality; Complementary Adjustments to (a) the General Cooperation Agreement in the Context of Public Security and (b) the Cultural Cooperation Agreement on Cooperation in the Area of Social Communication, as well as the Cooperation Agreement between Brazil and Mozambique on Fighting the Illegal Production, Consumption and Trafficking of Narcotics and Psychotropic Substances and on Combatting the Activities of Money Laundering and other Fraudulent Financial Transactions, and the Complementary Adjustment to the General Cooperation Agreement for Implementation of the Project 'Social Inclusion through Sports'.

in the areas of health and agriculture.[32] In 2008, Mozambique's Foreign Minister, Oldemiro Baloi, visited the cities of Brasília, Belo Horizonte and Rio de Janeiro. In October 2008, President Lula da Silva visited Mozambique for the second time when, in a solemn ceremony, the former Brazilian Studies Centre was renamed the Brazil–Mozambique Cultural Centre (the change of name occurring simultaneously at the dozens of cultural centres run by Brazil's embassies and consulates around the world). In July 2009, President Guebuza made his second official visit to Brazil. The 5th Joint Commission of Brazil–Mozambique Cooperation was held in Brasília in June 2010.

President Lula da Silva visited Mozambique on 9–10 November 2010.[33] In relation to technical cooperation, the basis of African policy, visible progress was evident in all areas with concrete action made by the ABC in partnership with the ministries of Foreign Affairs, Education, Culture, Development and Foreign Trade, Agriculture, Farming and Food Supply, and Science and Technology.[34] In this sense, the combination of socio-economic development and foreign policy provides a clear affirmation of the concept of South–South cooperation in which the Brazil–Mozambique relations are inserted.

The multilateral sphere also continued to act as a complementary instrument to bilateral relations. In July 2004, in a speech concluding Brazil's presidency of the community, President Lula da Silva argued that the CPLP had become 'a mature organization, capable of responding promptly to difficult situations' and had begun to enjoy 'the prestige of an institution dedicated to preventing situations of tension and conflict'. After 2003 especially, the relations formed with the creation of the CPLP in 1996 had gradually deepened.

---

32 Complementary Adjustment to the General Cooperation Agreement for Implementation of the projects 'Strengthening Food and Nutrition Initiatives', 'Support for the Urban Development of Mozambique' and 'Support for the Development of Horticulture and Fruticulture of Mozambique'; Executive Programme of the Cultural Agreement for the Years 2007–2010; Agreement on the Transfer of Condemned Persons and Complementary Adjustment to the General Cooperation Agreement for Implementation of the Project 'Strengthening the National Health Institute of Mozambique'.

33 On the occasion, Complementary Adjustments were signed in relation to the project, 'Support for the Rehabilitation of the Chamanculo C District as Part of the Global Strategy for the Reordering and Urbanisation of the Informal Settlements of Maputo Municipality', the project 'Increase in the Research Capacity and Technological Diffusion towards Agricultural Development of the Nacala Corridor, Mozambique', the 'Cooperation Programme between the Open University of Brazil (UAB), the Ministry of Education (MINED), the Pedagogical University (UP) and Eduardo Mondlane University (UEM) of Mozambique', the project 'Support for the Implantation of the Telehealth Centre, Library and the Distance Learning Programme in the Health of Women, Children and Youth of Mozambique', and the project 'Implantation of a Breastmilk Bank and Centre in Mozambique'.

34 In education, the Third Protocol of the Postgraduate Student Assistance Programme (PEC-PG) was signed in 2006. The Da Silva government gave special emphasis to amplifying cooperation agreements and development programmes with Africa, increasing the offer of places on the Postgraduate and Graduate Student Assistance Programmes (PEC-PG and PEC-G).

In sum, the period between 2003 and 2010 saw an intense resumption and deepening of Brazil's African policy. The eight years of the Lula da Silva government can be regarded as the most fertile in terms of bilateral relations, given the number and quality of the high-level bilateral contacts, the increase in cooperation projects (and their results), the visibility of Africa in Brazil and Brazil in Africa, and especially the policies of historical–cultural recuperation, which form the bedrock to legitimising these relations. The constant renegotiation of the debts of PALOP countries to Brazil during the period (including the partial write-off of Mozambican and Cape Verdean debts) was also part of this foreign policy pursued by the Lula da Silva government, including the aim of facilitating Brazilian exports of products with higher aggregate value to these countries and their neighbours. The increase in bilateral contacts and the cooperation agreements signed and implemented add ballast to this claim and the legitimisation of South–South cooperation as the basis for these relations.

Final considerations: A new phase or a decline in bilateral relations?

Cooperative action has served as a basis of Brazil–Mozambique relations and, indeed, Brazil–PALOP relations since 1974. A combination of deep forces was transformed into an internal conditioning factor of these countries, rooted in deep structural deficiencies, which underlay the high level of demand for technical cooperation projects and initiatives (training of human resources, assistance in education, health, capacity-building in farming programmes and so on), with cooperation figuring as Brazil's main line of action for these Lusophone states.

However, this action should not be understood as devoid of political interests: by establishing the African continent as a 'regional area' in its foreign policy, specifically within the parameters of the South Atlantic, Brazil has been able to consolidate its presence in the PALOP countries – initiated through cooperation, but maintained and deepened through the political dimension of this activity. This can be identified, for example, in an increase in Brazil's direct investments in these countries, an increase in bilateral trade, in the support of these countries for Brazilian proposals at multilateral bodies like the United Nations, CPLP and G-20, and even in the preference offered to Brazilian companies to operate in national markets (especially Petrobrás and Vale do Rio Doce, or the construction firms, Odebrecht and Andrade Gutierrez).

The government of President Dilma Rousseff (2011–2016) has maintained the proactive African policy inherited from President Lula da Silva, albeit more discretely, with fewer high-level relations with Mozambique. President Dilma visited Maputo in October 2011. In March 2013, at a BRICS meeting in South Africa, President Dilma and President Guebuza met to discuss the deepening of bilateral cooperation, especially in relation to the continuation of coal mining in Moatize.

The persistent thread running through these bilateral relations has been cooperative action. The key concept behind this cooperation was redefined, however, during three distinct phases: 1) from 1974 to 1990, by horizontality; 2) from 1990 to 2002, by technical cooperation; and 3) from 2003 to 2010, by South–South cooperation, implemented as technical cooperation projects by the ABC – projects called 'Brazil–PALOP Cooperation' by the Brazilian government. The emphasis has been on human-resource capacity-building and training, institutional strengthening and meeting the basic needs of these populations, bilateral cooperation initiatives that first emerged in the 1970s. These demands, which were discussed with the beneficiaries, were identified during the regular Brazilian technical missions to the PALOP countries and analysed in the meetings of the Joint Commissions, especially in the 1980s.

Brazil–Mozambique relations are, therefore, embedded in a wider logic of deepening South Atlantic relations as a central axis of Brazil's foreign policy, rooted in a political understanding of this approximation, evident since the 1970s. Hence historical constraints are evident in the formulation of these bilateral relations, and in the Brazil–PALOP relations more widely. However, they retain their specificities, which, to a large extent, reflect the institutional and political changes experienced in both countries over this period, spanning more than three decades. Beyond sharing numerous historical and cultural aspects, Brazil–Mozambique–PALOP are located at the same level as actors within the world system; their peripheral situation forms a crucial and determinant point in the relations between themselves, especially through the notion of cooperative action, which has provided the basis and stimulus for these relations.

References

Amorim, C (2003) O Brasil e o renascimento africano. *Folha de São Paulo*, 25 May 2003. *Resenha de Política Exterior do Brasil*, No. 92, pp 238–40.

Amorim, C (2009) Discurso do Ministro das Relações Exteriores, embaixador Celso Amorim, durante a cerimônia em homenagem ao Dia do Diplomata, Brasília, 07/05/2009. *Resenha de Política Exterior do Brasil*, no.104, pp 103–05.

Amorim, C (2010) Brazilian foreign policy under President Lula (2003–2010): An overview'. *Revista Brasileira de Política Internacional*, **53** (Special Edition), pp 214–40.

Azeredo da Silveira, AF (1974a) Objetivos da revolução na política exterior. Pronunciamento do Ministro de Estado das Relações Exteriores feito a uma Estadocadeia de rádio e televisão, em 28 de março de 1974. *Resenha de Política Exterior do Brasil*, **1**, pp 23–4.

Azeredo da Silveira, AF (1974b) Políticos e diplomatas: o diálogo indispensável. Discurso do Ministro de Estado das Relações Exteriores na Sessão conjunta de Relações Exteriores do Senado Federal e da Câmara dos Deputados, em 19 de junho de 1974b. *Resenha de Política Exterior do Brasil*, **1**, pp 41–4.

Azeredo da Silveira, AF (1974c) Discurso do Chanceler brasileiro, Antônio F. Azeredo da

Silveira, na abertura da XXIX Assembleia Geral das Nações Unidas, em Nova York, em 23 de setembro de 1974c. *Resenha de Política Exterior do Brasil*, No. 2, pp 39–44.

Bauer, G and Taylor, SD (2005) *Politics in Southern Africa: State and society in transition*. Boulder, CO: Lynne Rienner Publishers.

Bueno, C and Cervo, AL (2008) *História da política exterior do Brasil*, 3rd edition. Brasília: Ed. Universidade de Brasilia.

Comunicado conjunto da visita do Senhor Joaquim Alberto Chissano, Presidente da República Popular de Moçambique ao Brasil, (09/04/1988). Available at: http://dai-mre.serpro.gov.br/atos-internacionais/bilaterais/1988/b_21 (accessed 10 April 2013).

Esteves, RCV (n.d.) *Programa Alfabetização Solidária: uma estratégia de sucesso para a educação de jovens e adultos no Brasil*. Available at: http://unpan1.un.org/intradoc/groups/public/documents/CLAD/clad0044529.pdf (accessed 19 April 2013).

Hill, C (2003) *The Changing Politics of Foreign Policy*. New York: Palgrave.

Hirst, M and Pinheiro, L (1995) A política externa brasileira em dois tempos. *Revista Brasileira de Política Internacional*, **38** (1), pp 5–23.

Iglesias Puente, CA (2010) *A cooperação técnica horizontal brasileira como instrumento de política externa: a evolução da cooperação técnica com países em desenvolvimento – CTPD, no período 1995–2005*. Brasília: FUNAG.

Lampreia, LF (2005) Discurso do Ministro das Relações Exteriores, Embaixador Luiz Felipe Lampreia, no Seminário 'A importância do relacionamento comercial e cultural entre o Brasil e os países africanos', comemorativo ao Dia da África, promovido pela Comissão de Relações Exteriores do Senado Federal, em Brasília, em 25 de maio de 1995. *Resenha de Política Exterior do Brasil*, **76**, pp 202–03.

Lima, MR Soares de and Hirst, M (eds) (2009) *Brasil, Índia e África do Sul: Desafios e oportunidades para novas parcerias*. São Paulo: Paz e Terra.

O Primeiro-Ministro de Portugal Marcello Caetano, visita esta semana o Brasil, numa ofensiva para tirar seu país do isolamento político que lhe deixou só dois amigos na África – Rodésia do Sul e República da África do Sul – e quase nenhum apoio nos outros continentes e na ONU. *Veja*, 9 July 1969, p 33.

Oua Pede Ajuda ao Brasil (1974) *Resenha de Política Exterior do Brasil*, No. 1, p 67.

Pavia, JFLZ (n.d.) *A Dimensão Internacional da Transição Pós-Autoritária em Moçambique: As Proposições de Laurence Whitehead*. Lisbon. Available at: http://www.cepese.pt/portal/investigacao/working-papers/relacoes-externas-de-portugal/a-dimensao-internacional-da-transicao-pos-autoritaria-em-mocambique-as-proposicoes-de-laurence-whitehead/A-Dimensao-Internacional-da-Transicao-Pos.pdf (accessed 18 April 2013).

Pinheiro, L (1989) Brasil, Portugal e descolonização Africana (1946–1960). *Contexto Internacional*, **5** (9), pp 91–111.

Problema Português na África: Brasil Define Posição (1974) *Resenha de Política Exterior do Brasil*, **1**, p 67.

Ribeiro, CO (2009) As relações Brasil-África entre os governos Collor e Itamar Franco. *Revista Brasileira de Ciência Política*, **1**, pp 289–329. Available at: http://seer.bce.unb.br/index.php/rbcp/article/viewFile/6600/5325 (accessed 18 April 2013).

Ricupero, R (2010) À sombra de Charles De Gaulle: uma diplomacia carismática e intransferível. *Novos estudos CEBRAP*, **87**, pp 35–58.

Rizzi, KR (2012) *O Grande Brasil e os Pequenos PALOP*. PhD thesis in Political Science, Postgraduate Program in Political Science, Federal University of Rio Grande do Sul, Brazil, 2012.

Silva, LI Lula da (2003a) Discurso do Presidente da República, Luiz Inácio Lula da Silva, no Congresso Nacional em 1 de janeiro de 2003. *Resenha de Política Exterior do Brasil*, **30** (92), 1st semester 2003, pp 13–20.

Silva, LI Lula da (2004) Discurso do Presidente da República, Luiz Inácio Lula da Silva, na cerimônia de abertura da 7ª Cimeira Brasil–Portugal, No Palácio Itamaraty, em 8 de março de 2004. *Resenha de Política Exterior do Brasil*, **31** (94), 1st semester, pp 70–1.

Silva, LI Lula da (2005) Discurso do Presidente da República, Luiz Inácio Lula da Silva, durante a Reunião Ampliada Brasil-Guiné-Bissau, Bissau, no dia 13 de abril de 2005. *Resenha de Política Exterior do Brasil*, **32** (96), 1st semester, pp 109–10.

Visentini, PGF (2004) *O descompasso entre as nações*. Rio de Janeiro: Record.

Visentini, PGF (2010) África na política internacional. Curitiba: Juruá.

Visentini, PGF (2012) *Os países africanos: diversidade de um continente*. Porto Alegre: Editora Século XXI/CEBRAFRICA.

Chapter 3

What Brazil–Mozambique relations tell us about South–South cooperation

Robert Myles McDonnell

As so-called emerging states[35] have sought a greater role in international affairs, the practice of 'South–South cooperation' (SSC) has developed and become a frequently encountered term in both academic and non-academic literature. SSC is usually taken to mean a form of cooperation between Southern or developing countries, which excludes richer Northern countries, and is ostensibly based on various principles, as will be discussed in more detail later.

However, SSC itself has not been fully explained yet. Is it in fact distinct from North–South cooperation (NSC) and, if so, how? Why do states choose to cooperate in this fashion? Why would aid recipients, with scarce resources, choose to become donors who divert resources away from their own state, and why do their publics accept this? Does SSC display the same characteristics as the so-called 'traditional aid' of richer, more established, donors? With a lack of empirical knowledge, we also have a lack of theoretical clarity. What can theories of international relations (IR) tell us about SSC and vice-versa?

One notable recent aspect of this form of international cooperation is the growth in foreign assistance transactions, or aid, between these states, with some countries existing simultaneously as aid recipient and donor, such as Brazil. There are some common claims made in the literature about why Brazil and Mozambique would choose to work together in this way, such as humanitarian, linguistic or cultural reasons, for economic opportunity, or in the name of security, geopolitics and alliance-building. This chapter seeks to place SSC, specifically Brazil's aid relationship with Mozambique, in an appropriate theoretical context in relation to IR theory.

South–South cooperation

While there is little concrete agreement on what exactly constitutes SSC, and no universally accepted definition that would allow us to neatly encapsulate

---

35 The terms 'emerging', 'developing', 'Southern' are used interchangeably throughout this chapter. It should be noted that many states have co-existing developed and developing regions, and that there is no consensus on the appropriateness of these terms for describing the global political economy. See, for example, Rosenbaum and Tyler (1975:244–5)

the intricacies of it, one thing many observers readily accept is its 'distinctly different flavour' (Ladd, 2010:6). Those working in the SSC literature, especially the non-academic literature, assume that since North–South relations involve opposites, South–South may be understood as relationships between equals – a position enthusiastically espoused by the states themselves. Sanahuja (2010:19) describes this view:

> South–South cooperation is portrayed as more 'developmental' – that is, detached from the selfish political, economic or strategic interests of rich countries; 'fair' – rooted in principles such as self-determination and solidarity, focused on social justice and free of hidden governmental agendas; 'horizontal' – it takes place between developing countries in a relationship of equals, without the power asymmetries and conditionality usually found in North–South cooperation; and 'more effective' – based on more cost-effective instruments and resources, and better adapted to the specific development needs and local contexts of recipient countries.

Abdenur (2007) similarly splits Brazilian aid into the following three categories: *pragmatism*, *altruism* and *strengthening cultural ties*. We can see these views reflected in the grandiose diplomatic language of 'horizontal cooperation', 'mutual benefit', 'solidarity' as championed by the states involved, particularly Brazil (Cabral and Shankland, 2013:5).[36] It is also common in the SSC literature. Investigating whether SSC relationships really are different to North–South ones is more than an academic exercise, because SSC is rapidly growing, attracting both admirers and critics.[37]

One of the most notable aspects of SSC rhetoric is the recurrent and powerful idea that SSC adheres to a principle of non-interference in the internal affairs of the recipient (Davies, 2010). This is pointed out as one of the most distinct and essential differences between NSC and SSC, and is used as one of the key justifications as to why SSC is such an important new development, especially by the states involved. It is a point of contention between those who believe that such 'untied aid' allows repressive regimes to continue their 'bad behaviour' and those who see it as emblematic of the more egalitarian nature of SSC. In the mainstream media, one prominent example of a modern-day SSC manifestation is the BRICS group of states (Brazil, Russia, India, China and South Africa). The BRICS are commonly referred to as a single unit, implying

---

36 See http://www.itamaraty.gov.br/temas/cooperacao-tecnica for an official description of Brazilian aid, or technical cooperation. Also see Martins (2011).
37 See, for example, Chichava *et al* (2013:15).

coherent preferences and objectives, a view summarily dismissed by some (such as Sharma, 2012). Although the BRICS has received much attention, the IBSA group of states (India, Brazil and South Africa) represents, in many ways, a much more significant realisation of SSC (Vieira, 2013).

The following sections detail the academic literature on aid and where it meets the concept of SSC. Thereafter, the relationship between Brazil and Mozambique is analysed in view of the theories detailed in these literatures.

Foreign aid

The scholars involved in the political science and IR literature on foreign aid can agree on one thing: there are many disagreements when it comes to foreign aid, such as how to define it and how to measure it.[38] As Morgenthau wrote as far back as 1962, of 'the seeming and real innovations which the modern age has introduced into the practice of foreign policy, none has proven more baffling to both understanding and action than foreign aid' (1962:301).

Academic work has argued that aid is inefficient (Collier and Dollar, 2002) and that even something as superficially non-political as food aid is dominated by geopolitical concerns (Ball and Johnson, 1996). On the donor side, there is much literature on the motivations that drive states to give aid (Alesina and Dollar, 1998; Berthélemy and Tichit, 2004). US aid, especially, has been shown to respond to political pressure, whether the pressure is due to Communism, the War on Terror or domestic politics (Otter, 2003; Boschini and Olofsgård, 2007; Fleck and Kilby, 2010; Tingley, 2010). International organisations, too, have been found to shape their aid and loan programmes according to the political wishes of their powerful members; Kilby (2009) finds evidence of US influence on the World Bank, while Reynaud and Vauday (2009) demonstrate the 'over-influence' of the United States and the G7 on the International Monetary Fund's (IMF) board of directors.[39]

Aid can buy favourable United Nations General Assembly votes (Dreher, Nunnencamp and Thiele, 2006), and temporary membership of the United Nations Security Council brings with it increased aid loans for the duration of membership (Dreher, Sturm and Vreeland, 2009). Overall, most of the academic work done on donor motivations has come to one generally agreed conclusion:

---

38 The word 'aid' here is an umbrella term to unify the many varying descriptions of this type of cooperation, such as foreign assistance, humanitarian assistance, technical cooperation, and so forth. As emerging donors often purposely avoid using the word 'aid' for political reasons, and, therefore, invent innumerable variations, I feel it is justified for the sake of simplicity.

39 This is not to imply some negative connotation; many would believe that it is entirely rational for a donor to demand (reasonable) concessions from the recipient. Indeed, the domestic politics of these donor countries would surely demand that aid money is not wasted. Also, there is nothing untoward in a state helping domestic commerce find a foothold in foreign markets.

states give aid *only* if it is in their interest to do so, a point of view markedly different from the altruistic and 'solidarity' rhetoric of emerging donors.

On the recipient side, Werker, Ahmed and Cohen (2008) show that aid given to non-democratic regimes is associated with spending on non-capital goods and correlates with a large outflow of funds from the recipient state. This implies that this aid money was not spent on development for the recipient but, instead, stashed in offshore bank accounts or spent on luxury goods, a finding consistent with selectorate theory work by Bueno de Mesquita and Smith, who find that aid is used to buy the political support necessary to stay in power (Bueno de Mesquita and Smith, 2007; 2009). Alesina and Weder found that the more corrupt a state is, the more aid it receives (1999).

There is also the not insignificant fact that no one seems to be able to get past the substantial methodological hurdles to obtain concrete answers with regard to the question of whether aid causes growth or growth attracts aid, and to understand how exactly aid functions in relation to foreign direct investment and economic growth (see, for example, Boone, 1995; Burnside and Dollar, 2000; Kosack and Tobin, 2006; Minoiu and Reddy, 2009).[40] Another demonstration of the lack of agreement in the literature is the finding that there is no evidence that aid promotes democracy (Knack, 2004) and the finding that aid does, indeed, promote democracy, depending on who gives it (Bermeo, 2011).

Finally, some scholars see aid as just one of many options in the foreign-policy portfolio, whether the donor chooses 'change-seeking' or 'maintenance-seeking' policies (Palmer *et al*, 2002), or chooses to foster dependency or signal commitment (McKinlay and Little, 1978) – views that link back to Morgenthau's assertion that aid is but one of the 'weapons in the political armoury of the nation' (1962:309), even if it is one that is more valuable in terms of 'soft power'. The following section discusses the meeting point of SSC and aid; in other words, the appearance of so-called 'emerging' donors.[41]

Where South–South cooperation and foreign aid meet

What is interesting for the aid literature is the emergence of states that are both recipient and donor, which characterises India, Brazil and China, among others. Brazil's aid receipts from the Organisation for Economic Development

---

40   There is a significant problem with selection bias in aid analysis, since countries are selected beforehand by donors for aid based on their suitability, and so aid is not randomly donated. There is also an issue with endogeneity, as the work done on the causal relationship between aid and growth demonstrates.
41   These donors are assumed to be new entrants to the world of aid. Most have, in fact, been giving aid in one form or another for decades (Rosenbaum and Tyler, 1975; Cervo, 1994).

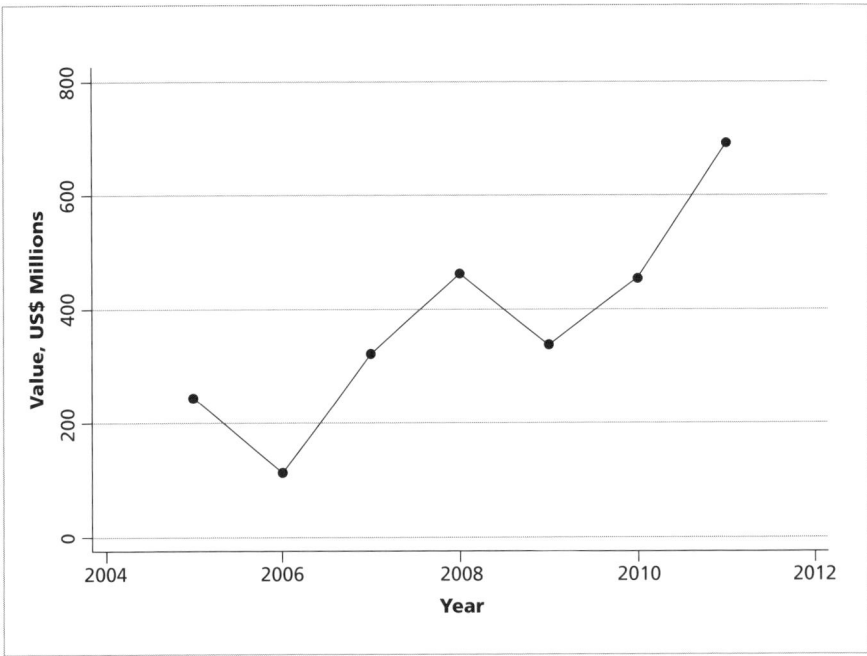

Figure 3.1: OECD aid to Brazil 2005–2011
Source: Author from OECD statistics

(OECD) countries for the years 2005 to 2011 are shown in Figure 3.1. This illustrates quite clearly that while Brazil's foreign assistance is growing (shown in Figure 3.2), its aid receipts are doing likewise.

Brazil does not offer aid in the form of loans or grants, as it is legally difficult to do so (Cabral and Weinstock, 2010:10), although it has cancelled or reduced many debts from African states (Pino, 2010:4). Its aid programme is dispersed across different government agencies and is rather unorganised, including the Agência Brasileira de Cooperação (ABC), the International Affairs Office of the Health Ministry, the Osvaldo Cruz Foundation, the Brazilian Agricultural Research Corporation (known by its Portuguese acronym, Embrapa, and linked to the Ministry of Agriculture) and SENAI (the National Service for Industrial Learning), not to mention Itamaraty, the Foreign Ministry.

'Establishing Brazil's quantitative profile as an aid donor is an arduous task, given the scarcity of official statistics, varying methodologies on what should be measured as development aid and the divergence between the estimates of international organisations and journalistic and academic sources,' notes Pino (2010:4). Estimates of Brazilian aid put it at US$4 billion dollars a year (*The Economist*, 2010), others at around US$1 billion (Cabral and Weinstock, 2010), yet others at US$365 million (ECOSOC, 2008). ABC has certainly been

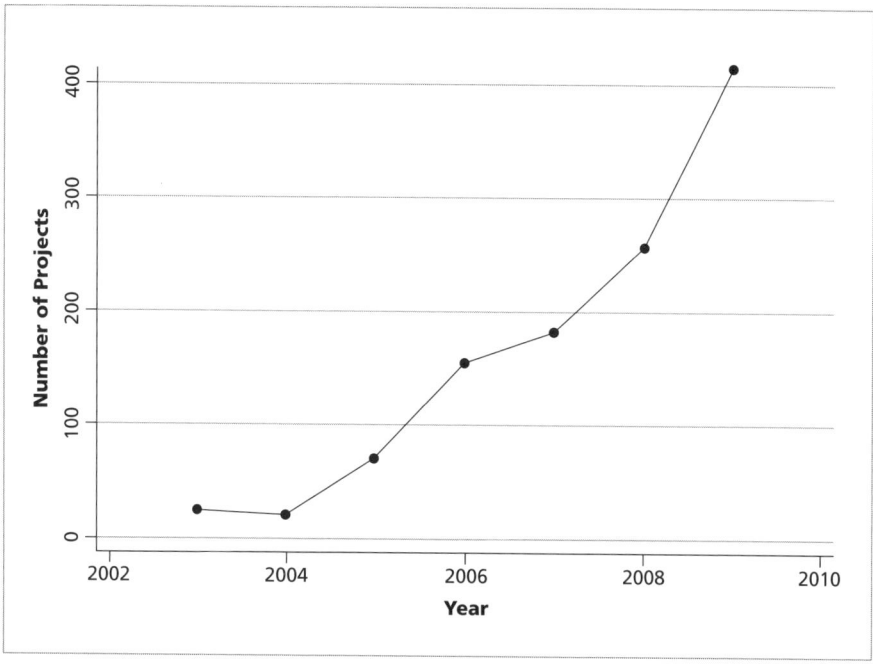

Figure 3.2: The number of technical cooperation projects initiated by Brazil annually, 2003–2009
Source: Author from ABC figures

ramping up both the magnitude and number of its projects over recent years with no sign of stopping any time soon, as is evident from Figure 3.2. Indeed, in 2013 President Dilma Rousseff promised the cancellation or restructuring of US$900 million of African debt (*Folha de São Paulo*, 2013).

Although the Brazilian Government prefers the term 'technical cooperation' to describe Brazilian activities in countries like Mozambique, it is widely recognised that foreign policy concerns play their part, which is one reason it is referred to here as aid (Puente, 2010). This technical cooperation involves the transfer of Brazilian technological expertise, usually in the areas of tropical agriculture, education, health (particularly AIDS-related) and energy, particularly biofuels (Vaz and Inoue, 2007).

It is also worth pausing briefly to note that Brazil is just one of many donors involved with Mozambique, with aid in various forms amounting to 23 per cent of Mozambican gross domestic product (GDP) in 2004, for example. The IMF calculated that 48 per cent of the government's budget was from aid in the same year and observers have raised concerns of aid dependence and the fraudulent use of funds (Renzio and Hanlon, 2007). It is also important to remember that most of Brazilian aid goes to Latin American countries (IPEA, 2010).

Scholarly analysis of South–South aid has focused heavily on China, as the biggest emerging donor in absolute terms, and particularly on China's involvement with Africa (see, for example, Kurlantzick, 2006; Davies *et al*, 2008; Woods, 2008). However, China is hardly representative of the states involved in SSC, because its economy is massively larger than other emerging states and it is now considered a world power, certainly in economic terms. Indeed, placing China in the picture serves only to confuse further; for example, China is a heavy investor in Brazil, with projects and activities in agriculture and infrastructure, which mirror Brazil's activities in Africa. Thus, to date the debate is a confused one due to the lack of availability of facts and figures regarding aid flows, and the lack of clarity in theoretical understanding.

One thing that we should recognise is that the logic underpinning the SSC is not new, neither is the term (Rosenbaum and Tyler, 1975; Pino, 2009). Realist theories detail the 'balancing' and 'bandwagoning' behaviour of states because of their position in the international system, a position determined by their power status, which in turn is informed by their material capabilities (see, for example, Waltz, 1979). According to this logic, states in the South, generally having less power, can 'bandwagon' by allying themselves with the strongest side, or they can choose a strategy of maintaining some autonomy by 'balancing'. The logic of the latter would explain SSC: states join forces to stand a better chance of achieving their goals (Rosenbaum and Tyler, 1975), a point of view also found in coalition theory work. However, the sharing of goals is often based on an assumption of shared underlying interests – a flawed assumption, as Oliveira and Onuki show in relation to the India–Brazil–South Africa Dialogue Forum (IBSA) (Oliveira and Onuki, 2010), one of the supposed new showcase institutions of SSC.

International political economy (IPE) scholars, including those informed by game theory, advocate both the use of rational-actor approaches and the dismantling of the idea that the state is a unitary actor in international politics (for example, Milner, 1997). In such an approach, cooperation, of any kind, is the result of the incentives (primarily domestic) that drive such behaviour. While incentives, or preferences, may be many and varied, this is the basic model through which SSC should be judged, according to IPE scholars. Following this logic, we might conclude that SSC is a product of domestic politics, supposing, for example, that right-wing governments are more likely to want to engage in foreign trade, or left-wing governments to give aid. It also implies that sub-national entities, such as sectoral interest groups and private companies, pursue the realisation of their preferences through the government. This would lead us to assume SSC is driven, at least in part, by Southern state governments seeking to provide benefits for these sectors of their society; for example, by negotiating aid agreements that benefit domestic producers. While this work has been done extensively with rich-world countries, there is not yet a comparable literature on developing states.

In earlier related literature, liberals who emphasised the growing interdependence, or globalisation, of the world political economy in recent decades (such as Keohane and Nye, 1974) have shown that developing states have sought to internationalise their economies, either to take advantage of perceived benefits, or because the failures of their previous systems led to international pressures from organisations such as the IMF, who insisted on neoliberal reform as the price for financial help. These failures of neoliberal economics could logically lead low- and middle-income states to collaborate to resist or reverse some of the damage that these policies have wrought on their economies, or, in the analogy of Chang, to fight to get back on the ladder to development (Chang, 2002). Much of the language of SSC is explicitly concerned with a 'more just' world economic order, as a reaction to the failures of neoliberalism in preceding decades.

In the popular imagination, perhaps the seeds of the 'common identity' (Sá de Silva, 2010) of the South were sown by US President Harry Truman in 1949, when he spoke of 'the underdeveloped regions of the world', which the United States had a duty to help. Sá de Silva sees this speech as the birth of the idea of the distinction between the developed world and the developing world, the latter of which can be observed, in various permutations, throughout the ensuing 60 years: the Non-Aligned Movement; the G77; the typology of 'Second' and 'Third' World; the G20; and currently represented by SSC institutions such as IBSA (Sá de Silva, 2010). Similarly, Cabral and Weinstock (2010:24) give a historical overview of SSC, tracing it back to the 1955 Bandung Conference. Constructivist theorists would surely argue essentially the same point: that a notion such as SSC has been transmitted over time and spread in the same way as norms, such as human rights, eventually spread.

What this discussion illustrates is that there is divide between academia, on the one hand, and think tanks, NGOs, diplomats and various commentators, on the other. One side believes that SSC, with all its concomitant manifestations (the BRICS concept, IBSA, etc.), is just simple international cooperation, as has been already studied in detail, and that IR theories do a good job of explaining SSC, either through notions of self-interest, interdependence or the spread of norms. The other side see it as a new form of cooperation that heralds a new era of more egalitarian relations between rich and poor states. Hopefully, the following analysis will help to develop the discussion.

Empirics

As mentioned previously, determining whether aid 'works' is a methodologically tricky task; or more to the point, it is still too early to tell if Brazilian aid is more 'effective', given that the purpose of it is unclear. However, there is some qualitative information available on the quality of Brazil's interactions with Mozambique. Given that the over-riding opinion of aid in the academic literature is that it is given for selfish motives, the onus is on examining if SSC is different from NSC, working from the assumption that it is not.

Firstly, we should deal with a patently false concept. In an egalitarian or horizontal relationship between states, there should be no large asymmetries, either in terms of power or economic size. Clearly, there are *enormous* economic differences between Brazil and Mozambique, just as there are huge differences between Chinese power and influence and the power of South Africa. Ranked by GDP, Brazil was the seventh largest economy in the world in 2010, whereas Mozambique was at number 124. In 2011, the GDP per capita in the countries was US$12 500 in Brazil and US$534 in Mozambique. The population of Brazil is almost 10 times that of its smaller partner, and Brazil has 45 internet users per 100 people compared to 4.3 in Mozambique.[42] We could continue in this fashion, but it is obvious that any talk of 'horizontal' relations is just diplomatic hot air, which should be taken with several pinches of salt. However, another aspect of the 'equal' relationship position lies in the shared culture and experience argument, which helps endow emerging donors with the heightened sensitivity (apparently lacking in states in the North)[43] necessary for successful relations with other developing states.

With respect to emerging donors 'knowing local recipient contexts better', Cabral and Shankland (2013) point out that Brazil's 'official presence in partner countries – which, with few exceptions, is almost exclusively confined to diplomatic representation – remains insufficient to generate an in-depth understanding of the local context'. Others have also noted the superficial, and likely unsustainable, nature of Brazil's engagement with Africa and the fact that it seemingly has more embassies than it can adequately staff (Stuenkel, 2013:34). Local Mozambicans are also complaining that many projects in the country, such as the joint Brazil and Japan ProSavana project, are 'top-down and fail to involve farmers and civil society in a meaningful way' (Chicava *et al*, 2013:15).

---

42 All the above data were gathered from World Bank statistics. Available at: http://databank.worldbank.org/

43 Not all Northern donors are alike. Many, such as the Netherlands and Ireland, place a great deal of emphasis on their aid money being used to combat poverty, and receive high ratings on an 'alignment' score.

Indeed, we can make the argument that Brazilian aid is *less* geared towards the non-elite in the recipient country than were traditional donors. For example, Ireland, a traditional OECD donor, is ranked number one in the world for the 'alignment' aspect of its aid programme. 'Alignment' ranks states by the non-conditional nature of their aid, the reliability of it being delivered, but also considers the quality of the donor's use of local systems of policy management, the coordination of the donor's aid policies with the recipient's policies (IPEA, 2010). States like Ireland and the Netherlands place very explicit demands on the recipients to use the aid to help those in real need, as opposed to helping Irish companies or Dutch political objectives. When Irish media outlets recently published stories of aid money going missing in Uganda, there was a public outcry and the Irish government immediately cut all aid to Uganda. In fact, the Ugandan government ended up paying back the misappropriated funds (*The Journal*, 2013).

Regarding the oft-mentioned cultural affinity, as exemplified in former Brazilian President Lula da Silva's claim that Brazil has a 'historic debt' to Africa (*The Economist*, 2012), it seems that Lula neglected the 'limited influence of Brazilian afro-descendants ... in formal Brazilian institutions. At the elite level, black Brazilians remain largely absent from the diplomatic corps and the upper ranks of Brazilian technocrats, as well as from prestigious scientific institutions such as Embrapa' (Cabral and Shankland, 2013:19). It is also worth mentioning that emphasising African links is not a new tactic for Brazilian diplomacy. The military dictatorship pursued a similar policy in the 1970s (Rosenbaum and Tyler, 1975:246).

Brazilian mining company Vale has faced protests from villagers, angry at its actions in Moatize, in northern Mozambique (*The Economist*, 2012). Chichava *et al* also mention the attitudes of the Mozambican blogosphere (which is admittedly small) regarding Brazilian activities in the country: Brazilian aid is a 'Trojan horse' which portends 'Brazilian neo-colonialism' (Chichava *et al*, 2013:15). The BBC has also reported on the tension between Brazilian companies and locals in Mozambique:

> Vicente Adriano, a teacher of long standing in Moatize, says that few of his former pupils have been employed by the mining companies and those that have are either 'guards or chauffeurs'. Furthermore, Mr Adriano says, the impression is that those getting the jobs come from other parts of Mozambique or from neighbouring countries. He says he worries there could be a violent backlash. 'We can already hear the mumbling on the streets and the issue has found its way into songs and poems. That's always where it starts,' he says (BBC, 2013).

Apparently, Mozambicans in Brazil are similarly not feeling their shared cultural links. The *New York Times* reported the story of a Mozambican living in Brazil who was a victim of police harassment. 'The police asked, "Where's Mozambique?" said Mr Nhantumbo, 33. They didn't know that there existed a country with this name' (Romero, 2012). The ignorance goes both ways: 'for instance, the Brazilians have found that the African masses know little more about Brazil than that their country produces outstanding soccer teams. Because of illiteracy, poor communications, and disinterest, they are unaware that some Brazilians share a partial cultural legacy with them' (Rosenbaum and Tyler, 1975:246). Clearly, the 'shared cultural ties' are not particularly well shared, although it should be noted that Brazilian television soaps are very popular across the Lusophone world, and the Brazilian brand of Pentecostalist churches are likewise influential.

Quantitative analysis shows that there is a clear correlation between the growth of Brazilian aid projects in Mozambique, shown in Figure 3.2, and Brazilian exports to Mozambique, as shown in Figure 3.3. However, due to the inherent endogeneity problems associated with aid, it is not possible to draw any firm conclusions about causal links from this fact. As more and more data become available on the relationship between Brazilian aid and Mozambique, in-depth analysis could make progress on this problem; however, for the time being, the relationship between Brazilian aid and exports to Mozambique suffers from the same endogeneity problem that affects much of the aid literature. Therefore, the liberal argument that SSC (in this case) exists to open up beneficial markets finds only *very* qualified support from the analysis.

However, there are examples of domestic interests benefitting from the increased cooperation between Brazil and Mozambique. Forty Brazilian farmers, from the state of Mato Grosso in the interior of the country, were invited en masse to Mozambique in 2011 by the Mozambican government. These farmers were offered huge tracts of land, equivalent to 'three Sergipes (a northern state in Brazil)' (6 million hectares) for concessionary prices, and for terms of 50 years with the possibility of a 55-year extension. The president of the Mato Grosso Association of Cotton Producers, Carlos Ernesto Augustin, described Mozambique as a 'Mato Grosso in the middle of Africa, with land for free' (*Folha de São Paulo*, 2011). While we may conclude little from a single case, the selectorate theory of Bueno de Mesquita *et al* predicts exactly this type of arrangement between powerful domestic groups (in this case the farmers' association) and government policy (Bueno de Mesquita *et al*, 2005). In this understanding, Brazilian aid is not altruistic and free of self-interest, but is pursued for reasons like those of the traditional aid donors. Domestic groups, which are important supporters of the executive, are rewarded with favourable policies, in this case the opportunity

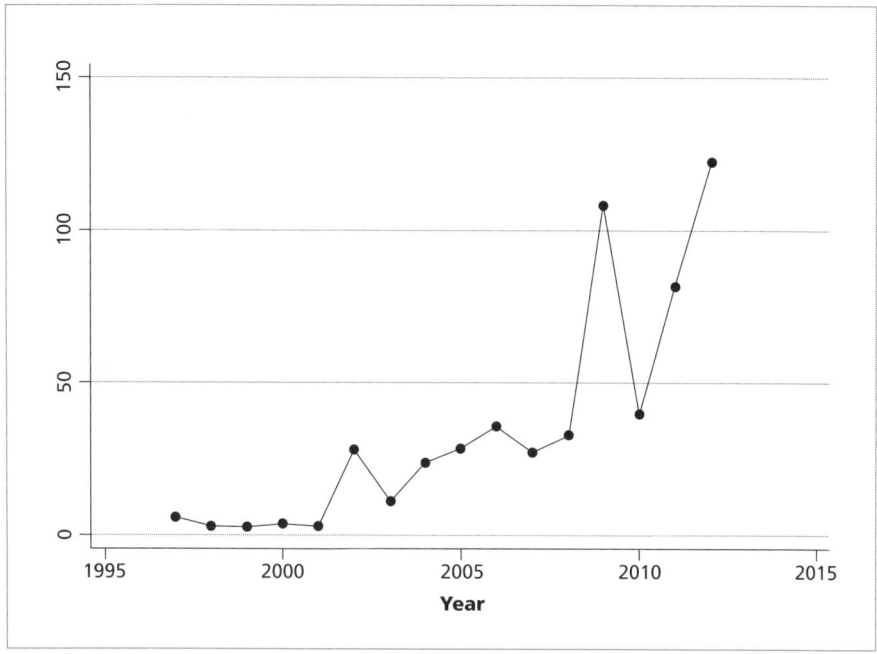

Figure 3.3: Brazilian exports to Mozambique in US$
Source: Author from UN Comtrade Statistics

of getting land 'for free' in a partner state. Some observers have noted that the Brazilian government has done this with land inside Brazil, and that countries like Mozambique offer a chance to continue the practice. Clements and Fernandes (2012) discuss how land-grabbing in Mozambique is mirrored by the experience of the 'cerrado miracle' in Brazil.

An important argument in the academic literature is that geopolitical objectives are key when it comes to foreign-aid policies. Measuring geopolitical rewards is often done by comparing the voting positions of the states in the United Nations General Assembly (UNGA). In the case of Brazil and Mozambique, data from the UNGA, specifically Voeten's database, were analysed. Little of value was gained from this analysis, as Mozambique's voting records shadow Brazil's almost perfectly. Mozambique votes in the UNGA, rated on an affinity score,[44] range from 0.75 to 0.98. This tells us that Mozambique votes consistently in the same way as Brazil, a pattern that does not correlate

---

44 The 'affinity' score, drawn from Strezhnev and Voeten's variable *s3un*, assigns values to UNGA votes using three categories: 1 = 'yes' or approval for an issue, 2 = abstain, 3 = 'no' or disapproval for an issue. A score of 0 implies no affinity and a score of 1 implies perfect affinity (i.e. the states vote the same way all the time).

with the different periods of Brazilian foreign policy, which concentrated (or not) on Mozambique (the two that did focus on Mozambique being the military dictatorship in Brazil and the recent period since 2003). Hence, using standard means of analysis of geopolitics, we cannot yet say anything definitive about Brazil's relationship with Mozambique with respect to Brazil's geopolitical objectives, and certainly cannot make any statements regarding the causal relationships between Brazilian aid and Mozambican UNGA voting.

The last main argument of the academic literature, being the 'demand-side' mirror of the selectorate theory, argues that aid is used by the recipient to reward essential supporters. Given that Brazilian aid is generally not in the form of fungible resources (i.e. cash), as was the case in Werker, Ahmed and Cohen (2008), this argument also cannot be definitively rejected or accepted. However, a corollary of this hypothesis is that we should expect to see little benefit accruing to everyday Mozambicans, since they are unlikely to be part of the group of essential supporters in a small winning coalition regime such as Mozambique's.[45] In a small-coalition regime, the rewards available for disbursement to supporters go to the very few. Rewards that improve the lot of the many, which are disbursed as public goods such as improved services in education or health, for example, are not often disbursed in small-coalition regimes; in fact, they usually arrive only in situations of absolute necessity for the leader or close to election time. Do Rosário makes the point in relation to Mozambican domestic politics: 'Politically-driven policies adopted by the ruling elites have generally discriminated against the majority of agricultural producers, who continue to be poor, vulnerable and dependent [on] handouts from government, donors or NGOs' (Do Rosário, 2012:2).

Agriculture accounts for 80 per cent of the Mozambican workforce and so, if public goods are to be distributed with the aim of pleasing a wide selectorate, we should expect to see investments made by the Mozambican government in this area, resulting in improvements in the lives of regular agricultural workers. While the agricultural sector in Mozambique has certainly witnessed political attention from the ruling party, FRELIMO, this attention has not been lavished on ordinary Mozambicans. 'The way resources are distributed to the local level is not intended to create support infrastructures or to strengthen the productive

---

45 Briefly stated, a small winning coalition regime is one in which the leader is reliant on few to keep him in power. These regimes are typical of many poorer countries, which may be autocratic or semi-democratic with rigged elections. For more on these terms, and how leaders behave with groups of essential and non-essential supporters within their polity, see Bueno de Mesquita *et al* (2005). I believe Mozambique may be classified as a small-coalition regime. Although it has mass elections, these are often dismissed by the opposition and independent observers as frauds. Also, as mentioned in the text, the benefits of economic growth and aid deals in Mozambique go to the elite few and not the masses, typical of a small-coalition regime as per Bueno de Mesquita *et al*.

Rural Areas (percentage)

Perception	All households			Male-headed household			Female-headed household		
	All	Poorest tercile	Richest tercile	All	Poorest tercile	Richest tercile	All	Poorest tercile	Richest tercile
Better	26.8	11.0	45.6	32.2	16.6	48.1	13.0	4.7	30.8
Worse	40.6	61.5	24.4	37.2	54.2	23.3	49.4	69.7	30.7
No change	32.6	27.5	30.0	30.6	29.2	28.6	37.6	25.6	38.5
Total	100.0	100.0	100.0	100.0	100.0	100.0	100.0	100.0	100.0

Source: Authors' calculations based on data PVS 2006.
Note: Sample is not representative.

Urban Areas (percentage)

Perception	All households			Male-headed household			Female-headed household		
	All	Poorest tercile	Richest tercile	All	Poorest tercile	Richest tercile	All	Poorest tercile	Richest tercile
Better	25.2	11.7	42.7	28.4	17.7	43.4	19.2	4.1	41.2
Worse	37.7	51.4	23.9	37.3	45.2	25.3	38.4	59.2	20.6
No change	37.1	36.9	33.4	34.3	37.1	31.3	42.4	36.7	38.2
Total	100.0	100.0	100.0	100.0	100.0	100.0	100.0	100.0	100.0

Source: Authors' calculations based on data PVS 2006.
Note: Sample is not representative.

Figure 3.4: Perceptions of change in household poverty
Source: Fox (2008)

capacity of small peasant families, but to strengthen and consolidate local elite groups with the capacity to produce, expand, and feed major projects taking place in the cities' (Do Rosário, 2012:13). Viewed in this light, Brazilian technical cooperation, which has a strong agricultural element focused on cash crops for export, is ideal for strengthening the capacities of large-scale farms. These farms typically produce cash crops like sugar and not food, which is left to small-scale subsistence farmers. The latter farmer receives little of the benefits of this technical cooperation. Indeed, econometric analysis of inequality in Mozambique shows that urban centres, such as the capital Maputo, are the main beneficiaries of development in the country (James, Arndt and Simler, 2005).

This point is certainly borne out by qualitative data on the opinions of regular Mozambicans. Figure 3.4 shows perceptions of change in quality of life in Mozambique in the five years preceding 2006. Although the data are not representative, information like this is not in great supply, so it is useful for present purposes. What the data show is that the poorer households, in both urban and rural areas, are not feeling any benefit from the aid flowing into Mozambique, which, let us not forget, is regarded as a great success by the World Bank. Richer households are more likely to perceive an improvement in their lives, whereas poorer households are noticeable for their pessimism, particularly in the rural areas heavily dominated by agriculture, which are supposedly a focus of Brazilian aid efforts.

Apart from perceptions of poverty and wellbeing, there are other indicators regularly used to assess government performance in delivering public goods to the population. These indicators, frequently taken from the World Bank's development database, contain measures such as the percentage of citizens with access to electricity, the infant mortality rate, the number of births attended by midwives, etc. Unfortunately, a lot of data are missing for Mozambique in the World Bank's development indicators, which again means we are limited when it comes to quantitative analysis. One indicator, government's spending on health, measured as a percentage of GDP, shows that expenditure, which was 17.9 per cent in 2000, had fallen to a little over 12 per cent in 2010. However, the poor availability of data like this from Mozambique means that survey information, such as that presented in Figure 3.4, is more demonstrative.

Conclusion

This discussion and analysis has presented the academic literature on both SSC and foreign aid, illustrating the divide between academia, on the one hand, and non-academic literatures, on the other. In the former, we find the constant opinion that aid is given in the interests of the donor and, depending on the characteristics of the recipient, is often used for selfish purposes by the leaders of these aid recipient states. We have also seen that the latter literature regularly appraises SSC as emblematic of a new era of international cooperation, free of the selfish motives and commercial concerns that are associated with Northern donors.

The analysis presented here has shown that arguments in favour of SSC based on *egalitarianism* and *shared cultural experience* can be dismissed. In terms of the Brazilian government using foreign assistance to reward domestic supporters, although only limited evidence to support liberal and IPE theories was found, the findings certainly do not indicate that Brazilian SSC is free from commercial interests and is, therefore, markedly different from traditional North–South relations. Indeed, the argument can be made that Brazilian assistance is less focused on helping the common citizen in Mozambique than is the case with some Northern donors. It has, likewise, been demonstrated that there are rising tensions and suspicions in Mozambique regarding SSC, and that the benefits of economic growth in Mozambique are accruing mainly to elites.

While the analysis has not been exhaustive due to missing or unavailable data, hopefully the discussion has progressed the debate over SSC and emerging donors. The argument that the practices of emerging donors are 'distinctly different' from traditional donors finds no support from this analysis of Brazil–Mozambique relations. In fact, when we compare Brazilian aid practices with those of highly rated Northern donors, such as Ireland, we find that Brazilian assistance is less geared to helping everyday people in the recipient state than is the case with some traditional donors. Indeed, it is the very aspects of SSC, held up to be 'egalitarian' (that is, no strings attached, or conditions to the provision of assistance) that allows the benefits of this cooperation to flow away from regular Mozambicans and to the elites, as predicted by selectorate theory. It is little wonder then that elites in Southern states are so quick to enthusiastically proclaim the wonders of SSC, since it benefits them directly.

References

Abdenur, A (2007) *The Strategic Triad: Form and content in Brazil's triangular cooperation practices*, The New School, International Affairs Working Paper No. 2007-06.

Alesina, A and Dollar, D (1998) *Who Gives Foreign Aid to Whom and Why?* NBER Working Paper Series, Working Paper No. 6612. Cambridge, MA: National Bureau of Economic Research.

Alesina, A and Weder, B (1999) *Do Corrupt Governments Receive Less Foreign Aid?* NBER Working Paper Series, Working Paper No. 7108. Cambridge, MA: National Bureau of Economic Research.

Ball, R and Johnson, C (1996) Political, economic, and humanitarian motivations for PL 480 food aid: Evidence from Africa, *Economic Development and Cultural Change*, **44** (3), pp 515–37.

Bermeo, S (2011) *Foreign Aid and Regime Change: A role for donor intent*, Working Paper. Available at: http://papers.ssrn.com/sol3/papers.cfm?abstract_id=1780357 (accessed 3 April 2013).

Berthélemy, JC and Tichit, A (2004) Bilateral donors' aid allocation decisions: A three-dimensional panel analysis, *International Review of Economics and Finance*, **13** (3): 253–74.

Boone, P (1995) *Politics and the Effectiveness of Foreign Aid*, Discussion Paper No. 272, Centre for Economic Performance, London School of Economics.

Boschini, A and Olofsgård, A (2007) Foreign aid: An instrument for fighting communism? *The Journal of Development Studies*, **43** (4), pp 622–48.

Bueno de Mesquita, B, Smith, A, Siverson, RM and Morrow, JD (2005) *The Logic of Political Survival*. Cambridge, MA: The MIT Press.

Buenode Mesquita, B and Smith, A (2007) Foreign aid and policy concessions, *The Journal of Conflict Resolution*, **51** (2), pp 251–84.

Bueno de Mesquita, B and Smith, A (2009) A political economy of aid, *International Organization*, **63** (2), pp 309–40.

Burnside, C and Dollar, D (2000) Aid, policies and growth, *The American Economic Review*, **90** (4), pp 847–68.

Cabral, L and Shankland, A (2013) *Narratives of Brazil–Africa Cooperation for Agricultural Development: New paradigms?* Future Agricultures, Working Paper No. 51. Future Agricultures Consortium, University of Sussex.

Cabral, L and Weinstock, J (2010) Brazilian technical cooperation for development: Drivers, mechanics and future prospects, Overseas Development Institute, Report, 6 September.

Cervo, A (1994) Socializando o desenvolvimento: Uma história da cooperação técnica internacional do Brasil, *Revista Brasileira de Política Internacional*, **37** (1), pp 37–63.

Chang, HJ (2002) *Kicking Away the Ladder: Development strategy in historical perspective*. London: Anthem Press.

Chichava, S, Duran, J, Cabral, L, Shankland, A, Buckley, L, Lixia, T and Yue, Z (2013) *Chinese and Brazilian Cooperation with African Agriculture: The case of Mozambique*, Future Agricultures, Working Paper No. 49, Future Agricultures Consortium, University of Sussex.

Clements, EA and Fernandes, BM (2012) Land grabbing, agribusiness and the peasantry in Brazil and Mozambique. Paper presented at the Global Land Grabbing II conference, 17–19 October, Cornell University, Ithaca, New York.

Collier, P and Dollar, D (2002) Aid allocation and poverty reduction, *European Economic Review*, **46**, pp 1475–500.

Davies, M, Edinger, H, Tay, N, and Naidu, S (2008) How China delivers development assistance to Africa, Research paper, Centre for Chinese Studies, University of Stellenbosch.

Davies, P (2010) South–South cooperation: Moving towards a new aid dynamic, *Poverty in Focus*, **20**. Geneva: International Policy Centre for Inclusive Growth, United Nations.

Do Rosário, D (2012) *From Negligence to Populism: An analysis of Mozambique's agricultural political economy*, Future Agricultures, Working Paper No. 34. Future Agricultures Consortium, University of Sussex.

Dreher, A, Nunnencamp, P and Thiele, R (2006) *Does US Aid Buy UN General Assembly Votes? A disaggregated analysis*, Kiel Working Paper No. 1275.

Dreher, A, Sturm, J-E, and Vreeland, A (2009) *Development Aid and International Politics: Does membership on the UN Security Council influence World Bank decisions?* Research Paper, Globalisation and Development Centre, Bond University.

The Economist (2010) Speak softly and carry a blank cheque, 15 July.

The Economist (2012) A new Atlantic alliance, 10 November.

Fleck, R and Kilby, C (2010) Changing aid regimes? US foreign aid from the Cold War to the War on Terror, *Journal of Development Economics*, **91**, pp 185–97.

Folha de São Paulo (2011) Moçambique oferece terra à soja Brasileira. Available at: http://www1.folha.uol.com.br/fsp/mercado/me1408201102.htm (accessed 10 April 2013).

Folha de São Paulo (2013) Dilma anuncia revisão de US$ 900 mi em dívidas de países africanos. Available at: http://www1.folha.uol.com.br/mundo/2013/05/1284994-dilma-promete-rever-us-900-mi-em-dividas-de-paises-africanos.shtml> (accessed 03 October 2013).

Fox, L (2008) *Beating the Odds: Sustaining inclusion in Mozambique's growing economy*. Washington, DC: World Bank.

Instituto de Pesquisa Econômica Aplicada (IPEA) (2010) *Cooperação Brasileira para o Desenvolvimento Internacional: 2005–2009*. IPEA.

James, R, Arndt, C and Simler, K (2005) *Has economic growth in Mozambique been pro-poor?* FCND Discussion Paper No. 202. International Food Policy Research Institute.

The Journal (2013) Uganda repays 4 million in Irish Aid funding that was misappropriated. Available at: http://www.thejournal.ie/irish-aid-money-repaid-744456-Jan2013/ (accessed 12 April 2013).

Keohane, R and Nye, J (1977) *Power and Interdependence*, 4th edition. London: Pearson.

Kilby, C (2009) The political economy of conditionality: An empirical analysis of World Bank loan disbursements, *Journal of Development Economics*, **89**, pp 51–61.

Knack, S (2004) Does foreign aid promote democracy? *International Studies Quarterly*, **48** (1), pp 251–66.

Kosack, S and Tobin, J (2006) Funding self-sustaining development: The role of aid, FDI and government in economic success, *International Organization*, **60**, pp 205–43.

Kurlantzick, J (2006) *Beijing's safari: China's move into Africa and its implications for aid, development, and governance*, Policy Outlook, Carnegie Endowment for International Peace, China Program.

Ladd, P (2010) Between a rock and a hard place: LDCs in a G-20 World, *Poverty in Focus*, **20**. Geneva: International Policy Centre for Inclusive Growth, United Nations.

Martins, R (2011) A Política da Solidariedade, *Carta Capital*. Available at: <http://www.cartacapital.com.br/internacional/a-politica-da-solidariedade/ (accessed 4 April 2013).

McKinlay, RD and Little, R (1978) A foreign-policy model of the distribution of British bilateral aid, 1960–1970, *British Journal of Political Science*, **8** (3), pp 313–31.

Milner, H. 1997. *Interests, Institutions, and Information*. Princeton, NJ: Princeton University Press.

Minoiu, C and Reddy, S (2009) *Development Aid and Economic Growth: A positive long-run relation*, IMF Working Paper No. WP/09/118. Washington, DC: International Monetary Fund.

Morgenthau, H (1962) A political theory of foreign aid, *The American Political Science Review*, **56** (2), pp 301–09.

Romero, S (2012) Brazil gains business and influence as it offers aid and loans in Africa, *The New York Times*, 7 August.

Oliveira, A and Onuki, J (2010) India, Brazil and South Africa: Collective action, divergent positions, *New Global Studies*, Manuscript No. 1087.

Otter, M (2003) Domestic public support for foreign aid: Does it matter? *Third World Quarterly*, **24** (1), pp 115–25.

Palmer, G, Wohlander, SB and Morgan, TC (2002) Give or take: Foreign aid and foreign policy substitutability, *Journal of Peace Research*, **39** (1), pp 5–26.

Puente, C.A (2010) A cooperação técnica horizontal brasileira como instrumento de política externa: a evolução da cooperação técnica com países em desenvolvimento no período 1995–2005', FUNAG.

Pino, BA (2009) South–South Cooperation (SSC) and multilateral governance of the aid system: The implications for Spanish aid, Fundación para las Relaciones Internacionales y el Diálogo Exterior, FRIDE Comment, June.

Pino, BA (2010) *Brazilian Cooperation: A model under construction for an emerging power*, Real Instituto Elcano, ARI Paper No. 143/2010.

Renzio, P and Hanlon, J (2007) *Contested Sovereignty in Mozambique: The dilemmas of aid dependence*, Global Economic Governance, Working Paper No. 2007/25.

Reynaud, J and Vauday, J (2009) Geopolitics and international organizations: An empirical study on IMF facilities, *Journal of Development Economics*, **89**, pp 139–62.

Rosenbaum, HJ and Tyler, WG (1975) South–South relations: The economic and political content of interactions among developing countries, *International Organization*, **29**, pp 243–74.

Sá de Silva, M (2010) '*How did we get here?' The pathways of South–South cooperation*, Poverty in Focus, No. 20. Geneva: International Policy Centre for Inclusive Growth, United Nations.

Sanahuja, JA (2010) Post-Liberal Regionalism: S-S Cooperation in Latin America and the Caribbean, *Poverty in Focus*, No. 20, Geneva: International Policy Centre for Inclusive Growth, United Nations.

Sharma, R (2012) Broken BRICS: Why the rest stopped rising, *Foreign Affairs*, **91** (6). Published on the web. 12 April 2013. Available at: http://www.foreignaffairs.com/articles/138219/ruchir-sharma/broken-brics (accessed 12 April 2013).

Stuenkel, O (2013) *Brazil in Africa: Bridging the Atlantic?* KAS International Reports 1/2/2013.

Tingley, D (2010) Donors and domestic politics: Political influences on foreign aid effort, *The Quarterly Review of Economics and Finance*, **50**, pp 40–49.

Vaz, AC and C Inoue, C (2007) *Emerging Donors in International Development Assistance: The Brazil Case*, IDRC/CDRI Report.

Vieira, M (2013) Interview with Marco Vieira, *Análise Caeni*, **1** (2), pp 11–14. Available at: http://

www.caeni.com.br/images/cursos/ficha-matricula/Analise_Caeni_12_Junho_2013_VF.pdf (accessed 3 October 2013).

Waltz, K (1979) *Theory of International Politics*. Boston, MA: Addison-Wesley.

Werker, E, Ahmed, FZ and Cohen, C (2008) How is foreign aid spent? Evidence from a natural experiment, *American Economic Journal: Macroeconomics*, **1** (2), pp 225–44.

Woods, N (2008) Whose aid? Whose influence? China, emerging donors and the silent revolution in development assistance, *International Affairs*, **84** (6), pp 1–18.

Databases

Strezhnev, A and Voeten, E (2013) United Nations General Assembly Voting Data. Available at: http://dvn.iq.harvard.edu/dvn/dv/Voeten/faces/study/StudyPage.xhtml?studyId=38311&studyListingIndex=0_dee53f12c760141b21c251525332 (accessed 10 April 2013).

United Nation Trade Statistics Commodity database (Comtrade). Available at: http://comtrade.un.org/db/ (accessed 10 April 2013).

World Bank Databank. Available at: http://databank.worldbank.org/data/home.aspx (accessed 10 April 2013).

Chapter 4

The role of Brazil in the consolidation of an extractive model of development in Mozambique

Carolina Milhorance

Mozambique is Brazil's main development cooperation partner in Africa, and this is marked by a discourse of exchange of experiences (Chichava *et al*, 2013). Despite the recent slowdown in interchange initiatives, there are still few analyses that capture the concrete impact of this intensification of relations in the first decade of this century. In this chapter, we seek to show the role of Brazilian stakeholders in the consolidation of a development model based on agricultural modernisation and on strengthening an 'extractive economy'. The influence of Brazil in this case refers to an incremental change in political strategies, providing technical, political and financial resources for the implementation of a project already under way in the country.

The analysis is based on government and private initiatives in Mozambique, mainly the tripartite cooperation programme for the agricultural development of the tropical savannah of Mozambique (ProSavana) and the investments of the company Vale in rehabilitating the Nacala Corridor railway. In addition, the chapter considers initiatives such as the More Food International Programme and the Agricultural Research and Technological Innovation Platform (Piait).[46]

The approach adopted in this chapter stresses the conflicts and alliances between the various coalitions of international and Mozambican actors, based on the work of Sabatier and Jenkins-Smith (2014). It is argued that 'international pressure' or 'the mechanical import of foreign models' into Mozambique (Mosca, 2010; Bellucci, 2003) do not, on their own, explain the adoption of the Brazilian initiatives. The social, economic and political interests in conflict should be considered, and the development trajectory supported by the international actors, and by the national governments and other interests (Castel-Branco, 2011). This perspective recognises the agency of the Mozambican actors, who represent the degree of freedom (margin for

---

46 This study is derived in part from a doctoral thesis, for which 280 semi-structured interviews were held between 2013 and 2015, with decision-makers, private-sector stakeholders, representatives of civil society and researchers of both countries. Network analysis tools were also used in an illustrative and complementary manner.

manoeuvre) and of influence (power) as well as the resources mobilised, despite the structural constraints (Brown and Harman, 2013).

Despite the political and financial asymmetry in the relations between Brazil and Mozambique, a series of factors helps to increase the margin for manoeuvre of the Mozambican actors – for example, the absence of political conditions in Brazilian cooperation, the low capacity of the Brazilian government to finance and implement international projects, and the importance of African diplomacy for the international insertion of Brazil, mainly in multilateral fora and for the internationalisation of Brazilian companies.

The favourable national and international context for foreign investment in natural resources

Since the civil war ended in 1992, Mozambique has passed through an intense process of economic growth (an annual average growth rate of 7 per cent) (World Bank, 2015). These results are partly related to the development of mega-projects based on foreign investment (Brito *et al*, 2010). The discovery of vast mineral resources has contributed to consolidating an economy structured around the extraction and export of natural resources and agricultural produce (Mosca and Selemane, 2012).

This 'mega-projects' model is being consolidated in the country's political agenda and remained in place after President Filipe Nyusi took office in 2015. The new National Development Strategy (ENDE, 2015–2035) prioritises extractive and manufacturing industries, agriculture and tourism, based on fiscal incentives, public–private partnerships and international financing. It also stresses the importance of the development corridors and of the growth poles, particularly based on Special Economic Zones (ZEE). According to representatives of Mozambican rural movements, the formulation of strategies for the rural sector, such as the National Agricultural Sector Investment Plan (Pnisa), is also conditional on this context of investment in mineral and agricultural resources (Vunjanhe and Adriano, 2015).

The Mozambican economy is essentially agricultural and in 2014 this sector accounted for 23 per cent of GDP according to the Ministry of Agriculture. Almost 70 per cent of the population lives in the rural areas, which are their primary source of income and the basis of their food and nutritional security (World Bank, 2015). In this context, the land question takes on an important symbolic force in the political and social thinking of the country (Mitha Ribeiro, 2008). According to Galli (2003), land is the historical battle ground: Mozambicans identify themselves with land and they engage in struggle for land. Accordingly, this is the question that most clearly opposes national political interests. Hence the relationship between the 'extractive economy' and the land attracts the attention of non-governmental organisations (NGOs) and social movements, in addition to generating new political tensions.

Furthermore, the potential of the 'mega-projects' model to produce income for the local population has been questioned. One aspect raised is the risk of sharpening social and regional inequalities, starting from the concentration of the productive and accumulation base. It is also worth recalling that the activities of this sector are guided by fiscal incentives and the profits from investments are frequently repatriated. Furthermore, the services are concentrated on poorly paid labour and do not create enough jobs for an economic transition (Cunguara *et al*, 2012; Mercandalli, 2013). The projects are also high risk because of the volatility of the international prices of mineral commodities.

As for agriculture, foreign investments increased after the food crisis of 2007–2008 (FAO, 2012). A series of authors argue that the convergence of multiple crises (food, energy and financial) contributed to a wave of agricultural investments based on land acquisition (Borras *et al*, 2012). According to Anseeuw *et al* (2012), the interest of the investors was stimulated by the rise in food prices at the end of the decade. However, this 'race for land' is marked by strong regionalism (Hall, 2011) and is associated with long-term trends such as population growth, increased demand for biofuels and raw materials, and financial speculation. Sub-Saharan Africa is one of the regions that has felt the most impact from these investments, expressed through long-term concessions (Boche, 2015).

But it is also worth noting that many of the approved investments in agriculture across the globe have not been implemented (Anseeuw *et al*, 2012). This context is attributed to a series of factors, such as: 1) underestimating technical and management difficulties; 2) absence of the necessary attributes faced with high transaction costs; and 3) the speculative position of certain investors. Furthermore, the international promotion of biofuels, which partly contributed to the increased investments, was faced with the fall in the price of oil, and the reduction in the expansion objectives of these sources of energy in European policy, as well as the failure of some projects (Wilkinson, 2014). Finally, the high institutional and political risks, faced with opposition from social movements, contributed to delaying some of these initiatives, as was the case with the Brazilian initiatives in Mozambique.

In general, these projects face significant difficulties in Mozambique. By 2015 the land surface they effectively occupied amounted to only 8 per cent of the total announced (Boche, 2015). Many initiatives are proving non-viable because of the system of prices, capital costs, and transaction and implementation costs, apart from technical and management difficulties. In this context, many of the projects are co-financed by international development agencies.

These habitually make their support conditional on initiatives for including smallholder farmers, such as production contracts, allocation of land titles and subsidised access to inputs. In the institutional environment of Mozambique, investors rarely opt independently for agriculture by contract (Boche, 2015). Some private actors promote this modality as a component of social and environmental responsibility, or as a means of access to credit from the international institutions (Smart and Hanlon, 2014). Hence, the relation between land-based investments and the resources of international cooperation has proved close in this country. However, most of the farmers benefitting from these contracts are the 'emerging' farmers who have greater financial, technical and land resources (Hanlon and Smart, 2012; Boche, 2015). And most of the jobs created have been precarious (Mosca, 2010).

In addition to the focus on foreign investments, a modernising perspective has dominated the country's main arenas of rural policies (Zanella and Milhorance, 2016). Many of the interviews with Mozambican political officials revealed the goal of transforming peasants into modern farmers integrated into the market. This perspective is also aligned with the recommendations of certain international agencies such as the World Bank[47] for the promotion of agricultural growth and poverty reduction. It gains legitimacy in a context where agricultural productivity in the country remains low (Cunguara *et al*, 2012:30).

The goals of modernisation and of promoting the private sector have thus proved central in the national strategies for rural and agricultural development. For example, the Agricultural Sector Development Strategic Plan (PEDSA) rests on the Green Revolution Strategy, which reaffirms the aim of 'transforming an essentially subsistence agriculture into a commercial agriculture' (MINAG, 2011:1). Its guiding principles include: acting along the value chain according to the agro-industrial model, the development of public-private partnerships, the structuring of a framework favourable to investment and commercial operations, the promotion of technological innovations and the spread of technology to increase production and productivity (MINAG, 2011:33).

This plan seeks to facilitate action by the private sector in agricultural production and in guaranteeing services, focused on the adoption of 'technological packages' and on the promotion of mechanisation. Public investments are basically guided to products and zones regarded as of 'high agricultural potential' (MINAG, 2011:1).

PEDSA is the plan that makes Pnisa operational, drawn up in line with

---

47   See: World Bank (2007) *World Development Report 2008*. Washington, DC: World Bank. Available at: https://openknowledge.worldbank.org/handle/10986/5990.

the Comprehensive African Agriculture Development Programme (CAADP). The goals of Pnisa include increasing agricultural productivity and a supply of services oriented towards the establishment of agro-industrial complexes and the development of poles of agricultural and commercial potential. The plan guides agricultural policies for specific crops, envisaging the participation of up to 60 per cent of the private sector in its financing. The document also validates the approach of development corridors and proposes strengthening value chains, such as those of soya, sunflower and sesame, with the international market. As for the rural sector, one of the main initiatives of ENDE, presented earlier, was the creation of the Ministry of Land, Environment and Rural Development out of the former Ministry for the Coordination of Environmental Action. The visions that guide the political strategies for the Mozambican rural sector are not homogeneous, and multiple strategies co-exist (Castel-Branco, 2013; Mosca, 2010). However, a constant aspect in governmental plans is the focus on increasing production and productivity, on developing value chains per product, and on the role of foreign investment and of the private sector as engines of development.

Adjusting Brazilian actions to the political strategies of Mozambique
Cooperation between Brazil and Mozambique for the rural sector has guided much of the initiatives for the development of commercial products. The ProSavana programme, which brings together the governments of Japan, Brazil and Mozambique, is the largest in the portfolio of the Brazilian Cooperation Agency (ABC). The initiative was launched in 2009 with the mission to 'improve and modernise agriculture with a view to an increase in productivity and production, and the diversification of agricultural production' (ProSavana Website, 2013). The Mozambican government considered the programme a priority, as stated by the Minister of Agriculture, José Pacheco, in a public hearing in 2013. In Brazil, the programme attracted the attention of investors interested in the potential of Mozambique's agricultural and land market (Nishimori and ProSavana, 2012). The region chosen for implementing the initiative – the Nacala Corridor – displays favourable conditions for producing agricultural surpluses, mostly because of the fertility of the soils and the rainfall, but it is also the most populous region of the country, and faces high rates of food insecurity (PAMRDC, 2010; FAO and WFP, 2010).

The investments of Vale began in 2004, based on the government's concession to operate the Moatize coal mines. Right from the initial stages, logistical and infrastructure questions proved one of the main challenges for making the project profitable. Thus, the company became involved in rehabilitating 682 kilometres of the Nacala railway, which connects the Moatize mines to the Nacala-à-Velha deep-water terminal in Nampula Province, crossing the territory of Malawi. The strategy of integrating the infrastructure and the development of agro-industrial complexes had already been noted in Brazil, for example, in the case of building a railway to move the production of the Carajás mines in the north of the country (Shankland and Gonçalves, 2016).

The development corridors have been promoted because of their potential for structuring agro-industrial complexes, the integration of regional markets, the promotion of investments and the expansion of infrastructures (Kaarhus, 2011). This approach was also stressed by the strategies of the Comprehensive African Agriculture Development Programme (CAADP) and the New Alliance for Food and Nutritional Security of the G8. Agricultural investments are often justified internationally because of their potential for disseminating new agricultural technologies and reducing poverty (Liu, 2013). They are also inserted into the regional integration under way, linking Mozambique, Malawi and Zambia by means of logistical infrastructures. The railway rehabilitated by Vale and by the Japanese company Mitsui could potentially transport the copper from Zambian mines. In addition, the World Bank, the African Development Bank, the Exim-Bank of South Korea and JICA of Japan are financing a road linking the cities of Nampula and Lichinga in Mozambique.

ProSavana, according to representatives of the Ministry of Agriculture, constituted the operational arm of the agricultural policies for the Nacala Corridor.[48] The programme promotes a vision of the private sector as the 'driving force of development' and of the public sector as a facilitator and a 'supervisor of public policies' (ProSavana-PD, 2014:7). This vision is aligned with the national strategies drawn up in Mozambique, which point to an increase in agricultural productivity, the structuring of value chains, and the orienting of peasants towards the market. According to the preliminary version of the Master Plan, 'through the out-grower system, local farmers expect benefits from the guarantee of stable markets, obtaining good quality agricultural inputs and acquiring better cultivation techniques' (ProSavana-PD, 2014:14). On the Brazilian side, according to one of the interlocutors of the programme, 'Africa is seen as the last frontier for this type of large scale investment'.[49]

Thus, faced with the challenges of the institutional environment of Mozambique, presented in the previous section, and the national and regional context of the promotion of foreign investment, ProSavana tied its implementation to an integrated strategy, including: 1) access to the logistics infrastructure developed by Vale for the transport of agricultural produce; 2)

---

48 Declaration of the Niassa Provincial Director, Consultative Meeting, Lichinga, June 2014.
49 Interview with representative of the programme, Brasília, June 2013.

institutional security characteristic of an inter-governmental cooperation project; 3) agricultural research for the adaptation of crop varieties by the Brazilian Agricultural and Livestock Research Company (Embrapa); 4) domestic and international market prospects; and 5) prospects of setting up a financial mechanism (the Nacala Fund) (Milhorance, 2015). These mechanisms were designed to overcome the lack of knowledge of investors about the rural and institutional reality of Mozambique and the high costs of the projects.

Hence, the Brazilian initiatives of ProSavana and the Vale logistics investments in the Nacala Corridor contributed to consolidating the dominant benchmark in the country's public policies, based on an extractive political economy and on the objective of promoting a 'green revolution'. These initiatives proved to be coherent – from the institutional and cognitive viewpoints – with the preferences of the Mozambican political elites, despite the strong criticisms from civil society organisations. The Master Plan of ProSavana is aligned with PEDSA, Pnisa and ENDE and with other national strategies regarding their fundamental principles. The priority crops are common to all these plans, as are the Quick Impact Projects (QIP) of ProSavana and even of PEDSA. The role of the state is that of facilitating the actions of the private sector, in a context of low public investment in agriculture (approximately 1.5 per cent of GDP in 2010). Peasant access to agricultural inputs is tied to contract agriculture and to the private distribution companies structured into clusters (ProSavana, 2013).

Historical dialogue for promoting investments and agro-business
Beyond the alignment with current strategies, certain aspects of the Brazilian initiatives in Mozambique have been discussed for several years between public and private actors of both countries and other traditional cooperation agencies. Research into the archives of the Brazilian Foreign Ministry (MRE) has shown that since the start of the 2000s, the triangular nature of the cooperation between Japan, Brazil and Mozambique was already known; its connection with Brazilian agribusiness and its relationship with Vale's investments.

The agreement with Japan had been mentioned in internal correspondence of 2003, when the then Brazilian Ambassador in Maputo recorded the interest expressed by the Japanese International Cooperation Agency (JICA) in establishing triangular arrangements with Brazil in agriculture. Furthermore, the interest of the Brazilian government in establishing conditions for internationalising agribusiness and for the transfer of technology was also recorded in official correspondence since 2003 (MRE, 2003b). An agreement signed in the same year between Embrapa and the Mozambican Ministry of Agriculture established 'unequalled opportunities for cooperation between

Brazil and Mozambique, and may also leverage business for Brazilian companies in the area of agribusiness' (MRE, 2003a). Other correspondence spoke of the interest of the Mozambican government 'in acquiring Brazilian technological experience for soya production' through the promotion of joint ventures between Brazilian and Mozambican companies (MRE, 2003d). According to reports of official meetings, soya was 'one of the crops the development of which the Agriculture Ministry [of Mozambique] regards as a priority, bearing in mind the existence of agreements on the preferential acquisition of this product by Norway at preferential prices' (MRE, 2004).

Finally, the association between the cooperation project and the Vale investments was also stressed since the initial stages of the formulation of ProSavana. The negotiations for collaboration between the two countries in mining dates from the 1970s, as shown by the studies of Ribeiro (2014). The prospect of establishing a project on logistical infrastructures are found in studies since the 1970s, but Vale was directly involved in the negotiations only in the early 2000s. Representatives of the company were received by President Chissano during their mission to Maputo in May 2003. At the time, Brazilian diplomats stressed the opinion of the Director of the Zambezi Valley Development Planning Office (GPZ)[50] about the fact that 'the plans of Vale could not be restricted only to the movement of coal, but should cover other development projects in the region, particularly in agriculture and agribusiness'. Furthermore, the archives show that there was a shared conception about the interest of orienting Embrapa to this initiative (MRE, 2003c).

In this context, the shape of the initiative and its association with the investments in infrastructures are the result of a longstanding dialogue. Unlike what some analyses claim (Garcia et al, 2013; GRAIN et al, 2012; Brautigaum, 2012), the Mozambican political elites expressed their interest right from the conception of the initiatives. Furthermore, contrary to the official statements, the interest of representatives of Brazilian agribusiness was present right from the first stages of negotiation.[51] The declared inspiration of ProSavana in the Brazilian Programme for the Development of the Cerrado (Prodecer) was the main source of criticism.

The latter programme benefited from Japanese institutions for the consolidation of an agricultural development plan based on producing commercial crops, using mechanisation and for export. Despite the later efforts of those in charge of ProSavana to separate the two initiatives, this association

---

50 Today, the Zambezi Valley Development Agency (ADZ).
51 Interview with a representative of ABC, Maputo, March 2013; Interview with a representative of the Mozambican Ministry of Agriculture, Maputo, March 2013.

had been formulated right from the launch of the programme (FGV Projetos, 2014; *Canal Terraviva entrevista Cleber Guarany*: Terraviva TV Channel). As informed by a Brazilian diplomat in Mozambique, 'the attempt was to adapt Prodecer, including agribusiness and family agriculture. The private actors are interested in the fertile land of Mozambique.'[52] This connection led to criticisms from NGOs and social movements. As one of their representatives said: 'We know that this experience was chaotic for communities and for the environment in Brazil.'[53] A series of studies also indicated the possible impacts of ProSavana based on the known results of Prodecer (Schlesinger, 2013; Ekman and Macamo, 2014; Funada *et al*, 2014).

Innovations in the technical and technological modernisation project
The promotion of a public system of agricultural research is the main innovation of the Brazilian initiative regarding the programmes under way in Mozambique. The previous strategies depended basically on occasional projects and a variety of national and international institutions. The Platform for Agricultural Research and Technological Innovation (Piait) was supported by Embrapa and by the US Agency for International Development (USAID), with the participation of the universities of Florida and Michigan. This platform sought to strengthen the institutional and financial capacity of the Mozambican Agricultural Research Institute (IIAM) based on joint action from a consortium of international institutions.

Embrapa has contributed, since its foundation in the 1970s, to the development of a public system of research and development for tropical agriculture in Brazil. The institution values the approach by value chains and by eco-region, based on a systemic perspective combining productive techniques with the use of 'modern' inputs. This technical and methodological project for producing and spreading technologies consolidated the notion of 'technological package' by product, inspired in the guidelines of the 'green revolution' (Aguiar, 1986). And, as some of its researchers state, one of the main goals behind setting it up was to support the Brazilian private sector (Reifschneider *et al*, 2010:68).

According to the national director of the IIAM, the Embrapa model was not the only one considered for structuring the Institute, but it had a preponderant impact on defining the goals to be prioritised: 'The IIAM is the result of a reform process based on several research institutions … A series of assessment studies was undertaken by several institutions, but it was with Embrapa that the IIAM

---

52 Interview with a Brazilian diplomat, Maputo, March 2013.
53 Interview with a representative of the social movement in Mozambique, Maputo, October 2014.

sought to work.'⁵⁴ Other representatives of the IIAM, Embrapa and USAID confirm this data: 'Embrapa strongly supported us in drawing up our strategic plan and in making this plan operational';⁵⁵ 'The institutional strengthening [of the IIAM] was inspired in the experience of Embrapa';⁵⁶ 'In formulating the Strategic Plan [of the institute] there was clear leadership by Embrapa'.⁵⁷ Such objectives were considered positive, including by representatives of Brazilian civil society, despite criticism aimed at the technological product adopted: 'The work of Embrapa in the institutional strengthening of the IIAM is a good thing … the problem is the production method adopted'.⁵⁸

Brazilian support in developing a 'technological package' adapted to the reality of Mozambique was well received by the Mozambican interlocutors in the government, since the work of this institution around tropical agriculture is widely recognised.⁵⁹ According to a representative of Piait, Embrapa studies are frequently used in Mozambican university agriculture faculties: 'We all went there; we know the work of Embrapa. It's a reference point for our tropical reality.'⁶⁰ According to the IIAM director, its perspective 'is to develop technological packages for Mozambican reality, including hybrid seeds and fertilisers'.⁶¹ This perspective was also confirmed by one of the IIAM's field agents: 'we work [in ProSavana] on a variety of hybrid maize which is oriented towards agribusiness. This will comprise technological packages which will be at the disposal of IIAM.'⁶² The initiatives received support from USAID, given the agency's interest in the implementation of triangular projects with emerging countries and the alignment with other initiatives already implemented in Mozambique, such as the programme 'Feed the Future'.⁶³

However, unlike the Brazilian system of agricultural research, which is structured with the support of public power, the participation of the Mozambican government in financing IIAM is low. As its director explains, 'we have a public budget, but more than half the resources are used to pay wages to the staff. We don't have financial autonomy.'⁶⁴ In this context, 'we have worked so that IIAM may become a self-sufficient enterprise based on the sale of services'.⁶⁵

---

54   Interview with representative of IIAM, Maputo, April 2014.
55   Interview with representative of IIAM, Nampula, March 2013.
56   Interview with representative of Embrapa, Brasília, July 2013.
57   Interview with representative of Usaid, Maputo, April 2014.
58   Interview with representative of civil society in Brazil, Brasília, June 2013.
59   Interview with representative of IIAM, Maputo, April 2014.
60   Interview with representative of Piait, Maputo, April 2014.
61   Interview with representative of IIAM, Maputo, April 2014.
62   Interview with representative of IIAM, Lichinga, June 2014.
63   Interview with representative of USAID, Brasília, June 2013.
64   Interview with representative of IIAM, Maputo, April 2014.
65   Interview with representative of IIAM, Nampula, March 2013.

Thus, the initiatives to support consolidation of a national research system and the development of technological packages adapted to the agro-ecological conditions of Mozambique have proved coherent with the objectives of the government actors and of the IIAM representatives. However, the role of the Mozambican government in implementing and financing activities fell short of that expected by the representatives of Brazilian cooperation. The attraction of international and private finance remains the main line of the institution.

The goals of agricultural modernisation present in the Mozambican government's strategies had repercussions on the implementation of other Brazilian cooperation programmes. For example, the programme 'More Food International', originally associated with Brazilian policies to promote family farming, was adopted in Mozambique as an initiative fundamentally oriented towards agricultural mechanisation at preferential prices. The programme combines preferential credit for the import of Brazilian agricultural machinery and technical assistance for designing specific policies for family farming. The broader interests of the Brazilian counterpart in establishing 'an emancipatory system of technical assistance and food security oriented towards family farming'[66] were considered secondary in implementing the strategy (Zanella and Milhorance, 2016). This initiative took shape in Mozambique through the Agricultural Mechanisation Programme, for which the government mobilised resources envisaged in Pnisa and in the Agricultural Development Fund (FDA). Other actors confirm this argument, showing that the goals of promoting family farming gradually gave way to the commercial component of the initiative (Cabral, 2015).

The Brazilian instruments, internationalised by the initiatives analysed in this chapter, were translated into national public-policy instruments by hybridising the elements present in the two countries. These strategies inform a cognitive and public-action system based on the promotion of agricultural modernisation, the structuring of value chains by product, the orienting of peasant farmers to the market through contracts, attracting foreign investment by means of fiscal incentives, and the centrality of the private sector in the supply of agricultural services. However, this is not a reorientation of the cognitive and action framework of the country's sector strategies. The 'exchange of experiences' in this case was the object of an incremental change consolidating an existing political and institutional apparatus established by the political elites of the sector and by the main traditional donors.

---

66 Interview with representative of the Ministry of Agricultural Development of Brazil, Brasília, June 2013.

Conflicts and alliances in the orientation of development strategies

As shown in the previous section, the strategies of accumulation and of combatting rural poverty in Mozambique were, to a large extent, oriented towards the goals of agricultural modernisation, the promotion of private investment and the development of an extractive economy. The regional trend of promoting the development corridors and the international context of intensified investment contributed to consolidating political instruments favourable to these dynamics. In this context, the Mozambican administrative elites have been particularly receptive to the technical and financial cooperation initiatives of ProSavana, of Piait and of the More Food International programme, and to the Vale investments. However, this model has been severely criticised by a series of actors from Mozambican and international civil society, and has been counter-balanced by other projects such as the PAA Africa Programme, which sought to establish institutional markets for family farmers. This latter initiative will not be discussed in this chapter.

A heterogeneous group of social organisations has consolidated an informal network of interchange and social mobilisation. Since 2012, this network has acted through publicity campaigns, seeking to draw public attention to the risks for peasant populations associated with foreign, and particularly Brazilian, investment. Denouncing 'land grabbing', a phenomenon that received great international attention at the end of the decade of 2000 (Boche and Anseeuw, 2013), the first campaigns sought to associate ProSavana with the development model of the Brazilian cerrado region. The symbolic power of this model refers to the historic dispute over public resources and land experienced by the rural population of this region. As mentioned by Shankland and Gonçalves (2016), the use of simple graphic and audio-visual artefacts was crucial for building and spreading a 'political imaginary' associating the savannah with the cerrado. As reported by the representative of a Mozambican NGO,

> The subject of ProSavana appeared when we began to observe the first official visits in which land was offered. First, the Minister of Agriculture said that land was available in Mozambique. Later he went to Brazil and said that land in Mozambique was not expensive and there were fiscal incentives. The perspective was to develop Prodecer in the Nacala Corridor. But the provincial governments were not informed. That was when we decided to investigate.[67]

Mobilisation intensified faced with a scenario that was not transparent in

---
67 Interview with representative of an NGO in Mozambique, Maputo, April 2014.

drawing up the programme, mainly the Master Plan. This context contributed to the spread of alarmist ideas. Japanese civil society was also invited to join the mobilisation effort through the platform of the international peasant movement, Via Campesina. On the Mozambican side, in addition to the National Union of Peasants (Unac), a series of organisations in Maputo and in the provinces in which ProSavana and the Vale investments would be implemented (Nampula, Niassa, Tete, Zambézia) joined this movement. Organisations such as Academic Action for the Development of Rural Communities (Adecru), the Rural Mutual Aid Association (Oram), Environmental Justice (Justiça Ambiental, JA) and the Nampula Civil Society Platform (Plataforma Provincial das Organizações da Sociedade Civil de Nampula, PPOSC-N) contributed strongly to the first stages of mobilisation. Other actors that were part of the International Coordination of those Impacted by Vale, such as the Association of Support and Legal Assistance to Communities (AAJC), also became involved. Interviews with representatives of these organisations showed that Mozambican civil society had rarely experienced this level of mobilisation, equivalent only to the Land Campaign[68] during the formulation of the Land Law in the late 1990s.[69]

The continual flows of financial resources from international NGOs such as Oxfam guaranteed a process of socialisation among the actors of this network: an exchange of information;[70] production of videos in several languages that were distributed among farmers and the international community;[71] drawing up reports following the programmes;[72] numerous meetings of Mozambican and international organisations;[73] and open letters addressed to heads of state.[74] It is worth noting that this movement was accompanied by practical initiatives of exchange of experiences, but this form of action remained limited.

Initially, criticism was built on information that was available on the Brazilian case. Civil society representatives then sought a dialogue with peasant associations and a survey of specific cases of the impacts of ProSavana. It should

---

68 According to Negrão (2003), the approval of the Land Law (No. 19/1997) was largely due to this social movement, which involved more than 200 organisations in revising and distributing the drafts of the law, concerning the new legal framework, seeking to avoid privatisation of the land.
69 Interview with representative of an NGO in Mozambique, Maputo, October 2014.
70 See, for example, publication of a preliminary version of the Master Plan (GRAIN and Environmental Justice, 2013).
71 '*ProSavana e FACE OCULTA Do Prodecer*', 2013, made by Mozambican and Brazilian organisations; '*ProSavana: Land Grabbed, Life Stolen*', 2015, made by Mozambican organisations with international support; '*Daqui a Nada*', 2015, made by Brazilian researchers with the support of ActionAid; '*Mozambique: les grands exploitants agricoles délogent les petits fermiers du Nord*', 2016, made by the French newspaper *Le Monde*.
72 See: Funada (2013); Schlesinger (2013); Unac (2014); Adecru (2015).
73 Triangular conferences of the peoples against ProSavana, Maputo, August 2013; July 2014; November 2015.
74 'Open Letter to Halt the Programme Urgently', 2013.

be noted that the relations between central power in Mozambique and civil society were, to some extent, conflictual during the decade of 2000, because of the association between this group and international aid to the 'good governance' reforms (Bellucci, 2003). Political elites and private actors sought at several moments to discredit the mobilisations, saying that they were not representative of the rural population.[75] On numerous occasions the critics of ProSavana were regarded as opponents of the development of Mozambique, as illustrated by the words of the Niassa Provincial Director at a public meeting:

> The external pressures come for Niassa to remain in poverty. That's not what we want. We want to produce food and we have land for this. We have to wake up… We have to pay attention to the outside pressures that want to block our development.[76]

This discourse met opposition from actors of civil society:

> We find that the government has difficulty in criticising private companies. When we demonstrate, they criticise us for acting against the country's development. We had problems with Vale resulting from this lack of dialogue. These companies are close to the government because they know the doors are open… Only when there are strikes or demonstrations do they [the government] seek us out.[77]

Civil-society organisations mainly sought to influence changes in the government's behaviour through actions of direct confrontation and publicity campaigns (Milhorance and Bursztyn, to be published). The mobilisation effort was of great scope in 2013 and 2014, and achieved some of its demands, such as: 1) greater publicity for information on the initiatives; 2) the removal of the objectives of population displacement from the ProSavana Master Plan; 3) reassessment of the strategy for population displacement in the rehabilitation of the Nacala railway; and 4) the formulation of technical-assistance activities for smallholder farmers by means of the rural extension component of ProSavana (ProSavana-PEM). The pressures opposed to the programme also contributed to weakening the Nacala Fund, which had not been successful in its initial raising of finance (Fase, 2014). Additionally, the increase in mobilisation led some investors interested in operating in the country to reconsider their

---

75 Interview with representative of the Ministry of Agriculture, Maputo, April 2013; Interview with consultant of JICA, Nampula, April 2013; Interview with representative of Vale, Tete, May 2014.
76 Provincial Director of Niassa in a consultative meeting with civil society, Lichinga, June 2014.
77 Interview with a representative of civil society of Tete, Tete, May 2014.

projects.⁷⁸ Finally, the Mozambican government promised to draw up a new legal framework for mining.

However, these changes were not regarded as sufficient by many civil society actors, who were seeking to transform the draft programme and the privileged model of strengthening the extractive economy (Mosca, 2014). As shown in the 'Open Letter', these organisations were striving for the 'immediate suspension of all actions and projects currently under way', demanding 'that all human, material and financial resources allocated to the ProSavana programme [be] reallocated to defining and implementing a sustainable National Plan to Support Family Farming' and that 'the Mozambican government [adopt] policies centred on support for peasant agriculture'.⁷⁹

After the first stage of mobilisation, divergences were noted among the members of the coalition concerning the goals and the methods used. The divergences became sharper after the launch of the 'No to ProSavana' campaign in June 2014. The campaign's goal was to block the programme completely. While most of the organisations were opposed to the Brazilian support for the mega-projects and to the strengthening of an extractive model of development, they diverged over the total rejection of these initiatives. Some local peasant associations and NGOs based in Nampula and Niassa were committed to participating directly in implementing the programme, through initiatives to strengthen the capacity of the peasant farmers faced with the investments, and in allocating land titles.⁸⁰

Furthermore, opposition to the Brazilian projects did not extend to an equivalent criticism of similar initiatives to promote agribusiness, financed by other international donors, which helped to discredit the criticism. The perception of certain international donors on the speculative nature of denunciations about land appropriation in the Nacala Corridor also led to a decline in sources of political and financial support.

To sum up, this movement grew, based on the socialisation of a common perspective on the risks of internationalising agribusiness, the symbolic material for which referred to the historical trajectories of the Brazilian agrarian movements. However, after an initial phase of mobilisation, the movement gradually fragmented, while the coalition of governmental actors and private promoters of these initiatives remained relatively cohesive. According to Tarrow (cited in Borras, 2010), the continuity of waves of social mobilisation is based on the density of networks and on effective structures of interaction oriented

---

78   Interview with representative of Embrapa, Brasília, July 2013.
79   'Open letter to halt urgently the ProSavana programme', June 2013.
80   Interviews with representative of civil society in Nampula and Lichinga, June 2014.

towards action. In this sense, the internal dynamics of this coalition – which Borras (2010) characterises as the politics of mobilisation – had a considerable impact on its results. The main factors of divergence were the goals of the mobilisation, the privileged forms of action, and the cohesion of the receivers of the message (the government).

Hence the interactions between and among the coalitions of actors of the rural sector of Mozambique influenced the adoption of the initiatives analysed. Table 4.1 shows the main coalitions of actors involved in this process, their resources and the main instruments comprising their perspective of action. The actors identified in this analysis possess asymmetric resources in terms of formal authority and the material (financial) resources necessary for the consolidation of public policies.

Figure 4.1 then illustrates a simplified structure of the regular interactions between the actors and coalitions shown in Table 4.1, using the network analysis tool.[81] It identifies the main organisations operating in the formulation, implementation or criticism of the initiatives analysed. We can note three main groups, which correspond to the coalitions of actors, and are defined by the intensity of interactions between each group (Blondel *et al*, 2008). The first two coalitions (C1 and C2) tend to collaborate in the promotion of private investments, despite thematic differences, since the second operates in the agricultural area. Together they represent a dense and influential group in defining the country's development options. The third coalition corresponds to the group of civil society organisations that have participated in criticism of and negotiations with the actors in the first two coalitions.

In general, the measures of centrality assess the relative importance of a vertex (an organisation in this case) in a network, and it can be measured in different ways. The larger the sphere, the greater the centrality of the actor represented by it. In the present study, eigenvector centrality was used (Bonach, 2001), which informs the importance of an actor as a function of the importance of their neighbours (in the same coalition). If an actor is linked to others who are in a central position in the network, that actor will have a high centrality. This measure is frequently used to analyse the socialisation of information and of behaviour, as well as their influence in the system, as in the case of the coalitions of actors presented here. It should be noted that this tool

---

81   This tool analyses the interdependence (functional, cognitive, relational, etc.) between the members of a political system, identifying social and political resources, as well as power differentials between the actors. In our case study, the relations considered were those of 1) collaboration, 2) technical or financial support, and 3) institutional affiliation. The data for drawing up the base were collected from semi-structured interviews, institutional reports of the organisations and reports of meetings. The tool calculates the existence or not (1 or 0) of these types of relation between organisations. The centrality of an actor is, thus, measured based on the series of its positive relations.

is used for illustrative purposes, complementary to the analysis developed over this chapter.

Table 4.1: Main coalitions of actors of the initiatives analysed

	Extractive Industry (C1)	Agricultural Modernisation (C2)	Opposition (C3)
Main members	**Public:** Ministry of Trade (MIC) and of Mines (MIREM), Investment Promotion Centre (CPI), National Directorate of Forestry and Land (DNTF) **International:** World Bank, Exim Banks **Private:** GAPI, Vale, Odebretch, Camargo Correa, Rio Tinto, Jindal	**Public:** Ministry of Agriculture (MASA), Agricultural Research Institute of Mozambique (IIAM) **Civil Soc:** OLIPA, iTC **International:** USAID, Clusa, Gates Foundation, World Bank, FIDA, AGRA, CGIAR, Getúlio Vargas Foundation (FGV), JICA, Embrapa **Private:** GAPI, Ikuru, Malonda, Technoserve, IITA, AgDevCo, others	**Civil Soc:** Unac, Adecru, Oram, AAJC, PPOSC-N, Human Rights League (LDH), Kulima, Environmental Justice (JA), Land Forum, iTC, ROSA, others. **International:** Oxfam, WWF, Care, ActionAid, Brazilian NGOs (Fase)
Belief system	Promotion of trade and of investments in natural resources and in infrastructures, structuring of growth poles along the corridors or in special economic zones	Development of technological packages, promotion of investments and of the private sector, structuring of value chains by product, promotion of contract agriculture, technical assistance to producers	Promotion of social participation, conservation of natural resources and maintenance of land rights, opposition to agrarian capitalism and the extractive model
Resources	Financial, technical, formal authority	Financial, technical, formal authority, international legitimacy	Public opinion, international legitimacy, social legitimacy

Source: Drawn up by the author

The 'extractive' coalition shows in pride of place actors such as Vale and the Mozambican Investment Promotion Centre (CPI). The 'modernising' coalition confirms the predominance of actors such as USAID, IIAM and the Ministry of Agriculture, as well as Embrapa itself. In the 'opposition' coalition, embodied by civil society, the position of centrality is shared between actors such as Oram and Unac, who came into disagreement after the launch of the 'No to ProSavana' campaign. As explained earlier, the internal divergences in the opposition movement, over the nature of the struggle and forms of action, contributed to diminishing it. These divergences were even more compelling at provincial level, but for reasons of space, the territorial dynamics will not be looked at in depth in this text. As complemented by Chichava and Alden (Chapter 7), these cleavages are related to various factors, such as the search for prominence by some organisations, but they also underscore a deep regional division in Mozambican civil society. Hence the author considers the divergences as based on the struggle by organisations from the centre and north of the country for emancipation from the organisations based in Maputo, apart from the dispute for the resources of the initiatives of Brazil and Japan. Despite the effectiveness of the mobilisation actions in attaining certain objectives, ProSavana, Vale and the projects to modernise agriculture have remained central to the political agenda of the Mozambican government.

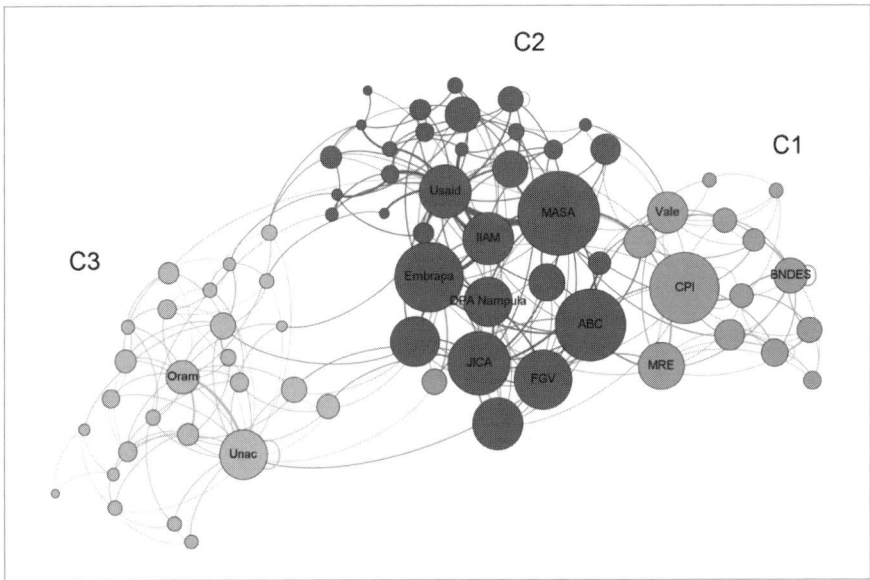

Figure 4.1: Simplified representation of the coalitions of actors
Source: Compiled by the author with Gephi

Conclusion

The Brazilian initiatives analysed in this chapter are part of a broader context of promoting private investment in natural resources, mainly mineral and agricultural resources. Both Mozambican and international interests have converged to maintain public policies favourable to these goals. The political change observed was thus incremental: the main coalition of the Mozambican rural sector benefitted from Brazilian support to consolidate its project of productivist modernisation and of strengthening the economy with an extractive base, which brings in foreign currency. This process was driven by the national and international context, which favoured agricultural investments.

In the cases of ProSavana and Vale, these initiatives have contributed to consolidating the existing political strategy. In the complementary cases of the 'More Food International' and Piait programmes, the promoters of these initiatives on the Mozambican side prioritised the development instruments of 'technological packages', although their significance was often broader or even separate from these initiatives in the Brazilian context. These strategies were widely criticised by a coalition of NGOs and social movements, which benefitted from political and financial resources channelled by Brazilian and international organisations, critical of the agribusiness model and of the activities of Vale.

Initially, this effort to socialise aspects of transnational agrarian struggles and of political mobilisation attracted great visibility and achieved some of its goals. However, the system of beliefs and actions of the Mozambican government was not transformed by these campaigns, which fragmented at a later stage. The internal divergences hinged mainly on the nature of the mobilisation and its forms of action; so while, on the one hand, the opposition coalition lost in density of its mobilisation and in coordination over time, on the other hand, the political elites in favour of the agricultural and mining investments continually reorganised themselves when faced with resistance by these movements. Understanding the dynamics of interaction between the national and international actors in the distribution of resources, the dispute over models and the structuring of networks has proved fundamental in analysing the process and impact of mobilisation by social movements in Mozambique. This approach reaffirms the active role of Mozambican actors in defining the trajectories of the country's development, despite international injunctions.

References

Adecru (2015) Governo do Distrito de Malema persegue e ameaça camponeses que rejeitaram o ProSavana. Acção académica para o desenvolvimento das comunidades rurais. Available at: https://adecru.wordpress.com/2015/05/11/governo-do-distrito-de-malema-persegue-e-ameaca-camponeses-que-rejeitaram-o-prosavana/ (accessed 5 April 2016).

Aguiar, R (1986) *Abrindo o Pacote Tecnológico: Estado e pesquisa agropecuária no Brasil*. São Paulo: Polis.

Anseeuw, W, Boche, M, Breu, T, Markus, G, Lay, J, Messerli, P and Nolte, K (2012) *Transnational Land Deals for Agriculture in Global South: Analytical report based on the Land Matrix Database*. Bern/Montpellier/Hamburg: CDE/CIRAD/GIGA.

Bellucci, S (2003) Le Mozambique à l'heure néo-libérale: Bonne gouvernance et ONG. Thèse Etat. France, Université de Paris-Sud.

Blondel, D, Guillaume, J, Lambiotte, R and Lefebvre, E (2008) Fast unfolding of communities in large networks, *Journal of Statistical Mechanics: Theory and Experiment* (10), pp 1–12.

Boche, M (2015) Contrôle du foncier, agricultures d'entreprise et restructurations agraires: Une perspective critique des investissements fonciers à grande échelle: Le cas de la partie centrale du Mozambique. PhD thesis, Paris, Université Paris XI Sud.

Boche, M and Anseeuw, W (2013) *Unravelling 'Land Grabbing': Different models of large-scale land acquisition in Southern Africa*. LPDI Working Paper No. 46, Institute for Poverty, Land and Agrarian Studies, University of the Western Cape.

Borras, S (2010) The politics of transnational agrarian movements, *Development and Change*, **41** (5), pp 771–803.

Borras, S, Franco, J, Gómez, S, Kay, C and Spoor, M (2012) Land-grabbing in Latin America and the Caribbean, *The Journal of Peasant Studies*, **39** (3–4), pp 845–72.

Brito, L, Castel-Branco, C, Chichava, S and Francisco, A (eds) (2010) *Economia Extractiva e Desafios de Industrializaçao em Moçambique*, 1st edition. Maputo: Instituto de Estudos Sociais e Económicos.

Brown, W and Harman, S (eds) (2013) African agency in international politics. *Routledge Studies on African Politics and International Relations*. London and New York: Routledge.

Cabral, L (2015) *Priests, Technicians and Traders? The discursive politics of Brazil's agricultural cooperation in Mozambique*. Working Paper No. 10, China and Brazil in Africa Agriculture Project. Sussex: Institute for Development Studies.

Canal Terraviva entrevista Cleber Guarany (2013) Available at: http://fgvprojetos.fgv.br/noticias/canal-terraviva-entrevista-cleber-guarany (accessed 22 October 2014).

Castel-Branco, C (2011) *Dependência de Ajuda Externa, Acumulação e Ownership: Contribuição para um debate de economia política*. Cadernos IESE No. 7/2011. Maputo, Moçambique, Institute of Social and Economic Studies.

Castel-Branco, C (2013) *CAADP and Agrarian Options for Mozambique: Contribution for a political economy analysis*. Available at: http://www.iese.ac.mz/lib/noticias/2013/CNCB_CAADP_PEAPAConference_18-20.03.13.pdf (accessed 24 February 2015).

Chichava, S, Duran, J, Cabral, L and Shankland, A (2013) Brazil and China in Mozambican agriculture: Emerging insights from the field, *ids Bulletin*, **44** (4), pp 101–15.

Cunguara, B, Fagilde, G, Garrett, JL and Uaiene, R (2012) Growth without change? A case study of economic transformation in Mozambique, *Journal of African Development*, **12** (2), pp 105–30.

Ekman, S and Macamo, C (2014) *Brazilian Development Cooperation in Agriculture*. Working Paper No. 138. Bogor, Indonesia: Centre for International Forestry Research.

Food and Agriculture Organisation of the United Nations (FAO) and WFP (2010) *FAO/WFP Crop and Food Security Assessment Mission to Mozambique*, August 2010. Special Report. Maputo: Food and Agriculture Organization/World Food Programme.

Food and Agriculture Organisation of the United Nations (FAO) (2012) *Trends and Impacts of Foreign Investment in Developing Country Agriculture: Evidence from case studies*, p 200. Rome: FAO.

Fase (2015) *Fundo Nacala: Estrutura original e desdobramentos*. Available at: https://fase.org.br/wp-content/uploads/2015/04/Fundo_Nacala_Final.pdf (accessed 27 May 2017).

FGV Projetos (2014) *Nacala Corridor Fund*. Available at: http://www.oecd.org/forum/issues/nacala%20corridor%20fund-fgv%20Projetos.pdf (accessed 16 January 2014).

Funada, S (2013) *Fukushima, ProSavana and Ruth First: Examining Natalia Fingermann's 'Myths behind ProSavana'*, pp 85–114.

Funada, S, Watanabe, N and Akimoto, Y (2014) *ProSavana Civil Society Report 2013. Findings and Recommendations* (English Summary), (10 April). Available at: http://www.ngo-jvc.net/jp/projects/advocacy/data/prosavana-ikenkoukan-9-7.pdf (accessed 27 May 2017).

Galli, R (2003) *Peoples' Spaces and State Spaces: Land and governance in Mozambique*. Lanham, MD: Lexington Books.

Garcia, A, Kato, K and Fontes, C (2013) *A Historia Contada Pela Caça Ou Pelo Caçador? Perspectivas sobre o Brasil em Angola e Moçambique*. Rio de Janeiro: Instituto Politicas Alternativas para o Cone Sul (PACS).

GRAIN, UNAC and Via Campesina Africa (2012) *Brazilian Megaproject in Mozambique Set to Displace millions of peasants*, 29 November 2012. GRAIN. Available at: http://www.grain.org/article/entries/4626-brazilian-megaproject-in-mozambique-set-to-displace-millions-of-peasants (accessed 6 May 2014).

Hall, R (2011) Land grabbing in southern Africa: The many faces of the investor rush, *Review of African Political Economy*, **38** (128), pp 193–214.

Hanlon, J & Smart, T (2012) *Soya boom in Gúruè has produced few bigger farmers – so far*, p 9. Available at: http://www.open.ac.uk/technology/mozambique/sites/www.open.ac.uk.technology.mozambique/files/pics/d136343.pdf (accessed 23 October 2014).

Jenkins-Smith, H, Nohrstedt, D, Weible, C and Sabatier, PA (2014) The advocacy coalition framework: Foundations, evolution, and ongoing research. In PA Sabatier and CM Weible (eds). *Theories of the Policy Process*, 3rd edition. Boulder, CO: Westview Press, pp 183–223.

Kaarhus, R (2011) Agricultural Growth Corridors Equals Land-Grabbing? Models, Roles and Accountabilities in a Mozambican Case. In *International Conference on Global Land Grabbing*, LDPI, Sussex.

Liu, P (ed) (2013) *Trends and Impact of Foreign Investment in Developing Country Agriculture: Evidence from case studies*. Rome: Food and Agriculture Organization of the United Nations.

Mercandalli, S (2013) Le Rôle Complexe Des migrations dans les reconfigurations des systèmes d'activités des familles rurales: La circulation comme ressource? Localité de Leonzoane, Mozambique 1900–2010. Doctoral thesis. Paris: Université Paris Sud-Paris XI.

Milhorance, C and Bursztyn, M (to be published) South–South civil society partnerships: Increasing ties of political contention and policy building, *Development Policy Review*.

Milhorance, C (2015) *Emerging Trends in Global Commodities Markets: The role of Brazil and China in contemporary agrarian transformations*. Available at: http://www.iss.nl/fileadmin/ASSETS/iss/Research_and_projects/Research_networks/BICAS/BICAS_WP_12-Milhorance.pdf (accessed 19 August 2015).

MINAG (2011) *Plano Estratégico para o Desenvolvimento do Sector Agrario (2011–2020)*.

Mitha Ribeiro, G (2008) O pensamento social sobre o politico em Moçambique: Estudo de caso da cidade de Tete. Doctoral thesis. Lisbon, Instituto Superior de Ciências do Trabalho e da Empresa (ISCTE).

Mosca, J and Selemane, T (2012) Mega-projectos no meio rural, desenvolvimento do territorio e pobreza. In: *Desafios para Moçambique 2012*. Maputo, IESE, pp 231–255.

Mosca, J (2010) *Políticas Agrárias de (em) Moçambique (1975–2009)*, 1st edition. Lisbon and Maputo: Escolar.

Mosca, J (2014) *ProSavana*. Available at: http://omrmz.org/images/publicacoes/DR5.pdf (accessed 7 August 2014).

MRE (2003a) CTPD. Brasil–Moçambique. EMBRAPA-MADER. Projeto Na Área de Agricultura. Assinatura de Memorando de Entendimento, 13 January.

MRE (2003b) CTPD. Cooperação com o Japão para projetos em Moçambique. Visita de funcionários da Cooperação Japonesa em Maputo, 24 January.

MRE (2003c) Brasil–Moçambique. Projetos de desenvolvimento. Visita da CVRD. Embrapa, 26 May.

MRE (2003d) Brasil–Moçambique. Agricultura. Assinatura do Protocolo de Entendimento entre o Instituto de Desenvolvimento Industrial de Minas Gerais e o MADER, 18 December.

MRE (2004) Brasil–Moçambique. Agricultura. Plantio de soja e pecuária. Protocolo de intenções entre empresários brasileiros e moçambicanos, 26 January.

Negrão, J (2003) *A propósito das relações entre as ONGs do Norte e a sociedade civil moçambicana*. Available at: http://www.sarpn.org/documents/d0000650/P662-Relacoes.pdf (accessed 5 July 2014].

Nishimori and ProSavana (2012) Brasília: Palavra Aberta Available at: http://www2.camara.leg.br/camaranoticias/tv/materias/palavra-aberta/422013-dep.-luiz-nishimori-(psdb-pr)--relacoes-exteriores.html (accessed 13 April 2013).

PAMRDC (2010) Plano de Acção Multissectorial Para a Redução Da Desnutrição Crónica Em Moçambique (2011–2014).

ProSavana Website (2013) *O que é o ProSAVANA?*. Available at: http://www.prosavana.gov.mz/index.php?p=pagina&id=27 (accessed 3 March 2015).

ProSavana (2013) *Elaboração do Plano Director do Desenvolvimento Agrícola no Corredor de Nacala: Nota Conceitual*. Available at: https://www.prosavana.gov.mz/pdf/note_pt.pdf (accessed 14 January 2014).

ProSavana-PD (2014) *Formulação do Plano Director de Desenvolvimento Agrícola no Corredor de Nacala: Versão preliminar*

Reifschneider, F, Henz, G, Ragassi, C, Dos Anjos, UG and Ferraz RM (2010) *Novos Ângulos da História da Agricultura no Brasil*. Brasília: Embrapa Informação Tecnológica.

Ribeiro, A (2014) Tete: Historical meeting place for Brazilian and Mozambican developmentalist elites? Conference Presentation at the IV International Conference of IESE, Maputo, October. Available at: http://www.iese.ac.mz/lib/publication/IV_Conf2014/Tematicas/Tematica%206/2%20Ana%20Ribeiro.pdf (accessed 27 May 2017).

Sabatier, P and Jenkins-Smith, H (eds) (1993) *Policy Change and Learning: An advocacy coalition approach*. Theoretical Lenses on Public Policy. Boulder, CO: Westview Press.

Schlesinger, S (2013) *Cooperação e Investimentos do Brasil na África: O caso do ProSavana*, 1st edition. Maputo: FASE.

Shankland, A and Gonçalves, E (2016) Imagining agricultural development in South–South cooperation: The contestation and transformation of ProSavana, *China and Brazil in African Agriculture*, **81**, pp 35–46.

Smart, T and Hanlon, J (2014) *Chickens and Beer: A recipe for agricultural growth in Mozambique*. Maputo: Ciedima.

Unac (2014) *Pesquisa Sobre os Impactos Actuais Resultante da Prática da Actividade de Plantação de Eucaliptos e Pinheiros Levado a Cabo Pela Chikweti Forest do Niassa*, Maputo.

Vunjanhe, J and Adriano, V (2015) Segurança Alimentar e Nutricional em Moçambique: Um Longo Caminho Por Trilhar, *Textos para Discussão 6*. Rio de Janeiro: Reference Centre in Food and Nutritional Security/ Federal Rural University of Rio de Janeiro.

Wilkinson, J (2014) *Brazilian Bio-diplomacy in Africa: The case of biofuels*. Rio de Janeiro: ActionAid.

World Bank (2015) *World Development Indicators*. Available at: http://databank.worldbank.org/data/views/reports/tableview.aspx (accessed 19 February 2015).

Zanella, M and Milhorance, C (2016) Cerrado meets savannah, family farmers meet peasants: The political economy of Brazil's agricultural cooperation with Mozambique, *Food Policy*, **58**, pp 70–81.

Chapter 5

Brazilian interventions in the Nacala Corridor development programme: From rhetoric to practice in South–South development cooperation

Isabela Nogueira de Morais and Ossi I Ollinaho

Important changes have been taking place in the development cooperation architecture as emerging donors have consolidated their programmes in recent years. What had traditionally been a North–South relationship, clearly framed by the Development Assistance Committee (DAC) of economically advanced countries, has now become much more diffuse. Woods, for example, argues that a 'silent revolution' is taking place, with an increasing number of Southern donors 'offering alternatives to aid-receiving countries' (Woods, 2008:1220–1). Although South–South development cooperation (SSDC) is not a new phenomenon or concept, it has gained prominence in a changing international order characterised by the economic and political strengthening of middle-income countries (Muggah and Hamann, 2012). Not only has aid from Southern donors been growing over the last decade, but SSDC has also come to represent a powerful set of developmental principles (Mawdsley, 2012:65).

After decades of foreign aid being poured into sub-Saharan Africa and no clear structural results being achieved, the arrival of new donors, with a distinct discourse and sectorial preferences, has aroused expectations that cooperation could lead to significant achievements in poverty reduction. One of the poorest countries in the world, Mozambique, is a case in point. It has experienced consistent economic growth and high levels of foreign aid and foreign investments,[82] yet recent official statistics indicate that extreme poverty

---

82 From 1993, one year after the peace agreement that ended almost three decades of civil war, until 2012, average real GDP growth has been around 8 per cent a year, one of the fastest growth rates in Africa, behind only a few oil-exporting countries. Rates have been especially stable in the last decade and, since 2001, annual GDP real expansion has never dropped below 6 per cent (World Economic Outlook Database, April 2013. Available at: http://www.imf.org/external/pubs/ft/weo/2012/01/weodata/index.aspx).

has not been declining.[83] Growth has been pulled along by a few enclave megaprojects in the mineral and energy sectors, financed with foreign investments. These are capital intensive, rely heavily on imported intermediates and export most of their production, which means that they create few jobs and have few linkages to the public budget due to widespread tax exemptions. Therefore, they exacerbate the extractive nature of the Mozambican economy (Virtanen and Ehrenpreis, 2007; Castel-Branco, 2008; Sonne-Schmidt et al, 2009).

For its part, the agricultural sector has been characterised by declining per capita food production and land productivity; it clearly lags behind. In 2008, both food per capita and food per hectare were lower than in 2002 (MPD, 2010; Cunguara, 2012; Cunguara and Hanlon, 2012). Although there is general recognition of the capacity of agricultural development to help reduce poverty, the sector received only 3 per cent of government spending in the first decade of this century and 7.6 per cent of the total Official Development Assistance (ODA) from traditional donors and agencies between 2005 and 2011 (Mosca, 2012).

In a context marked by disillusionment regarding traditional donors' capacity to reduce poverty, coupled to fast Chinese expansion in sub-Saharan Africa and Brazil's recent success in reducing its own poverty, cooperation with Brazil should sound a promising avenue. Indeed, Brazilian technical aid puts emphasis on the agricultural sector compared to traditional donors. This sector accounted for 22 per cent of Brazilian global aid initiatives between 2003 and 2010 (RFB, 2011), and for 24 per cent of its aid allocations in the case of Mozambique.[84] Brazilian officials have also been one of the clearest voices in the international arena supporting SSDC as an alternative to traditional North–South cooperation.[85] The main arguments are that most Southern donors do not have a colonialist past and do not impose political or macroeconomic conditionalities. Instead, they claim to hold the principle of non-interference in internal affairs and to be in a better position to capture the

---

83   In fact, poverty incidence, measured by the national poverty line, still found room to rise, going from 54.1 per cent of the population in 2002–2003 to 54.7 per cent in 2008–2009 (MPD, 2010). A similar tendency can be observed in more long-term food-security indicators. Chronic child malnutrition has seen 'little substantive progress' according to UNICEF: in children under five years, it went from 47.1 per cent in 2003 to 46.4 per cent in 2008/09. Acute child malnutrition in fact rose from 5.1 per cent to 6.6 per cent in the same period (MPD, 2010).
84   Interview with Brazilian Cooperation Agency (ABC) official, Maputo, 13 March 2013.
85   Brazilian diplomats managed to include a critical paragraph at the Accra Agenda for Action of the Third High Level Forum on Aid Effectiveness, held in 2008, synthesising its view of SSDC: 'South–South co-operation on development aims to observe the principle of non-interference in internal affairs, equality among developing partners and respect for their independence, national sovereignty, cultural diversity and identity and local content. It … is a valuable *complement* to North–South cooperation' (p 18, emphasis added. Available at: http://www.oecd.org/dac/effectiveness/34428351.pdf).

social complexity of developing countries, due to their own recent experience with development. In government documents, Brazilian rhetoric claims that SSDC should be 'demand-driven', 'nonprofit, unlinked to commercial interests', 'without impositions or political conditionalities', 'inspired by the concept of solidary diplomacy' and 'participatory'. Projects and programmes should have a 'structural approach' leading to sustainable results and higher social-economic impacts (ABC, n.d.; ABC, 2010; IPEA 2011:32–3; MRE, 2013).

This chapter has two aims. The first is to critically examine some Brazilian cooperation practices in the agricultural sector in Mozambique vis-à-vis broader tendencies in the global development architecture after the growing concerns over land grabbing. Second, it analyses to what extent such practices are distanced from the principles that Brazilian political leaders claim to endorse with the cooperation. We empirically investigated Brazilian cooperation practices in the framework of an ambitious trilateral agricultural programme, ProSavana. The research is based on analysis of government documents and 38 semi-structured interviews with Mozambican, Brazilian and Japanese informants working in or affected by the programme. These interviews were combined with multi-sited ethnography in Nampula and districts around the Nacala Corridor from March to April 2013.

This chapter compares the discourse of SSDC and the actual practice of Brazilian development cooperation in ProSavana, identifying some sound ruptures between these. It is argued that the programme is well-inserted into the post-land-grabbing mainstream development cooperation trend, and goes against some of the principles that Brazil supports in the international policy arena. Instead of being unlinked to commercial motivations, private business interests, in fact, play an inherent part in the programme. It is not demand-driven, as the discourse claims, but was, instead, proposed by the donors. Lastly, ProSavana is hardly participatory but is, instead, characterised by top-down and outside-inside conduct. In what follows, we first briefly outline the programme in its context before showing how the actual practices break with the promises in SSDC. Then, we argue that these ruptures are in line with the most recent mainstream development cooperation trend. We conclude by discussing some possible implications of Brazilian cooperation practices within ProSavana for Mozambican development.

Cooperation profile and investments in the Nacala Corridor

Mozambique has been facing enormous constraints in its agricultural sector. It has not been able to increase per capita food production for the past decade, and thus has not been able to properly feed its population and increase rural incomes. In this context, the ambitious regional agricultural programme,

ProSavana, a trilateral initiative run by the governments of Japan, Mozambique and Brazil, provides a great opportunity. It is a long development project spanning 20 years, allowing structural changes to be carried out in the socio-economic system in the 19 districts of the provinces of Nampula, Niassa and Zambezia, where some 4.3 million people live.

ProSavana is by far the biggest Brazilian development programme in the area of technical agricultural cooperation in Mozambique (Table 5.1), even when one compares other trilateral initiatives. Its first phase, from 2011 until 2019, is organised around three components. The first is a technological one (ProSavana-PI), executed mainly by the Brazilian Agricultural Research Corporation (Embrapa) in cooperation with the Mozambican Agrarian Research Institute (IIAM). It was to be implemented from 2011–2016 with a budget of US$13.5 million. A second component, the Master Plan formulation (ProSavana-PD), executed together by Oriental Consulting (a Japanese consulting team), FGV Projetos (a Brazilian consulting company), and Mozambican counterparts, was implemented between 2012 and 2013 with a total of US$7.7 million. A third component, focusing on agricultural extension and models (ProSavana-PEM), was in its formulation phase in mid-2013 and should run until 2019, with a preliminary budget estimated at around US$15 million.[86] At the beginning of 2013, it became clear that the main agricultural development model supported by the programme would seek to integrate large-scale foreign investments with small-scale, local farmers in a contract-farming scheme. Small-farmers would get inputs (such as improved seeds, fertilisers, inoculants, pesticides and extension services) from investors in exchange for their production.

As the agricultural body of the broader Nacala Corridor development plan, ProSavana is located within a large web of foreign, private and public investments that are taking place in the region (Figure 5.1). If all these investments materialise, they will represent one of the most impressive and concatenated infrastructure development initiatives in this part of Africa. These include investments from the Brazilian mining company Vale, which are not officially related to the programme but overlap in practical terms (see the following section). In addition, several other infrastructure projects are being financed by the Japanese government, such as the modernisation and expansion of the Nacala Port and upgrading of the main roads along the corridor, including the routes Nampula–Cuamba, Cuamba–Mandimba and Mandimba–Lichinga, totalling more than 650 kilometres. From a Japanese strategic interest

---

86   For a more detailed description of ProSavana, see Chichava *et al* (2013).

Table 5.1: Budget, duration and type
Ongoing Brazilian programmes in the agricultural sector in Mozambique

Project name	Total budget (US$)	Duration	Type
Technical cooperation			
ProSavana PI+PD+PEM*	36 207 210	2011–2019	Trilateral (with JICA)
Plataforma	14 688 802	2010–2014	Trilateral (with USAID)
Food security	2 406 724	2011–2013	Trilateral (with USAID)
Food acquisition programme	500 000	2012–2013	Multilateral (with FAO and WFP)
Traditional seeds	363 500	2011–2014	Bilateral
Concessional loan + technical cooperation			
'More Food' Mozambique	97 590 000	Signed in 2011	Bilateral

* ProSavana-PEM does not yet have an approved budget. Estimation is based on non-official technical staff forecast.

Source: ABC and MDA (personal correspondence). For details on the programmes, see, for example, Chichava et al (2013), Cabral and Shankland (2013) and Patriota and Pierri (2013).

perspective, these investments, like ProSavana itself, are aimed at increasing world food production and, thus, stabilising global food prices – an understanding shared by different ProSavana staff members in both private and public meetings.[87]

Notwithstanding these opportunities, ProSavana has become by far the most contested Brazilian programme in Mozambican civil society[88] and has provoked several critical academic papers.[89] The highly opaque management and incoherencies in the scarce information that has been shared with the public, combined with delays in launching the programme's 'social part' (extension services for peasants), have induced a wave of criticism and fear

---

[87] The Mozambican national coordinator for ProSavana, for instance, publicly shared this understanding in a meeting with members of civil society held in Nampula on 21 March 2013.

[88] All major national social movements have publicly expressed their concern over the programme. See the pronouncements from the National Peasant's Union (Unac) published in October 2012 (http://www.unac.org.mz/index.php/7-blog/39-pronunciamento-da-unac-sobre-o-programa-ProSavana), from the Platform of Civil Society in Nampula (Plataforma) published in November 2012 (*Reflexão, inquietações e recomendações sobre o ProSavana*) and from Environmental Justice/Friends of the Earth Mozambique released in January 2013 (http://farmlandgrab.org/post/view/21566). A collective pronouncement, signed by three Mozambican and 20 African and Latin American organisations, was released in April 2013 raising concerns over the ProSavana Master Plan (http://farmlandgrab.org/post/view/21996) (all links last accessed May 2013).

[89] See, for instance, Cabral *et al* (2012), Clements and Fernandes (2013) and Funada-Classen (2013).

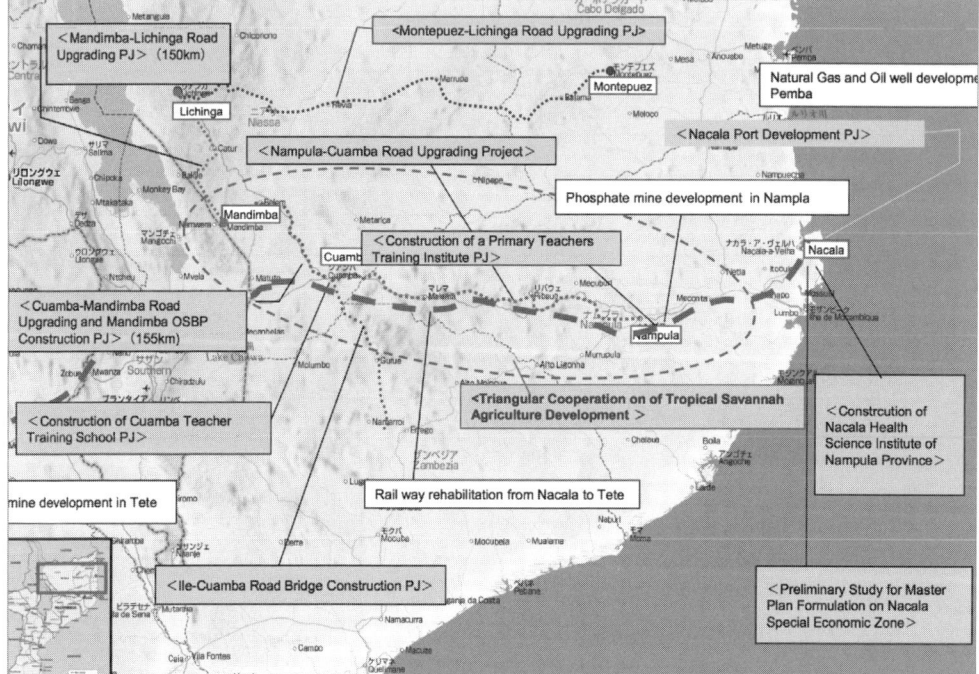

Figure 5.1: Foreign-financed investments in the Nacala Corridor
Source: JICA and ABC (2011)

related to land grabbing, resettlements, reduced food security and growing inequality. Why is this? Should the Brazilian cooperation not be welcomed by recipient countries once it embraces principles such as no links to commercial interests, a demand-driven approach and a participatory framework? We show in the following section that ProSavana does not follow some of the most salient principles of SSDC, rendering the criticisms both understandable and legitimate.

Ruptures between discourse and practice in Brazilian cooperation
From 'no links to commercial or economic motivations' to 'private investors as the dynamic force for development'
Officially based on the concept of 'solidary diplomacy', Brazilian cooperation is often presented as 'non-profit and unlinked to commercial interests', although a recent article called for an *aggiornamento* (updating) of this principle once it has been 'bypassed in practice in recent programmes'.[90] In fact, both interviews and project documents speak clearly that private and foreign investors are 'the

---
90   Patriota and Pierri (2013).

main dynamic force for development' in ProSavana. The March 2013 version of the Master Plan precisely formulates an agricultural development plan that 'contributes to social and economic development by engaging private investment to promote a sustainable production system and poverty reduction in the Nacala Corridor' (ProSavana-PD-QIP:1.1). The plan also foresaw the implementation of Quick Impact Projects that were expected to produce rapidly visible impacts as a way 'to attract local and foreign companies to invest in agriculture and agribusiness projects in the Nacala Corridor' (ProSavana-PD-QIP:4.1).

Indeed, due to the centrality of private investors in the operationalisation of ProSavana, the plan often resembled a business plan more than a development plan. For example, in a project for integrated grain cluster in the Majune district, 'feasibility indicators, at a discount rate of 10%, show that the project has high profitability and the IRR was calculated at 20.3% and the payback is 9 years' (ProSavana-PD-QIP, 2013:3.43). This project demanded 60 000 hectares, 'incorporating family farmers in the business through promotion, contracts, including hand labor and the establishment of production villages in case when resettlement in needed [sic]' (ProSavana-PD-QIP, 2013: 3.43). The plan adds: 'the Nacala port will be the main route of the cluster's production flow' (ProSavana-PD-QIP, 2013:3.45), a phrase found in other projects where no concerns are raised over internal food supply. While no other project in ProSavana demands such vast quantities of land, the private-investor perspective predominates in many of them. Another project, for grain and cotton in Lioma, demands 'tax incentives mechanisms' to attract investors and 'identification of areas available for expansion' (ProSavana-PD-QIP, 2013:3.50; 3.51). Half of the Quick Impact Projects are to be taken forward by the private sector, including agribusiness investors already operating in the Nacala Corridor. The plan suggests 'an affordable agricultural loan at a low interest rate' to 'widely promote' the out-grower scheme for soybean production for companies already operating in Lichinga and Lioma (ProSavana-PD-QIP, 2013:4.36). In the case of one soybean producer, whose plan was to expand his cultivation area to 2 500 hectares by 2015, an 'affordable agricultural loan' was also required 'to cover 50% of the above cost of implementing the out-grower scheme' (ProSavana-PD-QIP, 2013:4.32).

The line between ProSavana as a development programme and the private interventions in the Nacala Corridor are often blurred. Two big investments in the Nacala Corridor, while not officially associated with the programme, are being carried out by Vale, the Brazilian mining company that operates the Moatize coal mine in Tete Province (Figure 5.1). One investment aims to rehabilitate the export terminal port in Nacala and the railway that runs from

Nacala to Tete, passing through Malawi. Vale has the concession to operate both the railway and the associated coal-export terminal at the deep-water seaport of Nacala-à-Velha. Once this infrastructure is completed, the company expects to be able to transport and export at least 18 Mt/y of coal, against 6 Mt/y now through the Beira Port.[91] The rehabilitation includes revamping 682 kilometres of existing railroads right in the heart of ProSavana and laying a new 230-kilometere section.[92] Under another concession, Vale has also made an investment to build a mine to access the Evate phosphate deposits – the largest in Mozambique – in Monapo, Nampula Province. It was expected to become another large-scale mining operation after 2014, but this has not happened yet. To process the phosphate, Vale planned to build a complex in the coastal district of Nacala-à-Velha to produce fertilisers.[93]

Motivated by its interests in the region, Vale sponsored the first agro-climatic zoning in Mozambique, which aimed to assess the agricultural potential of different zones. The zoning was part of a larger viability study prepared between 2010 and 2011 in Mozambique and three other African countries to produce biofuels. These studies were requested by the Brazilian government, sponsored by Vale, and executed by a team from FGV Projetos, the same consulting company that has prepared the Master Plan. By initiative of FGV Projetos, the scope of the zoning was broadened to include not only biofuels, but also other crops such as corn, soya and cotton.[94] The fact that a private mining company has been financing a prospective cooperation programme in its planning phase could be regarded as both an indication of its interest in the region and of the limited capacity of Brazilian official cooperation to respond to demands.

ProSavana is often presented as a 'package' that can reduce the costs and risks for investors. This is notably done by the Nacala Fund, an investment fund that was also elaborated by FGV Projetos, which, in 10 years, aimed to raise US$2 billion to finance agribusiness investors along the corridor. Brazilian stakeholders usually emphasise that the Nacala Fund does not have any formal connection with ProSavana. It is worth noting, however, that the fund does appear in the list of projects proposed by the March 2013 version of the Master Plan, although stating that 'the project sheet will be completed after confirming the situation of the Nacala Fund' (ProSavana-PD-QIP:3.35). By 2013, the

---

91 http://www.miningweekly.com/article/vale-reveals-progress-in-moatize-expansion-and-nacala-corridor-development-2013-03-08 (last accessed April 2013).
92 Vale, Railroads website: http://www.vale.com/brasil/EN/business/logistics/railways/Pages/default.aspx (accessed May 2013).
93 http://www.macauhub.com.mo/en/2012/10/09/brazil%E2%80%99s-vale-starts-quantifying-phosphate-reserves-in-mozambique/ (accessed May 2013).
94 Interviews with FGV Projetos staff, 18 March 2013 and 3 June 2013.

Nacala Fund had already selected 10 Brazilian farmers, who, according to a business plan, should work in cooperation with four Mozambican farmers with medium-sized farms. They were to operate around three production clusters: cotton (to be further developed into a textile cluster), corn and soya (both also for producing cooking oil and animal feed).[95] The fund was planned to be registered as an Investment Company Risk Capital (SICAR) in Luxembourg, and was marketed as offering 'investments with low risk and high return', once risks had been minimised by ProSavana's 'institutional package' (FGV Projetos, 2012:58).

By 2013, at least four large foreign agribusiness companies were already operating or beginning operations in the Gúruè (usually in the Lioma region) and Lichinga districts, producing mainly soya on a contract-farming scheme, as proposed by ProSavana. The companies are Hoyo Hoyo (Portugal), Africa Century Agriculture (registered in Mauritius and based in London), Rei do Agro (United States) and the controversial Agromoz, a partnership between Grupo Pinesso (Brazil), Grupo Américo Amorin (Portugal) and Intelec Holdings, owned by the Mozambican president, Armando Guebuza (Hanlon and Smart, 2012). This last partnership obviously raises questions about the Mozambican political leaders' personal interests in attracting foreign investments in agriculture as they argue for improving national food security.

Brazilian investors will not be the only beneficiaries of the ProSavana interventions, but still one of the main groups. The Mozambican focal point in Nampula reported that 'Brazilian investors are the ones that come in larger numbers within the scope of ProSavana'. 'There have been two big [Brazilian] missions, and in one of them they have hired a full Boeing, with 70 investors in November 2012… Last Saturday there was a Brazilian team to search for land to work in here. But they left with a bit of a deception, because land here is not what they had imagined. To find 20 000 ha here is not easy … there is a lot of hidden land but the investor comes and looks around the road. With the zoning done by ProSavana it will be easier.'[96] Besides Grupo Pinesso, up to mid-2013 at least three Brazilian agribusiness companies were waiting for the approval of their DUAT, the state-granted land use right.[97]

The central role of the large-scale private sector in the ProSavana project has not been unproblematic. In the first stages of the elaboration of the Master Plan, the Japanese counterparts claimed that large-scale agribusiness 'would not be feasible', as one FGV Projetos staff member pointed out. Officials from

---

95 Interview with FGV Projetos staff, 3 June 2013.
96 Interview on, March 2013.
97 Interview with MINAG official, 9 April 2013.

the Mozambican Ministry of Agriculture (MINAG) have also reported facing difficulties in dealing with the expectations of Brazilian partners regarding large-scale investments. 'The biggest challenge with Brazil is that we have different perceptions. What is small in Brazil is not the same thing in Mozambique. So, for big farms … [t]his is a big challenge for us: how to correspond to private investors' expectations in practical terms.'[98] Nonetheless, a strong characteristic of the March 2013 draft of the Master Plan is the role of foreign, private investors in fostering family production through contract farming.

The high population density in the 14 districts immediately around the railway line was reported to be the main reason for expanding ProSavana interventions to 19 districts. The programme now includes five new districts with lower population density where it could be easier to implement large-scale farming, for example in Majune.[99] In a context marked by limited operational and policy capacity on the part of ABC (more later) and by the implicit need to defend 'national interests' through cooperation,[100] it should not be surprising that organised private interests have been able to take the lead in certain Brazilian SSDC projects.

From a 'demand-driven' to a 'donor-proposal' approach

Brazilian South–South development cooperation is, according to the official discourse, 'demand-driven' (ABC, 2013) and based on principles that promote 'local ownership' (Patriota, 2009) and 'local leadership'. Projects and programmes should take place 'in response to the demand from developing countries' (ABC, n.d.) and should be aligned with national development plans. Instead of being original SSDC principles, these concepts have been derived from the so-called Aid Effectiveness Agenda, which has been orienting traditional donors' practices since the 2005 Paris Declaration. The idea behind ownership is that developing countries should be formulating their own national development strategies. In practical terms, however, recipient countries have had less policy space to define social, economic and political strategies due to the proliferation of strategy papers, often written with the intention of pleasing foreign donors. These documents have come to form the main framework of recent donor–recipient relations in Africa (Oya, 2006; Oya and Pons-Vignon, 2010; Castel-Branco, 2011).

ProSavana is, indeed, aligned with a couple of Mozambican national strategies, notably with the Strategic Plan for Development of the Agrarian Sector (PEDSA). However, to what extent these national plans were developed

---

98 Interview with MINAG official, 9 April 2013.
99 Interview with FGV Projetos and JICA staff members, 18 March 2013.
100 Interview with former ABC director, 6 March 2013.

to respond to new trends in development cooperation is subject to further investigation. What we know is that ProSavana was not a product of a request or a demand from the Mozambican government.[101] It was initially an initiative of the Japanese counterparts, operationalised by JICA and motivated by the Japanese desire, as said earlier, to balance 'the supply and demand for food in global standards by increasing food production' (ProSavana, 2009). ProSavana is based on the decade-old 'Japan–Brazil Partnership Programme' (JBPP) agreed on 28 March 2000 in Tokyo, which takes the same type of triangular form that Japan has used in its partnerships with several other Southern countries.[102] The partnership was reactivated at the initiative of the Japanese during a visit of the Senior Vice-President of JICA, Kenzo Oshima, to Brasília in April 2009. During these meetings, JICA proposed spreading the results of the Prodecer (Brazil–Japan Cooperation for the Development of Brazilian Cerrado) to the African savannah. This led to the signing of an agreement between Oshima and the former Director of ABC, Marco Farani, on 3 April 2009, confirming a common interest in using the JBPP framework for cooperation in the development of the African tropical savannah.

It was only then that the first beneficiary country of the agreement began to take part in the formulation of the plan. As the ProSavana Master Plan's Terms of Reference put it, 'as a result of a combined decision between the governments of Japan and Brazil ... ProSavana aims at repeating in the African continent the development experience of Brazilian cerrado, and Mozambique was defined as the first country to receive the program's actions' (ProSavana ToR, 2011:14). The first formal entrance of officials from the Ministry of Agriculture of Mozambique into the planning of the programme was during a roadshow visit to the Brazilian cerrado, organised in May 2009, to present Brazilian large-scale agriculture and the techniques that could be transferred. A subsequent Japan–Brazil joint mission to Mozambique in June 2009 formed an initial perception that there would be 'an extensive area of non-used arable land' available for investments (ProSavana, 2009). Finally, in July 2009, the programme was given high-level political approval during a meeting between the Japanese Prime Minister Taro Aso and the Brazilian President Lula da Silva at the G8 summit meeting in L'Aquila – without the presence of a Mozambican authority.

From a 'participatory' to an 'explanatory' framework
Probably the two most criticised characteristics of ProSavana have been its

---

101 Based on interviews with former and current ABC and JICA staff members, Mozambique Ministry of Agriculture and on the minutes of the meeting of 17 September 2009 (ProSavana, 2009).
102 This framework was first used with Brazil in a partnership for capacity-building in Josina Machel Hospital in Angola in 2007 (JICA, n.d.).

opaque management from the public's perspective and the incoherence between different stakeholders over time.[103] In a civil-society meeting held in Maputo,[104] this incoherence was illustrated in a debate over the displacement of local communities. A Brazilian representative of the study team categorically stressed that no displacement would take place in the first phase (until 2019), and this was followed by a Mozambican intervenient who affirmed that 'I cannot say if there will be displacements or not. We want to minimise conflicts … but it doesn't mean that they cannot happen.'

Both in personal interviews and public events, government officials and the programme staff have admitted that problems of communication are an important failure, and have stated that they are trying to fix it through meetings at village level and the dissemination of information to civil society. Since February 2013, teams consisting of Mozambican officials and Japanese and/or Brazilian consultants have been visiting districts to present ProSavana to local communities. After presenting the programme, the teams open the floor to questions and suggestions from farmers, to learn about the constraints they are facing. However, the methodology seems to focus merely on presenting the project as it has already been planned, rather than allowing locals real participation. According to officials at the Mozambican focal point in Nampula,[105] there has been 'divulgation' to local communities to avoid 'disturbance'. The methodology is to 'spread information' and 'explain' the programme. A member of the Japanese study team shared this view: 'We have started the divulgation of ProSavana in local communities as a way to oppose the criticism.'[106] Only one consultant interviewed reported some knowledge of a participatory approach: 'I ask them about their dreams. How do they see themselves in the future?'[107]

Genuine 'participation' does not imply asking someone's opinion before doing what has been already planned (and what would be done anyway, in many cases). Participation should mean planning together and sharing each other's opinions transparently in the process of planning. Interventions that fail to put such a process into practice risk a low level of local ownership by the community and a high probability of gross mistakes. However, a participatory approach was not an official orientation of the ABC at the formulating phase of the Master Plan, and it was left to consultants to decide their approach. 'If

---

103 See Funada-Classen (2013) for a systematisation of the volatility in ProSavana discourse from a Japanese perspective.
104 Attended by one of the authors, 18 March 2013.
105 Interview, 21 March 2013.
106 Interview, 1 April 2013.
107 Interview, 27 March 2013.

we had asked for it to be participatory, there would be no chance to conclude the study within the period defined in the contract for the delivery of the final product', reported an ABC staff member.[108]

The March 2013 draft of the ProSavana Master Plan was elaborated by the Japanese and Brazilian consulting teams with very limited input, not only from local communities and organised civil society but also from the Mozambican government. This is to say that the planning of the programme was not only imposed in an 'outside-inside' manner, that is, proposed by donors, but also in a 'top-down', that is, a non-participatory manner. 'We haven't got much involved. We are waiting to see what they are going to propose', responded one high official from MINAG.[109] The lack of involvement of the Mozambican government, a problem reported also by Brazilian and Japanese stakeholders, is a matter of methodology. Other projects that Brazil has developed in Mozambique, like the formulation of the strategic plan for the Institute of Agrarian Research (IIAM) in partnership with Embrapa, have adopted a participatory approach from the beginning. 'Otherwise they don't feel it is their plan and they won't use it', summarised the Embrapa representative in Maputo.[110]

The exclusion of local communities and Mozambican civil society organisations (MCSOs) led them to harshly criticise the ProSavana programme, saying that it will reproduce the same problems created by Prodecer in Brazil, namely, environmental degradation; expropriation of small farmers to benefit the agro-industry and the big companies and political elites of Mozambique, Japan and Brazil. Some MCSOs supported by their Brazilian and Japanese counterparts called to completely stop the programme, replacing it with another that favours the small farmers, while others asked for its reformulation, a process in which they should be included along with local communities (Chichava and Alden, Chapter 7 in this volume).

ProSavana as a manifestation of the post-land-grabbing mainstream trend
ProSavana seems to be a precise manifestation of the mainstream development cooperation trend that has emerged as a response to growing apprehension over the phenomenon of land grabbing in poor countries. Since 2007, a large number of reports on land grabbing have been commissioned by different organisations.[111] These studies raise concerns over issues ranging from food

---

108 Phone interview, 17 May 2013.
109 Interview, 9 April 2013.
110 Interview, 14 March 2013.
111 For example, the United Nations Food Agricultural Organization (FAO), United Nations Development Programme (UNDP), International Land Coalition (ILC), The Oakland Institute, and Land Deals Politics Initiatives. For a review, see Fernandes et al (2012).

security, land conflicts and the incapacity of past land deals to reduce poverty, to their concentrated benefits in terms of corporate profits.[112] As a response to these threats, some 'opportunities' were identified in the 2011 World Bank report (Deininger *et al*, 2011), whereby large investors' resources and interest in land would be used to help low-income countries to increase smallholder productivity and improve local livelihoods. This development agenda uses the 'win-win' discourse to argue that large-scale foreign direct investments are the answer to low agricultural productivity in Africa if coupled with two things: a beneficial policy environment and a code of conduct for transnational corporations. As Borras and Franco summarise, 'the dominant storyline of land grabbing as a threat is slowly ceding ground to a new storyline – that of the new land deals as a potential opportunity for rural development, if they can be harnessed properly to minimise or avoid possible negative social and environmental effects' (Borras and Franco, 2010:509).

The policy framework that, according to the 2011 World Bank report, would lead to large-scale investment in agriculture and land acquisition, as well as the enhancement of 'opportunity', is the same policy framework that orientates the ProSavana Master Plan. The defining principles are: 1) well-defined and demarcated land rights; 2) clear identification of land and its availability through agro-ecological zoning; and 3) facilitation of contract farming or other out-grower schemes (Borras and Franco, 2010; Deininger *et al*, 2011). Often, these are not interventions formulated with pro-poor interests in mind, in the sense of 'proceeding from a social-justice-driven analysis of the causes of rural poverty and the need to protect and advance rural poor people's land access and property interests' (Borras and Franco, 2010:511). The main issue to be tackled is rather an 'investment problem', which will supposedly be overcome through facilitation of foreign investments.

However, why should foreign, private investors 'promote development' once large plots of land are sold or rented out to them on a commercial or concessional basis? According to Borras and Franco (2010), the answer – the 'magic bullet' – in the new narrative is a voluntary international code of conduct for investors; that is, a self-regulation guideline that should orient investors towards 'good practices'. In the ProSavana Master Plan, this is materialised as the Principle of Responsible Agricultural Investment (PRAI), essentially a reproduction of seven principles prepared by the FAO, IFAD (International Fund for Agricultural Development), UNCTAD (United Nations Conference on Trade and Development) and World Bank Group (FAO et al, 2010),

---

112 For applied research on land grabbing in Mozambique, see The Oakland Institute (2011) and Aabo and Kring (2012).

which 'private investors interested in agricultural development in the Nacala Corridor will be requested to comply with' (ProSavana-PD-QIP, 2013:5.3). The list includes several vague requirements without enforcement mechanisms, allowing for a high degree of interpretation and discretion; for example, it is requested that 'continuing access to food is assured' or that 'strategies to reduce potential instability of supply are adopted'. In other cases, investors are requested to adhere to what should be their most basic practices in any case, such as 'comply[ing] with laws, regulations, and policies applicable in the host country'. The Master Plan also discusses the creation of an agency to address Principles for Responsible Agricultural Investment (PRAI) issues, recommending that 'this agency or unit will not possess legal power to impose sanctions or penalties' (ProSavana-PD-QIP, 2013:5.8).

The critical aspect to be highlighted here is not the presence of foreign private capital in development strategies per se, but the centrality it has gained in policy formulation and operationalisation, and in terms of self-regulation, as opposed to state regulation. As Chichava *et al* (2013:6) have observed, the emphasis on the private sector has been present in development cooperation ever since the structural adjustment agenda emerged. What is new, they argue, 'is the central role attributed to the private sector in operationalizing public policy', coupled with the optional self-regulation guidelines, we would add. As a consequence, this development agenda minimises the responsibility of the state in promoting development and blocks the possibility of imposing contract conditionalities on foreign investors, although these have been proven to be crucial elements in development (Chang and Gabrel, 2004; Oya, 2006). Thus, ProSavana does not impose size limits for foreign farms, ceilings on exports or shares of the production that must stay in the local market. Indeed, these are not even mentioned, and yet one of the expected results is increased food security. In the same way, although the plan foresees the creation of industrial linkages through agro-processing facilities, no binding contracts to add value locally are discussed.

How have organised private interests come to gain so much space in policy planning and operationalisation of ProSavana? There are several possible interpretations, but this discussion goes beyond our objective in this chapter. What we would like to emphasise is that, on the Brazilian side, the programme involves several different institutions, some of them known for their different approaches to the 'agrarian question'. And, above all, general coordination, which should be taken forward by ABC, is missing due to limited staff and resources and the lack of policy orientation (Cabral and Shankland, 2013). In the agribusiness sector, one influential figure in conceptualising the programme has been Roberto Rodrigues, a former Minister of Agriculture and a former president of the Brazilian Agribusiness Association, who is currently coordinator of the FGV Center for Agribusiness. One of his arguments is that Brazil has developed large-scale tropical agricultural technology that no other country has, and it should make efforts to become a world provider of this technology – the more people use it, the more valuable it becomes.[113]

However, this technology is suitable only for certain types of agrarian systems, notably agribusiness with relevant scale. It is also highly dependent on the use of inputs (seeds, fertilisers and pesticides) certified by major agricultural companies. It is, therefore, no coincidence that the ProSavana Master Plan does not include any project that employs agro-ecology systems, such as organic fertilisers or improved native seeds – areas in which Brazil also has a good knowledge base – which can provide local and autonomous solutions, reducing pressures on the national budget and balance of payments while improving food sovereignty.[114] It is also striking that a programme of such magnitude ignores the internal demand side of the agricultural system, again an area in which Brazil has acquired much relevant knowledge via national food acquisition programmes. In early 2013, the Ministry of Agrarian Development (MDA), which is responsible for family farming in Brazil, had refused to take part in the ProSavana programme, stating that the reason was 'not believing in the model' that was being proposed.[115] It finally decided to take part in the elaboration of ProSavana-PEM in April 2013 as a way of strengthening family farming in the programme.

Conclusion

In this chapter, we have argued that ProSavana is a precise manifestation of the recent mainstream development storyline that perceives foreign land deals in Africa as a potential opportunity for rural development, a straightforward reaction to the concerns raised by the literature on land grabbing. Following this trend, ProSavana defends a stance in which private investments as a 'dynamic force' are the answer to low agricultural productivity in Mozambique – when coupled with a beneficial policy environment and a self-imposed code of conduct for transnational corporations. These conditions include a responsible investment approach and a fast expansion of the contract-farming scheme for accommodating large-scale farmers (without automatically dispossessing local smallholder peasants).

The responsible investment approach has helped to bypass issues surrounding socio-economic impacts of large-scale investments and contract farming, taking for granted that 'development will naturally follow' economic growth.

---

113 Interview with FGV Projetos and JICA staff members, 18 March 2013.
114 Altieri and Toledo (2011).
115 Interview with MDA and ABC staff members, 31 January 2013 and 18 February 2013.

This has meant, however, that the numerous risks associated with contract farming have been ignored, such as the risk of a decrease in food production due to an emphasis on monocultures for export, the risk of higher vulnerability and dependence (price and access) of small producers on imported inputs, and the risk of strengthening the already predominantly extractive nature of the Mozambican economy.[116] Organised local cotton producers, who have been working on a contract-farming basis for decades in the Nacala Corridor, have reported difficulties in price bargaining and serious difficulties in ascending the value chain due to large contractors' dominant market power.[117]

In the case of ProSavana, the mainstream agenda has given legitimacy to cooperation practices that are strongly influenced by organised, private interests around commodity exporting sectors. The critical aspect that we have emphasised is not the presence per se of private actors in a development strategy, but the central role they have come to play in terms of policy formulation, operationalisation and self-regulation. In such a context, private investment behaviour is not to be controlled or oriented by the state or public actors, but it is to be guided by suggestions that lack enforcement. Given the high degree of fragmentation in the institutional framework governing Brazil's development cooperation, coupled with limited coordination capacity on the part of ABC, a lot of space has been opened for organised private interests to take the lead in this specific Brazilian SSDC project.

Our fieldwork provides evidence that ProSavana goes against at least three central pillars of Brazilian SSDC principles. First, contrary to the official discourse on the lack of economic motivations, the centrality of private investors as the dynamic force for development has led to a Master Plan that, in its March 2013 version, resembles a business plan rather than a development plan. Second, and contrary to the official principle of a demand-driven approach, ProSavana was not borne out of a request from the Mozambican government – although all local officials interviewed supported the programme and expressed hope that it would boost local agricultural production. Third, any participatory aspects in the ProSavana Master Plan have been forced into it by the fierceness of the criticism from civil society and peasants' organisations; at first, at least with local populations, the programme contained no participatory element at all. The plan follows not only a top-down but also an outside-inside direction, since the Mozambican government authorities are not equal partners in the project.

Mozambique, like various other sub-Saharan countries, faces some undeniable challenges in terms of food security and sheer material poverty. In

---

116 Mosca (2012) provides an introduction to this discussion.
117 Interview, 29 March 2013.

such a context, agribusiness derives its legitimacy from the failure of peasants to produce sufficiently. Enduring and rapid economic growth in recent decades has not helped to alleviate these basic problems; in fact, it has deepened the extractive nature of the Mozambican economy. Development programmes that ought to have the best impacts with respect to poverty reduction are such that they represent a break from this extractive logic.

Agro-ecology-based production systems helping to reduce dependency, structural projects solving the internal demand side of agricultural constraints, and a structure of land distribution that avoids excessive concentration when allocating resources should be regarded as fundamental components of an inclusive development plan. So far these have been absent from ProSavana. Moreover, although the programme has merit in its emphasis on agro-processing, it has failed to introduce an inclusive strategy for carrying out structural change that will enhance the condition of the masses and add value locally. While remaining sensitive to all these components, there is a serious need for a genuinely participative, bottom-up and publicly backed regional development programme. If Brazil were to stand by the principles it expresses in official discourse, inclusive development in ProSavana would not have to represent a utopia.

References

Agência Brasileira de Cooperação (ABC) (n.d.) *Brazilian Technical Cooperation*. Available at: http://www.oecd.org/swac/events/49257793.pdf (accessed January 2013).

Agência Brasileira de Cooperação (ABC) (2013) *Cooperação Técnica Brasileira, Agricultura, Segurança Alimentar e Políticas Sociais*. Available at: http://www.abc.gov.br/training/informacoes/ABC.aspx (accessed April 2013).

Agência Brasileira de Cooperação (ABC) (2010) *A Cooperação Técnica do Brasil para a África*. Brasília: Agência Brasileira de Cooperação, Ministério de Relações Exteriores.

Altieri, M and Toledo, VC (2011) The agro-ecological revolution in Latin America: Rescuing nature, ensuring food sovereignty and empowering peasants, *Journal of Peasant Studies*, **38** (3), pp 587–612.

Aabo, E and Kring, T (2012) The political economy of large scale land acquisitions: Implications for food security and livelihoods/employment creation in rural Mozambique, UNDP Africa Policy Notes, 2012–2004.

Borras Jr, S and Franco, J (2010) From threat to opportunity? Problems with the idea of a 'code of conduct' for land-grabbing, *Yale Human Rights and Development Law Journal*, **13**, pp 507–23.

Cabral, L and Shankland, A (2013) *Narratives of Brazil–Africa Cooperation for Agricultural Development: New paradigms?* FAC Working Paper No. 051, Future Agricultures Consortium.

Cabral, L, Shankland, A, Locke, A and Duran, J (2012) Mozambique's agriculture and Brazil's cerrado model: Miracle or mirage? *GREAT Insights*, **1** (10), December.

Castel-Branco, C (2008) Os mega projectos em Moçambique: que contributo para a economia nacional? *Apresentação Feita no Fórum da Sociedade Civil sobre a Indústria Extractiva, Museu de História Natural*, Maputo, 27–28 November, Available at: http://www.iese.ac.mz/lib/noticias/Mega_Projectos_ForumITIE.pdf (accessed 30 May 2017).

Castel-Branco, C (2011) Dependência de ajuda externa, acumulação e ownership: Contribuição para um debate de economia política, *Cadernos IESE*, 7, Maputo: Instituto Estudos Sociais e Económicos (IESE).

Chang, HJ and Gabrel, I (2004) *Reclaiming Development: An alternative economic policy manual*. London: Zed Books.

Chichava, S, Duran, J, Cabral, L, Shankland, A, Buckley, L, Tang, L and Zhang, Y (2013) *Chinese and Brazilian Cooperation with African Agriculture: The case of Mozambique*. FAC Working Paper No. 049, Future Agricultures Consortium.

Clements, E and Fernandes, B (2013) Land grabbing, agribusiness and the peasantry in Brazil and Mozambique, *Agrarian South: Journal of Political Economy*, **2** (1), pp 41–69.

Cunguara, B (2012) An exposition of development failures in Mozambique, *Review of African Political Economy*, **39** (131), pp 161–70.

Cunguara, B and Hanlon, J (2012) Whose wealth is it anyway? Mozambique's outstanding economic growth with worsening rural poverty, *Development and Change*, **43** (3), pp 623–47.

Deininger, K, Byerlee, D, Lindsay, J, Norton, A, Selod, H and Stickler, M (2011) *Rising Global Interest in Farmland*. Washington, DC: World Bank.

FAO, IFAD, UNCTAD and World Bank Group (2010) *Principles for Responsible Agricultural Investment that Respect Rights, Livelihoods and Resources*. Available at: http://siteresources. worldbank.org/INTARD/2145741111138388661/22453321/Principles_Extended.pdf (accessed May 2013).

Fernandes, B, Welch, C and Gonçalves, E (2012) *Land Governance in Brazil*. Framing the Debate Series No. 2. Rome: International Land Coalition.

FGV Projetos (2012) Agricultural investment in Africa: Brazilian expertise to promote sustainable agriculture investments. Presentation to the G-15 Training Workshop: Best Practices on Renewable Energies, Dakar, Senegal, 5–7 November 2012.

Funada-Classen, S (2013) *Analysis of the discourse and background of the ProSavana program in Mozambique: Focusing on Japan's role*, (20 January). Available at: http://afrikagrupperna.se/sodraafrikaidag-uploads/2013/06/ProSavana-Analysis-Japanese-University.pdf (accessed May 2013).

Hanlon, J. and Smart, T (2008), *Do bicycles equal development in Mozambique?* Rochester, NY: James Curry.

Instituto de Pesquisa Econômica Aplicada (IPEA) (2011) *Cooperação Brasileira para o Desenvolvimento Internacional: 2005–2009*. Brasília: IPEA.

Japan International Cooperation Agency (JICA) (n.d.) *Partnership Program: Challenge to inclusive and dynamic development through triangular cooperation with new partners*. Tokyo: JICA.

Japan International Cooperation Agency (JICA) and ABC (2011) Tropical Savannah Agriculture Development Program: Japan–Brazil–Mozambique triangular cooperation. Presentation at the G-20 Conference on Agriculture Research for Development, Promoting Scientific Partnership for Food Security, Montpellier, France, 12–13 September.

Mawdsley, E (2012) *From Recipients to Donors: Emerging powers and the changing development landscape*. London: Zed Books.

Mosca, J (2012) *Porque é que a produção alimentar não é prioritária?* Documento de Trabalho No. 1. Maputo: Observatório do Meio Rural.

Ministério da Planificação e Desenvolvimento de Moçambique (MPD) (2010) *Pobreza e bem-estar em Moçambique: Terceira avaliação nacional*. Maputo: Direcção Nacional de Estudos e Análise de Políticas.

Ministério de Relações Exteriores do Brasil (MRE) (2013) *Cooperação Técnica em Agricultura*. Website of the Ministry of External Relations of Brazil. Available at: http://www.itamaraty.gov.br/temas/cooperacao-tecnica-en/agricultura (accessed April 2013).

Muggah, R and Hamann, E (2012) Le Brésil et sa généreuse diplomatie: Un dragon amical ou un tigre de papier? *Revue internationale de Politique de Développement*, **3**. Available at: http://poldev.revues.org/955 (accessed February 2013).

Oya, C (2006) The political economy of development aid as main source of foreign finance for poor African countries: Loss of policy space and possible alternatives from East Asia. Paper presented at the Second Annual Conference of the International Forum on the Comparative Political Economy of Globalization, 1–3 September, Renmin University, Beijing, China.

Oya, C and Pons-Vignon, N (2010) Aid, development and the state in Africa. In V Padayachee (ed.) *Political Economy of Africa*. London: Routledge.

Patriota, G (2009) Statement by Minister Plenipotentiary Guilherme de Aguiar Patriota to the Permanent Mission of Brazil to the United Nations. II Committee, Agenda item 55: Globalization and interdependence, New York, October 2009.

Patriota, TC and Pierri, FM (2013) Brazil's cooperation in agricultural development and food security in Africa: Assessing the technology, finance and knowledge platforms. In F Cheru and R Modi (eds), *Agricultural Development and Food Security in Africa*. London: Zed Books, pp 125–44.

Ministério da Agricultura (2010). *Plano Estratégico para o Desenvolvimento do Setor Agrário, 2010–2019 (PEDSA)* Maputo.

ProSavana (2009) Minutes of Meeting on Triangular Cooperation for Agricultural Development of the Tropical Savannah in Mozambique, Maputo, 17 September 2009.

ProSavana-PD-QIP (2013) *Agriculture Development Master Plans in the Nacala Corridor in Mozambique*. Report No. 2, Quick Impact Projects, Triangular Cooperation for Agricultural Development of the Tropical Savannah in Mozambique, written by MINAG, DPA, Getulio Vargas Foundation, Oriental Consultants, NTC International and Task, March 2013. Available at: http://www.grain.org/article/entries/4703-leaked-prosavana-master-plan-confirms-worst-fears (accessed May 2013).

ProSavana-TEC (2011) Projeto de Melhoria da Capacidade de Pesquisa e de Transferência de Tecnologia para o Desenvolvimento da Agricultura no Corredor de Nacala em Moçambique – Resumo Executivo. Brazilian Cooperation Agency and Embrapa, June 2011.

ProSavana ToR (2011) Termos de Referência – Solicitação de Propsta No. 14740/2011. Contratação de Consultoria Pessoa Jurídica para Prestação de Serviços Técnicos Especializados na Elaboração do Plano Diretor para o Desenvolvimento da Agricultura do Corredor de Nacala, em Moçambique. UNDP, December 2011.

República Federativa do Brasil (RFP) (2011) *Brazilian Technical Cooperation: Agriculture, food security and social policies*. Fact sheet presented at the 37th Session of the United Nations Food and Agriculture Organization (FAO) Conference, Rome, June 24.

Sonne-Schmidt, C, Arndt, C and Magaua, M (2009) Contributions of mega-projects to GDP in Mozambique. Paper presented at the II IESE Conference 'Dinâmicas da Pobreza e Padrões de Acumulação Económica em Moçambique', 22–23 April, Maputo: IESE.

Virtanen, P and Ehrenpreis, D (2007) *Growth, Poverty and Inequality in Mozambique*. Country Study No. 10. Brasília: International Poverty Centre (IPC) and United Nations Development Programme (UNDP).

Woods, N (2008) Whose aid? Whose influence? China, emerging donors and the silent revolution in development assistance, *International Affairs*, **84** (6), pp 1205–21.

Chapter 6
Brazil in international cooperation: A study of the ProAlimentos project in Mozambique

Natalia N Fingermann

The expansion of South–South cooperation, especially in countries like China, Brazil, India and South Africa, has established a new framework for aid within the international system. As part of the debate on Brazilian foreign policy, diverse recent studies have sought to explore what this more active role means for international development cooperation (IDC) (Soares de Lima, 2005; Vigevani and Cepaluni, 2007; Ribeiro, 2010; Saraiva, 2010; Menezes and Ribeiro, 2011). Although Brazil's cooperation portfolio is much smaller than that of some other emerging countries, like China,[118] amounting to an estimated US$2.9 billion for the period 2005–2009 (IPEA, 2010), the country has attracted attention with the substantial expansion of its activities in Africa, primarily through technical cooperation policies linked to areas of national expertise, such as agriculture, health care and social development.

Another factor that singles out Brazilian cooperation is its openness to partnerships with international organisations and developed countries through trilateral agreements, despite its discourse of differentiating itself from the practices of traditional donors[119] (Costa Vaz and Inoue, 2007). Based on the demands of its partners and on the principles of solidarity, reciprocity and non-intervention, Brazilian South–South cooperation presents itself as an alternative to African countries. This idea of the development partnership that is heralded in official government discourse is not accepted unanimously by academics. The debate would appear to interpret the growth of Brazilian cooperation on the African continent in three distinct ways: 1) as a development partner (Saraiva, 2010; 2012); 2) as sub-imperialism or colonialism (Clements and Fernandes, 2013; Curado, 2010; Visentini, 2010); and 3) as self-interest (Soares de Lima, 2005; Vigevani and Cepaluni, 2007; Menezes and Ribeiro, 2011).

---

118 Brautigam (2009:168) projects that China disbursed approximately US$1 billion on development cooperation to Africa in 2008 and US$1.4 billion in 2009.

119 Traditional donors are regarded as the developed countries belonging to the Development Assistance Committee of the Organisation for Economic Cooperation and Development (DAC-OECD) and international bodies like the United Nations, the World Bank, the International Monetary Fund (IMF) and others.

The development-partner view argues that Brazil's closer links with Africa, achieved through the growth in cooperation policies, are related to its recognition of its 'historical debt' to African peoples, and its aim 'to transform ties of friendship ... into economic and social progress for mutual benefit' (Amorim, 2003). The sub-imperialism view, on the other hand, sees the development cooperation projects as a mechanism for promoting imperialist policies of territorial occupation, designed to further Brazil's domestic business interests. Clements and Fernandes (2012) claim that the ProSavana programme[120] in the north of Mozambique is one example of this Brazilian colonial attitude, intended to assist the entry of national agribusiness. Visentini (2010), though, argues that it is still too early to decide whether the Brazil–Africa relation is based on an imperialist agenda or simply a search for prestige. Finally, the self-interest view provides two motives: one focused on maintaining the international equilibrium and the other aimed at the country's own socio-economic development. Vigevani and Cepaluni (2007), for example, emphasise that development cooperation forms part of a strategy of 'autonomy through diversification' in which 'South–South cooperation [aims] to achieve greater equilibrium with the countries of the North, making adjustments, increasing the country's international role and consolidating changes' (Vigevani and Cepaluni, 2007:283). Finally, Soares de Lima (2005:24) stresses the instrumental role performed by South–South cooperation in maintaining socio-economic development in Brazil itself by facilitating the participation of national capital at the global level.

The literature, thus, reveals a considerable effort to determine *why* Brazil has invested in IDC. However, there is still relatively little research on precisely *how* these activities are implemented. And there are even fewer analyses of *how* Brazilian technical cooperation takes place in the context of trilateral agreements, which include a traditional donor as a partner. Long (2002) emphasises the need to comprehend the *process* of international development cooperation, rather than limiting analysis to the *whys* of the project formulators. He argues that an actor-oriented approach shows that the social practice of human agents constantly restructures the conception of cooperation policy. Thus, the relations between local actors, project executors and researchers establish 'battlefields of knowledge', arenas in which the interests and values of the different actors collide with one another and inform the direction taken

---

120 The ProSavana programme is one of Brazil's largest trilateral cooperation projects involving the Japanese International Cooperation Agency (JICA), the Brazilian Cooperation Agency (Agência Brasileira de Cooperação: ABC) and the Mozambique Ministry of Agriculture (MINAG). The programme aims to lever agricultural development in the Nacala Corridor, located in the north of Mozambique.

by technical cooperation (Long, 2002; Bourdieu, 2011; Buckley, 2011; 2013).

To understand *how* Brazilian trilateral cooperation works on the ground, therefore, this research, which is grounded in an actor-oriented approach, focuses on a case study, the Nutrition and Food Security Programme Technical Support Project, better known as ProAlimentos (ProFood). This project is a triangular cooperation initiative involving the Brazilian Cooperation Agency (ABC), the Brazilian office of the United States Agency for International Development (USAID-Brazil) and the Mozambique Ministry of Agriculture (MINAG), aimed at strengthening the strategic capacities of the production and distribution of horticultural crops in the 'green belt' region of Maputo. The data for this research were collected mostly in the months of March and April 2013,[121] using ethnographic participant-observation techniques and 22 semi-structured interviews[122] with key actors involved.

Through the analysis of this case study, the research seeks to understand not only *how* the relations between the American–Brazilian executors and the Mozambican beneficiaries occur in practice, but also *how* relations develop between individuals who are familiarised in such apparently distinct paradigms, like North–South and South–South cooperation. With this aim in mind, this chapter begins by delineating the concept of trilateral cooperation and its scope in terms of Brazilian cooperation in Mozambique. Thereafter ProAlimentos is presented, including information on the objectives, coverage, resources and executing entities involved. Finally, the chapter analyses the principal results of the data collection in the field. It concludes that the process of Brazilian trilateral cooperation is neither linear nor continuous: there are constant negotiations and tensions involved in the tripartite system. These arenas of negotiation establish a new model of cooperation, which, although weakening the principles of South–South cooperation by complying with North–South strategies, also strengthen them by maintaining a horizontal form of collaboration between the actors and, crucially, focusing on institution building.

ABC and trilateral cooperation

The expansion of trilateral cooperation results from the search for new development models in a context of the transformation in the framework of international aid. In general terms, this modality aims to combine the traditional donors' experience in cooperation with the technical knowledge of emerging countries. However, there is no clear consensus on the definition of

---

121 Another two interviews were conducted in Brazil, in July and August 2012, as indicated in the Appendix.
122 A list of interviews is provided in the Appendix.

trilateral cooperation, also known as triangular or tripartite cooperation. The United Nations Economic and Social Council, for example, defines triangular cooperation as the arrangement in which 'OECD/DAC donors or multilateral institutions [provide] development assistance to Southern governments to execute projects/programmes with the aim of assisting other developing countries' (ECOSOC, 2008). Fordelone (2009), meanwhile, in her research for the Development Assistance Committee (DAC) of the Organisation for Economic Cooperation and Development (OECD), defines trilateral cooperation as a partnership between donors from DAC-OECD and a pivot country, that is, an emergent leading country in South–South cooperation working in a third beneficiary country.

Stahl (2012) limits the definition of the concept to three categories of actors by taking triangular cooperation to imply only partnerships between recognised traditional donors, emerging donors and African beneficiaries. Furthermore, Stahl also excludes partnerships with traditional multilateral donors, such as the United Nations and the World Bank, due to the need for triangular cooperation to follow more flexible principles and norms than those set by these institutions. Grimm (2011), on the other hand, goes in the opposite direction by expanding the concept of trilateral cooperation to any tripartite schema, including those agreed between countries exclusively from the South, such as the India–Brazil–South Africa initiative (IBSA).

None of these approaches, however, matches the one informing Brazil's trilateral cooperation projects. According to the Brazilian Cooperation Agency (ABC), trilateral cooperation should always be based 'on principles of horizontality with more dialogue between the parties',[123] without any pre-established division of tasks between the partners. In this vision, the traditional donor, either a developed country or a multilateral institution, should act based on equality, adhering to the principles of Brazilian South–South cooperation, without any clear distinction between funder and executor. In fact, examples of trilateral cooperation projects for ABC include short-term technical training provided in Brazil to individuals from third countries.

To develop the trilateral cooperation projects in accordance with its principles of horizontality, ABC looks to sign Memorandums of Understanding, 'umbrella' agreements with traditional donors. The most recent data published by the agency indicate that memorandums were signed with the following developed countries: Japan (2000), Italy (2007), Spain (2009), Israel (2009), the United States (2010), Germany (2010) and Australia (2010)

---

123 Definition given by ABC's Coordinator of Received and Trilateral Technical Cooperation, interviewed in Brasília/DF, 15 July 12012.

(ABC, 2013). In the case of the partnership with the United States, it can be observed that ABC and USAID-Brazil went further by developing a joint 'Trilateral Development Partnership Strategic Framework' (2011), which aims to streamline the coordination of the partner countries' activities.

ABC's trilateral cooperation in Mozambique

Mozambique is the principal beneficiary of Brazilian technical cooperation, representing 16 per cent of the total resources, with 21 projects currently being executed (ABC, 2011). This rapprochement between the Brazilian and Mozambican governments is also reflected in the increase in trade relations. Brazilian exports to Mozambique, for instance, have seen an average annual growth of 37 per cent, rising from approximately US$2.8 million in 2001 to US$122.3 million in 2012. The same upward trend is observed in the importation of Mozambican products into Brazil, which jumped from US$0.9 million (2001) to US$24.1 million (2012); in other words, an annual average rise of 31 per cent over the period (MDIC, 2013).

In terms of technical cooperation, Mozambique appears to be not only the main beneficiary of ABC's portfolio of projects, but also the country with the most innovative projects, such as the ProSavana programme, the community seed bank, the antiretroviral factory, and various others. Among these projects, the agricultural sector stands out due to one characteristic, namely, that most of the projects fit into the trilateral cooperation model. As Table 6.1 shows, 11 of the 15 listed projects are classified as trilateral (ABC, 2013).

However, many of the projects classified by ABC under this modality are short-term capacity-building courses offered in Brazil to technicians from Portuguese-speaking African countries (PALOPs) and Latin America. For example, seven of the projects targeted at Mozambique's farming sector are training courses – five of them forming part of the Third Countries Training Programme (TCTP) established between the Japanese International Cooperation Agency (JICA) and ABC. It is important to mention that three of the five courses promoted under the TCTP programme have already been concluded, while at that stage two still had activities planned until 2015, reflecting the fact that the agreement for each type of capacitation project covers a five-year period (JICA, 2013).

Table 6.1: Trilateral projects

Project name	Objective	Type	Local institutions involved	Beneficiaries	Brazilian executing institutions	Modality	Status
ABC–JICA–MINAG cooperation: ProSavana programme	Develop family and commercial farming in the Nacala Corridor in northern Mozambique. The programme is long-term and its activities involve three projects: Director Plan, Research Plan, and Extension and Models Plan.	Structuring technical cooperation; financial cooperation	MINAG, IIAM, DNEA, CEPRAGI, CIP, Provincial directorates of Nampula and Niassa	Local technicians. Direct impact on small, medium and large rural producers.	FGV Projects, Embrapa, SENAR and EMATER	Trilateral	In progress
ABC–USAID cooperation: Mozambique–MINAG Technical Support Project for the Mozambique Farming Innovation Platform	Strengthen the institutional capacity of IIAM, with support for the elaboration of IIAM's Strategic Plan, the establishment of the Seed and Territorial Management System, as well as communication and information tools	Structuring technical cooperation	IIAM/MINAG	Local technicians. Indirect impact on agricultural producers.	Embrapa	Trilateral	In progress
International training: Course in Sustainable Production of Horticultural Crops	Cooperation agreement between JICA–ABC, Third Countries Training Programme (TCTP) for PALOP countries (2011–2015). Held in Brazil.	TCTP training	IIAM/MINAG	Local technicians. Indirect impact on agricultural producers.	Embrapa	Trilateral	In progress

Project name	Objective	Type	Local institutions involved	Beneficiaries	Brazilian executing institutions	Modality	Status
ABC–USAID–Brazil-MINAG cooperation: Mozambique Nutrition and Food Security Technical Support Project	Strengthening IIAM and the strategic capacities in producing and distributing horticultural produce in Mozambique, in support of the nutrition and food security programmes.	Structuring technical cooperation	IIAM/MINAG and Provincial Agricultural Directorates of Maputo and Gaza	Local technicians. Indirect impact on small agricultural producers.	Embrapa	Trilateral	In progress
International training: Course in Production, Post-Harvesting and Industrial Processing of Brazil Nuts and Cashew Fruit	Cooperation agreement between JICA–ABC, Third Countries Training Programme (TCTP) for PALOP countries (2011–2015). Held in Brazil.	TCTP training	IIAM/MINAG	Local technicians. Indirect impact on agricultural producers.	Embrapa	Trilateral	In progress
International training: Course in Manioc Production and Processing	Cooperation agreement between JICA–ABC, Third Countries Training Programme (TCTP) for PALOP countries.	TCTP training	IIAM/MINAG	Local technicians. Indirect impact on agricultural producers.	National Centre of Manioc and Tropical Fruit Crop Research	Trilateral	Concluded
Brazil–France Project for Capacity Building of Mozambican Technicians in Conservation Agriculture	Share Brazilian and French experience in conservation agriculture with agricultural specialists in Mozambique.	Training	N/A	N/A	EMBRAPA	Trilateral	Concluded

Project name	Objective	Type	Local institutions involved	Beneficiaries	Brazilian executing institutions	Modality	Status
Seminar: Towards French–Brazilian Cross Cooperation in Haiti and Africa	Held in Brasilia, DF, Brazil.	Training	N/A	N/A	Brazil–BRA	Trilateral	Concluded
Biotech seminar: Biotechnology as a Tool for Sustainable Development in Agriculture	Held in Maputo, Mozambique. In partnership with the United States Embassy and USAID.	Training	IIAM/MINAG	Students, technicians and researchers from local institutions and civil society	Embrapa	Trilateral	Concluded
Implantation of community seed banks and capacity building in recovering, multiplying, storing and using traditional/native seeds in family farming areas in Mozambique and South Africa	Project involves the exchange of experiences of family farmers and social movements in three countries: South Africa, Brazil and Mozambique. The objective is to contribute to the organisational and economic strengthening of family farming in the countries.	Technical cooperation	National Peasants Union (UNAC) in Mozambique; Trust for Community Outreach and Education (TCOE) in South Africa	Small family farming producers	Embrapa, IBASE, Movement of Peasant Women (MMC) and Popular Peasant Movement (MCP)	Plurilateral	In progress

Project name	Objective	Type	Local institutions involved	Beneficiaries	Brazilian executing institutions	Modality	Status
Project for Stimulating the Purchase of Local Foods, as part of the Food Purchase Programme for Africa (PPAAfrica)	Initiative of the General Coordination of International Actions for Combatting Hunger (CG Combate à Fome) of the Ministry of Foreign Affairs (MRE), which aims to guarantee food security for small farmers, with initiatives for purchasing products through the WFP. The project is also implemented in the following countries: Senegal, Ethiopia, Malawi and Niger.	Technical cooperation, with transfer of funds to international bodies	MINAG	Smallholder family farming producers	FAO Rehabilitation Coordination Units and local WFP offices, with monitoring by CG Combate à Fome	Multilateral	In progress
More Food for Africa programme	Through family farming, increase food production, jobs and income in the rural world. Lines of credit available to fund machinery purchases. The project is also implemented in the following countries: Senegal, Kenya, Ghana and Zimbabwe.	Technical cooperation, with access to loans	MINAG	Smallholder family farming producers	Ministry of Agrarian Development (MDA)	Plurilateral	In progress
International training: Course on Tropical Fruit Production	Cooperation agreement between JICA–ABC, Third Countries Training Programme (TCTP) for PALOP countries.	TCTP training	IIAM/MINAG	Local technicians. Indirect impact on agricultural producers	Embrapa	Trilateral	Concluded

Project name	Objective	Type	Local institutions involved	Beneficiaries	Brazilian executing institutions	Modality	Status
Support for the Development of Fruit Growing in Mozambique	Contribute to the development of fruit production in Mozambique through capacity building courses for IIAM technicians.	Structuring technical cooperation	IIAM/MINAG	Local technicians. Indirect impact on agricultural producers.	Embrapa	Bilateral	Concluded
International training: Course in Sustainable Horticultural Production	Cooperation agreement between JICA–ABC, Third Countries Training Programme (TCTP) for PALOP countries.	TCTP training	IIAM/MINAG	Local technicians. Indirect impact on agricultural producers.	Embrapa	Trilateral	Concluded

Source: Various: ABC website (2013); JICA–Brazil website (2013); MDA and MRE website; official documents collected during field research. Author's elaboration

Meanwhile, the other trilateral projects being implemented in 2013 involved a 'structuring' type of technical cooperation,[124] seeking to integrate human-resource training with organisational strengthening and institutional development (Almeida *et al*, 2010). These projects include: the ProSavana programme, a partnership between ABC, JICA and MINAG; the Platform Support Programme, a partnership between ABC, USAID-Mozambique and MINAG; and ProAlimentos, a partnership between ABC, USAID-Brazil and MINAG (chosen as the case study for this research project). There are also diverse multilateral and plurilateral projects, such as the Project to Stimulate Local Food Purchases and the Community Seed Bank Implantation Project, respectively.

ProAlimentos

ProAlimentos was the first agreement signed between ABC, USAID-Brazil and the Mozambique Ministry of Agriculture. Ratification on 3 March 2010 of the Memorandum of Understanding between the governments of Brazil and the United States on the Implementation of Technical Cooperation Activities in Third Countries was followed by the elaboration of the Trilateral Development Partnership Strategic Framework (2011) (MRE-SCI, 2013).

Beginning in March 2011 and ending in 2014, with financial resources estimated at approximately US$2.4 million, ProAlimentos's overall objective has been to strengthen the strategic capacities for producing and distributing horticultural produce in Mozambique. The direct beneficiaries of the project are the professionals from the Mozambique Institute of Agrarian Research (IIAM), the rural extensionists working in the Provincial Farming Directorates of Maputo and Gaza, and the families of small agricultural producers from Moamba and Boane, districts located in Maputo's so-called 'green belt' (ProAlimentos, 2011).

The institutions responsible for executing the project are Embrapa (the Brazilian Agricultural Research Company) on behalf of ABC, the University of Florida (UF) and Michigan State University (MSU), selected by USAID and IIAM, the counterparty of MINAG. The financial resources are distributed as follows: USAID is primarily responsible for covering the purchase of machinery and equipment; ABC funds the trips made by the Embrapa team, including travel and accommodation expenses; and Embrapa and IIAM pay for the hours worked by their respective researchers and agrarian technicians. Overall, 46 per

---

124 The concept of structuring technical cooperation involves the successful integration of human-resource training, organisational strengthening and institutional development among the government entities of the beneficiary country (Almeida *et al*, 2010).

cent of the total financial resources are covered by USAID, 24 per cent by ABC, 22 per cent by Embrapa and 9 per cent by IIAM.[125]

The content of the ProAlimentos project (2011) is highly detailed and defines the implementation of three integrated components:
1. Socio-economic survey of local producers;
2. Strengthening of production activities; and
3. Capacity-building in post-harvest handling and agro-processing.

The first component, the socio-economic survey, was undertaken jointly by researchers from MSU, Embrapa and IIAM, with the support of the UF. This component involves four studies with local agricultural producers: 1) a description of the horticultural production and commercialisation systems; 2) a study of the composition, structuring and performance of the horticultural production chain; 3) an analysis of the production costs and sales prices of horticultural produce; and 4) a study of dietary habits. The second component, strengthening production activities, was implemented by researchers and technical staff from the University of Florida, Embrapa and IIAM, with the assistance of agronomy students from the region. This component included plans to test various seed varieties brought by the American and Brazilian partners to IIAM's Umbeluzi Agricultural Station, as well as trials of different systems and techniques for managing irrigation and soil fertility. Plans were also included for researchers from the executing institutions to provide capacity-building courses for IIAM staff and rural extensionists, prior to the transfer of technologies and knowledge to producers from the green zones of Maputo and Moamba.

The final component, training in post-harvest handling and agro-processing, had yet to begin at the time of the field research – March and April 2013. This component was also planned to be executed jointly, including diverse capacity-building and monitoring activities. However, it is worth emphasising that USAID is expected to play a key role in this component by financing the reconstruction of the Collective Agrofood Processing Unit at the Umbeluzi Agricultural Station, the space used for training the local farm-producers associations.

In general terms, the ProAlimentos document aims to boost the horizontality of the tripartite relations by establishing three coordination mechanisms: 1) the Project Coordination Committee (*Comitê de Coordenação do Projeto*: CCP), comprising representatives from ABC, USAID, UF, MSU and Embrapa; 2) the Project Technical Committee (*Comitê Técnico do Projeto*: CTP), including the focal actors from each executing institution; and 3) the Evaluation Committee, which curiously only indicates the participation of Embrapa. The same

---

125 Information provided via e-mail by the ABC office in Mozambique.

document also highlights the principles of structuring cooperation, focusing on IIAM's institutional strengthening through capacity-building initiatives in Mozambique, 'Brazil and the United States directed towards IIAM's technical team in order to train multipliers to disseminate the technologies and knowledge generated by the project' (ProAlimentos, 2011:31).

These collaborative relations, based on the principles of structuring and horizontal technical cooperation, are observable in the implementation process, although this does not mean an absence of conflict over how the work should be executed. The implementation process does not unfold in a linear and continuous form, in fact, much the opposite: clashes are apparent between the agents in the tripartite system, generated by the different social practices and perceptions. These tensions have been apparent since the very beginning of the agreement, centring on the political motives of each agency, their degree of involvement in elaborating the proposal, and their work practices in the field. Nonetheless, it should be stressed that the negotiations and conflicts related to ProAlimentos are allayed in large part by the pre-existing networks of relations between the actors, which enable greater flexibility between the parties during decision-making processes (Shrum *et al*, 2007).

Political motives behind the triangulation

Before analysing ProAlimentos itself, it is important to grasp the political motives that, in this case, led Brazil and the United States to cooperate in Mozambique. Brazil, which usually opposes the initiatives of traditional donors, in many cases opts to develop activities in the trilateral mode, as shown in Table 6.1. What are the political interests of Brazil and the United States in this tripartite scheme?

According to the information collated, the motivations of ABC and USAID are markedly different. For USAID-Brazil, the participation in trilateral cooperation projects stems from the idea of running USAID offices in countries classified as having already 'graduated' from the agency's system, such as India and Brazil. This strategy is openly stated by the general coordinator of USAID-Brazil: 'trilateral cooperation is a format that USAID agencies may adopt in graduated countries; instead of us leaving the country, we continue with a small agency but working alongside the country in a third country'.[126] ABC, for its part, sees trilateral cooperation as a political mechanism for boosting its credibility in the international system as an aid provider. This becomes clear in the remarks of the agency's former director: 'ABC assures its respectability by managing to negotiate with large agencies from developed countries, which in

---

126 Interview, Maputo, 26 March 2013.

the past treated us as inferiors, while today we work side-by-side in a horizontal form.'[127]

It is worth emphasising that the success of this joint venture is important to both agencies, especially USAID, which depends on the progress of this pilot project to keep its administrative office open in Brazil. Mozambique became the first such trilateral experience for various reasons, which will become clearer when we analyse how the ProAlimentos proposal has been elaborated. It is important to stress, though, that USAID-Brazil–ABC have since launched similar projects in Haiti and Honduras (Feed the Future, 2013).

Elaborating the ProAlimentos project

One of the advantages presented by the official discourse of Brazilian cooperation, vis-à-vis traditional donors, is the fact that it stems from the demand of the recipient countries. However, the data gathered in the field indicate that the demand originated without the participation of all the actors, with a consequent impact on the project design. Another point that emerged in the research was the asymmetry in the information exchanged between the parties, with limited participation of the American executing institutions. Although the non-participation of these institutions was anticipated in the USAID–ABC Strategic Framework, this fact ended up significantly delaying the start-up of the activities.

The coordinators of ABC[128] and IIAM[129] both stated that the idea for the proposal emerged from informal talks during negotiations between ABC, USAID-Mozambique and IIAM-MINAG over the Platform Project. When USAID-Brazil obtained funds through the Feed the Future initiative[130] and proposed to engage in trilateral cooperation with Brazil in 2010, ABC suggested using these funds to meet two interconnected demands that had been discussed with the Mozambican government: the Nutrition and Food Security Programme and the School Meals Project. The initial proposal was, thus, based on Brazil's concept for the World Food Programme, which creates a link in the supply chain by directing smallholder farm produce to local schools. However, ABC indicated that since the demand emerged in the context of IIAM, focused on the issue of food security, there were problems in matching the project to the interests of Mozambique's Ministry of Education (MINED),

---

127 Interview conducted in São Paulo via Skype, 8 August 2012.
128 Interview with ABC's Coordinator in Mozambique, Maputo, 9 March 2013.
129 Interview with IIAM's Coordinator General of ProAlimentos, Maputo, 3 April 2013.
130 The Feed the Future initiative was launched by the Obama government in 2010 as a strategy to fight hunger and guarantee global food security. This initiative includes 19 underdeveloped countries, including Mozambique, and three partner countries in agricultural development: South Africa, Brazil and India (Feed the Future, 2013).

which was responsible for running the School Meals Project. Although the idea was for these two proposals to begin simultaneously and assist the same region of the country, this proved impossible: while the first project was quickly signed by MINAG in March 2011, the second was sent for analysis by MINED, where it was still in the final stages of negotiation at the time of writing.

Another point worth highlighting is the form in which ProAlimentos was elaborated, specifically the participation of each of the institutions. It can be noted that, irrespective of USAID's commitment to collaborating in the initiative proposed by ABC, Embrapa had already been developing the concept of the ProAlimentos project with researchers from IIAM, without any involvement from the American implementing entities. As IIAM's general coordinator for the project made clear, Embrapa travelled to Mozambique in July 2010 to discuss the proposal, and 'as we were discussing the ideas for the project, we received advice that only the American institutions would be able to use the American money, meaning that neither Embrapa nor IIAM would be able to manage the American resources'.[131] Consequently, the Embrapa researchers were unsure about whether the American partners would be involved so they had elaborated the basic elements of the project without taking their participation into account. It was only in January 2011, when the American partners were chosen through an international selection process run by USAID, that 'a video conference was held at the American Embassy in Brasília with these US partners. [As we discussed the production part of the proposal] the Florida people asked: how do you think you can help us with the production component? That completely threw us: how would we respond? What now? What could they add to this process?'[132]

The non-involvement of the American institutions from the very outset, as well as the negotiation between all the institutions over the final document of the Cooperation Technical Project (*Projeto Técnico de Cooperação*: PCT), delayed the start of its implementation, meaning that the activities of the socio-economic and production components started only in July 2012, over a year after the planned date. This lack of synchronisation in the elaboration of the PCT generated disagreements on technical questions concerning how to implement the activities. For example, the general coordinator of the project at IIAM told of the difficulty he encountered in reaching a consensus on the daily rate to be paid by each of the countries to its researchers, since the

---

131 Interview with IIAM's Coordinator General of ProAlimentos, Maputo, 3 April 2013.
132 Remarks made by the coordinator of the production component of ProAlimentos during an interview with a group from Embrapa, including the coordinator of the socio-economic component of ProAlimentos, an agronomist from the production component of ProAlimentos, and the technical coordinator of the Embrapa office in Mozambique, 13 March 2013.

daily rate set by USAID differed from that of ABC. In addition, the American institutions, which had already received funds from USAID, were unsure of whether they should begin implementing the activities ahead of the Brazilians, who were still waiting for adjustments in the PCT.

The practices involved in implementation

The areas of dispute in the ProAlimentos project are found both between the donor institutions and between the executing institutions and the recipient country. In the case of the executing entities, it is crucial to stress the personal trajectory of each and the existence of prior relations, since this factor has had a positive impact on the project's progress, as clearly pointed out by Shrum *et al* (2007). In the socio-economic component, for example, there is a close relation between the researchers of MSU and IIAM, based on MSU's 20 years of work in the country, although there was no prior relationship between MSU and Embrapa. In the production component, close links have been formed with researchers from the UF, most of whom are Brazilians or former employees of Embrapa. Furthermore, there is an indirect link between IIAM and Embrapa, since the Coordinator General of ProAlimentos and two of IIAM's researchers all did their postgraduate studies at Brazilian universities and participated in the capacity-building courses offered by Embrapa on many occasions. This network of prior relationships and the fact that the executors of the US counterparty are Brazilian or speak Portuguese fluently is cited as an advantage by the Coordinator General of ProAlimentos at IIAM: 'At the end of the day, we realised that we are working with Brazil, because the colleagues who came from Florida are Brazilian ... despite the agreement being trilateral.'[133] This is reinforced by MSU's coordinator in Mozambique: 'It seems that by speaking the same language we can understand each other better ... although Brazilian and Mozambican Portuguese are different. But there are closer ties on the cultural and historical sides. And the fact that Brazil can also add its experience of the tropical zone.'[134]

However, this by itself does not guarantee an absence of conflict in the social practices of the institutions and agents involved, since each of them represents different discourses and interests. One of the first clashes in the ProAlimentos project emerged in the institutional sphere due to the distinct organisational structures and bureaucratic practices of the funding agencies. On one hand, USAID has a decentralised administrative structure, which transfers financial resources to UF-MSU for the latter to manage directly, without any

---

133 Interview with IIAM's Coordinator General of ProAlimentos, Maputo, 3 April 2013.
134 Interview with MSU's coordinator in Mozambique, Maputo, 25 March 2013.

interference in organising the missions or purchasing materials and equipment. By contrast, ABC has assumed a much more centralising role in the planning of each mission. The absence of a national cooperation law[135] means that each mission must be planned far in advance. Its realisation depends on the transfer of resources via the United Nations Development Programme (UNDP) and the advance publication of the Embrapa research mission in Brazil's *Federal Official Gazette*. Indeed, the coordinator of ABC in Mozambique recognised that Brazilian cooperation has a 'slower timing'[136] due to these financial constraints and the late payments.

These organisational differences are factors hindering the implantation of ProAlimentos. For example, the interviewees mentioned two moments, in April 2011 and December 2012, when missions took place involving only staff from MSU and UF, respectively. However, the non-attendance of the technical team from Brazil may have been mitigated thanks to the presence of the Coordinator General of the Embrapa-Mozambique Programme, based at the Maputo office. Furthermore, the hiring of a Brazilian administration manager by the UF in Maputo, to help streamline the missions and the advance purchase of material, has had a positive impact on the coordination of activities.

Paradigm conflicts also exist between MSU-UF and Embrapa over how to carry out the work. In the socio-economic component, for example, there was an initial divergence in the methodology to be used in collecting the material: while MSU's coordinator of ProAlimentos took a quantitative approach, the Embrapa researcher tended towards a more qualitative solution. This situation was exacerbated by Embrapa's absence from the first MSU mission in 2011, when the American counterparty took decisions without consulting the Embrapa technicians, that is, without following the principles of horizontality. This top-down approach from MSU was not well received by Embrapa. After this incident, Embrapa's International Relations Office prohibited the exchange of information with other parties prior to signing the final version of the PCT.

In the production component, there are fewer clashes over working practices due to three factors: 1) the methodological alignment of the executing teams due to pre-existing connections within Embrapa; 2) the Brazilian origin of the members of the implementation teams; and 3) IIAM's recognition of the need to strengthen its research capacities. However, areas of dispute over knowledge remain, especially between the UF-Embrapa mission and IIAM. One example concerned alterations in the way that soil compost for seedlings is made. The

---

135 Cabral and Weinstock (2010) analyse the various limitations experienced by ABC due to the lack of a cooperation law, highlighting the shortcomings in the agency's speed of implementation caused by its dependence on the financial intermediation of UNDP to execute its activities abroad.
136 Interview with ABC's coordinator in Mozambique, Maputo, 8 March 2013.

dialogue that unfolded during a visit by the USAID-Brazil mission to the Umbeluzi Agricultural Station, on 26 March 2013, shows this clearly:

> *IIAM researcher*: 'One important area that brought a lot of good results was the alteration in the soil compost used for seedling production. The first Embrapa mission that came here examined the Agromix used, picked up the sack and noticed it was very light. That meant its density must have been low. They asked us, "what's in this?" They tried reading the packaging and it didn't say anything. We went to the sellers and they had no information either. So we began to develop a new mixture with them. They used organic compost, organic fertiliser like fresh and dried manure, ashes to avoid disease propagation, NPK12-84-12, an artificial fertiliser available here, and loose river sand to increase porosity. So, a sack of Agromix with this new composition doubles the yield. That means not only a better output, there are also savings for the rural producer.
> *USAID visitor*: 'But why do they need Agromix then?'
> *IIAM researcher*: 'Agromix is a commercial product, it's imported from South Africa. It already has a good structure, and we add organic fertiliser, for example, to increase the nutrient content.'
> *USAID visitor*: 'Have you tested it without Agromix?'
> *IIAM researcher*: 'Without Agromix it wouldn't have the same effect, it's not worth testing it.'[137]

After hearing this dialogue, I decided to check with the executing institutions what the reasons were for not conducting trials without the Agromix commercial compost. According to the feedback provided, these experiments were not conducted due to resistance from IIAM's researchers. This was quickly confirmed during the conversations that ensued with the institute's Mozambican technicians. They affirmed that Agromix is of 'good quality' for a 'commercial' product – that is, an industrial product imported from South Africa. The IIAM team believed, therefore, that soil compost made from organic material is ineffective. This perception is linked to the imagination of Mozambique society, which still thinks of all imported products as being better than those produced locally through artisanal techniques. This reflects an economy that is entirely dependent on the outside market. For example, when I asked the researchers whether they perceived any contradiction between the high quality of South African horticultural produce and the low quality of the Agromix, they said no,

---

137 Conversation heard while accompanying the USAID-Brazil mission's visit on 25 March 2013.

since they believe that 'Agromix in fresher condition must work well'.[138]

Despite the occurrence of this clash, a horizontal collaboration can be observed between the three teams, without any signs of a vertical relation. There is a partnership with the researchers from UF-Embrapa to strengthen the technical knowledge concerning horticultural crops, especially in relation to IIAM's soil management and irrigation, but also a direct involvement of IIAM's researchers. This fact was observed during the ethnographic encounters at the Umbeluzi Agricultural Station, where the teams worked side-by-side until dusk and then left together to eat at a restaurant. This point was also emphasised in the interview with Embrapa's technical coordinator in Nampula: 'At Umbeluzi we have an agronomist ... he's a local person very interested [in the project], Dr Ecole ... he's well-known ... very articulate, he does a good job and he works to ensure IIAM's members can participate: Hipólito, Celestino, Fagima and Máximo.'[139]

However, some Mozambican members point to the weakness of the project itself and its lack of horizontality when it comes to knowledge transfer. ProAlimentos supplies open pollination seed varieties that can be easily reproduced in Mozambique. However, the project does not promote the complete independence of IIAM's technicians since they are not instructed on how to produce these seeds. This issue appears in the remarks of MSU's coordinator in Mozambique: 'It's not that the variety testing is completely useless, it's a continuous process, from hybridisation onwards: how you cross this with that; when you have a variety, how to test which to select, how the trial is conducted, how the results are analysed.'[140]

Furthermore, the field research discovered that, despite the project's very strong focus on IIAM's institutional strengthening, a problem exists concerning the continuation of the research into horticultural crops at the Umbeluzi Agricultural Station once the project is concluded. The fact that some IIAM researchers receive extra wages to work on the ProAlimentos project demonstrates a clear overlap of American practices with the process of implementing the South–South cooperation agenda. This practice of buying 'ownership' in response to the low wages paid by government institutions is very common in programmes involving traditional donors in Mozambique. However, this can jeopardise the continuity of projects and even cause a 'brain drain' to partner institutions. As one of ProAlimentos's researchers very clearly stated, although this project is a priority for IIAM's staff, it is not a priority for

---

138 Interview with ProAlimentos's chief agronomy engineer, Boane, 2 April 2013.
139 Interview with the technical coordinator of the Embrapa office in Mozambique, Nampula, 22 April 2013.
140 Interview with MSU's coordinator in Mozambique, Maputo, 25 March 2013.

MINAG, which paradoxically seeks to stimulate agriculture without investing in one of its main tools, namely research work: 'The way in which public funds are distributed does not help IIAM carry out its mandate. On the contrary, it distracts IIAM because, imagine, up until last week not a single penny had been deposited in IIAM's account to carry out any research whatsoever.'[141]

Conclusion

The analysis based on an *actor-oriented approach*, focused on the ProAlimentos case, can help elucidate *how* Brazilian trilateral cooperation occurs on the ground by identifying the constant processes of negotiation and agreement between the agents. Although the conclusions of this study cannot be generalised because the research is limited to a single case, it does show that Brazilian trilateral cooperation, to a certain extent, maintains the relation of horizontality promoted in Brazil's official discourse, focused on the institutional development of IIAM. However, this relation of horizontality does not occur in linear form: clashes occur over practices and how the work is understood. In this case, though, the clashes are mitigated for two reasons: the smoother working relationship enabled by a shared language and the pre-existing networks of relations formed in Embrapa.

Furthermore, it was noted that the horizontality of Brazilian cooperation in the ProAlimentos project is weakened by the absence of capacity building in seed production. This training would be the best strategy to end IIAM's external dependency, accommodating the practices of traditional donors at the same time. Brazilian cooperation's acceptance of the University of Florida's payment of extra wages to IIAM's technicians is an example of the cooperation model developing in the new framework of international aid, where North–South and South–South borders are becoming increasingly blurred.

Finally, it was observed that low wages and the absence of funding for IIAM's highly qualified researchers discourages the continuity of ProAlimentos. This problem is not exclusive to this project, however, but applies to all projects in Mozambique in the agricultural sector which seek to strengthen research activity. The 'brain drain' to locally based international institutions is a recurrent phenomenon in Mozambique, and this is a scenario that may occur if funding alternatives are not found for IIAM's highly skilled researchers. All the interviewees possessed professional and academic experience outside the country and, despite being excited by the ProAlimentos project, foresaw few career prospects working for the state.

---

141 Interview conducted with the Coordinator General of ProAlimentos, Maputo, 3 April 2013.

Appendix: List of Interviewees

Interviewee	Institution	Date	Location
Coordinator General of USAID-Brazil	USAID-Brazil	26 March 2013	Maputo, Mozambique
IIAM agricultural technician	IIAM	2 April 2013	Boane, Mozambique
IIAM General Coordinator of ProAlimentos	IIAM	3 April 2013	Maputo, Mozambique
IIAM agricultural engineer	IIAM	2 April 2013	Boane, Mozambique
Coordinator of the socio-economic component for MSU	MSU	10 March 2013	Maputo, Mozambique
Coordinator of the socio-economic component of ProAlimentos for Embrapa	Embrapa	13 March 2013	Maputo, Mozambique
Coordinator of the production component of ProAlimentos for Embrapa	Embrapa	13 March 2013	Maputo, Mozambique
Agronomist from the production component of ProAlimentos for Embrapa	Embrapa	13 March 2013	Maputo, Mozambique
Technical coordinator of the Embrapa office in Mozambique	Embrapa	13 March 2013 and 22 April 2013	Maputo and Nampula, Mozambique
Head agricultural engineer of ProAlimentos	IIAM	2 April 2013	Boane, Mozambique
Coordinator of the socio-economic component for IIAM	IIAM	3 April 2013	Maputo, Mozambique
Researcher for the socio-economic component for MSU	MSU	3 April 2013	Maputo, Mozambique
First Secretary of the Brazilian Embassy in Mozambique	Brazilian Embassy	16 April 2013	Maputo, Mozambique
Coordinator General of the Embrapa office in Mozambique	Embrapa	9 April 2013	Maputo, Mozambique
Agricultural engineer from UF	UF	10 April 2013	Maputo – Skype, Mozambique
Former director of ABC	ABC	8 August 2013	São Paulo – Skype, Brazil
MSU coordinator in Mozambique	MSU	25 March 2013	Maputo, Mozambique
Intern from ProAlimentos	IIAM	2 April 2013	Boane, Mozambique
ABC coordinator in Mozambique	ABC	8 March 2013	Maputo, Mozambique
Adviser from the Ministry of Agriculture	MINAG	21 May 2013	Maputo, Mozambique
UF International Programmes Director	UF	23 March 2013	Maputo, Mozambique
Coordinator of ABC Received and Trilateral Technical Cooperation	ABC	15 July 2013	Brasília, DF, Brazil

References

Agência Brasileira de Cooperação (ABC) (2011) Fact Sheet issued by the Brazilian Cooperation Agency, Rome, June 2011. Available at: http://www.brasil.gov.br/para/press/press-releases/june-1/brazil-to-highlight-south-south-cooperation-initiatives-at-fao-side-event/files/fact-sheet-brazilian-technical-cooperation-final.pdf (accessed 8 May 2013).

Agência Brasileira de Cooperação (ABC) (2013). Available at: www.abc.gov.br (accessed 10 April 2013).

Amorim, CLN (2003) O Brasil e o 'renascimento africano', *Folha de São Paulo*, p A3, 25 May 2003.

Brautigam, D (2009) *The Dragon's Gift: The real story of China in Africa*. New York: Oxford University Press.

Bourdieu, P (2011) *O Senso Prático*. Translation by M Ferreira, 2nd edition. Petrópolis, RJ: Vozes.

Buckley, L (2011) Eating bitter to taste sweet: An ethnographic sketch of a Chinese agriculture project in Senegal. Paper presented at the International Conference on Global Land Grabbing, 6–8 April. Available at: http://fac.dev.ids.ac.uk/publications/research-and-analysis/doc_details/1274-eating-bitter-to-taste-sweet-an-ethnographic-sketch-of-a-chinese-agriculture-project-in-senegal#.UbrNR5wWlNM (accessed 5 April 2013).

Buckley, L (2013) Chinese land-based interventions in Senegal, *Development and Change*, **44** (2), pp 429–50.

Cabral, L and Weinstock, L (2010) *Brazilian Technical Cooperation for Development: Drivers, mechanics and future prospects*. London: Overseas Development Institute, pp 1–45.

Clements, EA and Fernandes, BM (2013) Land grabbing, agribusiness and peasantry in Brazil and Mozambique, *Agrarian South: Journal of Political Economy*, **2** (1)1, pp 41–69.

Costa Vaz, A and Inoue, CYA (2007) *Emerging Donors in International Development Assistance: The Brazil case*. One of five reports on the role played by emerging economies in funding international development policy series. Ottawa: International development Research Centre, Partnership and Business Development Division.

Curado, PRF (2010) O Brasil na América do Sul: Sub-imperialismo ou liderança regional benigna? Paper presented at the VI Colóquio de la Sociedad Latinoamericana de Economia Política y Pensamiento Crítico (SEPLA). Available at: rediu.org/ROCHA.mesa8.pdf (accessed 13 May 2013).

United Nations Economic and Social Council (ECOSOC) (2008) Trends in South–South and triangular development cooperation. Background study for Development Cooperation Forum, April. Available at: http://www.un.org/en/ecosoc/docs/pdfs/south-south_cooperation.pdf (accessed 5 May 2013).

Fordelone, TY (2009) Triangular cooperation and aid effectiveness. Can triangular cooperation make aid more effective? Paper presented to the Policy Dialogue on Development Cooperation, Mexico City, 28–29 September. Available at: http://www.oecd.org/dac/46387212.pdf (accessed 5 May 2013).

Feed the Future (2013) Feed the Future website. Available at: http://www.feedthefuture.gov (accessed on 17 May 2013).

Grimm, S (2011) *Engaging with China in Africa: Trilateral cooperation as an option?* EDC2020 Policy Brief No. 9, February. Bonn: European Association of Development Research and Training Institutes (EADI). Available at: http://www.edc2020.eu/fileadmin/publications/EDC2020_-_Policy_Brief_No_9_-_Engaging_with_China_in_Africa_–Trilateral_Cooperation_as_an_Option.pdf (accessed 5 June 2013).

Instituto de Pesquisa Econômica Aplicada (IPEA) (2010) *Cooperação Brasileira para o Desenvolvimento Internacional: 2005–2009*. Brasilia-DF: Instituto de Pesquisa Econômica Aplicada.

Long, N (2002) An actor-oriented approach to development intervention, *Rural Life Improvement in Asia*, Japan, 22–26 April, pp 47–61.

Japanese International Cooperation Agency Website JICA (2013) Website. Available at: http://www.jica.go.jp/brazil/portuguese/office/activities/triangular03_01.html (accessed 12 May 2013).

Ministério do Desenvolvimento Agrário (MDA) (2013). Available at: http://www.mda.gov.br/portal/noticias/item?item_id=9220490 (accessed 10 May 2013).

Ministério do Desenvolvimento, Indústria e Comércio Exterior (MDIC) (2013) (accessed 15 May 2013).

Menezes, RG and Ribeiro, CO (2011) *A Cooperação Sul-Sul revisitada: A política externa do Governo Lula da Silva e o Desenvolvimento Africano*. Anais do I Circuito de Debates Acadêmicos. Code 2011, IPEA. Available at: www.ipea.gov.br/code2011/chamada2011/pdf/.../area10-artigo12.pdf (accessed 20 May 2013).

Ministério das Relações Exteriores (MRE-SCI) (2013) Website of the Integrated Consular System. Available at: http://dai-mre.serpro.gov.br/ (accessed 10 May 2013).

Organisation for Economic Cooperation and Development (OECD) (2009) Triangular cooperation: What do we know about it? Overview prepared for the OECD Policy Dialogue on Development Cooperation, Mexico City, 28–29 September.

Instituto de Investigacao Agrária de Moçambique (IIAM) and Plataforma de Investigação Agrária e Inovação Tecnológica (PIAIT) (2011) *ProAlimentos Projeto de Apoio Técnico aos Programas de Nutrição e Segurança Alimentar de Moçambique*. Cooperação Trilateral Brasil-Estados Unidos-Moçambique. Available at: http://bricspolicycenter.org/homolog/uploads/trabalhos/5977/doc/1861634885.pdf (accessed 30 May 2017).

Ribeiro, CO (2010) A política africana do governo Lula (2003–2006), *Tempo Social Revista de Sociologia da USP*, **21** (2), pp 185–209.

Saraiva, JFS (2010) The new Africa and Brazil in the Lula era: The rebirth of Brazilian Atlantic Policy, *Revista Brasileira de Política Internacional*, **53**, pp 169–82.

Saraiva, JFS (2012) *África Parceira do Brasil Atlântico: Relações Internacionais do Brasil e da África no início do Século XXI*. Belo Horizonte: Editora Fino Traço.

Soares de Lima, MR (2005) A política externa brasileira e os desafios da cooperação Sul-Sul, *Revista Brasileira de Política Internacional*, **48** (1), pp 24–59.

Stahl, AK (2012) *Trilateral Development Cooperation between the European Union, China and Africa: What prospects for South Africa?* Discussion Paper for the Centre for Chinese Studies, Stellenbosch University, August. Available at: http://www.ccs.org.za/wp-content/uploads/2012/09/Discussion-Paper_AnnaStahl_FINAL.pdf (accessed 13 May 2013).

Shrum, W, Genuth, J and Chompalov, I (2007) *Structures of Scientific Collaboration*. Cambridge, MA: MIT Press.

Vigevani, T and Cepaluni, G (2007) Lula's foreign policy and the quest for autonomy through diversification, *Third World Quarterly*, **28** (7), pp 1309–1326.

Visentini, PF (2010) Cooperação Sul-Sul: Diplomacia de Prestígio ou *Soft* Imperialismo? As relações Brasil-África do Governo Lula, *Revista SÉCULO XXI*, Porto Alegre, **1** (1), Jan–Dec, pp 65–84. Available at: http://sumario-periodicos.espm.br/index.php/seculo21/article/viewFile/1706/31 (accessed 20 May 2013).

Chapter 7

Civil society and the opposition to ProSavana in Mozambique: End of the line?[142]

Sérgio Chichava and Chris Alden

The concept of civil society occupies an important position within the canon of theory of liberal democracy.[143] Standing between the state and the private sphere, civil society is an instrument for holding the government and business interests accountable to the values and needs, usually codified in the Constitution, of wider society. But to do so, it requires a legal structure that guarantees autonomy and freedom of action. Operating in this political space, somewhat paradoxically, 'not only restricts state power but legitimises state authority when that authority is based on rule of law'.[144]

In developing countries in Africa, the position of civil society is often characterised as precarious, representing, for instance, primarily an urban constituency in societies that may still be fundamentally rural or heavily scrutinised by hostile governments, anxious to reduce their scope for influence and action.[145] Weak institutions and strong regimes or cross-cutting societal forces all challenge the capacity of civil society to perform the functions that theorists ascribe to it in these settings. Presented in different guises in the local discourses and academic representations, ranging from an 'authentic' collective voice of local communities to that of a putative instrument of state or foreign interests, a thriving civil society is, nonetheless, as central to the functioning of a liberal democracy in developing countries as elsewhere.[146]

Mozambique's civil society, emerging out of the socialist period, which saw state-sanctioned organs and foreign solidarity organisations occupy that narrow political space into the onset of the democratic era in 1994, has been recognised as a vocal intermediary in a society coping with the multiple challenges of development in a post-conflict environment. Its weaknesses are evident to many observers, with some going so far as to say that 'with the

---

142 This is based partially on an article by Sergio Chichava, 'A Sociedade Civil e o ProSavana em Moçambique', *Desafios Para Moçambique 2016*, IESE, Maputo.
143 For a short survey by ardent advocates of this school, see Carothers and Barndt (1999:18–29).
144 Larry Diamond, cited in Grugel and Bishop (2001:94).
145 Goren Hyden (2010).
146 Fukuyama (2001:7–20).

exception of a few standouts ... Most Mozambique civil society organizations are weak and lack the capacity to be effective watchdogs on behalf of the public interest'.[147] For others, it is not the lack of power as such but the composition of Mozambique's civil society, specifically the rise of foreign NGOs and Pentecostal churches as important elements in associational life, that is problematic.[148] These portrayals ignore the seminal role that national and local organisations played in the context of contentious debates around the government's efforts to privatise land in the late 1990s and early 2000s. The mobilisation of Mozambicans, across different regions and walks of life, to combat the disassociation of land from rural smallholders in favour of an influx of private investors and corporate entities, stymied these state-led efforts and was an unprecedented demonstration of civil society activism in the country.[149]

It should, therefore, come as no surprise that Mozambican civil society organisations (OSCMs), supported by partners from other countries (mainly Brazil and Japan), have been very critical of ProSavana, the trilateral agricultural development programme between Mozambique, Brazil and Japan. This is the most ambitious and newsworthy programme of Brazil and Japan in the recent history of their international cooperation in development projects in Africa. The success of Prodecer, a Japanese–Brazilian development partnership, in transforming the tropical savannah of Brazil into one of the most productive agricultural regions in the world, is one of the arguments put forward for the conception of ProSavana.[150] The OSCMs say that this programme will benefit mainly Brazilian and Japanese capital and the Mozambican elite, by expropriating and marginalising small local producers and leading to a rural exodus, reproducing the same problems created by Prodecer in Brazil. Consequently, the OSCMs began a series of protests demanding that the governments of the three countries suspend and rethink the programme.

However, the promoters of ProSavana see the situation differently from the OCSMs, believing that the programme will revolutionise agriculture in Mozambique, transforming the Nacala Corridor in the north into a highly productive agricultural area, and definitively solving the question of food insecurity.

But while, at the beginning, the OSCMs involved in the struggle against ProSavana displayed a certain consensus about the need to stop and reformulate the programme, in coordination with the interested and affected parties, today they are deeply divided. Some are calling for the definitive suspension

---

147 Manning (2010:162).
148 Pfeiffer (2004:359–72).
149 Alden (2001); West and Kloeck-Jensen (1999:482–83).
150 For more information on Prodecer, see: http://www.campo.com.br/proceder/?lang=es.

of the programme, while others call for its adoption if their positions are accommodated.

This chapter has two objectives: the first is to analyse the various forms used by the OSCMs to oppose ProSavana; and second, to show and explain the divergences among these organisations. It is structured as follows: first it succinctly presents ProSavana, then it introduces the various forms of protest of the OSCM and, finally, it analyses the divergences among the OSCMs towards ProSavana.

ProSavana in brief

As mentioned earlier, the experience of the development of the cerrado in Brazil, based on a 30-year cooperation programme with Japan – Prodecer (1979–2001) – inspired the formulation of ProSavana. The promoters of Prodecer say that this programme was responsible for the transformation of the Brazilian cerrado into one of the most productive regions in the country, and the second largest producer of soya in the world, after the United States. Brazil gained important know-how regarding agricultural development of the tropical savannah through this support from Japan. Based on this, in 2009 Kenzo Oshima, then the deputy chairperson of the Japanese International Cooperation Agency (JICA), and Marco Farani, at the time the director of the Brazilian Cooperation Agency (ABC), signed a memorandum committing themselves to a Programme of a Brazil–Japan Partnership for the Development of the African Tropical Savannah, which would reproduce the experience of the Brazilian cerrado in Mozambique, through ProSavana.

Implementation of ProSavana began in 2011, and it was envisaged that it would occupy an area of 14 million hectares in the Nacala Corridor, covering the provinces of Cabo Delgado, Nampula, Niassa, Tete and Zambézia, over a period of at least 20 years. ProSavana envisaged the development of large-scale systems of commercial production, alongside subsistence family agriculture, through state-of-the-art technology from the Brazilian and Japanese experiences and agricultural conservation techniques. The programme is divided into three components, each with its own institutional provisions and implementing bodies, to be implemented over three phases, namely, ProSavana-PI, ProSavana-PD and ProSavana-PE.[151]

ProSavana-PI is centred on research and on the modernisation and institutional capacity building of the Mozambique Agricultural Research Institute (IIAM). Lasting for five years (2011–2016), this component of the programme was undertaken by the Brazilian Agricultural and Livestock

---

151 This information on ProSavana is available at: http://www.prosavana.gov.mz/?lang=pt-pt.

Research Company (Embrapa) in coordination with the IIAM and the International Agricultural Science Research Centre of Japan (JIRCAS).

The second component, which was scheduled to begin in 2012 and end in 2014, has not yet been implemented, for reasons we shall explain later. This component involves a Master Plan (ProSavana-PD) for the agricultural development of the Nacala Corridor, and is coordinated by JICA, ABC and the Mozambican Ministry of Agriculture (MINAG).[152]

The third component, ProSavana-Extension and Models Project (ProSavana-PEM), scheduled for implementation between 2013 and 2019, has the objective of increasing the levels of agricultural production in targeted areas of the Nacala Corridor, through the adoption of agricultural development models. MINAG, JICA and ABC are also responsible for the implementation of this component.

According to Embrapa, it is expected that the project will directly benefit 400 000 small and medium producers and, indirectly, 3.6 million (Embrapa, 2012). According to the ProSavana implementing agencies, the choice of the Nacala Corridor is because this region possesses agro-ecological characteristics like the Brazilian cerrado. This aspect is not exclusive to ProSavana, since Brazil believes that its development experience is more generally applicable to the African continent, given that they share the same type of tropical climate. Thus most, if not all, of the Brazilian development cooperation programmes in Africa, and particularly Mozambique, are a replica of those implemented in Brazil that were regarded as successful (Chichava et al, 2013). This is one of the formative disputes between OSCM and the proponents of ProSavana, since the former believe that Prodecer was a total failure, while the latter think the opposite, and argue that it can be exported to Mozambique and other parts of Africa.

Opposition of Mozambican civil society to ProSavana

The start of OSCM activism against ProSavana dates from 2011. The criticism of ProSavana took place essentially through open letters, and the organisation of workshops, conferences or seminars, which denounced the possible damaging effects of this programme on Mozambique.

The OSCM, who have stood out in the fight against ProSavana, include the National Union of Peasants (Unac),[153] Environmental Justice (JA),[154] the Rural Mutual Aid Association (ORAM), the Nampula Provincial Platform

---

152 Currently the Ministry of Agriculture and Food Security (MASA).
153 Based in Maputo, this is the largest organisation that represents and defends peasants in Mozambique. It was set up in 1987.
154 An organisation set up in 2004 in Maputo, which fights for equity and defence of the environment.

of Civil Society Organisations (PPOSC-N)[155] and Academic Action for the Development of Rural Communities (Adecru).[156] Unac, JA, Adecru and ORAM have their head offices in the capital, Maputo, while PPOSC-N has its headquarters in Nampula. This detail is important because, as we shall see, this marks these organisations' positions towards ProSavana.

The first public declaration against ProSavana came from Unac, through its provincial nuclei in Cabo Delgado, Nampula, Zambézia and Niassa, at a meeting held in Nampula in October 2012. According to Unac, there were basically two problems with ProSavana: not only had Prodecer, which inspired ProSavana, favoured large-scale ago-industry, degraded the environment, and expropriated and marginalised the indigenous populations of the cerrado, but there was also a lack of information and little transparency about how this programme would be implemented in Mozambique (Unac, 2012), and they wanted to ensure that the negative effects of Prodecer would not be repeated here.

Hardening and internationalising their actions, in May 2013, 23 Mozambican civil society organisations (OSCMs), with the support of 43 international organisations, addressed an open letter to the heads of government of Mozambique, Japan and Brazil, demanding the immediate suspension of ProSavana, to allow a reflection on and reformulation of the programme, involving not only the associations that support and defend peasants, but also the peasants themselves, through an inclusive and democratic dialogue (Adecru *et al*, 2013).

Although directed specifically at the presidents of the three countries implementing ProSavana, there was something in common in the demands of these organisations: a request to focus more on family agriculture, which occupies most of the rural population of Mozambique, instead of agro-business which, in their opinion, would benefit only the multinationals. They accused Brazil, for example, of hiding behind a discourse of solidarity to facilitate the entry of multinationals, and they demanded that Brazil, among other things, give greater priority to the '*Mais Alimentos*' (More Food) programme.[157] According to these organisations, *Mais Alimentos* gives primacy to smallholder farmers, unlike

---

155 Set up in 2009 and based in Nampula, this defines itself as a coordinating mechanism of initiatives of civil society organisations, integrated into thematic and sector networks. It is intended to facilitate communication with partners in the public and private sectors, in pursuing provincial development initiatives.
156 Set up in 2007, it focuses on the defence of rural communities and the promotion of local and inclusive development.
157 This is a programme of the Ministry of Agricultural Development of Brazil (MDA) to finance and build the capacity of family agriculture. The programme is also being implemented in Mozambique. For more details, see http://portal.mda.gov.br/portal/saf/maisalimentos/.

ProSavana, which prioritises agro-business. Japan was accused of investing in mega-infrastructures in the Nacala Corridor with the sole purpose of moving the produce that would result from ProSavana in favour of the multinationals, ignoring peasant agriculture. They reminded the Mozambican president that family agriculture – which occupies 80 per cent of the Mozambican population and is responsible for producing at least 90 per cent of the food produced in the country – has always been the vanguard at the most crucial moments in the country's history and should be protected against agro-business, otherwise serious privations would be created, not only in this sector, but in the whole country (Adecru *et al*, 2013).

As mentioned earlier, the OSCMs received very important support from their Brazilian and Japanese civil society partners. Thus, in August 2013, a 'Triangular Conference of the Peoples' (Japan, Brazil and Mozambique) was organised in Maputo, where, once again, the OSCMs repeated their positions towards ProSavana. The Brazilian and Japanese organisations insisted on the negative impacts of Prodecer in Brazil, demanding that it not be implemented in Mozambique (Justiça Ambiental, 2013).

For example, considering that the open letter of May 2013 had not received an answer and that ProSavana was already under way, five Japanese organisations, namely, ATTAC Japan, Oxfam Japan, the Japan International Volunteer Centre (JVC), the Africa–Japan Forum (AJF) and Citizens Concerned with the Development of Mozambique (CCDM), drew up a new open letter in September 2013, specifically addressed to the Japanese Prime Minister, Shinzo Abe. In this they called not only for an immediate halt to ProSavana but also a fundamental review of this programme (ATTAC Japan *et al*, 2013).

On 2 June 2014, only a year after the open letter was issued and in what could be described as a culminating moment in this process, nine OSCMs launched a national campaign entitled 'No to ProSavana', demanding a total and immediate halt to the programme. They insisted once more on the negative impacts on the environment and the local population that this programme would bring in the absence of dialogue and transparency over its design and implementation. These organisations also denounced cases of intimidation by the Mozambican authorities against local people who opposed ProSavana. They said that, with a view to implementing this programme, the people were being coercively and compulsively expelled from their territory. According to these organisations, the campaign 'No to ProSavana' was a response to the 'silence' of the governments of Japan, Brazil and Mozambique to the open letter of May 2013 (Adecru *et al*, 2016).

Table 7.1: OSCMs that launched the campaign 'No to ProSavana'

Unac
ADECRU
Environmental Justice/Friends of the Earth
Human Rights League
Women's Forum
Action Aid Mozambique
Association of Legal Support to Communities (AAAJC)
Livaningo
Kulima

This position was repeated in the 2nd Triangular Conference of the Peoples, held in Maputo on 24 July 2013. Here the participants said that they had already witnessed some negative impacts of ProSavana. For example, Unac observed that in the Monapo district alone, in Nampula Province, ProSavana had expropriated about 3 000 hectares of land from local producers to hand over to agro-business for soya production (Suzete, 2014) – a claim that was difficult to confirm.

While in the initial years of ProSavana's implementation, the criticisms were directed more at Brazil's participation in the programme because it was regarded as primarily benefitting Brazilian agro-industry and Brazilian farmers, more recently Japan has been heavily targeted – a position seconded by Japanese civil society organisations. It should be mentioned that, during the visit by the Japanese Prime Minister to Mozambique in 2014, the local OSCMs were very critical, believing that, although masked in speeches of friendship and solidarity, the visit had a hidden 'imperialist' agenda, intended only to consolidate Japanese interests to the detriment of Mozambican interests (Vujanhe, 2014).

Splits among the OSCMs: Manipulation, search for protagonism or struggle for survival?

The actions of the OSCMs have had some positive effects, leading those responsible for drafting ProSavana to make efforts to give it more transparency and to include the OSCMs in the debates about the programme.

The first meeting organised by MINAG to present ProSavana and consult the civil society organisations was held in Cuamba, in Niassa Province, in September 2013. According to MINAG, the idea was to present and discuss ProSavana-PD with the OSCMs. Likewise, after the OSCMs had presented their concerns at a conference on 24 July 2014 in Maputo, MINAG was again forced to reply, restating the willingness of Mozambique, Japan and Brazil to hold a transparent dialogue about ProSavana with the representatives of the OSCMs and their Brazilian and Japanese counterparts.[158] Since then, the government has been publishing information about ProSavana on a page in its website dedicated to the programme. MINAG has also distributed leaflets in Portuguese and in Mozambican language to the local population, explaining ProSavana.

However, some OSCMs, such as Unac and Adecru, look with suspicion at the openness of the proponents of ProSavana and the creation of the Civil Society Mechanism for the Development of the Nacala Corridor (MCSC) in February 2016, stating that this is not an honest and transparent initiative, and that some organisations have been manipulated and co-opted to legitimise the programme, weakening their fight against ProSavana (Adecru, 2016; Unac, 2016).

Among the organisations considered as having been co-opted are: PPOSC-N, the Niassa Forum of Non-Governmental Organisations (*Fórum das Organizações Não Governamentais do Niassa*, Fonagni), the Forum of Zambézia Non-Governmental Organisations (*Fórum das Organizações não Governamentais da Zambézia,* Fongza) and the Network of Organisations for the Environment and Sustainable Development of Zambézia (*Rede de Organizações para Ambiente e Desenvolvimento Sustentável da Zambézia*, Radeza). Curiously, these all come from regions in which ProSavana is being implemented. The Countryside (Rural) Observatory (*Observatório do Mundo Rural* OMR; one of the few OSCMs based in Maputo that agreed to join the MCSC) is also seen as having been co-opted (Adecru *et al*, 2016; Unac, 2016). It should be mentioned that the MCSC is led by PPOSC-N, and that OMR is coordinator of the technical group, the purpose of which is to issue opinions and suggestions for improving ProSavana-PD. ORAM (another OSCM from Maputo) completes the list of OSCMs who are members of the MCSC.

Adecru, JA and Unac, assisted by, among other organisations, Livaningo, LDH and the Women's Forum, also accuse the World Wide Fund for Nature (WWF) – in collusion with the promoters of ProSavana – of using its position as a donor to induce some OSCMs to not only accept the programme, but also to join the MCSC. Adecru, JA and Unac believe that WWF (whom they also regard as acting in an ambiguous and camouflaged manner, not opening any space for dialogue) should leave the role of leadership in this process to the OSCMs (Unac *et al*, 2016a). JA, for example, argues that it makes no sense to set up an MCSC to reflect on a programme widely contested by society and which runs against the interests of the people, and thus reiterates its commitment to the campaign 'No to ProSavana' (Justiça Ambiental, 2016).[159]

---

158 For more details, consult: http://www.prosavana.gov.mz/index.php.
159 On the position of JA, see also *Pambazuka News* (2016).

For their part, PPOSC-N, Fonagni and Fongza, unlike Adecru and Unac, believe that the MCSC will be a space where 'the Civil Society Organisations and the communities can hold a dialogue in an efficient way and perform their role with the government and its partner in ProSavana in planning, implementation and monitoring'(PPOSC-N *et al*, n.d.). These organisations also believe that this space will allow the revision and finalisation of ProSavana-PD by including and safeguarding the concerns of the OSCMs, which, as we have seen, are at the centre of the discord among the advocates of ProSavana. Because of the pressure of the OSCMs, ProSavana-PD, which should have begun in 2013, had still not been implemented by the first half of 2016.

To see the division among the OSCMs, it is enough to look at the results of the vote of the 39 organisations who took part in the proposal to revise ProSavana-PD in Nampula, in January 2016: four voted no to continuing ProSavana; seven voted against, but agreed to negotiate if their conditions for dialogue were accepted; two were indecisive; 19 voted in favour of dialogue with ProSavana, if some alterations to ProSavana-PD were made to accommodate their concerns; and seven organisations, designated as governmental, did not take any position. Some members of Unac were also accused of having preferential access to travel to Japan, to the detriment of the other organisations (Majol, 2016).

Another example of the divergences among the OSCMs is when Unac, supported by Adecru, by the OMR and by the Land Forum, denounced the fact that in the Nampula meeting its members were intimidated and suffered attempted assaults by the subscribers of ProSavana (namely, a JICA consultant) because they did not agree with the terms of the programme. At the same time, according to members of PPOSC-N, some Unac members at the meeting spread lies about their organisation (Majol, 2016).

The splits between the OSCM of the south and those of the centre and north can also be noted in the fact that the campaign 'No to Prosavana', launched on 2 June 2014 (as its slogan indicates), argues that there is no place for ProSavana, and that it simply should be abandoned and replaced by an agriculture that gives primacy to the family sector. The campaign has been supported by most of the OSCMs in the south of the country (see Table 7.1). This shows the different approaches to this programme – for while the OSCMs in the south favour the end of ProSavana, those in the north and centre favour its revision. These differences and oppositions can also be read through this extract of the interview with António Mutuoa of the Civil Society Mechanism:

Table 7.2: OSCMs that signed the joint statement on ProSavana in August 2016

UNAC
Environmental Justice
Academic Action for Community Development (Adecru)
World March of Women (MMM)
Women's Forum (FM)
Livaningo
Mozambique Human Rights League (LDH)
Friends of the Earth Mozambique (ATM)
Nacala Diocesan Justice and Peace Commission (CDJPN)
Justice and Peace Commission of the Nampula Archdiocese (CajuPaNa)

You know that the ProSavana programme was heavily opposed and many voices of civil society organisations took the lead … because there was no understanding, there was no openness, there was no dialogue, the dialogues were minimised, and they took a decision to deter ProSavana, but some voices of civil society said, OK you have to stop, so we reflected and created a mechanism which could be inclusive, interactive and sustainable. It was then that … the other organisations said … no to ProSavana and they march, they marched, but we in the Nacala Corridor as organisations and the Alliance of organisations that we create in Maputo, we think we should [work] with the government, what should be the best way, what would be the alternative to reactivate the programme (Miramar, 23 February 2016).

In August 2016, Unac and another nine OSCMs assisted by, among others, Japanese, Brazilian and African organisations (Table 7.2), produced a document claiming that the organisations who had agreed to participate in the MCSC had done so naively because they were unaware that its creation was part of a 'communication strategy' devised by the governments of Japan, Brazil and Mozambique immediately after the first denunciation of ProSavana by Unac. The aim of this 'communication strategy' was to co-opt, contain, manipulate and divide the OSCMs and weaken their struggle against ProSavana. For these reasons Unac and its supporters advised the organisations who were members of the MCSC to reconsider their positions and their commitment to ProSavana (Unac *et al*, 2016b). It is interesting to note that two OSCMs based in Nampula, namely, the Nacala Diocesan Justice and Peace Commission (CDJPN) and the Justice and Peace Commission of the Nampula Archdiocese (CajuPaNa), both linked to the Catholic Church, signed the document.

All these aspects demonstrate that there was a deepening division among the OSCMs, which served to discredit their activism against ProSavana. These splits may constitute a search for pre-eminence on the part of some organisations, but they may also represent a struggle for emancipation by organisations from the centre and north of the country from those of the south, more specifically from Maputo. In other words, it may be a way for the OSCMs of the centre and north to create their own space and free themselves from the tutelage of the OSCMs of Maputo; and show that they, rather than the OSCMs of Maputo, have their own ideas and interests and that the situation in the Nacala Corridor, although a national question, primarily affects them. Finally, one should not lose sight of the possibility that these splits may also constitute a struggle for survival, because there are those who believe that only some organisations are benefitting from partnerships with their counterparts from Japan and Brazil.

Conclusion

This chapter has discussed the reasons that make the OSCMs critical of the ProSavana programme. Basically, opposition has been waged through open letters, and the organisation of public seminars and debates, with the participation of international civil society organisations, particularly from Japan and Brazil. Since the programme is still in its early stages, so that nothing specific can be said about its real impacts, the criticisms are based essentially on the negative experiences of Prodecer in the Brazilian cerrado, particularly the marginalisation of smallholder farmers in favour of large capital, and the pernicious effects on the local environment.

This chapter also discussed the emerging fissures within Mozambican civil society, highlighting the gap between communities in different regions of the country as well as the ever-present urban–rural divide. The relationships among the OSCMs opposing ProSavana show that some favoured abandoning it, while others called for it to be revised. This has led to some distrust among these OCSMs. This division can be classified as regional, since most of the OSCMs from the south are in favour of the 'No to ProSavana' campaign, while those from north of the Save River (Sabi River) want a 'reformulation' of the programme so that it does not damage the local population. This 'reformulation' should be undertaken with the involvement of the various interested parties. These rivalries between the OSCMs of the south and those from north of the Save River can also be read as the latter seeking to free themselves from the tutelage of the former, or in terms of access to resources. Furthermore, these cleavages hint at ethnic divides that overlap with these same regional distributions.

The appearance of massive investments in Mozambique made by the so-called 'emerging powers' of the South, particularly Brazil and China, drew the attention of the OSCMs to the impacts of these investments, especially in agricultural and mining projects, which normally include the displacement and resettlement of the local population. What comes under criticism is not the investment itself, but what is regarded as a lack of transparency and the non-inclusion of the local people in the discussion and implementation of the project. The OSCMs are also concerned with the enormous areas of land required for these projects. The opposition has had some positive results, forcing the proponents of the programme to give explanations and to respond to the protests of the OSCMs.

The main concern expressed by the OSCMs about mega-projects such as ProSavana, which combine international development cooperation with foreign direct investment, lies in the fact that they believe that these projects benefit only the local political elite and the multinationals, that there is no open and inclusive discussion with the interested parties and those who could be affected, and that there is little information about how these programmes are to be implemented.

However, and without taking merit away from the OSCMs and their fight against ProSavana, it must be stressed that the arguments advanced to criticise this programme are not endogenous, and do not result from experience of or findings from this programme. Instead, their opposition is based on the arguments and experiences advanced by their Brazilian and Japanese counterparts in relation to Prodecer in Brazil. More than any other mega-project, the critique of ProSavana has the specificity of involving a significant number of international civil society organisations, particularly from Japan and Brazil, who have contributed to internationalising the opposition and giving it greater visibility. This relationship seems to underscore the importance of both domestic sources and international linkages as part of the effective mobilisation of Mozambican civil society aimed at challenging certain state-led policies. Significantly, it suggests that these links enhance its ability to act on behalf of community interests rather than, as some observers have suggested, tilt its orientation unduly towards outside interests. The nature of the issue – land, smallholders and rural livelihoods – is also crucial to the depth and sustainability of local activism. Meaningful to local communities and important to their advocates in the national context, as well as resonating with civil society counterparts outside Mozambique, the issues raised by ProSavana brought together a 'perfect storm' of interests, which were able to effectively challenge the project. Maintaining this degree of coherency and activism, as demonstrated in this study, is less likely as the centrifugal forces of localism and competition increasingly assert themselves in this debate.

References

Adecru et al (2013) Carta aberta para deter de forma urgente o Programa ProSavana – Notas Públicas – Associação Brasileira de Organizações Não Governamentais. Available at: http://www.abong.org.br/notas_publicas.php?id=6219 (accessed 7 May 2016).

Adecru et al (2016) Depois de desperdiçados mais de 560 milhões de ienes para elaboração do Plano Director do ProSavana, os governos optam pela cooptação da Sociedade Civil. *Adecru*, January. Available at: https://adecru.wordpress.com/2016/01/11/depois-de-desperdicados-mais-de-560-milhoes-de-ienes-para-elaboracao-do-plano-direc-tor-do-prosavana-os-governos-optam-pela-cooptacao-da-sociedade-civil/ (accessed 7 May 2016).

Alden, C (2001) *Mozambique and the Construction of the New African State*. Basinstoke: Palgrave.

ATTAC Japan et al (2013) Japanese civil society statement on ProSavana: Call for an immediate suspension and fundamental review, 10 November. Available at: http://cadtm.org/Japanese-civil-society-statement (accessed 9 May 2016).

Banks, N and Hulme, D (2012): *The Role of NGOs and Civil Society in Poverty Reduction*, Brooks World Poverty Institute, Working Paper No 171. Available at: <civil20.org/upload/iblock/9b1/rolengo.pdf> (accessed 12 May 2016).

Carothers, T and Barndt, W (1999) Civil society, *Foreign Policy*, **117**, pp 18–29.

Chichava, S et al (2013) *Chinese and Brazilian Cooperation with African Agriculture: The case of Mozambique*, Working Paper No. 49, Future Agriculture Consortium.

Embrapa (2012) Avançam ações de projeto conjunto entre Brasil, Japão e Moçambique. Portal Embrapa, 31 January. Available at: https://www.embrapa.br/en/busca-de-noticias/-/noticia/1461641/avancam-acoes-de-projeto-conjunto-entre-brasil-japao-e-mocambique (accessed 12 May 2016).

Fukuyama, F (2001) Social capital, civil society and development, *Third World Quarterly*, **22** (1), pp 7–20.

Goren H (2010) Civil society in Africa: Constraints and opportunities for democratic change. In C Shabir and V Powposki (eds) *Engaging Civil Society: Emerging trends in democratic governance*. Tokyo: United Nations University Press, pp 249–64.

Grugel, J (2002) *Democratization: A critical introduction*. London: Palgrave.

Hanlon, J (2004) Do donors promote corruption? *Third World Quarterly*, **25** (4), pp 747–63.

Justiça Ambiental (2013) O disse não disse de quem não quer dialogar. Available at: https://justicaambiental.wordpress.com/2013/08/ (accessed 9 May 2016).

Justica Ambiental (2016) *Comunicado. Prosavana em discussão no seio das organizações da sociedade civil em Nampula*, Maputo.

Majol (2016) Acta do Encontro de Sociedade Civil sobre ProSavana. Available at: https://adecru.files.wordpress.com/2016/02/acta-worshop-11-e-12-janeiro-final.pdf (accessed 8 May 2016).

Manning, C (2010) Mozambique's slide into one party rule, *Journal of Democracy* **21** (2), pp 151–65.

Miramar (2016) ProSavana: Partes alcançam consenso, 23 February. Available at: http://www.miramar.co.mz/Jornalismo/Mz-no-Ar/Destaques-23-de-Fevereiro/PROSAVANA-partes-alcancam-consenso (accessed 5 September 2016).

Pambazuka News (2016) *Moçambique: Emergência de divisões na luta contra o Prosavana?* Available at: http://www.pambazuka.org/pt/human-security/mo%C3%A7ambique-emerg%C3%AAncia-de-divis%C3%B5es-na-luta-contra-o-prosavana (accessed 17 June 2016).

PPOSC-N et al (n.d.) Comunicado de imprensa. Available at: http://awsassets.wwfmz.panda.org/downloads/comunicado_de_imprensa_em_portugues.pdf (accessed 17 June 2016).

Suzete, I (2014) Mozambique: Civil society organizations decided to globalize the 'No to ProSavana' campaign and promise to give legal responsibility to 'perpetrators. La Via Campesina. Available at: http://viacampesina.org/en/index.php/actions-andeventsmainmenu-26/stop-transnational-corporations-mainmenu-76/1643-mozambique-civil-society-organizations-decided-to-globalize-the-no-to-prosavana-campaign-and-promiseto-give-legal-responsibility-to-perpetrators (accessed 21 June 2016).

Pfeiffer, J (2004) Civil society, NGOs and the Holy Spirit in Mozamibuq, *Human Organization*, **63** (3), pp 359–72.

UNAC (2012) Land grabbing for agribusiness in Mozambique: Unac statement on the ProSavana program. Available at: http://viacampesina.org/en/index.php/main-issues-mainmenu-27/agrarian-reform-mainmenu-36/1321-land-grabbing-for-agribusiness-on-mozambique-unac-statement-on-the-ProSavana-programme (accessed 8 May 2016).

Unac et al (2016a) *Denúncia da parceria entre WWF e Prosavana, A Verdade*. Available at: http://www.verdade.co.mz/vozes/37-hora-da-verdade/57154-selo-denuncia-da-parceria-entre-wwf-e-prosavana- (accessed 6 September 2016).

Unac et al (2016b) *Comunicado Conjunto e Questionamentos da Sociedade Civil de Moçambique, Brasil e Japão sobre o ProSAVANA com Relação aos Documentos do Governo Recentemente Vazados*, 27 August. Available at: http://fase.org.br/wp-content/uploads/2016/09/TICAD-ProSAVANA-Comunicado-Conjunto-pt5Sept2016.pdf (accessed 21 September 2016).

Vujanhe, J (2014) Às vésperas de uma visita imperial, Adecru, 16 January. Available at: https://adecru.wordpress.com/2014/01/ (accessed 17 June 2016).

West, H and Kloeck-Jensen, S (1999) Betwixt and between: 'Traditional authority' and democratic decentralization in post-war Mozambique, *African Affairs*, **98** (39), pp 455–84.

Wischermann, J, Bunk, B, Kollner, P and Lorch, J (2016) *Do Associations Support Authoritarian Rule? Tentative answers Algeria, Mozambique and Vietnam*, GIGA Working Paper No. 295, December, pp 1–30.

Chapter 8

Foreign direct investment inflows and transfer of tacit knowledge: The Brazilian company Cine Group in Mozambique

Roberto Gonzalez Duarte, José Márcio de Castro and Renata Borges Guimarães

The governments of the African continent have adopted a whole series of policies, including privatisation, tax cuts, the strengthening of regulatory frameworks and improvements to social and physical infrastructure to stimulate economic growth in their countries (McKinsey, 2010). One of the leading examples is Mozambique's economy, which, since the signing of the Peace Agreement in 1992, bringing an end to 16 years of civil war, has expanded on average at over 6 per cent per year (World Bank, 2015). Having grown at 7.0 per cent and 7.4 per cent in 2011 and 2012, respectively, an average growth of 7.8 per cent is forecast between 2014 and 2017 (EIU, 2013). This outlook has made the country increasingly attractive to multinational companies (MNCs). The country, which in 1992 received just US$25 million in foreign direct investment (FDI) inflows, saw this volume rise to almost US$6 billion in 2014 (UNCTAD, 2012; World Bank, 2015). Some of the MNCs that have invested are Brazilian in origin, of various sizes and from diverse sectors, such as Vale in the primary sector, Odebrecht in the infrastructure sector and, more recently, the Cine Group in the service sector.

Among the potential impacts of the FDI inflows, the transfer of resources – including the transfer of technology, knowledge, know-how and organisational practices (Jones, 2005) – can have a variety of effects on the destination economy, ranging from the improvement of organisational practices to leveraging the country's economic growth. Discussing knowledge transfer specifically, Dunning and Lundan (2008) argue that MNCs, by connecting people from different institutional contexts, create training and qualification opportunities for the employees of the subsidiaries located in different countries.

Knowledge transfer can be understood as a process of exchanging tacit and explicit knowledge between two agents (Kumar and Ganesh, 2009). However, this transfer is neither a simple nor easy task, since it presumes the simultaneous maintenance and recreation of a set of complex routines in a new context (Szulanski, 1996). Moreover, understanding the complexity of knowledge transfer as an activity also means understanding it as a process. It therefore matters how this process is configured and what factors compose and affect it (Szulanski 2000). In these terms, knowledge transfer between the parent company and subsidiaries of MNCs is a complex and time-consuming process, the results of which can be shaped by, among other factors: 1) the type of knowledge transferred; 2) the mechanisms used to transfer the knowledge; 3) the institutional, cultural and organisational barriers to transfer; and 4) last, but not least, the absorptive capacity of the receiver.

A consensus exists in the literature that the most valuable type of knowledge transferrable by one firm to another is tacit (Gold, Malhotra and Segars, 2001; Bock *et al*, 2005). This knowledge includes technical elements ('know-how', competencies and habits) and cognitive elements (mental models that help people mediate and interpret the world) (Nonaka and Takeuchi, 1995). This type of knowledge is important to these organisations because it enables improvements to the quality of services and, strategically, to the capacity for innovation, as well as the increase and improvement of organisational performance (Chen and Edgington, 2005). Although more valuable, tacit knowledge is also the most difficult knowledge to evaluate (Arvidsson, 2000). Tacit knowledge (insights, intuition and suppositions) is highly personal and hard to formalise, and is linked to actions, processes, routines, ideas, values and emotions (Nonaka and Takeuchi, 1995). This type of knowledge is also difficult to transfer (Kogut and Zander, 1993; Nonaka and Takeuchi, 1995), primarily due to the conditions in which it is produced. The specificity of the socio-cultural–institutional context in which it is created (Easterby-Smith, Lyles and Tsang, 2008) makes this knowledge difficult to transfer between distinct national and organisational contexts (Bock *et al*, 2005). The adequate use of transfer mechanisms can, however, improve social integration and the capacity for absorption, and consequently increase the effectiveness of the intra- and inter-organisational transfer of knowledge (Bjorkman, Stahl and Vaara, 2007).

The appropriate choice of mechanisms for transferring knowledge, especially tacit knowledge, is particularly important since some are more suitable than others because they allow organisations to overcome the difficulties inherent in the transfer process. Among the diverse mechanisms available, those involving social integration (training, technical visits, team work, expatriation, and so on) are the most appropriate for transferring tacit knowledge. First, these mechanisms allow the construction of relations of trust and the creation of a shared vision among the parties, improving social integration between the organisations involved in the transfer of knowledge (Bjorkman, Stahl and Vaara, 2007). Secondly, they help reduce the gap between the potential absorptive capacity and the real capacity of the receiver; in other words, their use increases the firm's capacity to exploit and utilise the knowledge received. Both social integration between the parties and the increase in the absorptive capacity of the recipient firms are crucial to enhancing the effectiveness of the knowledge-transfer process (Bjorkman, Stahl and Vaara, 2007).

Social integration mechanisms are, by their very nature, personalisation mechanisms: their purpose is to transfer tacit knowledge between individuals and groups (face-to-face). By working to increase the connectivity between their different units and, therefore, make the outside knowledge more familiar, organisations can facilitate its exploitation by the receiving firm (Bresman, Birkenshaw and Nobel, 1999; Jansen, Van den Bosch and Volberda, 2005). This, in turn, will help increase the innovation of the organisation's products, processes and services, and consequently its competitive advantage. Without this connectivity, there is a risk of transferring and receiving only formal and explicit knowledge, which although potentially useful and more easily shared and disseminated (Kogut and Zander, 1993; Hansen, 1999; Jasimuddin, 2007), may not be critical knowledge, given that it is easy to imitate and even replace (Pérez-Nordtvedt et al, 2008). Nonetheless, the attempt to transfer tacit knowledge can be fruitless if the real absorptive capacity is low, making its exploitation and utilisation inviable.

The objective of this chapter is to discuss the question of tacit knowledge transfer in the context of the investments made by MNCs from the services sector operating in Mozambique. More specifically, it seeks to comprehend the challenges that this type of transfer represents for these MNCs. With this aim in mind, we analyse the case of a Brazilian company from the audio-visual sector, which began operating in Mozambique in 2008. We describe the social integration mechanisms used to transfer a certain kind of knowledge – audio-visual production – which is by nature essentially tacit, as well as the role of these mechanisms in improving the absorptive capacity of the receiving company for exploiting and utilising outside knowledge. In addition, some of the barriers related to knowledge transfer between the Brazilian and Mozambican units are discussed. This case illustrates two key factors, both interrelated, that are necessary for any successful transfer. The first relates to the social mechanisms used to share and transfer knowledge. The second concerns the absorptive capacity – leveraged by the mechanisms – which is especially important to the effectiveness of the transfer; that is, to the acquisition, assimilation, transformation and exploitation of the knowledge originating from an external source. Although a shared idiom can effectively facilitate the sharing, transfer and absorption of knowledge, it is notable that, in the case analysed in this chapter, idiom is also a factor hindering the process and should not, therefore, be overlooked.

Following this introduction, the chapter is structured in four sections. In the following one, we discuss the theoretical assumptions of this chapter. Afterwards, we present the case of Cine Group, highlighting the mechanisms used and the barriers faced in the transfer of knowledge, especially tacit knowledge, between the Brazilian parent company and the Mozambican branch. In the penultimate section, we discuss the main challenges that the transfer of tacit knowledge poses for MNCs investing in Mozambique. Finally, we present our conclusions.

Foreign direct investment in flows and transfer of knowledge

FDI inflows can have different effects on the destination economies (UNCTAD, 1992; Dunning, 1994; Jones, 2005; Dunning and Lundan, 2008). Jones (2005:262–82) identifies some of these effects, including the transfer of resources (knowledge, capital and employment); trade balance of the host economy (foreign subsidiaries may affect the volume and composition of imports and exports); market structure (multinationals may increase competition or concentration); the creation of linkages with local companies and spill-overs (professionals trained in the MNCs may switch jobs, for example, transferring the acquired knowledge to other organisations); cultural factors (MNCs may alter consumer habits), and so on. These impacts can vary according to the economic sector, the MNC, the mode of entry, the nature of the destination economy, and local government policies towards MNCs.

Since the MNCs are usually important agents of innovation, their subsidiaries generally have access to knowledge, technologies and organisational practices (managerial, administrative and productive), both from the parent company and from other subsidiaries, allowing them to offer products and services that are more competitive in the local market. If this indeed happens, it may generate the so-called 'demonstration effect' (Jones, 2005): in other words, local companies seek to improve their own products and/or services, aiming to be more competitive. Often this improvement occurs through the adoption of similar organisational practices (isomorphism) to those used by their foreign competitors. Another channel for knowledge transfer to the host economy is through the connection established between the MNC subsidiaries and local firms (Duarte, 2001; UNCTAD, 2001). Becoming a supplier for an MNC in many cases entails the need to adopt certain organisational practices and respond to certain demands, such as those related to quality. In setting these requirements, the MNC may provide the supplier with access to its knowledge and technology, contributing to an increase in the competitiveness of the local supplier companies.

In either case, knowledge transfer can occur through the informal and/or formal development of human resources, both those of the subsidiaries and those of partner companies, such as suppliers. This development is particularly welcome in countries such as Mozambique where there is a shortage of qualified labour or where considerable financial or institutional difficulties exist in terms of developing human resources. Furthermore, the qualification of the workforce by the MNCs – whether undertaken internally or externally – can contribute to the spill-over of knowledge to the rest of the host economy. Professionals trained by the MNCs may change jobs and transfer their acquired knowledge to other firms (Jones, 2005:273).

As well as training its workforce, the MNCs, which tend to be intensive in knowledge, increase the demand for qualified staff in the labour market of the host countries. Slaughter (2002:16) argues that 'there is compelling evidence that affiliates' demand for skilled labour is stimulated by their receipt of parent technology and their investments in physical capacity'. A shortage of qualified labour, especially technical, can lead subsidiaries to bring in professionals from outside. These expatriates can be sources and channels for knowledge transfer, expertise and know-how. This transfer is not automatic, but depends on the existence of mechanisms for it to take place. Some governments have limited the number of foreigners that can be hired by the subsidiaries of the MNCs. The objective is to stimulate the recruitment of local staff. However, if no effective policies for training and qualifying local professionals are in place, this type of prohibition hinders the transfer of knowledge, which may be essential to the local economy.

The knowledge transferred between organisations (between parent companies and subsidiaries, for instance) may be explicit or tacit (Nonaka and Takeuchi, 1995). Grant (1996:111) argues that tacit knowledge may be associated with 'know-how' and explicit knowledge with 'knowing about facts and theories'. More precisely, explicit knowledge is the kind that can be systematically codified and transmitted through formal mechanisms of organisation, like manuals, systems and prototypes, for example (Nonaka, 1994; Nonaka and Takeuchi, 1995; Lubit, 2001). Tacit knowledge, on the other hand, is more difficult to codify since it is based predominantly on individual experiences, which are, in turn, anchored in the socio-cultural context in which these individuals live and work. According to Grant (1996), the degree of transferability from one to another varies, as do the mechanisms for its transfer. Zander and Kogut (1995:85) suggest that the ease with which an organisational capacity can be codified and taught indicates how tacit the knowledge is and how difficult it may be to communicate. Tacit knowledge, more difficult to codify, can only be observed during its application and acquired through practice; hence its transfer between people is a slow, costly, uncertain and, consequently, challenging process (Kogut and Zander, 1993). The paradox, as Arvidsson (2000) points out, is that while tacit knowledge is the most valuable, it is also the most difficult to transfer. Its transference depends on the interaction and integration between people.

Thus, the more frequent the communication between the individuals from the source and the recipient, the better the work environment and, consequently, the easier it is to transfer knowledge between the parties (Kogut and Zander, 1992). Visits, technical meetings and training courses allow more social integration and, potentially, more transfer of knowledge between the interacting sides. Moreover, increased social integration, using mechanisms of social integration, has a significant impact on the absorptive capacity of the recipient firm. This is because closer relationships intensify social exchanges, which can, for example, help members of the recipient firm to overcome problems related to understanding and using the external knowledge, reducing the barriers to the exchange of information within an organisation (Zahra and George, 2002).

Zahra and George (2002:186) define the absorptive capacity as a 'set of organizational routines and processes by which firms acquire, assimilate, transform and exploit knowledge to produce a dynamic organizational capability'. Absorptive capacity can be discussed and analysed at different levels, which are closely interrelated: country, organisation or individual. At the level of a country, the average formal qualification of its population determines its absorptive capacity and, in turn, its economic development. The cases of Japan some decades ago and China more recently illustrate how absorptive capacity can lever not only economic growth, but also the creation of a more diversified and dynamic economy through the creation of new technologies and new knowledge (Jones, 2005; Lin, 2011).

At the level of organisations, the degree of absorption is determined by individual absorptive capacities, since these are what facilitate the process of absorbing external knowledge (Cohen and Levinthal, 1990; Zahra and George, 2002). More specifically, an organisation's absorptive capacity depends on basic and prior knowledge in the recipient firm, which provides it with the capacity to evaluate, comprehend and absorb the knowledge from external sources (Cohen and Levinthal, 1990) to create value for the organisation. For external knowledge to be used creatively, therefore, the recipient organisation needs professionals with distinct capacities and experience. However, even though this is a *sine qua non* condition, it is not enough to merely recognise and assimilate new knowledge. Without its transformation and exploitation, there is no creation of the new knowledge (Cohen and Levinthal, 1990; George and Zahra, 2002). The absorptive capacity for recognising and assimilating

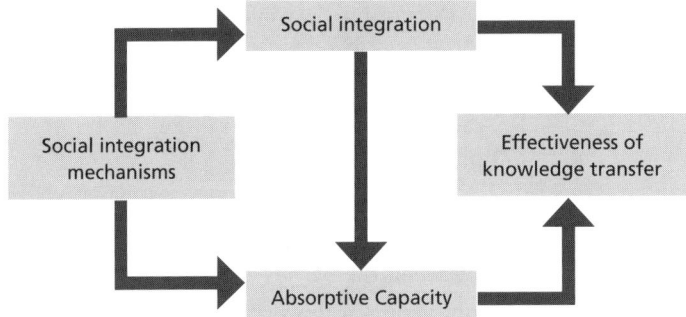

Figure 8.1: Social integration mechanisms and transfer of knowledge
Source: Authors (based on Zahra and George, 2002; Bjorkman, Stahl and Vaara, 2007)

outside knowledge is termed 'potential absorptive capacity'; therefore, the capacity for transforming and exploiting knowledge – that is, creating value (new knowledge) for the organisation – is termed 'realised absorptive capacity' (Zahra and George, 2002).

Thus, the absorptive capacity of a country or an organisation depends on the absorptive capacity of individuals. At least in theory, well-qualified and formally and informally trained individuals – that is those with more capacity to absorb, use and exploit the knowledge – are in a better position to transfer knowledge for real, both within organisations and between them. Hence the larger the potential absorptive capacity (acquisition and assimilation of external knowledge) and the realised absorptive capacity (transformation and exploitation of knowledge), the more effective the knowledge transfer (Zahra and George, 2002). Absorptive capacity is, therefore, directly related to social integration mechanisms, since by promoting greater integration between the individuals from the source company and the receiving company, these mechanisms contribute to reducing the gap between potential and realised absorptive capacities. In other words, the social-integration mechanisms not only contribute to increasing social integration, but they also help to improve the realised absorptive capacity of the recipient company through integration and relationship-building activities (George and Zahra, 2002). These ideas can are visualised in Figure 8.1, which guides the discussion of the case presented in this chapter.

As we argued earlier, MNCs can contribute significantly to the transfer of knowledge – both explicit and tacit – to the economies in which their subsidiaries are based, hence leveraging local economic development. This knowledge first needs to be transferred to the local economy and subsequently used and applied. One of the main challenges for MNCs is sharing and transferring this knowledge. This challenge has, in turn, knock-on effects for the human-resource policies and practices of the subsidiaries of these MNCs. To illustrate the points presented earlier, we discuss the case of the Cine Group, a Brazilian company from the audio-visual sector, which entered the Mozambican market in 2008.

The Cine Group case

Created in 1995, the Cine Group produces documentaries, institutional videos, series, interactive media, publicity films, and so on. The parent company is based in Brasília and has affiliates in São Paulo and Rio de Janeiro. Its first experience in the international market was in the 1990s, when it took part in an audio-visual project in South Africa. Later, in 2008, based on contacts established at an international television fair (MIPCOM), the Cine Group decided to open a subsidiary in Mozambique, the first outside of Brazil. Initially the firm operated with staff that included Brazilian professionals, who had previously worked at the parent company in Brazil, as well as Mozambican freelancers and Brazilians who split their time between offices in the two countries. Once set up in Maputo, the Cine Group's first concern was to create 'content nucleuses', kick-starting the process of becoming independent from the parent company. One of the first projects developed in the country was the television series *N'txuva: Vidas em Jogo*, comprising 15 episodes of 15 minutes, coproduced with a Mozambican television network. Over time, various other projects were developed – from institutional videos to TV series – not only in Mozambique but also across the African continent.

Although the Cine Group had initially used mainly Brazilian professionals, the goal from the outset was to gradually replace these with Mozambicans. This substitution posed a challenge, however: transferring the knowledge of the Brazilian professionals to the Mozambicans, while respecting the knowledge of the latter. Audio-visual production combines technical knowledge with tacit knowledge of the local context or, more specifically, knowledge of the cultural references predominant in a specific location. Among other aspects, this knowledge is related to visual culture, that is, the meanings ascribed to images by different social groups in a specific population. Only when these references are known or learnt can a story be told that elicits the interest of the public, ensuring that they receive the information and, at the same time, feel affected by it. Awareness is, thus, a key aspect of audio-visual production, but this is possible only if the particularities of a given cultural context are well known and understood.

While aware of the need to work with professionals immersed in the Mozambican context, the Cine Group needed to overcome a major challenge:

the shortage of skilled labour in the audio-visual sector in Mozambique. Firstly, as a result of decolonisation, the country lost knowledge and know-how, and the subsequent civil war meant relative isolation in relation to access to information and knowledge, in general, and particularly visual production. For example, the small number of television programmes and cinemas limited the constitution of a more diverse panorama of visual references. According to one of the partners and current director of the Mozambican unit, 'many people were left "stranded" when it came to receiving information from elsewhere in the world, especially since there weren't the same kind of advanced communications technologies that exist today'. Secondly, reflecting the absence of any institutions capable of training professionals in this area in contemporary technical requirements for audio-visual production, there were insufficient professionals available in the market. Success in Mozambique thus depended on educating and training locally based professionals. Therefore, during the recruitment phase, the company was keen to select professionals who were not only interested in the audio-visual field but, above all, also eager to learn. As one of the partners remarked, to transfer knowledge, it is first and foremost necessary for the recipient to have a genuine interest in learning. In his words, 'he [the candidate] also has to have an inner desire to absorb'. In sum, both prior knowledge in the audio-visual area and an interest in learning – or, more precisely, motivation – were prerequisites for the selection.

Once selected, the challenge was to pass on both explicit and tacit knowledge to the Mozambican professionals. While the former is easily mobilised and delivered to another individual or group, tacit knowledge depends on a number of socialisation strategies that stimulate integration between people and, as a result, the sharing of this kind of knowledge.

The president reflected on the importance of cultural aspects in the case of audio-visual production and, above all, the need to understand the relation between one and the other: 'communication is fundamentally linked to culture … In the case of television, I'm selling culture, I'm messing with people's minds, with their personalities. So, I have to take enormous care. That's why, the first point when we arrived there was to respect and understand the local culture.'

As the local director said: 'it's a process of construction and maturation, real "trial and error". I don't have a clear scientific methodology that defines it: "I'm going to give you a manual and this manual will teach you to see things differently." That's why an exchange of experiences is essential.' In summary, to minimise any possible negative effects stemming from socio-cultural differences, conviviality between the professionals from both countries was always encouraged. According to the president, the goal was to learn about the culture, live with the Mozambicans and mix with them to comprehend their way of life. For her, 'understanding their culture means living with them. Our first point was to tell our employees: "go out with the Mozambicans, mingle".'

Different social integration mechanisms were used to make this transfer possible. One was joint work: in other words, the Mozambican professionals worked alongside more experienced Brazilian professionals. One of the partners emphasised the importance of practice and joint work for training and the exchange of information and knowledge, and gave an example: 'I had a Mozambican director who spent two months "glued" to a Brazilian director.' Another mechanism was the exchange of information and experiences. A Brazilian who worked for some years in the Mozambican office cites the example of the director's training: '[the Mozambican director] shows what he is producing here and the directors from Brazil also show the new things that they are producing there; they swap information among themselves.' She gave an example of how this exchange occurs at an everyday level: '[the president of the Cine Group] sits down and says: "show us everything you've produced since the last time I came." She then instructs them: "this is beautiful, this here isn't, what happened?" Then he [the Mozambican director] gives his viewpoint, I'll give mine. There is a self-analysis and also support … that's what I think's great.' Another mechanism employed to share knowledge was the use of practical examples. One of the Mozambican professionals observes that: 'much more than speaking or forcing someone to do a particular thing, you have to do it, show it to them and they [the Brazilian unit] are the first to show how it's done'. The Brazilian journalist tells of a case that illustrates just how the use of these practical examples can help in training people: 'from going around with our team so much … [the driver] became a production assistant; he provides [technical] assistance without any problem … he knows how to carry equipment, how to help assemble and disassemble, the importance of making sure the work starts on time. They are people with a profile, we see that they have a profile, and we invest in the growth of these people.' In sum, by using these different mechanisms of social integration, the aim was to transfer knowledge and, with it, assumptions concerning the desired standards for audio-visual production.

The Cine Group's concern with the recruitment and selection of staff, the education and training of the professionals, and the effective participation of Mozambicans in the production of audio-visual content, ended up giving a Brazilian–Mozambican shape and character to the firm's African unit. Seven years after its arrival in Mozambique, the affiliate caters for almost 100 per cent of its Mozambican demand in the country. There are still some challenges to be surmounted to reduce the remaining dependency on the Brazilian office. The Mozambican director stated: 'there are some projects where we don't need any input from Brazil ... but there are others where we really do need them; for example, works that require computer graphics.' This exchange between the parties will continue because it is characteristic of the kind of company involved, but, as the president asserts, 'today, they [the Mozambicans] are now ready'. The combination of Brazilian and Mozambican knowledge brought undoubted benefits for the Cine Group. One is the comparative advantage, since, as the director of the Mozambican unit stresses, 'the major differentiating feature of Cine Group, however much it works locally, [is] the fact that we add the gloss and creativity of a Brazilian company'. This difference is based on the combination of local and technical knowledge – with both its explicit and tacit dimensions – transferred to the local professionals.

The challenge of transferring knowledge between Brazilian MNCs and Mozambican subsidiaries

The Mozambican economy has grown robustly and consistently for almost two decades, which has helped attract MNCs in a variety of sectors. The growing volume of FDI inflows is bound to affect the labour market, increasing the demand for a qualified workforce. If this workforce is unavailable, there are two possible solutions for MNCs. One is to use expatriates to meet existing demand. The other is to qualify and/or train a local workforce. Investments in primary sectors, such as the exploitation of resources, may require employees skilled in technical areas, a demand more quickly met by using expatriates. However, there are legal limits to the number of people that foreign companies can bring to Mozambique. Furthermore, this kind of solution is extremely expensive. In other sectors, though, training people is more than simply a response to legal demands: it may be essential to the kind of activity involved. The case of the Cine Group illustrates this point perfectly: while expatriates can quickly solve the workforce shortage problem, especially in relation to technical work, they lack a local comprehension or understanding – a Mozambican 'eye'– which, in certain areas like audio-visual production, makes all the difference. Script writing, for example, is an activity that requires awareness of technical issues but also an immersion in the local culture.

As we saw earlier, tacit knowledge is the most valuable, but also the most difficult to evaluate and transfer (Kogut and Zander, 1992; Nonaka and Takeuchi, 1995; Arvidsson, 2000). The value of this knowledge and the difficulty in transferring it is evident in the case of the Cine Group. Although technical knowledge determines the result of the company's audio-visual productions, it is the tacit element – that is, the most intangible – that effectively adds value to the productions. Possessing technical knowledge alone would thus be insufficient to create an audio-visual product. It is not easy, however, to separate the explicit and tacit elements contained in these two types of knowledge. This is a situation common to all the companies, although the proportion between technical and tacit knowledge can vary between sectors and between companies. At any rate, it is the proportion between one and the other, and the relevance of each that determines how and why particular forms of knowledge should, or should not, be transferred between the different units of the organisation.

In the case analysed in this chapter, the critical knowledge for the Cine Group is essentially tacit; in other words, valuable knowledge, like the construction of narrative content – 'how to tell a story' – can be shared and transferred only via social interaction. Staff exchange is one of the principal means for transferring tacit knowledge (Easterby-Smith, Lyles and Tsang, 2008). Given the contextual nature of this type of knowledge, the transfer of knowledge from the Brazilian unit to the Mozambican unit requires face-to-face encounters; that is, joint work involving Brazilian and Mozambican professionals. The objective is to pass on tacit elements of practice (Argote and Ingram, 2000; Bjorkman, Stahl and Vaara, 2007; Yakhlef, 2007). Although adequate in the case of the Cine Group, these same mechanisms may not be effective for other Brazilian MNCs operating in Mozambique. The decision about what mechanisms to use depends on the balance between the two types of knowledge, the relevance of each of them and the barriers to their transfer. In any event, the appropriate choice of mechanisms largely determines the success or otherwise of this transfer.

As discussed in the theoretical section of this chapter, there are barriers to transfer, related to the knowledge itself (the degree of transferability), the absorptive capacity of the country and recipient organisation, and the cultural contexts of the source and the recipient. In the case of the Cine Group, given the mostly tacit nature of its specialised knowledge and the difficulty of transferring this, the company has primarily used social-integration mechanisms – visits, joint work, the exchange of information and experiences – since these are the most effective in this situation. Moreover, although difficulties may exist in transferring this knowledge, due to the shortage of professionals in the audio-visual area or weaknesses in the formal training of existing professionals, the use of social-integration mechanisms helps improve the relationship, interaction and communication between the parties and, thus, enhance the process itself. Social-interaction mechanisms, which strengthen integration and the ties between foreign and local professionals, also enable an increase in the realised absorptive capacity. These mechanisms – joint work and the exchange of experiences and information – contribute to the process of learning among local professionals, enabling them not only to acquire relevant external knowledge, but also to absorb, exploit and use this knowledge while appreciating the importance of the local context.

The question of mechanisms takes us to human-resource policies and practices, especially those involving knowledge transfer between parent companies and subsidiaries. Expatriation can quickly solve problems relating to skilled labour shortages in the country in which the investment is being made. However, it is very often not the best solution because it is expensive, which reduces the company's competitiveness; there are legal restrictions on hiring foreigners; and the organisation's distinctive knowledge, which gives it a comparative advantage, is rooted either partially or wholly in the local context. As seen in the case analysed here, expatriates can sometimes minimise the problems described earlier – especially where technical aspects are concerned – but they may also face difficulties in producing audio-visual content that demands a deep knowledge of local particularities.

The financial and legal difficulties of expatriation can favour the implementation of initiatives to train local workers instead. Aside from these reasons, in certain cases training ends up being a determining factor in the company's competitiveness because audio-visual production is anchored in both technical knowledge, little influenced by the culture, and in a knowledge of visual references, which depends on an immersion in the culture and an understanding of the Mozambican reality. Although the Cine Group has technically highly skilled professionals in Brazil, they lack sufficient understanding of subtle and less tangible aspects of Mozambique's socio-cultural reality. More than training via traditional mechanisms, this case demonstrates the importance of on-the-job development practices, which encourage the swapping of experiences, information and knowledge. Stimulating and creating the conditions for the exchange of people between the parent company and the subsidiary, work-group training, the organisation of meetings and technical visits, which expand and strengthen connections and trustworthiness, are some examples of effective actions on the part of MNCs that need to transfer tacit knowledge to their Mozambican affiliates.

Conclusion

In this chapter, we discussed the relation between the entry of Brazilian MNCs in Mozambique and the transfer of knowledge between the parent companies and subsidiaries. High rates of economic growth and common cultural roots represent an attraction not only for those companies wishing to expand their presence on foreign markets, but also for those who wish to internationalise their operations. For the Mozambican economy, Brazilian MNCs – though not just Brazilian – comprise a source of resources, especially knowledge, technology, know-how, expertise, techniques, organisational practices and so on, which can potentially contribute to further economic growth or, more importantly, to the dynamisation and modernisation of the Mozambican economy and its organisations.

Transfer of knowledge does not occur automatically, though. Its success depends on the kind of knowledge to be transferred, the mechanisms used to transfer it and how the obstacles to transfer are confronted. We have seen that the transfer of tacit knowledge is more effective when social-integration mechanisms are used. These mechanisms increase integration, favouring the building of a more trusting relationship between the parties and, consequently, an increase in the absorptive capacity of the individual, enabling an effective transfer of knowledge between the parties. Beyond the choice of mechanisms, this case shows that social interaction also contributes to minimising the problems caused by socio-cultural differences. In this case, attenuating the effects caused by these differences is crucial since they can affect the result of any transfer, principally those enabled through social interaction, which is more susceptible to the effects of these differences.

The most important implication for managers is the need for defining practices, especially in relation to human resources, that favour the transfer of both explicit and tacit knowledge. Inadequate mechanisms (mechanisms suited to the transfer of explicit knowledge being used to transfer tacit knowledge) or an inadequate understanding of the dynamic and operation of the mechanisms (social interaction presumes the interest of both parties and the skill to build a trustful relationship) can compromise the effectiveness of the transfer. As well as the mechanisms, the absorptive capacity of people needs to be developed, since their capacity is the basis for the creation of new knowledge and, hence, the competitiveness of organisations. Qualifying, developing and training human resources, therefore, is one of the most challenging tasks for the managers of Brazilian MNCs working in (or intending to enter) the Mozambican market. By doing so they increase the likelihood of success of local operations.

References

Argote, L and Ingram, P (2000) Knowledge transfer: A basis for competitive and advantage in firms, *Organizational Behavior and Human Decision Processes*, **82** (1), pp 150–62.

Arvidsson, N (2000) Knowledge management in the multinational enterprise. In J Birkinshaw and P Hagstrom (eds), *The Flexible Firm: Capability management in network organizations*. Oxford: Oxford University Press, pp 176–93.

Bjorkman, I, Stahl, GK and Vaara, E (2007) Cultural differences and capability transfer in cross-border acquisitions: The mediating roles of capability complementarity, absorptive capacity, and social integration, *Journal of International Business Studies*, **38**, pp 658–72.

Bock, GW, Zmud, RW, Kim, YG and Lee, JN (2005) Behavioral intention formation in knowledge sharing: Examining the roles of extrinsic motivators, social-psychological forces, and organizational climate, *MIS Quarterly*, **29** (1), pp 87–111.

Bresman, H, Birkinshaw, J and Nobel, R (1999) Knowledge transfer in international acquisitions, *Journal of International Business Studies*, **30** (3), pp 439–62.

Chen, ANK and Edgington, TM (2005) Assessing value in organizational knowledge creation: Consideration for knowledge workers, *MIS Quarterly*, **29** (2), pp 179–309.

Cohen, WM and Levinthal, DA (1990) Absorptive capacity: A new perspective on learning and innovation, *Administrative Science Quarterly*, **35**, pp 128–52.

Duarte, RG (2001) Cross-border acquisitions and changes in domestic management practices: The case of Brazil, PhD thesis (unpublished), University of Cambridge.

Dunning, JH (1994) Re-evaluating the benefits of foreign direct investment, *Transnational corporations*, **3** (1), pp 23–51.

Dunning JH and Lundan, SM (2008) Multinational enterprises and the global economy, 2nd edition. Reading: Addison-Wesley.

Easterby-Smith, M, Lyles, MA and Tsang, EWK (2008) Inter-organizational knowledge transfer: Current themes and future prospects, *Journal of Management Studies*, **45** (4), pp 677–90.

Economic Intelligence Unit (EIU) (2013) Mozambique Economic and Political Outlook: Country Report, London.

Gold, AH, Malhotra, A and Segars, AH (2001) Knowledge management: An organizational capabilities perspective, *Journal of Management Information Systems*, **18** (1), pp 185–214.

Grant, RM (1996) Toward a knowledge-based theory of the firm, *Strategic Management Journal*, **17** (7), pp 109–22.

Hansen, MT (1999) The search-transfer problem: The role of weak ties in sharing knowledge across organization subunits, *Administrative Science Quarterly*, **44**, pp 82–111.

Jansen, JJP, Van den Bosch, FAJ and Volberda, HW (2005) Managing potential and realized absorptive capacity: How do organizational antecedents matter? *Academy of Management Journal*, **48** (6), pp 999–1015.

Jasimuddin, SM (2007) Exploring knowledge transfer mechanisms: The case of a UK-based group within a high-tech global corporation, *International Journal of Information Management*, **27**, pp 294–300.

Jones, G (2005) *Multinationals and Global Capitalism: From the nineteenth century to twenty-first century*, Oxford: Oxford University Press.

Kogut B and Zander, U (1992) Knowledge of the firm, combinative capabilities, and the replication of technology, *Organization Science*, **3** (3), pp 383–97.

Kogut, B and Zander, U (1993) Knowledge of the firm and the evolutionary theory of the multinational corporation, *Journal of International Business Studies*, **24**, pp 625–45.

Kumar, JA and Ganesh, LS (2009) Research on knowledge transfer in organizations: A morphology, *Journal of Knowledge Management*, **13** (4), pp 161–74.

Lin, J (2011) From flying geese to leading dragons: New opportunities and strategies for structural transformation in developing countries. WIDER Lecture, 4 May, Maputo. Available at: http://siteresources.worldbank.org/INTMOZAMBIQUE/Resources/WIDER_Lecture-Justin_Lin-05-03-11.pdf (accessed 15 May 2014).

Lubit, R (2001) Tacit knowledge and knowledge management: The keys to sustainable competitive advantage, *Organizational Dynamics*, **29** (4), pp 164–78.

McKinsey Global Institute (2010) *Lions on the Move: The progress and potential of African economies*, June.

Nonaka, I (1994) A dynamic theory of organizational knowledge creation, *Organization Science*, **5** (1), pp 14–37.

Nonaka, I and Takeuchi, H (1995) *The Knowledge-creating Company: How Japanese companies create the dynamics of innovation*, Oxford: Oxford University Press.

Pérez-Nordtvedt, L, Kedia, BL, Datta, DK and Rasheed, AA (2008) Effectiveness and efficiency of cross-border knowledge transfer: An empirical examination, *Journal of Management Studies*, **45** (4), pp 715–44.

Slaughter, M (2002) *Skill Upgrading in Developing Countries: Has inward foreign direct investment played a role?* Technical Papers No. 192, Paris: OECD Development Centre.

Szulanski, G (1996) Exploring internal stickiness: Impediments to the transfer of best practice within the firm, *Strategic Management Journal*, Special (17): 27–44.

Szulanski, G (2000) The process of knowledge transfer: A diachronic analysis of stickiness. *Organizational Behavior and Human Decision Processes*, **82**, pp 9–27.

United Nations Conference on Trade and Development (UNCTAD) (1992) *World Investment Report 1992: Transnational corporations as engines of growth*, New York: United Nations.

United Nations Conference on Trade and Development (UNCTAD) (2001) *World Investment Report 2001: Promoting linkages*, New York: United Nations.

United Nations Conference on Trade and Development (UNCTAD) (2012) *World Investment Report 2012: Towards a new generation of investment policies*, New York: United Nations.

World Bank (2015) 'Overview: Mozambique', Available at: http://data.worldbank.org/country/mozambique.

Yakhlef, A (2007) Knowledge transfer as the transformation of context, *Journal of High Technology Management Research*, **18**, pp 43–57.

Zander, U and Kogut, B (1995) Knowledge and the speed of the transfer and imitation of organizational capabilities: An empirical test, *Organization Science*, **6** (1), pp 76–92.

Zhara S and George, G (2002) Absorptive capacity: A review, reconceptualization, and extension, *Academy of Management Review*, **27** (2), pp 185–203.

Chapter 9

Mediascapes of Brazil's investments in Mozambique: Reporting on the Tete-Nacala Development Hub in the Brazilian press

Potyguara Alencar dos Santos

Over the past few years both digital and print newspapers in Brazil have been exploring in detail the geopolitical and economic shaping of the international flow of productive capital goods from Brazil to Mozambique. Rather than concentrating exclusively on the industrial and political sectors involved in the dynamics of the South–South globalisation of development models, these media sources and opinion-makers look to gather information on the macro-regions in which these dynamics unfold. This press coverage gives impetus to the speculation and discursive formulations already in existence concerning this 'plethora of the developmentalist expansion of Brazil's industrial sector' (*Folha de São Paulo*, 26 March 2013): an expectation that applies to the Tete-Nacala Development Hub, located in northern Mozambique.

This chapter aims to situate and analyse the various discursive formations used by Brazilian newspapers to report on development in Mozambique and the productive networks of mixed capital being invested in the country. Its hypothesis is that these 'mediascapes' (Appadurai, 1990) of the development networks involved in Brazil–Mozambique international cooperation act both as gateways and as informative and formative primers on the progressive rise in speculation between the countries involved. This phenomenon deserves as much attention as studies on the feasibility of installing business infrastructures in regional spaces (Diniz and Boschi, 2007), market research, international relations and the economic and political agendas between Brazil and Africa (Vaz, 2006) – topics that are becoming increasingly popular at a time when intercontinental exchanges of production are expanding at a global economic level.

Like other studies of press mediascapes, this chapter attempts to denaturalise some of the terminologies and interpretations produced by these newspapers in their attempt to model the interactions between the sectors involved in international cooperation. Another objective is to show how the various discourses concerning Mozambique and the Tete-Nacala Development Hub are fully embedded in the construction of a developmentalist mind-set in Brazil, with clear impacts on business groups interested in this dynamic. Consequently, a newspaper article like 'FGV develops a R$2 billion project for agribusiness in Africa' (*Folha de São Paulo*, 12 January 2012), published in São Paulo, the largest business metropolis in Latin America, can have an impact both in Mozambique and on the R$2 billion project designed for the country's north-eastern region – part of an agreement involving the Brazilian Agency for Cooperation (ABC) linked to the Federal Government of Brazil, the United Nations Development Programme (UNDP), the Japan International Cooperation Agency (JICA) and the Getúlio Vargas Foundation (FGV) for economic research (Brito, 2012). As a mediascape, this news item exerts an undeniable influence on political decision-making contexts. Indeed, theorists and ideologists of the mass media have long emphasised this influence (Wolf, 1995).

When it comes to exploring the spaces formed by these transnational development networks (Ribeiro, 1991; 2008), we need to recognise that while the logistical, political and scientific infrastructures of the projects physically shape the future of the states and their political economies, media coverage performs an equally important and complementary role of imbuing symbolic and ideological meaning to the transformational dynamics grounded in the real productive interactions involved in the exchange of capital through large-scale projects. In this sense, while political and business partnerships engage in raising capital and managing international cooperation policies, media portrayals associated with the state–capital nexus create a discursive practice that 'enrols' participants (Oliveira, 2006), enabling the recipient country and region to perform the co-actor role scripted by the world of economic development.

The mediatisation of developmental integration networks between Brazil and Mozambique: A theoretical–methodological approach

The concept of 'developmental integration', as employed by anthropology and other related disciplines, elicits two analytic concerns: how we conceive of large-scale projects (Ribeiro, 2008) and how we conceive of public–private initiatives categorised as 'productive regional integration policies' (Rolim, 1994:15) designed to intervene in regions identified as catalysts for development. Factors such as geographical location and local resource potential, tax incentives and the availability of basic infrastructures are just some of the regional conditions taken as favourable to large-scale infrastructure projects and a boost to the local economy enabled by these policies. As an example of an area meeting these criteria, the Tete-Nacala economic macro-region is seen to combine the diversity of conditions needed for the spatialisation of production equipment

– such as the incentives consistently given by the Mozambican government to partnerships between states over recent years – with the incipient growth of various market and infrastructural conditions that, though insufficient to meet the scale of the industrial development planned for the country, are gradually transforming into projects identified as 'initial infrastructural benefits to the process of expanding business' (*Folha de São Paulo*, 26 March 2013). Discussing regional developmental integration in the context of international cooperation between Brazil and Mozambique is, therefore, an unavoidable topic from an analytic viewpoint.

The concept of 'productive integration', for instance, is found in an extensive bibliography of interpretative texts on the topic. Attempting to contextualise the concept within a political analysis of Latin America and more specifically Brazil, Rolim (1994) emphasises that:

> the word integration has various meanings in economic analysis. Sometimes it refers to integration between firms, sometimes to integration within the same firm or the same economic sector, or sometimes to integration between countries in the context of international trade or, finally, to national integration (Rolim, 1994:151).

Going back to one of the first works to conceptualise the idea of 'developmental integration', Rolim (1994) cites *The History of Thought of Economic Integration* (1977) by Fritz Machlup in which the author defines the concept by recourse to three ideas:

> 1) economic integration basically refers to the division of labour; 2) it involves the mobility of resources or goods, or both; and 3) it is related to the differentiation or non-differentiation of resources and goods (regarding, for example, their origins or destinations) (Rolim, 1994, citing Machlup, 1977:152).

In the specialised literature on the topic, which is especially predominant in schools of political economy, the idea of 'integration' is widely related to a series of other terms. Souza (1981:21), for example, writes of the 'integration of the local regional economy'; Dathein (1992:1) analyses 'Latin-American economic integration' as one expression of this process; while other authors like Creuz (2008:211) explore the globalised context of project integration when they discuss the role of 'international economic integration and cooperation organizations'. In terms of the interests of the anthropological approaches to understanding development, and the concern with the specific value of the concept and its use in the context of the implementation of large-scale infrastructure projects are relatively new. Here we can highlight the ethnographic work of Nogueira (2009:7), which aims to 'analyse and discuss the way in which the multi-state telecommunications network Telesur is attempting to construct a Latin-American identity'. Another term interacting with the idea of 'integration' is the concept of 'consortiumisation' proposed by Ribeiro (1991), who describes the development projects as an assemblage of multiple sectors in a centrally planned productive process, constituted by: 'a cascading set of actions which – through the organization of new economic and administrative entities guided by specific tasks – connects international, national and regional capital within the same project' (Ribeiro 1991:100).

Among the spaces formed by the integration of economies, developmental projects and business initiatives responsible for generating closer links between Brazil and Mozambique over recent years, we can highlight the important role performed by the media in constructing a 'mediascape' of development. As Appadurai (2006) emphasises, this concept expresses the construction of discursive fields that publicise and strengthen global brands and projects, giving a sense of unity and credibility to the 'product'. In this case, the product in question is the exportation of industrial capital from Brazil to Mozambique. For example, using figures and interpretations of a future project, the media describe the Tete-Nacala Development Hub as a new experimental zone for the international expansion of Brazilian companies (*Folha de São Paulo*, 26 March 2013).

In the following interpretations, rather than focusing on a physical geographic area, I turn to news items published by the Brazilian media that function as dynamic scripts through which political–financial practices are highlighted, with the aim of stimulating the national industrial sector to invest in the internationalisation of capital goods.

The intention in this chapter is to present a 'hypertextual' study (Marcushi and Xavier, 2005) that synthesises ideas present in the narrative of the news articles through topical textual expressions. As Marcushi and Xavier (2005) explain, this formal concern with knowing, for example, how an expression may relate to another undeclared expression and how a concept reconstructs earlier concepts, involves the attempt to 'reconstruct meanings' through the argumentative logic of the ideas. A methodology that privileges the hypertextual analysis of the content of these news times aims to: 1) reconstruct the trajectory of certain ideas in the published texts through the comparison between different sets of news items; 2) foreground expressions relevant to the topics under analysis (such as regional development, public–private partnerships, productive regional integration, and so on); and 3) reconstruct the meaning of these textual constructions through the internal consistency of their arguments and ideas. All these methodological prescriptions are also applied by anthropologists, who propose, for example, to evaluate public policies based on the analysis of discursive contents and trajectories (Rodrigues, 2011).

Mediascapes of Brazil–Mozambique cooperation

Some Brazilian newspapers offer their readers weekly reports on the economic and political partnerships between Brazil and the Portuguese-speaking African countries (the PALOP group). In the last few years, since the end of Lula da Silva's second presidential term and the start of Dilma Rousseff's government (more precisely between 2008 and 2010), Mozambique and the Tete-Nacala Development Hub have received special attention from these newspapers. Among other topics, they have focused on the actions of the mining company Vale SA, operating in two land concessions in Moatize, and the construction company Camargo Correa, responsible for building the Mphanda Nkuwa Hydroelectric Dam on the Zambezi River. These two large-scale projects are the overseas business ventures that have received the most coverage in Brazil's domestic media – topics that have stimulated the publication of other information on the introduction of Brazilian productive capital in the African country.

The news reports analysed in this chapter were taken from two of Brazil's largest circulating newspapers, both based in the so-called business capital of Latin America, São Paulo, namely: the *Folha de São Paulo* and *O Estado de São Paulo*. Although some articles from other smaller newspapers are also cited, the high circulation of the information published by these two media outlets made them ideal for this research.

These news items emphasise the regional scales and conditions of viability in Mozambique that favour the business initiatives planned for the country. These reports – no less influential than the incentive policies between states – offer different alternatives and possibilities for the actors involved in the local developmental drama, serving as scripts able to guide the actions of state officials. So, for example, in one of the items we read that:

> An area in Mozambique (Southeast Africa) equivalent in size to the Brazilian Pantanal is set to be transformed into an agricultural mega-project, with technology and productivity similar to those of the *cerrado* [tropical savannah] of Brazil … In total, the region covers 140 000 square kilometres … As well as defining the *regional vocations* for farm production, FGV Projetos will also be responsible for negotiating with the Mozambican government concerning the legal framework for the entire development plan. This is a precondition necessary to give legal

protection to private investors. For example, private land does not exist in Mozambique: lands are controlled by the State and can only be explored through concessions (Brito, 2012:1; my emphasis).

As political geography has shown (Oliveira, 2006), the construction of the regional landscape through developmental capital depends on investing in the symbolic reconstruction of places through discourses emphasising the favourable characteristics of these spaces for economic production. Using this interpretative lens, we can identify terms in the excerpt above, such as 'regional vocations', that attempt to describe the region as a space ideal for agro-industrial developments in terms of infrastructure and wider business logistics. The 'vocations' in this case are regarded as an intrinsic, almost natural quality of the place, which justify, together with the networks of investors and accumulated capital, the implementation of the announced economic activities.

Another element highlighted in the above excerpt is the similarities between Mozambique and Brazil in terms of industrial practices and the size of their natural environments. The article attempts to draw a comparison between the biophysical environment of agricultural production in Mozambique and a productive landscape typical of Brazil, the cerrado, a biome located in the centre of the country. It observes that these investments will be made in an area 'equivalent in size to the Brazilian Pantanal ... with technology and productivity similar to those of the *cerrado*'. The affinity between these agricultural landscapes is not only constructed in terms of biophysical similarities, but also in terms of the economic potential that has historically characterised one of them, the cerrado, as an important zone in the expansion of Brazilian farming. Furthermore, the article suggests, given the existence of similar conditions and resources and a business network engaged in the project, the cerrado's productive model could be replicated on African soil.

The ProSavana project, for instance, coordinated by the ABC and Ministry of Agriculture and Food Security of Mozambique (MASA formerly known as MINAG) and JICA promotes the use of an agricultural technology that requires the presence of similar characteristics in these two biophysical landscapes: the Brazilian cerrado and the Mozambican Savannah.[160] Although depicted as a large-scale project of huge importance in the context of the international cooperation between the two countries, surprisingly there is no reference to this project in the newspaper sources used for this article. Perhaps the period chosen to collect these articles explains the lack of media coverage concerning this project. A survey of more recent material from these sources would probably encounter

---

160   Available at: http://www.cnpmf.embrapa.br/destaques/Mocambique.pdf (accessed 20 August 2013).

more information on this agricultural initiative, which unifies the two countries economically and technologically based on their biophysical similarities.

Another news item, published a year before the previous one, gives an account of the mobilisation of companies in the creation of partnerships involving the Brazilian and the Mozambican governments.

> Brazilian business leaders with projects in Mozambique this Wednesday presented the main Brazilian private investments in the country to President Dilma Rousseff. A large portion of the projects are related to the coal mining concession awarded to Vale in 2004 to explore the Moatize mines located in the north of the country. This project generated a kind of 'Brazilian hub' in the region. However, in order to make coal exportation viable, the company had to invest heavily in the Mozambican infrastructure since the region in question had no ports or railways compatible with the anticipated coal production. The mining company hired Brazilian construction companies such as Odebrecht and Camargo Correa to expand one port and revitalise a railway that had been inoperative for 20 years (*O Estado de São Paulo*, 19 October 2011, p 1).

This excerpt reveals an important moment in the rearrangement of political forces in Brazil, namely, the transition between the two governments of Luís Inácio Lula da Silva – considered by many analysts as the president who revived the history of cooperative relations between Brazil and Africa (Penna Filho and Lessa, 2007) – and the government of Dilma Rousseff, who came into power with the business sector expecting a continuation in international policies and domestic economic incentives.

At the level of international economic policies, the transitional period between the two governments coincided with the expansion of megaprojects in Africa involving Brazilian business partnerships. While the internationalisation of Brazilian capital was an emerging enterprise during Lula da Silva's government, still closely centred on state-diplomatic intervention and large-scale public–private initiatives, Dilma Rousseff's government saw an increase in ventures led by large corporations, which had begun to shape the future of partnerships and the spatialisation and integration of the capital of other Brazilian companies in Mozambique.[161] The above excerpt highlights Vale's leading role in these development networks, describing the company's

---

161 One of these leading Brazilian companies is Odebrecht, due to build the Nacala International Airport in Mozambique's Nampula Province, with funding from the state-owned Brazilian Development Bank (BNDES). Available at: http://www.odebrecht.com/sala-imprensa/noticias/noticia-detalhes-303 (accessed 16 October 2013).

main initiative in terms of aggregating other firms: 'The mining company hired Brazilian construction companies such as Odebrecht and Camargo Correa to expand one port and revitalise a railway that had been inoperative for 20 years' (*O Estado de São Paulo*, 19 October 2011, p 1).

Vale SA appears as both a gravitational centre, coalescing productive sub-units in diverse areas such as construction, and a model business initiative, given that it successfully established and maintained its active role, diversifying its business initiatives and contributing to the revitalisation of Mozambique's infrastructure, thereby creating the right conditions for the implementation of large-scale projects. Vale's leading role and the participation of other sectors in these business networks in the Tete-Nacala region – named in the news article as a 'Brazilian hub' in Mozambique – are cited by a series of news reports on the internationalisation of Brazilian capital as an example of an expansionist process that is 'safe', from an economic and continuity viewpoint, and based on an increasingly liberal international policy.

The following excerpt interview to the then Vale President Murilo Ferreira, shows clearly what we have said above:

'Internationally-speaking, this is Vale's first large infrastructural project', the company's president said. 'Vale has made similar infrastructural investments in Brazil, but never on this scale in another country.' He added that he was hopeful that the investments in the region would create a development hub, attracting farming and industry based on soya and ethanol production. 'Technicians from Embrapa are in Mozambique to assess the possibility of using the soil within the hub planned by Vale' (Gallas, 2011).

To set up operations in Africa, Brazilian businesses have to compete against the Chinese. But according to Odebrecht's director of new business, Fernando Soares:

> unlike the Chinese, the Brazilians have the advantage of employing local workforce. China always brings its own workforce. We are one of the biggest employers in Mozambique, with approximately 6 000 employees, and today between 90% and 92% of our workforce is Mozambican (Gallas, 2011).

This excerpt is an example of how the internationalisation of Brazilian megaprojects in Mozambique was treated as a novelty just a few years ago. The construction of an optimistic discourse, which looks to depict Brazilian entrepreneurship, the 'boldness' of some of its corporate sectors and the elaboration of a regional space in which Brazilian economic practices can be reproduced, are all clear in the context of the news report. Another excerpt from the same news article mentions, for example, that 'despite expectations, no other companies have shown an interest in setting up in the region, according to the Brazilian embassy in Maputo' (*O Estado de São Paulo*, 19 October 2011, p 1). Despite this claim, however, it is known today that the region was, indeed, a motive for competition between diverse interests. Unfortunately, the latitude with which the media report and interpret information often leads them to produce erroneous news items like this.

It is precisely by observing the emergence of a niche market and the need to boost market speculation in the context of developmental internationalisation that the mediascape of Brazilian investments in Mozambique attempts to reconstruct the history and composition of the business sectors involved in these projects. A significant proportion of the new reports on this topic treat the Tete-Nacala Corridor as a regional space that is open to the introduction of economic initiatives and set to obtain the infrastructural conditions needed to welcome diverse business initiatives. Hence we return to the same discursive strategy that reconstructs geographical spaces through an appeal to the 'vocations' that make them favourable to capital investment. This leads to the interpretation that the reproduction of these mediascapes strengthens the belief in the international expansion of the 'developmental model of the Lula era' to Africa. These news reports thus publicise and create symbolic representations concerning the conditions needed to strengthen and maintain a 'Brazilian hub' in the north of Mozambique. Far from being a concrete reality, when these articles were published (between 2011 and 2012), the Tete-Nacala Corridor was being presented to the Brazilian public as a projection of the Brazil state's desire for modernity, an internationalist profile and, some would say, an imperialist role (Fontes, 2010). As analysts have pointed out, this imperialism would be a repetition in Africa of a form of economic domination already practised by Brazil within the geopolitics of Latin America.

> Malawian authorities have announced that Vale will invest US$1 billion to build a new stretch of railway in Malawi, which will allow the company to transport the coal it extracts from Mozambique to the Port of Nacala. The Brazilian company will construct 138 km of railway in the south of Malawi, which will allow it to transport coal from the mine in Moatize (near Tete, in the northwest of Mozambique) to the Port of Nacala (in the northeast) where Vale is currently building a terminal. The section passing through Malawi, halted since 2005 due to diplomatic differences, should be completed in the next three years, according to the agreement signed by Vale and the government of Malawi (*Folha de São Paulo*, 30 December 2011, p 1).

When the newspapers describe the infrastructural dimensions of the large-scale projects being implemented by Brazilian companies in the Tete-Nacala Corridor, other issues emerge, which are not directly related to their physical occupation of Mozambican space. On the one hand, these reports publicise the gigantic size and socio-economic impacts of these projects. On the other, though, they also include some descriptive – albeit inconclusive – information about the intricacies of the international and macro-regional geopolitics involved in the implementation of these development initiatives.

In the newspaper article cited above, Vale's investments in an intermodal transport infrastructure (a railway and a port complex) for shipping coal are presented. The enterprise required the company to set up a committee to negotiate with the Malawian government agencies concerning the construction of a 138-kilometre stretch of railway crossing the country. The company's intervention in the region, together with its capacity to negotiate with national and local levels of government, demonstrate the transnational dimension of the broader project, as well as the level of political integration existing between the different sectors operating in these construction projects.

Seen from the viewpoint of the news report, a transnational company's construction of a railway line connecting countries is not problematised in terms of its partnerships, the diplomatic negotiations involved or the many setbacks occurring during the process. The article conveys the idea that everything is a foregone conclusion. It fails to explore the micro-political implications that arise from handing areas of national territory over to private-sector exploration. Neither does it measure the impacts or return benefits for the country occasioned by Vale's creation of an intermodal transport route. Likewise, many other aspects specific to the local development context are rendered invisible in favour of a more optimistic interpretation of the political and economic interactions involving the various institutional actors. In the end, the announcement that 'Vale will invest US$1 billion to build a new stretch of railway in Malawi' merely amplifies, and publicises to Brazilian readers, the speculative and exclusively positive dimensions of the project, treating any setbacks during the negotiations or negative social impacts as accidents, irrelevant in the face of the project's 'benefits'. This reductionism and the strategies used to give a positive spin to information, neutralise and diminish the inherent complexities in the cooperation policies between Brazil and Mozambique. By way of illustration, very few news reports dedicate a paragraph to exploring sociological or economic data on local contexts in which these projects are implemented.

Conclusion

Compiling and analysing newspapers reports on the internationalisation of Brazilian companies in Mozambique allowed me to: 1) re-analyse the recent history of South–South cooperation involving these two countries, and 2) explore the mediascapes (Appadurai, 1990) that discursively reconstruct the development networks structuring the large-scale projects implemented in the Tete-Nacala Corridor.

The diversity of the sectors involved and the increased transfer of productive capital between continents have raised many expectations among Brazilian companies competing in this niche market, and this economic consortium has been developing projects in mining, civil engineering, traffic engineering, agribusiness, and so on. The publication of news items on these negotiations – which reached a peak during the 'Lula era' (2003–2010) – shows the media's enthusiasm for a series of market interests. This same enthusiasm enables speculators to act and creates 'renewed' discourses on a diverse range of transactions between the Brazilian and Mozambican economies. While NGOs, Mozambican opinion-makers (Mabunda, 2011; Adelson, 2012) and other local leaders linked to civil society, such as Mozambique's National Peasants Union (Unac) and the Mozambican Environmental Justice movement, see social problems, neo-colonialist abuses and poorly planned economic projects, the Brazilian newspapers associated with big state–private capital see opportunities yet to be fully explored in a region of the world 'ideal for development'.

In the dispute for a legitimate language on South–South economic internationalisation, Brazilian newspapers reflect the vanity of the Brazilian expansionist ideology, which has emerged more vigorously over the last 10 years. Caught up in this scenario of media reports on 'two growing countries', the conceptual and geographical reconstruction of the landscapes forming the Tete-Nacala Corridor become absorbed into Brazil's corporate history. Though contested by some analysts, this history is still guided by traditional models of development based on the excessive concentration of private property, monopolies and monocultures supported by state subsidies, and predatory practices that endanger native biophysical environments, their populations and their natural resources.

These news articles not only lack an analysis of the Brazilian and Mozambican contexts but also, and especially, an analysis of Mozambique's situation in the light of Brazil's desire for progress. Also absent from these media sources are reports specifically discussing the state-funded cooperation projects between Brazil and Mozambique: in other words, they focus only on the discussion about private enterprises, a practice that obfuscates any information on the Brazilian state interventions in the country. This political game masks the state's real intentions concerning cooperation, while valuing the interests of private capital to the exclusion of all else. Nonetheless, the public debate promoted by organised civil society and the alternative popular press on Brazil's imperialistic developmentalism has played an important role in raising awareness about the facts and analyses that question the country's neo-colonialist ventures in the Mozambican state.

Domestic interpretations of the Mozambican context, surveys concerning the local population's response to these investments and a careful inquiry into the many different impacts caused by these development initiatives need to be conducted with just as much urgency and attention as the analyses imbued with business jargon and stuffed with economic growth figures. Perhaps the Brazilian media need to invert their gaze and shed light not on Brazil and its expansionist and modernising expectations, but on Mozambique, its current situation during the implementation of these private and interstate megaprojects, such as the ProSavana project, and the effects caused on the ground by the acceleration of these dynamics. Here I am not appealing to the paternalist media, which provide rational interpretative knowledge, filled with intellectual pretentions. Instead, I am talking about the media that promote dialogue in a solidary and sensitive form, willing to engage in the exchange of knowledge with Mozambican intellectuals, representatives of its organised civil society, and its grassroots political agents.

References

Adelson, R (2011) Neocolonialismo brasileiro em Moçambique, *O País Online*, Maputo, 23 August. Available at: http://macua.blogs.com/moambique_para_todos/2011/09/o-neocolonialismo-brasileiro-em-mo%C3%A7ambique.html (accessed 22 December 2012).

Appadurai, A (1990) Disjuncture and difference in the global cultural economy. In M Feathersonte (ed.) *Global Culture*, London: Sage Publications, pp 295–310.

Appadurai, A (2006) *Fear of Small Numbers: An essay on the geography of anger*, Durham, NC: Duke University Press.

Brito, A (2012) FGV desenvolve projeto de R$ 2 bilhões para agronegócio na África, *Jornal Folha de São Paulo*, São Paulo/SP, 5 September.

Creuz, LRC (2008) Organizações internacionais de integração e cooperação econômica: Revisões de uma teoria geral, *Revista da SJRJ*, **24**, pp 211–40. Available at: http://www4.jfrj.jus.br/seer/index.php/revista_sjrj/article/view/62 (accessed 14 November 2009).

Dathein, R (1992) Problemas e perspectivas da integração regional, *Indicadores Econômicos FEE*, Porto Alegre, **20** (3), pp 126–30. Available at: http://revistas.fee.tche.br/index.php/indicadores/article/viewArticle/716 (accessed 18 May 2009).

Diniz, E and Boschi, RR (2007) *A Difícil Rota do Desenvolvimento: Empresários e agenda neoliberal*. Belo Horizonte: Editora UFMG; Rio de Janeiro: IUPERJ.

Fontes, V (2010) *O Brasil e o Capital-Imperialismo: Teoria e História*. Rio de Janeiro: Editora UFRJ.

Gallas, D. 2011. Empresas Brasileiras enfrentam desafios de infra-estutura para produzir na África, *BBC Brasil*. Available at: http://www.bbc.com/portuguese/noticias/2011/10/111019_maputo_invest_dg_rc.shtml (accessed 27 May 2017).

Jornal Folha de São Paulo (2010) Brasil busca apoio político financiando etanol na África, São Paulo/SP, 7 October.

Jornal Folha de São Paulo (2011) Vale construirá ferrovia no Maláui para transportar carvão, São Paulo/SP, 30 December.

Jornal Folha de São Paulo (2012). Brasil 'cheio de charme' oferece ajuda de olho em negócios na África, diz 'NYT', São Paulo/SP, 8 August.

Jornal Folha de São Paulo (2012) ONG critica acordo Brasil-UE para etanol em Moçambique, São Paulo/SP, 14 September.

Jornal Folha de São Paulo (2013) Brics competem para ganhar terreno na África, São Paulo/SP, 26 March.

Jornal o Estado de São Paulo (2011) Empresas brasileiras enfrentam desafios de infraestrutura para produzir na África, São Paulo/SP, 19 October.

Mabunda, L (2011) Governo vendeu 24 distritos a brasileiros, *O País Online*, Maputo, 23 August. Available at: http://www.opais.co.mz/index.php/opiniao/86-lazaro-mabunda/16037-governo-vendeu-24-distritos-a-brasileiros.html (accessed 14 October 2012).

Machlup, F (1977) *A History of Thought on Economic Integration*. New York: Columbia University Press.

Marcuschi, LA and Xavier, AC (2005) *Hipertextos e Gêneros Digitais: Novas formas de construção de sentido*. Rio de Janeiro: Editora Lucerna.

Nogueira, SG (2009) A Identidade Latino-Americana e a Integração Regional: O Projeto da Rede de Comunicação Telesur, *Carta Internacional*, Universidade de São Paulo, **4**, pp 7–14. Available at: http://www.abant.org.br/conteudo/ANAIS/CD_Virtual_26_RBA/grupos_de_trabalho/trabalhos/GT%2023/SilviaNogueiraGT23l.pdf (accessed 15 November 2012].

Oliveira, CDM (2006) A complexidade territorial do turismo: atores, cenários e relacionamentos. In JB da Silva, J da Borzachiello, LCL Lima and EWC Dantas. *Panorama da Geografia Brasileira*, Vol. 1. São Paulo: Annablume, pp 12–25.

Penna Filho, P and Lessa, AC (2007) O Itamaraty e a África: As origens da política africana do Brasil, *Estudos Históricos*, Rio de Janeiro, **39**, pp 57–81. Available at: http://bibliotecadigital.fgv.br/ojs/index.php/reh/article/viewArticle/2561 (accessed 21 December 2012).

Ribeiro, GL (1991) *Empresas Transnacionais: Um Grande Projeto por Dentro*, São Paulo: Editora Marco Zero; ANPOCS.

Ribeiro, GL (2008) Poder, redes e ideologia no campo do desenvolvimento, *Novos Estudos*, março, **80**, pp 109–25. Available at: http://www.scielo.br/scielo.php?pid=S0101-33002008000100008&script=sci_arttext (accessed 17 October 2009).

Rolim, CFC (1994) Integração versus integração: a busca dos conceitos perdidos, *Indicadores Economicos Fee*, Porto Alegre, **22** (3), pp. 151–72. Available at: http://revistas.fee.tche.br/index.php/indicadores/article/view/859 (accessed 12 April 2011).

Rodrigues, LC (2011) Análises de conteúdo e trajetórias institucionais na avaliação de políticas públicas sociais: perspectivas, limites e desafios, *CAOS – Revista Eletrônica de Ciências Sociais*, João Pessoa, **16**, March, pp 55–73. Available at: http://www.cchla.ufpb.br/caos/n17/5.%20RODRIGUES,%20LEA%20AVALIA%C3%87%C3%83O%20EM%20PROFUNDIDADE%20UFC%2055-73.pdf (accessed 20 July 2012).

Souza, NJ de (1981) Economia regional: Conceitos e fundamentos teóricos, *Perspectiva Econômica*, Universidade do Vale do Rio dos Sinos, Ano XVI, **11** (32), pp 67–102. Available at: http://www.nalijsouza.web.br.com/teoria_econ_reg.pdf (accessed 14 September 2012).

Vaz, AC (2006.) *Intermediates States, Regional Leadership and Security: India, Brazil and South Africa*. Brasília: Editora da Universidade de Brasília.

Wolf, M (1995) *Teorias da Comunicação*. Lisboa: Editorial Presença.

Chapter 10
Brazilian South–South cooperation in public health: Dilemmas of the ARV factory initiative

Adriana Abdenur and Danilo Marcondes

The literature on South–South cooperation has been exploring the growing involvement in aiding development by countries like Brazil, which, until recently, had more often been aid recipients than providers (Mawdsley, 2012; Chin and Quadir, 2012). Indeed, cooperation in health has frequently been described as one of the most dynamic areas of South–South cooperation, with claims of innovative approaches by developing countries (Bliss, 2010). Setting out from this premise, we examine Brazilian South–South cooperation in the health arena, focusing specifically on the experience of fighting HIV/AIDS in Mozambique. Having analysed the Brazilian initiatives in this area over the last decade, especially the creation of a local capacity to supply antiretroviral drugs (ARVs) on a universal basis, we argue that Brazil (whose official discourse aims to export the Brazilian model of HIV/AIDS control to other developing countries) emphasises a specific element of this model – the production of generic drugs. However, Brazil's initiatives in Mozambique tend to overlook the range of experiences and institutions that helped shape the Brazilian approach in this area, including those related to the redemocratisation process after the military dictatorship ended in 1985, and democratic presidential elections were held in 1989 for the first time since the 1960s.

Furthermore, Brazil's attempt to promote the domestic production of antiretrovirals to other countries reflects its wider foreign-policy interests – particularly, the Brazilian government's efforts to expand support for its stance on compulsory licensing and equity within the pharmaceutical industries of developed countries. The installation of a pharmaceutical plant in Mozambique was, therefore, an attempt to disseminate the position adopted by the Brazilian government regarding the right to produce drugs deemed essential to the control of various epidemics. In the case of Mozambique, Brazilian cooperation has been seeking to work around the clashes between the Brazilian government and the government and pharmaceutical industry of the United States, including intellectual property rights. On the American side, this trilateral agreement could be explained, in part at least, as an attempt by the US agencies to acquire legitimacy by associating themselves with the Brazilian model for fighting HIV/AIDS. However, the attempts to establish triangular cooperation in Mozambique's health sector have yet to produce significant results, and Brazilian cooperation remains isolated from other efforts being implemented in Mozambique's health sector.

In this chapter, we first analyse the role of health in Brazil's foreign policy and its South–South cooperation initiatives in fighting the HIV/AIDS epidemic in Mozambique. Then we explore the main initiative of Brazilian cooperation in combatting HIV/AIDS in the country: the implementation of a pharmaceutical plant – the Mozambican Pharmaceutical Association (*Sociedade Moçambicana de Medicamentos*: SMM). We examine these initiative in the context of the debates on the approach developed by Brazil to combat AIDS at a domestic level. Finally, we analyse Brazil's relationship with some of the main local and foreign stakeholders involved in health cooperation. We conclude by examining several of the repercussions of the pharmaceutical plant experience for Brazilian South–South cooperation and propose some paths for future research on South–South cooperation in the health arena.

Fighting HIV/AIDS in Mozambique

Since the end of the civil war in 1992, Mozambique has received diverse forms of international assistance for development. Since the 1990s, various donor agencies and international organisations have established projects and programmes in the country, many working in the health sector. The proliferation of international NGOs has subsequently contributed to the complexity of this ecosystem of actors, as well as to the fragmentation of the Mozambican health sector (Pfeiffer, 2003; Zililo Piri, 2012). Since then, despite some social advances and a fairly high level of economic growth (GDP growth reached 7.2 per cent in 2011), Mozambique retains high levels of poverty. In the most recent Human Development Index published by the United Nations, the country is ranked 178th (from a total of 187 countries analysed; UNDP, 2014).

These problems are also reflected in the health sector. Mozambique is among the 10 nations most affected by the prevalence of HIV/AIDS. According to the National HIV/AIDS Council (CNCS), the epidemic affects 11.3 per cent of Mozambicans, with the female population (especially youths and adolescents) showing particularly high levels of infection. In 2012, of the approximately 1.4 million HIV-positive Mozambicans, just 250 508 adults and 23 053 children were receiving treatment with ARVs (corresponding to 51.7 per cent of adults and 19.7 per cent of children). Although this is a substantial improvement compared to 2003 levels when just 3 314 patients were receiving such treatment, it still represents a small portion of those affected (UNAIDS, 2012). Since

ARV therapy is central to the National Strategic Plan in Response to HIV/AIDS – through which the Mozambican government aims to improve disease prevention, advocacy, treatment and mitigation – making drugs available and administering them has become one of the priorities for the sector (Republic of Mozambique, 2010).

Over the long term, the challenges posed are amplified by the dependence on foreign assistance, a lack of trust between donors and the Mozambican government and endemic corruption (Renzio and Hanlon, 2009; Bidaurratzaga-Aurre and Colom-Jaén, 2012). One of the responses to this scenario has been the sector-wide approach (SWAp) to health, originally launched by the Mozambican government in 2000. SWAp aims to strengthen government leaders, with an emphasis on development policies and strategies to reduce foreign assistance costs. At the time of writing, a total of 26 partners use the SWAp structure to bolster the strategic dialogue between partners and the Ministry of Health. These partnerships include multilateral organisations such as the World Health Organization (WHO), UN agencies, the World Bank, the United Nations Development Programme (UNDP), the African Development Bank, the European Union, the Organisation for Economic Development (OECD) and the Global Fund; bilateral entities such as cooperation agencies from Britain (DFID), Japan (JICA), Germany (GTZ), Denmark (DANIDA) and the United States (USAID); and diverse NGOs. Although SWAp has alleviated some aspects of fragmentation, an evaluation by the Mozambican Ministry of Health concluded that bilateral actions by some donors hampered coordination of the actions (Martínez et al, 2005). At the same time, emerging countries like Brazil, China and India have been expanding their cooperation in this area, albeit with different approaches and very often working outside the SWAp framework.

Beyond these local-level dynamics, we need to consider wider changes in the field of international development after the turn of the millennium – all relevant to the Mozambican case. The Millennium Development Goals (MDGs), launched in 2001, include among their eight main goals three that are specific to health (Ameida et al, 2010). The Paris Declaration on Aid Effectiveness, endorsed in March 2005, complements the MDGs and serves as a basis for the Accra Agenda for Action, which brought together government leaders, representatives of organisations and civil society activists. This declaration is cited in the first paragraph of the SWAp Terms of Reference document, signed by the Mozambican Government in 2007, which reflects the importance of this agenda in the Mozambican strategy for health (Ministry of Health, 2007).

Despite the cited advances, problems with aid governance persist, including corruption (partly fomented by the lack of coordination between the donors themselves), which has led some countries like Sweden to cut their funding to the Mozambican programme for fighting HIV/AIDS (Agência de Informação de Moçambique, 2008). In September 2011, some international donors (including the World Bank), who financed a range of initiatives for combatting HIV/AIDS in Mozambique, announced that they would be drastically reducing their support (by US$17 million) of the operational budget of the National AIDS Control Council (CNCS). Created in 2000, the entity had initial expenses of around US$3 to 4 million per year, but by 2008, when the donors stopped their funding, its programmes were budgeted at around US$16 million. The reduction in foreign assistance forced the Mozambican state to fund the programmes for fighting and preventing HIV/AIDS. According to the CNCS, the donors said that they had stopped their funding because their input was not producing satisfactory results, given that infection levels in Mozambique remained high (OPLOP, 2012). According to the Mozambican government, the decision was related to the dwindling funds in the wake of the financial crisis (Valoi, 2012).

Having outlined the wider context of the fight against HIV/AIDS in Mozambique, we highlight the main components of Brazilian cooperation in this area and their impacts on the overall context of cooperation to control AIDS in the country.

Brazilian foreign policy and the fight against HIV/AIDS

Brazil's decision to intensify its cooperation in the fight against HIV/AIDS aligns with its move to strengthen the connections between its foreign policy and health (Almeida *et al*, 2009). In addition to cooperation with low-income countries, this initiative includes the creation of partnerships with other providers of South–South cooperation. Brazil, for example, cooperates with India in research projects and partnerships to influence the agenda on intellectual property rights over pharmaceutical drugs at the World Trade Organization (WTO) and the World Health Organization (WHO) (Chaturvedi, 2011).

To understand how Brazil negotiates, plans and implements cooperation in health, we need to go beyond the 'black box' of the state. In general, Brazilian cooperation is mostly a product of negotiations between states, with signed agreements serving as the basis for specific programmes and projects. Brazil's official rhetoric is to meet the demands made by its partner countries. For example, the document launching its international cooperation programme, divulged by the Ministry of Health in 2002, recognises its assumed position of international leadership and the considerable increase in demand from institutions and non-government organisations from various countries for Brazil to act more incisively to broaden the supply of ARV drugs to millions of people living with HIV/AIDS, who are currently unable to obtain these (Ministry of Health, 2002). At the same time, the Brazilian government also actively promotes its cooperation programmes, particularly those based on public policies implemented in Brazil that are regarded (inside and outside the country) as innovative. For example, in his two mandates, the former president, Luiz Inácio Lula da Silva, visited Africa 11 times (more than any other Brazilian president). These visits opened new cooperation relations and functioned as important occasions for announcing partnerships in areas such as health, agriculture and education; very often these were announced by the president himself, through what the Brazilian foreign policy literature identifies as 'active presidential diplomacy' (Danese, 1999). In the health field between 2003 and 2010, 53 bilateral cooperation agreements were signed with 22 African countries (MRE, 2010).

In terms of the agencies involved, Brazilian cooperation is driven primarily by implementing agencies, such as the Fundação Oswaldo Cruz (Oswald Cruz Foundation: Fiocruz), yet projects are formally coordinated by ABC (Brazilian Cooperation Agency, a subdivision of the Ministry of Foreign Affairs: MRE). ABC was created in 1987 and is tasked with coordinating official international cooperation, including South–South agreements. In budget terms, health corresponds to 19 per cent of the ABC budget, coming second only to agriculture (25 per cent). In terms of the overall distribution of the projects, the African continent has been receiving the majority; that is, 52 per cent of the total (Costa Leite, Suyama and Pomeroy, 2013:12). However, unlike many similar agencies, ABC's mandate and capacity are still limited, which makes the Ministry of Health and Fiocruz – its main executive institution in the area of cooperation – the true centre of gravity of Brazilian health cooperation (said to be capillary rather than centralised) (Abdenur, 2015). Even so, the organisational structures tend to create a fragmentation of cooperation: Fiocruz itself is neither a monolithic entity nor static – in fact, the institution has been implementing organisational changes as health cooperation expands. Since January 2009, for instance, Fiocruz has operated a division specifically focused on international health cooperation coordination and research – the Centre for International Relations in Health (CRIS). The creation of this division – which includes former Fiocruz presidents and other physicians and specialists with ample international experience – represents an important step in the professionalisation and specialisation of a team working in international cooperation. The CRIS team participates in building institutional networks and international cooperation programmes linked or not to ABC, fomenting what Kickbusch, Silberschmidt and Buss (2008) call 'health diplomacy' (for example, the National Public Health School, part of Fiocruz, runs an MA in Health Diplomacy). Despite this accumulation of capacity, Fiocruz's scale and organisational complexity – which, as well as administrative divisions, includes

17 technical–scientific units – means that many of its international cooperative projects are run by other divisions of the institution besides CRIS.

Even outside Fiocruz, the range of institutional actors involved in Brazilian health cooperation is remarkably complex. Many projects are realised in partnership with civil-society entities and private-sector companies – a pattern that, in many ways, traces back to the role played by non-state actors in the redemocratisation process in Brazil. In the fight against AIDS, the MRE and the Ministry of Health have been collaborating with the International Centre for Technical Cooperation (ICTC), an NGO founded in 2005 and with its head offices in Brasília, which receives funding from a wide spectrum of sources, including the Brazilian government, UNAIDS, the UK Department for International Development (DFID), GTZ (a German development agency) and the Inter-American Development Bank. Many of Brazil's cooperation agreements anticipate a role for civil society and other non-state actors. However, the institutional partners – even those forming part of the government structure – do not always operate harmoniously and there are identifiable contradictions, redundancies and fragmentation among the parties. Hence the expression 'Brazilian cooperation' requires the qualification that, despite the state's coordination efforts, the activities of the provider country do not necessarily involve a cohesive initiative undertaken by a monolithic actor.

Even so, in its foreign-policy discourse, the Brazilian government seeks to emphasise the cohesiveness of the state's interests and strategies. In the case of South–South cooperation, this rhetoric emphasises the ties of solidarity with other developing countries, especially Portuguese-speaking nations – which are among the leading partners of Brazilian South–South cooperation. The discourse also emphasises the principles of horizontality, the exchange of ideas and mutual benefit. The former president, Lula da Silva, frequently referred to Brazil's 'historic debt' to Africa – a reference to approximately 3.5 million Africans who were brought to Brazil as slaves (Dávila, 2010). Brazilian diplomacy also emphasises the idea that Brazil meets the demands of countries and partner institutions, in contrast to the assistance provided by the North, based on the imposition of models and ideas of the advanced countries. The Dilma Rousseff government (inaugurated in January 2010) continued this line of action, but with less presidential diplomacy and more emphasis on the economic benefits that cooperation with Africa provides to Brazil. Owing to budgetary restrictions related to the slowing down of the Brazilian economy, in 2011 the MRE budget was cut by 22.7 per cent and the ABC budget was frozen, after having tripled between 2008 and 2010 (Costa Leite, 2012). Overall, the MRE's share of the federal budget was reduced from 0.5 per cent in 2003 to 0.27 per cent in 2014 (Campos Mello, 2015).

In terms of cooperation, over the last decade Brazil has been stressing the importance of exchanging knowledge and implementing *structuring projects*[162] – which, unlike once-off interventions, have a systemic impact and are sustainable over the long term. To a certain extent, this approach implies recognition of the transitional nature of Brazilian projects – the aim is to have local institutions run with Mozambican administration and know-how. Moreover, other interests (not necessarily made explicit in foreign policy) motivate Brazilian South–South cooperation, including the quest to increase soft power (Nye, 2004). Insofar as South–South cooperation promotes a positive image of Brazil as an effective and supportive partner in cooperation for development, it contributes to the wider goals of Brazilian foreign policy. These goals include mobilising the support of partners (in the case of health, in Latin American and African countries) to provide backing to Brazil's interests in multilateral forums, including its lobby for a permanent seat on the UN Security Council. Finally, South–South cooperation facilitates the insertion of Brazilian companies in new markets, both directly (when it involves private-sector partners) and indirectly (by strengthening relations between the two countries). Hence, so long as this cooperation is welcomed by local stakeholders, Brazil benefits in diverse ways (Inoue and Vaz, 2012).

In the health arena, just as in other sectors, the Brazilian discourse on South–South cooperation looks to promote certain practices developed in Brazil as public-policy innovations. In HIV/AIDS prevention, these policies include preventive education, the regime of producing pharmaceutical drugs through compulsory licensing, and – more broadly – the construction of a public-health system and the capacity-building of health professionals. In Brazil, the 1988 Federal Constitution established access to health services as a universal right through the creation of a National Health System (*Sistema Único de Saúde*: SUS); in addition, ARVs for treating HIV/AIDS are distributed free through the public-health system as part of the Brazilian policy of universal access, as set out in Law 9313 (issued on 13 November 1996). The adoption of the local production of generic versions of pharmaceutical drugs, which are made available by national public laboratories, was a response to the mobilisation of civil society (Lima and Campos, 2010). In other words, non-state actors – in this case NGOs – were essential to the development of public policies that are now touted by the Brazilian State as part of its international cooperation activities.

After the turn of the millennium, domestic policy on confronting the HIV/AIDS epidemic assumed an important role in the international debate on combatting HIV/AIDS. The Brazilian government began to argue (for

---

162 On the Brazilian conception of structuring cooperation in the health area, see Almeida et al (2010).

example, in the WTO debates on the Agreement on Trade-Related Aspects of Intellectual Property Rights: TRIPS) for reducing the prices of imported drugs and for the national production of pharmaceuticals – measures deemed essential by the Brazilian government to guarantee the effective and egalitarian distribution of pharmaceutical drugs. In addition to the decisive role played by Brazilian civil society in this process, several international NGOs, like Oxfam and Médecins Sans Frontières, supported the Brazilian position of enabling access to ARVs (IPEA, 2010).

It is worth recalling that the role of the HIV/AIDS control programmes in Brazil's international cooperation initiatives predates the Lula da Silva government. For example, the AIDS issue has been part of Brazilian foreign policy since the Fernando Henrique Cardoso government in the 1990s (Nunn, 2009). In 1996, the Brazilian Congress approved Law 9313, assuring free access to ARVs for patients living with HIV/AIDS, based on the distribution of the drugs via the public-health system. The approach developed in fighting HIV/AIDS in Brazil led the government to adopt positions in international forums that were controversial, especially in relation to negotiations over reducing the price of pharmaceuticals to enable equitable patient access and the implementation of compulsory licensing for drugs, which was opposed by the pharmaceutical industry and developed countries. According to Chaves, Vieira and Reis (2008:180):

> Compulsory licensing revealed a government commitment to sustainable access to HIV/AIDS treatment in a context in which the drugs covered by patent protection are exorbitantly priced and inaccessible to the vast majority of developing countries. Moreover, the possibility signalled by the government of making use of compulsory licensing for other drugs is extremely positive since it aims to assure the sustainability not only of the National STD/AIDS Program but also of the entire public health system.[163]

The policies implemented domestically by Brazil began to have repercussions at international level with some international organisations, such as the World Bank and UN agencies, seeing the Brazilian model for fighting AIDS as an innovative policy.[164] From virtually the outset, this recognition led the Brazilian government to think about disseminating this approach to other developing countries. Back

---

163 Translation from the original version published in Portuguese.
164 Brasil é modelo, mas não pode relaxar, diz ONU, *Folha de São Paulo*, 26 November 2003. Available at: http://www1.folha.uol.com.br/fsp/mundo/ft2611200303.htm.

in 2001, the Minister of Health at the time, José Serra, who promoted various initiatives at the WTO in defence of Brazil's stance, stated that: 'Our example can serve as a model for other countries in Latin America, the Caribbean and even in Africa. Everyone worldwide has the right to access these therapies' (Wadia, 2001). As a more recent concrete example, we can highlight the Memorandum of Understanding signed in March 2010 between UNAIDS and the Community of Portuguese-speaking Countries (CPLP) to expand cooperation between UNAIDS and the member countries for the prevention and treatment of HIV/AIDS, which established the UNAIDS office in Brazil as a focal point.[165] In the context of Mozambique, many local stakeholders see Brazil as a model in terms of its attitude to combatting HIV/AIDS, especially given its leadership in proposing new channels for supplying medications to the population.[166]

Hence by promoting its models abroad, the Brazilian government helps legitimise its experience at domestic and international levels in the face of contestation by advanced countries and their pharmaceutical industries. For example, based on the perception of the relatively successful implantation of its public health system (SUS), launched in the 1990s, other developing countries have asked for assistance in implementing similar programmes. Even though SUS suffers from serious deficiencies, the demand for Brazilian cooperation in this area has allowed the Brazilian government to emphasise those aspects of the system that are regarded as successful. This is also the case of the breast-milk banks, already implemented in more than 20 countries in Africa and Latin America. In the case of fighting HIV/AIDS, cooperation not only helps strengthen public policy among the Brazilian population, it also supports Brazil's stance with respect to organisations such as the WTO and WHO (Russo, Cabral and Ferrinho, 2013).

Health cooperation between Brazil and Mozambique

The relations between Brazil and Mozambique date from September 1981, when the general cooperation agreement was signed between the two countries. Since then a series of agreements has been structuring Brazilian cooperation with Mozambique. In 2001, the two countries signed a bilateral

---

165 Additional information on the memorandum is available at: http://www.unaids.org.br/acoes/paises.asp. In an interview given to the international press concerning the Memorandum of Understanding, the Director of UNAIDS, Michel Sidibé, recognised Brazil's central role in the initiative in terms of sharing experiences developed domestically, but also in reference to the pharmaceutical plant in Mozambique. Available at: http://vihsidanoticias.wordpress.com/2010/03/18/em-entrevista-a-agencia-aids-michel-sidibe-diz-que-parceria-entre-unaids-e-cplp-deve-servir-de-modelo-para-o-mundo/.

166 Interview with Dr Noêmia Muíssa, Director of the Mozambican Pharmaceutical Association, Maputo, 19 November 2013.

protocol of intentions on technical cooperation in the health arena. In July 2005, in the middle of the first Lula da Silva government, a supplementary alteration was made to the general agreement, to focus on the implementation of the project 'Economic and technical viability study for the installation of a pharmaceutical plant in Mozambique to produce antiretrovirals and other drugs'. As part of a more comprehensive effort to deepen and diversify ties with Africa, the Brazilian government signed new cooperation agreements with Mozambique (Cau, 2011). Between 2005 and 2010, Mozambique became the main destination for Brazilian cooperation projects, accounting for 16 per cent of their total number (Costa Leite, Suyama and Pomeroy, 2013).

In September 2008, another supplementary alteration was made to implement the project 'Capacity building in the production of antiretrovirals and other drugs'. The aim of this initiative was to provide capacity and transfer knowledge on the production of ARVs and other pharmaceuticals in Mozambique (MRE, 2008). This programme also began to fund the training of more than 200 doctors and nurses in ARV therapy at Maputo Central Hospital.

In Mozambique, the official Brazilian cooperation developed within the framework of these agreements occur primarily through structuring projects in three priority areas: HIV/AIDS prevention and treatment, the implementation of a national health system and capacity-building in public health. There are also projects such as the breast-milk banks, which very often intersect with the structuring projects. In the arena of capacitation, for instance, Mozambique's first Master's in Health Sciences, created through a partnership with the National Health Institute (INS) of the Mozambican Ministry of Health (MISAU), trained its first group of students in 2010. As part of this agreement, professionals from Fiocruz undertook six working missions in Mozambique, while technicians from the INS undertook four working missions at Fiocruz (Cau, 2011). There was also a broader dialogue between the two institutions: Fiocruz and the INS collaborated on the drafting of a strategic plan to coordinate and negotiate health cooperation with Brazil.

In the HIV/AIDS area, Brazil works in Mozambique on prevention and capacitation programmes. Despite the distribution of Brazilian-produced ARVs, cooperation aims for greater sustainability through the local production of pharmaceuticals. Currently 80 per cent of the funds available for purchasing drugs in Mozambique come from donor countries. To reduce this dependency, Brazil has been cooperating on developing a pharmaceutical plant on land acquired by the Mozambican government in 2008 in Matola, on the outskirts of Maputo. This plant was offered by President Lula da Silva on a trip to Mozambique in 2003, in dialogue with Joaquim Chissano, the president of Mozambique at the time. Hence this cooperation initiative emerged at the highest political level. Even though the idea of constructing such a facility abroad was an unprecedented experience for Brazil, it formed part of Brazil's foreign policy of prioritising Africa post-2003.[167]

The possibility of technology transfer and the development of a laboratory to produce ARVs had already been mentioned in a speech by President Lula during a visit to Namibia in November 2003 (MRE, 2003).[168] A similar project had also been offered to South Africa (Nauta, 2011). However, neither of the two offers materialised. In the case of Mozambique, presidential diplomacy played a considerable role in advancing the proposal – one of the most ambitious projects of Brazilian cooperation, at an estimated cost of US$23 million (Sotero, 2009). The mining company Vale – which in 2012 launched a US$6 billion expansion project for mining coal in Mozambique – also entered with a donation of US$4.5 million to complete the plant; this represented 75 per cent of the expenses that would have fallen to the Mozambican government (Penha, 2012).[169]

The agreement to build the plant envisaged the transfer of technology and knowledge to produce five ARVs for adults and children, with the capacity to benefit around 2.7 million HIV-positive individuals in Mozambique. The head of Farmanguinhos (Institute of Drug Technology, Fiocruz) emphasised that the project's biggest benefit would be the transfer of technological knowledge: 'We wish to raise Mozambique to the level of a country capable of transforming technology' (Blog da Saúde, 2012). In a speech given in Mozambique in 2003, the Brazilian Minister of Health presented Brazilian cooperation as a question of responsibility: 'We shall have to use our knowledge and friendships to share responsibility for helping Mozambique and helping other African countries to confront the problem of AIDS in the way it should be confronted' (A Tarde, 2003).

The first stage in the implementation of the project (2003–2007) involved the negotiations and the elaboration of the plant viability study, followed by technical studies and the search for funding in the two countries (2008–2011). In 2009, the Brazilian Congress approved the financial resources for the project, allocating R$13.6 million. During the vote, government senators emphasised

---

167 Interview with Brazilian diplomat responsible for the health sector, Brazilian Embassy, Maputo, 27 November 2013.
168 In the case of the Namibian visit, the statement released by Brazil's Ministry of Foreign Affairs reported in relation to cooperation on fighting HIV/AIDS: 'The President of Namibia congratulated Brazil for its support in the fight against the terrible pandemic of HIV/AIDS. Along these lines, the President of Brazil agreed to continue collaborating with Namibia in the fight against the pandemic, including via technology transfer towards the installation of a laboratory for producing antiretroviral drugs in Namibia.' (MRE, 2003). Available at: http://www.itamaraty.gov.br/sala-de-imprensa/notas-a-imprensa/2003/07/comunicado-conjunto-sobre-a-visita-de-estado-a.
169 Interview with a Fiocruz representative, Maputo, 18 November 2013.

the humanitarian character of the project and Brazil's positive gesture in helping a sister country, while opposition senators criticised the measure, emphasising the precariousness of health care in Brazil, including the distribution of ARV drugs (Senado Federal, 2009).

Following approval of the funding, the ABC was assigned the task of carrying out the implementation process with the specialised know-how of Fiocruz and Farmanguinhos, which supplied the machines and technical knowledge. Construction work and the installation of equipment was undertaken from 2011. In mid-2012, the packaging line was initiated and about a year later, some pharmaceuticals were produced. Another five drugs were scheduled for production by December 2013.

Brazil's National Health Surveillance Agency (ANVISA) also took part in the process, assisting in the training of Mozambican professionals to create a regulatory body for the production and sanitary surveillance of pharmaceutical drugs in the country (FENAFAR, n.d.). These institutions worked with local counterparts: Mozambican technicians and other employees received capacity-building from Fiocruz, including in Brazil. Cooperation included Brazilian assistance at all stages, from the viability studies to the acquisition of equipment, technology transfer, technical qualification, registration and validation, and national and international accreditation. Institutional efforts also included the formulation of a plan for negotiations and guidance on questions of organisational sustainability (FIOTEC, 2012).

During Lula da Silva's visit to Mozambique in November 2010 – his last visit to an African country while President of Brazil – he referred to the project as a 'revolution' in the African fight against HIV/AIDS. During his following visit to the country in 2011, in a ceremony covered by the Brazilian and Mozambican media, he handed the Mozambican government the first shipment of ARVs manufactured in Brazil (Nevirapine 200 milligrams) but packed and labelled by the Mozambican plant (Mozambican Embassy, 2011). Over the course of the cooperation between the two states, 56 Mozambican employees were trained, five of whom received certificates from Lula da Silva for successfully completing the 'Production Technologies' module. This visit demonstrated Lula da Silva's commitment to implementing the plant and his influence on Brazil–Africa relations.

On the 21 July 2012, the Mozambican Pharmaceutical Association (SMM) was inaugurated in the presence of the vice-president of Brazil, Michel Temer, and the president of Fiocruz. This plant is important to Mozambique because, if successfully implemented in full, it will be able to help supply the internal demand for treatment. Furthermore, as the first fully public pharmaceutical plant in Africa, it would give Mozambique a prominent place on the continent (private companies produce small quantities of ARVs in Uganda, Kenya and South Africa). The plant began its operations with the packing, storage, quality control and distribution of Nevirapine produced in Brazil. The initial wave of production are three ARVs (Lamivudine/Zidovudine, Nevirapine and Ribavirin), with an annual total production of 226 million pharmaceutical units, and another five drugs are planned.

In addition to the ARVs, the production of 21 drugs is planned, including antibiotics, antianaemics, antihypertensives, anti-inflammatories, hypoglycaemics, diuretics, antiparasitics and corticosteroids – amounting to a projected annual production of 371 million pharmaceutical units, representing 226 million ARVs and 145 million other drugs (FIOTEC, 2012). Production at this scale would allow Mozambique to produce not only enough to treat its own population, but also a surplus that could be supplied to other African countries. If this materialises, this cooperation could affect the relationship between the Mozambican government and the international health system, and stimulate cooperation between Mozambique and other countries in southern Africa. Moreover, many of the agreements signed by Brazil with PALOPs, including Mozambique, contain clauses that permit triangulation to obtain funds from other international actors, including civil society entities (Torrontegui and Dallari, 2012). In Mozambique, some NGOs work in areas such as information campaigns and the distribution of condoms, two important examples being the Mozambican Aids Organization (MONASO) and the Italian Catholic NGO, *Comunidade de Sant'Egidio*. However, in general, these organisations have difficulty in participating or extending their activities due to funding shortages (Foller, 2013).

Other Brazilian actors – not linked to official cooperation – work in Mozambique and have a potential impact on health cooperation. Firstly, we can highlight a growing presence of Christian missionaries linked to Brazilian Evangelical churches, part of a movement described as transnational Brazilian Pentecostalism (Oro, 2004). Some of these missionaries participate in the care of people with HIV/AIDS (Kamp, 2011; BBC News Brasil, 2012). The growing activities of these churches can be related to the decline (and, possibly, contributing to the redefinition) of the role of traditional healers in Mozambique (Castro, 2010).

It is also worth highlighting the involvement of Vale in the health sector in Mozambique. As well as contributing to the construction of the plant in Matola through its social responsibility programme, Vale established – in partnership with USAID and the International Center for Reproductive Health – a nocturnal clinic in the region of Moatize, where the mining company operates. The clinic offers counselling and HIV/AIDS tests, and works in preventing sexually transmitted diseases.[170]

In relation to the interaction of Brazilian cooperation with the assistance of advanced countries, it is worth mentioning that, despite the SMM being a bilateral project, there are initiatives involving Brazil in other configurations in the health area, including the fight against HIV/AIDS in Mozambique. In 2010, Brazil (represented by the Ministry of Health, NAP and Fiocruz) entered into a triangular agreement with the United States (PEPFAR, Center for Diseases Control and Prevention and USAID) for a two-year project with an initial budget of US$3 million, aimed at strengthening the Mozambican response to combatting HIV/AIDS (Foller, 2013). This project – part of a wider agreement, which also includes components focused on food security and agriculture – aims to consolidate and expand cooperation projects already in progress with the Agricultural Research Institute of Mozambique (IIAM) and the Ministry of Education, among other institutions (O País, 2012).

The arrangement was surprising given that, between 2006 and 2008, a third of PEPFAR's funding was dedicated to sexual abstinence programmes, and partner institutions were obliged to sign a promise to repudiate prostitution, a fact that generated considerable controversy. PEPFAR was also initially criticised for funding brand ARVs rather than generic versions. In mid-2005, in protest to the restrictions imposed by PEPFAR's funding, the Brazilian government rejected US$40 million in assistance, which remained to be disbursed by the programme. In July of the same year, a telegram sent to Washington by the US Embassy in Maputo expressed a concern at the growth of Brazilian health cooperation in Mozambique. This document also recommended that the Brazilian experience in Mozambique was utilised, albeit with a degree of caution, given the political divergences. The text indicates that, already back in 2005, the US government had contemplated the possibility of collaborating with Brazil, in cooperation in Mozambique, in the fight against HIV/AIDS (Massad, 2011).

On the American side, the change in government (from Republican to Democrat) led to a partial relaxation of some of the norms relating to sexual abstinence, including in the PEPFAR, and may have opened new opportunities for cooperation. In relation to generics, the United States continues to press for stronger protection of intellectual property in the development and production of pharmaceuticals (Whitman, 2011). Despite these differences, the bilateral agreement was seen by the Brazilian side as an opportunity to combine forces. The ABC and MRE hosted a meeting in Brasília with representatives of the Ministry of Health, civil society and NGOs working on HIV/AIDS, as well as representatives of the CDC and USAID, with the objective of showing

---

170 Interview with Vale representative for corporate social responsibility, Maputo, November 2013.

the Brazilian response to the AIDS epidemic and to define the goals for the trilateral agreement (USAID, n.d.). This partnership was somewhat surprising given not only the divergences between US assistance and the Brazilian model of cooperation, but also because the Brazilian government is committed to negotiating compulsory licensing, which the US government opposes.

This turnabout is explained partly by the shrinkage in US funding. In 2010, the United States experienced wide-ranging budget cuts, and a trilateral agreement with Brazil – which has a degree of soft power in Mozambique – represented a way of supplementing US funds. Given that there already existed bilateral partnerships between Brazilian and US institutions such as Fiocruz and the CDC, the agreement would also allow better use of pre-established ties. Finally, the partnership with Brazil may also grant some legitimacy to USAID at a time when the agency has been widely criticised for channelling too much funding to hiring consultants. Although Brazilian cooperation in Mozambique is also subject to criticisms, thus far these have been concentrated primarily on the agricultural sector (Cabral and Shankland, 2012; Garcia, Kato and Fontes, 2012). However, it is important to emphasise that the project is just starting out: so far triangular cooperation in the HIV/AIDS area has not advanced in any substantial form.

Finally, it is worth emphasising the tenuous and irregular participation of the Brazilian cooperation institutions in more comprehensive arrangements in Mozambique's health sector, especially the Health Partners Group (HPG),[171] which aims to strengthen the coordination between diverse cooperation donors and providers. Brazil's irregular participation is in part due to being unable to maintain a fixed and constant presence of Fiocruz representatives in Maputo. Another factor is the Brazilian government's cautious posture in relation to the association with a forum in which so-called 'traditional donors' are present. Brazilian officials explain this position by pointing out that Brazil is not a 'donor' in Mozambique and that Brazil favours maintaining a bilateral relationship with Mozambique, avoiding any close association with the HPG's declarations or becoming formally connected to it.[172]

Conclusion

Brazilian cooperation in the fight against HIV/AIDS in Mozambique reflects the promotion of specific elements of a highly complex model developed at

---

171 For more details on the mechanism, see: http://www.afro.who.int/en/mozambique/who-country-office-mozambique/who-in-mozambique/partners-in-health-development.html.
172 Interview with Brazilian diplomat responsible for the health sector, Brazilian Embassy, Maputo, 27 November 2013.

domestic level in Brazil during the country's redemocratisation process in the 1980s. Seen by many states and organisations (inside and outside Brazil) as relatively successful, these elements are promoted by the Ministry of Health, in partnership with the ABC, as examples of public-policy innovation. In the case of HIV/AIDS treatment, the production of generic ARV drugs not only disseminates the Brazilian approach, it also serves to boost the nation's position in international debates on public-health policies. So far, however, implementation of the pharmaceutical plant has generated a series of challenges for the Brazilian government and local stakeholders alike. As well as the high cost of the plant, which has contributed to the slow pace of implementation, the cooperating parties have had to face the challenge of the project's long-term financial sustainability. Hence the process of establishing the SMM also illustrates a persistent limitation within Brazilian cooperation: its general inflexibility, given that any donation by Brazil requires a specific Bill, which once again highlights the importance of rethinking the existing legal structure, especially in a context in which Brazilian cooperation has acquired a higher profile and demands are greater.[173]

The installation of the pharmaceutical plant allows us to identify important lessons for Brazil. Firstly, the experience underlines the recognition of the importance of coordinating cooperation, which should be considered as important as the actual execution, as well as the recognition that both Brazil and the countries receiving Brazilian cooperation would benefit from a coherent institutional framework regulating its cooperation efforts. Secondly, the project highlights the importance of considering the political and institutional context in which a cooperation initiative is inserted. Unlike Brazilian civil society, which possesses a lengthy history of participation and activism in the health area, its Mozambican counterpart has few resources at its disposal and acts in a more restricted political context. Moreover, the state agencies in Brazil that are responsible for health are highly institutionalised (though not always efficient), while the Mozambican government has a lower level of organisational structuring. The construction of the SMM and its operationalisation may have a substantial impact in terms of fighting the HIV/AIDS epidemic in Mozambique, since – by allowing the local production of pharmaceutical drugs – the project, if implemented in full, would enable greater autonomy for the country in relation to treating the affected population. In terms of the relationship with international donors, the plant's operation will also strengthen the Mozambican state's capacity to respond to diseases like malaria, TB and hypertension, since the production of medications to control these diseases is also planned. However, we stress the need

---

173 Interview with Fiocruz Representative, Fiocruz Africa Office, Maputo, 18 November 2013.

for the ARVs used in Mozambique to be compatible with those used in other countries in the region, principally due to the high level of cross-border mobility, especially in relation to South Africa.[174]

This scenario generates a huge expectation regarding the plant's success and the response promoted by Brazilian cooperation. It also establishes the need for other donors to reconnect and reinvent their presence as the Mozambican state's capacity to act becomes stronger. While the relative isolation in which Brazilian South–South cooperation operates – despite the efforts to improve coordination between the outside actors working in Mozambique – does allow the Brazilian government to differentiate itself from these donors, it also limits the reach of Brazilian efforts. Consequently, the results of the plant – a unique and ambitious experiment for Brazilian cooperation as a whole – will be important, not only in fighting HIV/AIDS in Mozambique, but also in the wider debates on the possibilities and risks of South–South cooperation.

References

Abdenur, AE (2015) Organisation and politics in South–South cooperation: Brazil's technical cooperation in Africa, *Global Society*, **29** (3), pp 321–38.

A Tarde (2003) Fábrica contra o HIV custará US$ 23 milhões, 6 November. Available at: http://www.aids.gov.br/node/39761 (accessed 6 May 2013).

Agence France Press (AFP) (2012) Mozambique launches Brazil-funded drugs plant to battle HIV, 21 July. Available at: http://www.google.com/hostednews/afp/article/ALeqM5hMoQcsvKWZrFmNSyfx1SBz0NZQtA?docId=CNG.d4885a7204025260cf5dc5e7c1f26844.61 (accessed 6 May 2013).

Agência de Informação de Moçambique (2008) Tax revenue to fill any gap caused by Swedish aid reduction, 19 August.

Almeida, EL de and Kraychete, ES (2012) O discurso Brasileiro para a cooperação em Moçambique: Existe ajuda desinteressada? III Conferência Internacional do IESE, Moçambique: Acumulação e Transformação em Contexto de Crise Internacional, 4–5 September, Maputo, IESE.

Almeida, CM de, Campos, RP de, Buss, P, Ferreira, JR and Fonseca, LE (2009) Brazil's conception of South–South 'structural cooperation in health' in Global Forum Update on Research for Health 6.

Almeida, CM de, Campos, RP de, Buss, P, Ferreira, JR and Fonseca, LE (2010) A concepção Brasileira de cooperação Sul–Sul estruturante em saúde, *Reciis, Revista Eletrônica de Comunicação, Informação e Inovação em Saúde*, **4**, (1), pp 25–35, March. Available at: http://www6.ensp.fiocruz.br/radis/sites/default/files/pdf/a-concepcao-brasileira-de-cooperacao-sul-sul-estruturante-em-saude.pdf (accessed 6 May 2013).

BBC News Brasil (2012) Brasil cresce como 'exportador' de missionários cristãos, diz estudo, 2 March.

Bidaurratzaga-Aurre, E and Colom-Jaén, A (2012) HIV/AIDS policies in Mozambique and the new aid architecture: successes, shortcomings and the way forward, *The Journal of Modern African Studies*, 50 (2), pp 225–52.

Bliss, K (ed.) (2010) *Key Players in Global Health: How Brazil, Russia, India, China, and South Africa*

---

174 Interview with Dr Marco Vitoria, WHO, Geneva, 13 December 2013.

are influencing the game. Washington, DC: Center for Strategic and International Studies.

Blog da Saúde 'Aids' (2012) Cooperação entre Brasil e Moçambique vai produzir lotes contra o HIV, 5 January. Available at: http://www.blog.saude.gov.br/aids-cooperacao-entre-brasil-e-mocambique-vai-produzir-lotes-contra-o-virus-hiv/ (accessed 6 May 2013).

Buss, P (2011) Brasil: estruturando a cooperação na saúde, *The Lancet* (Saúde no Brasil). Available at: www.thelancet.com (accessed 6 May 2013).

Cabral, L and Shankland, A (2012) Brazil's agriculture cooperation in Africa: new paradigms?' III Conferência Internacional do IESE 'Moçambique: acumulação e transformação em contexto de crise internacional' 4–5 September, Maputo, IESE. Conference Paper No. 23.

Cabral, L and Weinstock, J (2008) Diplomacia da saúde e cooperação Sul–Sul: As experiências da Unasul Campos Mello, Patricia 'Itamaraty diz não ter como cobrir despesas' Folha de São Paulo, 29 January 2015. Available at: http://www1.folha.uol.com.br/mundo/2015/01/1579222-itamaraty-diz-nao-ter-como-cobrir-despesas.shtml (Accessed 3 December 2015).

Cabral, L and Weinstock, J (2010) *Brazil: An emerging aid player. Lessons on emerging donors, and South–South trilateral cooperation*, ODI Briefing Paper No. 64.

Castro, E (2010) Igrejas evangélicas Brasileiras crescem em Moçambique 'Agência Brasil, 24 December. Available at: http://agenciabrasil.ebc.com.br/noticia/2010-12-24/igrejas-evangelicas-brasileiras-crescem-em-mocambique (accessed 6 May 2013).

Cau, HS (2011) A Construção do Estado em Moçambique e as Relações com o Brasil, Tese de doutorado apresentada ao Programa de Pós. Graduação em Ciência Política da Universidade Federal do Rio Grande do Sul, Porto Alegre.

Chaturvedi, S (2011) *South–South Cooperation in Health and Pharmaceuticals: Emerging trends in India-Brazil collaborations*, Research and Information System for Developing Countries, Discussion Paper No. 172.

Chaves, GC, Vieira, MF and Reis, R (2008) Acesso a medicamentos e propriedade intelectual no Brasil: reflexões e estratégias da sociedade civil, *Sur, Rev. Int. Direitos Human*, **5** (8), pp 170–98.

Chin, G and Quadir, F (2012) Introduction: Rising states, rising donors and the global aid regime, *Cambridge Review of International Affairs*, **25** (4), pp 493–506.

Costa Leite, I (2012) Solidarity, interests and professionalization in Brazilian proivison of international cooperation: The More Food Africa case. In C Ayala and J Rivera (eds) *De la Diversidad a la Consonancia: La CSS latinoamericana*. Mexico, DF, Instituto Mora.

Costa Leite, I, Suyama, B and Pomeroy, M (2013) *Africa–Brazil Co-operation in Social Protection: Drivers, lessons and shifts in the engagement of the Brazilian Ministry of Social Development*, UN WIDER Working Paper No. 22.

Danese, S (1999) *Diplomacia presidencial: História e crítica*. Rio de Janeiro: Topbooks.

Dávila, JH (2010) *Hotel Trópico: Brazil and the challenge of African decolonization, 1950–1980*. Durham, NC: Duke University Press.

Embaixada de Moçambique (2001) Acondicionado na Matola: Lula da Silva procede a entrega de anti-retrovirais. Available at: http://www.mozambique.org.br/pt/index.php/100-acondicionado-na-matola-lula-da-silva-procede-a-entrega-de-anti-retrovirais (accessed 6 May 2013).

FENAFAR (n.d.) Brasil vai ajudar no combate à Aids em Moçambique' Federação Nacional dos Farmacêuticos. Available at: http://www.fenafar.org.br/portal/todos-os-artigos/1-ultimas-noticias/123-brasil-vai-ajudar-no-combate-a-aids-em-mocambique.html (accessed 6 May 2013).

FIOTEC (2012) The first antiretrovirals manufacturing site in Mozambique starts operations; project supported by Fiotec, Fundação para o Desenvolvimento Científico e Tecnológico em Saúde, Divisão de Comunicação Social da Fundação Osvaldo Cruz.

Available at: http://www.fiotec.fiocruz.br/institucional/index.php?option=com_content&view=article&id=1077:the-first-antiretrovirals-manufacturing-site-in-mozambique-starts-operations-project-supported-by-fiotec&catid=133&Itemid=364&lang=en (accessed 6 May 2013).

Follér, M-L (2013) South–South cooperation: Brazilian partnership with Mozambique and the construction of an AIDS drug plant, *Austral: Brazilian Journal of Strategy and International Relations*, **2** (3), pp 167–91.

Garcia, AS, Kato, K and Fontes, C (2012) A história contada pela caça ou pelo caçador? Perspectivas sobre o Brasil em Angola e Moçambique, *Políticas Alternativas para o Cone Sul*.

Global Health Strategies Initiative (2012) *The BRICS Report: How the BRICS are reshaping global health and development*, New York: GHSI.

Institute of Applied Economic Research (IPEA) (2010) *Cooperação Brasileira para o Desenvolvimento Internacional: 2005–2009*. Brasília, DF.

Inoue, CYA and Vaz, AC (2012) Brazil as a Southern donor: Beyond hierarchy and national interests in development cooperation? *Cambridge Review of International Affairs*, **25** (4), pp 507–34.

Kamp, L (2011) *Violent conversion: Brazilian Pentecostalism and the urban pioneering of women in Mozambique*. Amsterdam, VU University Press.

Kickbusch, I, Silberschmidt, G and Buss, PM (2007) Global health diplomacy: The need for new perspectives, strategic approaches and skills in global health, *Bulletin WHO*, **85** (3), pp 230–2.

Lima, TGF and Campos Mello, RP (2010) perfil dos projetos de cooperação técnica brasileira em Aids no mundo: explorando potenciais hipóteses de estudo' *RECIIS Revista Eletrônica de Com. In. Invo. e Saúde* **4** (1), pp 119–33.

Martin, M, Watts, R and Rabinowitz, G (2012) *Monitoring Implementation of the Busan Partnership Agreement: Why 'global light' and 'country-focused' must work together effectively*. Study prepared for Actionaid, Concord, Oxfam, Save the Children and UK Aid Network, April.

Massad, A (2011) EUA se preocuparam com modelo anti-AIDS brasileiro em Moçambique, *Pública*, 29 June. Available at: http://www.apublica.org/2011/06/wikileaks-eua-se-preocuparam-com-modelo-anti-aids-brasileiro-em-mocambique/ (accessed 6 May 2013).

Mawdsley, E (2012) *From Recipients to Donors: Emerging powers and the changing development landscape*. London: Zed Books.

McEwan, C and Mawdsley, E (2012) Trilateral development cooperation: Power and politics in emerging aid relationships, *Development and Change*, **43** (6), pp 1185–209.

Ministry of Health, Brazil (Ministério da Saúde do Brasil) (2002) Programa de Cooperação Internacional para Ações de Prevenção e Controle do HIV/AIDS para Outros Países em Desenvolvimento, Brasília, June.

Ministry of Health, Brazil (Ministério da Saúde do Brasi (2011) Alexandre Padilha Interview, em *Health Cooperation: Brazilian International Health Activities Bulletin* (4), May, pp 4–5.

Ministry of Health, Brazil (Ministério da Saúde do Brasil) (2012) Aids| Cooperação entre Brasil e Moçambique vai produzir lotes contra o HIV, 5 de janeiro de 2012. Available at: http://www.blog.saude.gov.br/aids-cooperacao-entre-brasil-e-mocambique-vai-produzir-lotes-contra-o-virus-hiv/ (accessed 6 May 2013).

Ministry of Health, Mozambique (Ministério de Saúde da República de Moçambique) (2007) Termos de Referência da Abordagem Sectorial Ampla (SWAp) Saúde. Maputo.

MRE (2003) Comunicado Conjunto sobre a visita de Estado à República da Namíbia do Presidente Luiz Inácio Lula da Silva (Windhoek, 6–7 November 2003), Nota à Imprensa No. 523, 7 November.

MRE (2008) Ajuste complementar ao acordo geral de cooperação entre o governo da República Federativa do Brasil e o Governo da República de Moçambique para a implementação do projeto 'capacitação em produção de medicamentos anti-retrovirais e outros medicamentos'. Brasilia, 4 September.

MRE (2010) *Balanço de Política Externa. Relações com África.* Tema: Saúde. Available at: http://www.itamaraty.gov.br/temas/balanco-de-politica-externa-2003-2010/2.2.4-africa-saude (accessed 6 May 2013).

Nauta, W (2011) Mobilising Brazil as a significant other in the fight for HIV/Aids treatment in South Africa: the treatment action campaign (TAC) and its global allies. In T Dietz, K Havnevik, M Kaag and T Oestigaard (eds) *African Engagements: Africa negotiating an emerging multipolar world*. Leiden: Brill Publishers.

Nunn, A (2009) *The Politics and History of AIDS Treatment in Brazil.* New York: Springer.

Nye, J (2004) *Soft Power: The means to success in world politics*. New York: Public Affairs.

O País (2012) Moçambique, Brasil e EUA acordam cooperação técnica na saúde e agricultura, 24 January. Available at: http://www.opais.co.mz/index.php/component/content/article/45-sociedade/18637-mocambique-brasil-e-eua-acordam-cooperacao-tecnica-na-saude-e-agricultura.html (accessed 6 May 2013).

OPLOP (2012) Em Moçambique, doadores cortam apoio ao Conselho Nacional de Combate ao Sida, *Boletim OPLOP*, **87**, 1 October.

Organização Mundial da Saúde (2013) *Partners in Health Development: Mozambique.* Available at: http://www.afro.who.int/en/mozambique/who-country-office-mozambique/who-in-mozambique/partners-in-health-development.html (accessed 6 May 2013).

Oro, AP (2004) A presença religiosa brasileira no exterior: O caso da Igreja Universal do Reino de Deus, *Estudos Avançados*, **18** (52), pp 139–55.

Penha, E (2012) Brasil vai inaugurar na África fábrica de remédio para tratamento da Aids, 13 July. Agência Brasil. Available at: http://agenciabrasil.ebc.com.br/noticia/2012-07-13/brasil-vai-inaugurar-na-africa-fabrica-de-remedio-para-tratamento-da-aids (accessed 6 May 2013).

PEPFAR (n.d.) Partnership to Fight HIV/AIDS in Mozambique: The United States President's Emergency Plan for Aid (PEPFAR). Available at: http://www.pepfar.gov/countries/mozambique/ (accessed 6 May 2013).

Pfeiffer, J (2003) International NGOs and primary health care in Mozambique: the need for a new model of collaboration, *Social Science & Medicine*, **56** (4), pp 725–738.

Renzio, P de and Hanlon, J (2009) Mozambique: Contested sovereignty? The dilemmas of aid dependence. In L Whitfield (ed.) *The Politics of Aid: African strategies for dealing with donors*. Oxford: Oxford University Press, pp 246–70.

República de Moçambique (2010) Plano Estratégico Nacional de Resposta ao HIV e SIDA, 2010–2014. Conselho de Ministros, Maputo.

Russo, G, Cabral, L and Ferrinho, P (2013) Brazil–Africa technical cooperation in health: What is its relevance to the post-Busan debate on aid effectiveness? *Globalization and Health*, **9** (2).

Smith, BH (1990) *More than Altruism: The politics of private foreign aid*. Princeton, NJ: Princeton University Press.

Senado Federal, 'Doação para Moçambique fabricar remédio contra Aids passa na CAE, 10 September 2009. Available at: http://www12.senado.gov.br/noticias/materias/2009/11/10/doacao-para-mocambique-fabricar-remedio-contra-aids-passa-na-cae (accessed 6 May 2013).

SIECUS (n.d.) Brazil rejects US HIV/Aids fund' Sexuality Information and Education Council of the United States. Available at: http://www.siecus.org/index.cfm?fuseaction=Feature.showFeature&featureid=1278&pageid=483&parentid=478 (accessed 6 May 2013).

Sotero, P (2009) Brazil as an Emerging Donor. Huge potential and growing pains. *Development Outreach*. Washington, DC: World bank, pp 18–20.

UNAIDS (2010) *Global Report. UNAIDS Report on the Global AIDS Epidemic, 2010*. Geneva: UNAIDS.

UNAIDS (2012) *Country Report for Mozambique. Global AIDS response progress report*. Source:

http://www.unaids.org/en/regionscountries/countries/mozambique/ (accessed 6 May 2013).

USAID (n.d.) *Triangular cooperation: United States, Brazil and Mozambique*. Mozambique delegation visits São Paulo and Brasília. Available at: http://brazil.usaid.gov/en/node/520 (accessed 6 May 2013).

Valoi, T (2012) Doadores cortam todo o financiamento ao CNCS, *O País*, 20 September. Available at: http://opais.sapo.mz/index.php/sociedade/45-sociedade/22269-doadores-cortam-todo-o-financiamento-ao-cncs.html (accessed 6 May 2013).

Wadia, R (2001) Brazil's AIDS policy earns global lauds, 16 August, CNN News. Available at: http://archives.cnn.com/2001/WORLD/americas/08/14/brazil.AIDS/ (accessed 6 May 2013).

Whitman, E (2011) Rich nations step up assault on generic Aids drugs, *The Guardian*, 10 June.

Zililo Piri, M (2012) The political economy of Mozambique twenty years on: A post conflict success story? *South African Journal of International Affairs*, **19** (2), pp 223–45.

Chapter 11

Resettled by Coal: Vale in Mozambique

Joana Pedro

'Resettled communities paralyse activities of Vale Moçambique.'
CanalMoz, 11 January 2012

On 10 January 2012, Cateme, one of Moatize neighbourhoods, made the headlines in Mozambican newspapers. Within a few days, the news had reached other corners of the world (see, for example, All Africa, 2012; Angola Press, 2012; *Jornal do Brasil*, 2012) and, over the year, the major global newspapers (Polgreen, 2012). In this area – where the Brazilian company Vale SA[175] had resettled more than 1 000 families between 2009 and 2011, removing them from the area of the new Moatize mine concession in Tete province, northwest Mozambique – the inhabitants blocked the Sena railway line transporting the mine's coal to the port of Beira to protest their living conditions. The government responded by sending in the army and the police which repressed the demonstration violently.

This situation was not unknown in Mozambique and some associations, such as Justiça Ambiental (Friends of the Earth Mozambique), the Centre for Public Integrity (CIP) and the World Wide Fund for Nature (WWF), had already been highlighting the discontent of the populations affected by resettlement for some time.

After this incident, many institutes, journalists and non-governmental organisations (NGOs) rushed to the locality, trying to conduct interviews and obtain testimonies. However, the government restricted visits to the resettlement to a minimum as if these populations lived under the protection of some sovereign agency (Santos, 2012). The Mozambican NGOs also wrote open letters to the then Mozambican president Armando Guebuza asking him to help humanise the resettlement process.[176]

In 2011, between the months of March and August, I had the opportunity to conduct fieldwork as part of my Master's research, investigating precisely the

---
175 A Brazilian mining company present in more than 37 countries.
176 See, for example: Liga dos Direitos Humanos *et al.* 2012.

resettlement process implemented by Vale. For 10 days, I conducted interviews and ran focus groups with the resettled populations and, for more than six months, I was able to interview diverse actors involved in the different stages of the process, including Vale employees and members of the local government.

The primary aim of this chapter is to explore ways of discussing the circumstances that led to the reported events, based on fieldwork carried out in 2011, and attempt to frame this resettlement programme within the relations between Mozambique and Brazil. The paper covers only a period until 2013. My aim is also to explore the strategies that are deemed necessary to prevent these kinds of news reports from returning to the newspaper headlines.

The coal rush

> 'At the start, Vale sent a team to woo us, saying that there was going to be a company arriving that was going to mine coal, meaning that we would be leaving, we'd be moving to Malupancha, meaning this place, Cateme. At the time we thought it was a lie, until we realised that it was true and that we really were coming here' (inhabitant of Cateme, interviewed in June 2011).

The history of coal exploration in Moatize, Tete Province, can be traced back to the colonial era, beginning in 1895. From 1982 onward, however, as armed conflict became widespread, a large proportion of mining activities were shut down (Rio Doce Moçambique, 2006a). In 2004, in a climate of increasing security and development in the country, Mozambique's Ministry of Mineral Resources and Energy announced an international tender to select a developer to mine the Moatize coal field (Aurecon, 2010). In parallel, a year earlier, the policies of the incoming president, Luiz Inácio Lula da Silva, had concretised Brazil's interest in Africa, which had already started flourishing in the 1990s (Almeida and Kraychete, 2012), by structuring them on more solid bases as part of the wider objective of expanding Brazil's global profile (World Bank, 2012; *The Economist*, 2012). In November of the same year, therefore, following two official state visits by Lula da Silva to Mozambique (Almeida and Kraychete, 2012), the Mozambican government granted mining rights to coal fields in Moatize to the Brazilian company Vale Moçambique (Aurecon, 2010).

However, this company is not the only mining firm in the region. The discovery of one of the world's largest coal deposits was followed by an enormous influx of mining companies and, currently, 34 per cent of Tete Province is already under concessions – a figure set to rise to 60 per cent if all the pending licenses are approved (Human Rights Watch, 2013) (Figure 11.1).

These undertakings, together with the construction of associated infrastructural works, such as highways, bridges and railways, have diverse social and environmental impacts, one of the most visible being the appropriation of lands occupied by communities that are subsequently forced to abandon these localities. This removal from the population's homeland should, from the outset, be accompanied by a resettlement process, implemented by the 'owner' of the project in cooperation with the government, followed by adaptation to the new reality – a process that spans from eviction to the creation of new communities, and referred to as 'forced resettlement'.

Development refugees

> 'It was the site where I grew up and always lived, which is why I felt so tied to there' (inhabitant of 25 de Setembro, interviewed in June 2011).

In socio-economic terms, forced resettlement affects the lives of people and communities, leading to the disruption of their everyday reality and a potential rupture in their networks of sociability. Change is a traumatic experience, which leads to the breakup of community ties established over years of interaction between the community and its spaces. According to Dowing (1996), although it might be thought in principle that this type of resettlement would be easier than those experienced by other kinds of refugees, given that the people involved do not lose contact with one another and maintain their families and neighbours, the truth is that the communities forced to leave their lands disintegrate, causing a social breakdown. Cernea (1996) adds that these populations suffer very similar traumas to war refugees or those fleeing natural disasters: they are 'development refugees'.

But unlike other types of refugees, these 'development refugees', as Colson (1994) also refers to them, cannot return home: their homes and the connections that tied them to their homeland are destroyed forever. Hence coercively resettled populations face rapid and massive changes that affect the very heart of their communities.

Recognising the inevitable social and economic costs for the affected communities, various authors have argued that resettlements should be avoided entirely, but if they do take place, should be undertaken accompanied by numerous safeguards (Cernea, 1997). In situations where resettlement is unavoidable, the following principles should be adopted (Cernea, 1996; World Bank Operation Evaluation Department, 2000):

- The existence of policies and norms protecting the rights of settled repopulations;
- Allocation of sufficient resources, internalising the costs from the initial phases;
- Empowerment of the resettled populations, giving them a voice and enabling them to participate in decisions and in the resettlement process;
- Planning for income-generation opportunities and ongoing assistance to the resettled population until it reinvents survival strategies;
- Joint work with NGOs, the private sector, government agencies and external donors to lower risks and increase the chances of success.

Ultimately, the main challenge of resettlement is prevention, seeking to avoid the impoverishment of the populations concerned (Cernea, 1997). As Clark (2000) points out, although the emphasis should not be placed on recuperating living conditions, which suggests a stagnation or deterioration resulting from the project's installation, but rather the immediate improvement of living conditions, which presumes the implementation of a community development project, in parallel with the economic development project that led to the resettlement.

In Mozambique, the importance of forced resettlements was legally recognised in 2012 with the approval of the regulation for resettlements on 8 August, through Decree 31/2012, after the Vale resettlement had already been concluded. This regulation establishes the rules and basic principles applicable to the resettlement process, with the aim of promoting the life quality of citizens and protecting the environment.

The New World

> 'There we had where to go and knew how to live, it was our native land. But here this land is new to us, everything is always new, everything is new to us' (inhabitant of Cateme, interviewed in June 2011).

In the case study presented here, 1 046 families living in an area of 10 912 hectares were resettled as part of the implementation of the Moatize coal project by the company Vale SA, in Tete Province in the northwest of Mozambique.

A Resettlement Action Plan (RAP) was elaborated in preparation, comprising three modules: knowledge of the real situation on the ground, the creation of the RAP and implementation of the RAP.

The set of actions involved in formulating the RAP was preceded by debates with the government, which led to the creation of a Resettlement

Committee in March 2006, with the objective of overseeing the planned works. This committee was composed of representatives from the provincial councils (including the sectors of Mineral Resources, Environmental Action Coordination, Public Works and Housing, and Agriculture), as well as the administrator of the Moatize district and the president of the Moatize Municipal Council, without any representation from the community leaders. The committee was headed by the permanent secretary of the Tete Province government (Pedro, 2011).

Analysing the territory involved, we can discern two types of human settlement. The first, which includes the communities from the districts of Chithata, Bagamoyo and Chipanga (30 per cent of the resettled population), shows peri-urban characteristics, located in Moatize town. The second, composed of scattered nucleuses belonging to the settlements of Mithethe and Malabwé (70 per cent of the resettled population), shows rural characteristics and is situated in the territory belonging to the administrative district of Moatize (Rio Doce Moçambique, 2006b).

According to their rural or urban classification, the transferred families were resettled either in Cateme (those considered rural) or 25 de Setembro, another Moatize neighbourhood (those considered urban). In addition, close to 25 per cent of all the families received two forms of compensation: assisted compensation (7.2 per cent), which involved help to families that declined to move to the resettled areas, helping them find and buy a new house elsewhere; and simple compensation (17.7 per cent), which involved the direct exchange of their assets for a determined amount (Aurecon, 2010).

The area in Cateme was chosen to resettle the rural population after being evaluated by the government and the company as suitable for farming activities and presenting the best topographical conditions in terms of supplying water and other forms of accessibility. The area was chosen to meet their housing needs, as well as establish conditions for access to land for crop cultivation. This is an area of approximately 3 800 hectares in the Moatize district, some 36 kilometres from Moatize town (previously, the people living furthest away were 10 kilometres distant) and 11 kilometres from the main highway (N7). The latter is reached along an unpaved road in a poor state of conservation, making access difficult (Pedro, 2011).

The 25 de Setembro neighbourhood, situated in the west zone of Moatize town, took in the affected population considered to pursue an urban lifestyle. Their location in Moatize town allows the resettled population continued access to their workplaces and other facilities to which they were accustomed before resettlement. Both the Cateme housing developments and those of 25 de Setembro were designed in linear plots in a grid formation alongside straight roads, nothing like the traditional patterns. The organisation in residential plots, non-residential plots and green areas follows the model of the communal villages (Raposo, 1999), a form of organisation contrasting strongly with the typically dispersed spatial organisation (Austral and Impacto, 2006), forcing the inhabitants to create new ways of living in this space.

As well as this grid-like form of organisation, very different from the traditional, it is impossible not to note the lack of free space, leisure areas and central spaces capable of functioning as meeting points for the population. In Cateme, non-habitational plots were left clear around the standpipes, intended for use by those wanting to open shops or traditional-style communal spaces, like churches. At the time of the research, though, this had yet to happen.

The houses for these new settlements were designed by an architectural office in Maputo and constructed by CETA, a Mozambican construction company owned by INSITEC group headed up by Celso Correia, current Minister of Land, Environnment and Rural Development and well connected with the former president Armando Guebuza. The houses include the main house, an open kitchen and a latrine/WC, as well as some annexed buildings. The housing model – the same for the rural and peri-urban populations – is much closer to the kind used by the population of the peri-urban area. This includes, for example, cement walls (for a population who derive one of their largest sources of income from making bricks) and glass windows (a fragile material, which is very difficult to replace for populations living in the rural zone).

The size of the new houses was based on the previous houses, without considering any expansion of the families. It will be difficult, therefore, for the residents to find the financial resources to increase the size of their dwellings, maintaining the current conditions. Some mismatch between the provided infrastructure and the population's reality is to be expected – already shown, for example, by the fact that many families have walled off the kitchen to use it as an extra room or even as a primary dwelling (Pedro, 2011).

In terms of construction quality, the houses already displayed a series of problems after about a year of use, including cracks, holes in the roofs and drainage problems in the latrines. Compounding these issues was the population's distrust of the building techniques used, especially the fact that the houses had been constructed without foundations, a point highlighted in all the focal groups and interviews.

These questions were exacerbated by the fact that the population had not been included in the process of building their own homes, which meant that they felt as if the homes were not really theirs – particularly relevant given that 90 per cent of people in the community had lived in houses built by themselves (Rio Doce Moçambique, 2006b).

While a model house was constructed initially for the community leaders to tour and suggest changes and improvements, the fact is that by this time there was little room to make any significant alterations. In terms of the organisational layout of the district itself, the only consultation made was over the choice of neighbours.

In relation to education and health care, two schools were built in Cateme, one primary and the other secondary, with the capacity to take in all the resettled children and young people, as well as those already living in the host area. A new health centre with a maternity unit was also constructed. These infrastructures were built by Vale but handed over to the government, which is responsible for their administration and management and for hiring staff.

In Cateme we can also highlight the construction of an *Estação de Conhecimento* (Knowledge Station), today called *Fazenda Modelo* (Model Farm), which aims to run technical courses for the local population. In the 25 de Setembro neighbourhood, no new schools were constructed, although existing schools were reformed in Moatize town to have the capacity to take in the new influx of students. Plans also existed for the construction of a health centre in the district. This finally opened in March 2013.

Only Cateme's main avenue has street lighting (all the homes that had and continue to have electricity were located around this street) and water is supplied via standpipes. Plans existed for the construction of a concrete water tank, which would supply the entire community via gravity feed. However, various plastic tanks were built first on wooden structures to feed the standpipes via gravity feed. This supply system has a short life span and depends on electric pumps to raise the water to the tanks.

In the 25 de Setembro neighbourhood, people have access to water piped to their own backyards, although most of the population uses the standpipes found in the neighbouring district as they lack the money to pay for the mains water. An identical situation occurs with the electrical supply, also installed in all the district's homes.

'So what are we going to live off now?'

> 'People don't live better here because there is no way of making money' (inhabitant of Cateme, interviewed in June 2011).

The main objective of the resettlements should be to improve, or at least restore, the survival strategies and everyday life of the affected populations (Cernea, 1999). In a resettlement, the infrastructure is normally the easiest thing to replace, the biggest difficulty is enabling people to recreate their spaces and survival strategies.

The resettled populations of both Cateme and 25 de Setembro depend on family farming for their subsistence (Austral and Impacto, 2006) and, indeed, it is the rhythms of agriculture that structure the everyday life of the populations and guarantee their survival, even those inhabiting the peri-urban districts.

Hence, one of the key elements of the sustainability of resettlement should be family farming. This includes, for instance, the transition from a dry farming system to an irrigation system and a form of agriculture using new, more productive and sustainable techniques (avoiding slash-burn agriculture with its negative impact on the environment), incentives for the population to organise in associations and cooperatives, and access to loans and farming subsidies.

In the 25 de Setembro resettlement, the families had no right to *machambas* (fields), contradicting earlier plans, since no land had been allocated by the government for this purpose. While it is true that all the families resettled in the area have at least one person with a fixed job, assuring some income, as the studies reveal, family farming continued to play a fundamental role in their monthly budget. Losing the *machambas* has had a very negative impact, therefore, further reducing their income options. In a district where, for example, water must be paid for, this can degenerate into serious and chronic situations of poverty. The importance of *machambas* for peri-urban families has been widely studied in the African context, evaluated as an important source of extra income for industrial workers (Andræ, 1992) and extremely important when faced with crises or problems (see, for example, Gefu, 1992; Mlozi, 1992). Hence these families should have been resettled after the government had decided not only on where the houses would be built, but also where the *machambas* would be located.

In Cateme, one hectare of *machamba* was allocated to each family, half the area previously agreed on. However, various problems have been observed in this case too. For example, the fact that some *machambas* were taken from previous owners raises another substantial problem: namely, that the main resettlement has also provoked another, smaller resettlement. Indeed, the Cateme area already had a resident population, which was resettled alongside the population coming from the Moatize area. *Machambas* also existed in this area and the owners had to be compensated for their loss.

The question of the low productivity of the *machambas* was also cited in all the focus groups. Explanations given included low soil fertility, the invasion of *machambas* by animals and the lack of water. This was ignored even if studies demonstrated the the poor agricultural potential of the soils where the population were relocated and this was a constant complaint in the discussion forums, principally the stony soil (Rio Doce Moçambique, 2006c; Human Rights Watch, 2013).

In terms of invasion by animals, the *machambas* allocated to the incoming population are situated very close to the houses, unlike the situation prior to resettlement, when more than half the population took more than an hour to reach their fields (Austral and Impacto, 2006). This was due, in part, to people looking for land with better agricultural potential for their plantations, but also because pet animals traditionally wandered freely through the village, destroying any *machambas* located too close to the settlements. The journey that people had to make every day to reach their *machambas* also frequently provided time for socialisation.

Another issue frequently raised, particularly by the Malabwé community that used to cultivate land along the shores of the Revúboè River, was the lack of water for agriculture and livestock. It is important to note that prior to resettlement, most of the population also cultivated various vegetable crops, especially in the low-lying areas close to rivers, which they basically used for their own subsistence (Austral and Impacto, 2006).

As well as agriculture, other survival strategies have been disrupted. Young people in Cateme, for example, said that in the past they would gather up a small bundle of firewood and take it by bicycle to the town of Moatize to sell. This has now become extremely difficult since the new settlement was built some 30 kilometres from the town.

Indeed, the resettlement of people and communities in zones far from their earlier places of residence, and thus the productive resources and markets to which they once had access, is considered an obstacle to the recuperation of survival strategies – something that seems to be happening already in Cateme.

In the rural housing development, an informal market had already emerged. However, this serves only local people, with little purchasing power, and no outside money enters to stimulate the local economy.

Other forms of work were also underestimated during the resettlement process, notably fishing, which the Malabwé population used to rely on. No study exists on this topic. There is also the question of the potteries (*oleiros* in Portuguese), who were producing clay bricks on the property that is now occupied by the mine and one of the groups harshly affected by the resettlement organised a series of demonstrations against Vale and not only blocked the Sena railway, but also the access to the coal mine.[177] The

---

177   For more details see Campbell (2013).

owners were given monetary compensation by Vale, but they considered it unsatisfactory and continued to protest. Equally, nothing was provided for other people who worked in the pottery sector, albeit informally. Pottery activities were not resumed in Cateme because the area is located far from the sales points, nor in 25 de Setembro because potters must now apply for a licence and people are unwilling to shift from the informal system, to which they were accustomed, to the formal system, normally inaccessible to populations with fewer financial resources (Pedro, 2011).

In fact, most of the resettled population is unemployed and it is a highly significant factor that people are now living at a greater distance from the areas in which the mining project was created. These populations, the most affected by the mining operation, have little access to the job opportunities created by it. In a context involving huge expectations for employment, this situation may well contribute to future social conflicts.

The Knowledge Station, which opened in 2012 under the name of Fazenda Modelo, offering professional training courses, is put forward as one solution to the unemployment issue. However, even with these courses, and considering the extreme importance of training, the definition of a survival strategy based on training alone will be insufficient to restore the economic wellbeing of these families. As Yunus (2006) emphasises, in the real world the poor are not poor because they lack training or are illiterate: they are poor because they cannot retain any income from their work.

Yunus (2006) also stresses that poor people do not need to be taught how to survive: this they already know. Rather, it is more important to give the resettled population access to loans or provide job opportunities, allowing them to put into practice skills that they already possess. The money that they earn then becomes a key instrument in enabling them to acquire new skills in the future, at which stage the Knowledge Station/Fazenda Modelo could, indeed, prove extremely important.

The risks of resettlements

> 'Now everyone's unemployed, there's no money' (inhabitant of 25 de Setembro, interviewed in June 2011).

Despite the studies undertaken on the social impact of resettlements, the kinds of mistakes identified in these works continued to be repeated with dramatic impacts on the social experiences of dislocated populations. Most resettlements fail to improve, or even recover, the survival strategies and everyday lives of the populations (Cernea, 1999).

Cernea (1999) identifies eight risks to avoid during resettlement, each of which can lead to the impoverishment of the resettled populations: the risk of becoming landless; the risk of unemployment; the risk of becoming homeless; the risk of marginalisation; the risk of food insecurity; the risk of increased mortality rates; the risk of losing access to collective resources; and the risk of social breakdown. According to Cernea, the success of a resettlement depends, to a large extent, on the capacity to avoid these risks. Consequently, each risk is analysed here to perceive how far they were considered in the Vale resettlement programme. Suggestions are also made as to how these mistakes could have been avoided or how they may still be remedied.

- **Risk of becoming landless:** In Cateme, though not a present reality, this risk exists due to the conflicts with the former occupants of the *machambas*, with a portion of the resettled population complaining that they have lost their lands. In 25 de Setembro, this risk became concrete as the population lost their agricultural lands and, thus, the basis for their productive systems and everyday livelihoods.

  In Cateme, perceiving how the customary systems of the local population operate, including the practices surrounding land acquisitions, would have helped to prevent this risk. Indeed, although the compensation required by Mozambican law had been awarded to the former owners of the *machambas*, they are likely to feel that the land is theirs still, believing that they have the right to use it or even grant access to it, but through the receipt of a monthly or annual rental fee, as various studies of communal villages have shown (Raposo, 1999; Geffray, 1991). Therefore, it will be important to resolve this problem by respecting traditional forms of land tenure and rights.

  In relation to 25 de Setembro, this risk could have been avoided had the removal and transfer of the population taken place only after the government had made land available for agriculture. To remedy this problem, while the new land is being found, access should be given to lands that are not yet in use within the Vale concession.

- **Risk of unemployment:** Given the distance of Cateme's inhabitants from Moatize town and the Vale mining project, an employment strategy based solely on training is likely to lead to chronic levels of unemployment among the population. To solve this situation, transportation schemes need to be created between Cateme and Moatize town and the mining project to provide transport for those wishing to benefit from the work opportunities in these areas. A loan system should also be considered for funding small projects, as well as financial and institutional incentives for cooperatives and small businesses.

The 25 de Setembro district is located within the urban perimeter of Moatize town, meaning that the population remains close to their jobs and they can also try to benefit from the new opportunities provided by the new mining project.

- **Risk of becoming homeless:** This risk was avoided since everyone had the right to housing. However, the fact that the houses were built using an unfamiliar construction style and from materials unavailable to the population could lead to critical issues in the future. This applies particularly to young people who will probably no longer wish to revert to the traditional type of house, but will also be unable to build a house in the new style. This risk could become a reality in both resettlement areas.

  The possibility of using construction techniques using earth should be studied, employing materials with which people are already familiar, but through the application of new and more resistant techniques, which are still, nonetheless, accessible to most of the population.

  Today the construction of some infrastructural works using earth-construction techniques could also be studied. These projects could employ a local workforce, allowing the population to learn the new techniques and stimulating them to build their own houses in the future, without needing to rely on the blocks of concrete used in the resettlement houses, which most people lack the financial means to purchase.

- **Risk of marginalisation:** In the case of Cateme, this risk was exacerbated by the distance at which the population was located from Moatize town. This barred its inhabitants from a series of job opportunities, both in the town and in the mining project. The resettled population was the victim of economic and geographic marginalisation, meaning that the Cateme resettlement should have been placed closer to where the population had previously resided. Since this risk is very closely linked to the risk of unemployment, the same remedial measures apply.

  Although there was no geographic marginalisation in the case of 25 de Setembro, the population lost one of its productive strategies – the *machambas* – which is likely to lead to impoverishment. At the same time, although the new mining projects in the region have created a new economy, including jobs for construction workers, these are barred to the population already living there. Therefore, this population is set to experience various forms of economic marginalisation.

- **Risk of food insecurity:** This risk is quite high given the low productivity of the *machambas* (in Cateme) or their complete absence (in 25 de Setembro) as well as the impoverishment of the population caused by their decline in productive activities.

In relation to 25 de Setembro, the mitigation measures should be those set out in the risk of becoming landless. In relation to Cateme, measures should be taken to make water available for agriculture and funds and credit should be made available for purchasing inputs or for use in other projects. Investments should also continue to be made in the extension system, with training and teaching in new cultivation techniques and assistance for small farmers.

- **Risk of increased mortality rates:** In Cateme, not only is this risk negligible, there is likely to be a reduction in the mortality rate in the next few years owing to the proximity of health centres and closer work with the population, particularly in terms of health education, which has already resulted in a clear increase in institutionalised childbirth, for example. The situation is different in the 25 de Setembro district because it is located further away from the hospital. However, the new health centre planned for the district should mean that it follows the same trend as Cateme.
- **Risk of losing access to collective resources:** The loss of collective resources was not included in the plans for either resettlement area, meaning that these factors were not compensated for and today constitute one of the main constraints on the level of survival strategies. This was especially true in Cateme, where the population lost water sources used for agriculture and livestock breeding, as well as firewood for use at home and for sale, reeds to make mats, and so on. For this reason, an inventory should have been made and the population compensated for the lost resources.

 Specifically, in relation to water, avoiding this risk can still be provided through the construction of a reservoir, or an irrigation system could be assembled for use by the population. In relation to reeds and other similar resources, studies could be undertaken to discover whether similar materials exist that could be used. Alternatively, studies could be made of other types of activities capable of replacing the previous ones.
- **Risk of social breakdown:** This risk is practically impossible to avoid. However, a substantial effort was made to maintain the relations between the various people in the communities, as well as the traditional power structures in both resettlement areas.

Three years after the resettlement programme, it is still very early to tell how the life of the populations will evolve in the future – to know whether the main resettlement risks have been avoided and whether the quality of life has improved. Ongoing work with the community is now essential, directed primarily at ensuring the sustainability of the resettlement, allowing it to continue to develop, even after the social officers have left the location. Writing along these lines, Scudder, cited by Windsor (2005), argues that resettlement takes at least two generations to become successful. Frequently, however, this success does not happen because the populations never recover from the economic and psychological disruption caused by the resettlement, the deterioration of their social structures and the loss of their 'spatial perception' (their 'sense of place').

This effort, however, will have to be done not *for* the population but *with* them. As Bénard da Costa (1994) emphasises, these populations are not passive victims waiting for help, but actors who develop their own strategies for their survival. Consequently, it is necessary, above all, to perceive the real capacities and strategies of the people concerned to avoid welfarism and ignoring their real needs.

A Brazilian company in Mozambique

> 'They [the region's inhabitants] lack the creativity to make a bench for their children to sit on at school' (Vale technician, formerly responsible for the Knowledge Station, interviewed in the documentary *Trapping Goats* in 2010).

The activities relating to Vale's resettlement programme were always implemented by subcontracted companies. The first studies of the territory, conducted in 2006, were elaborated by two Mozambican companies: Impacto and Austral. After these studies, arguing that they already had a history of collaborative ventures in Brazil, Vale hired the company Diagonal (at that time without any experience in Mozambique) to coordinate the entire resettlement process.

Made up of senior Brazilian technicians, Diagonal itself hired several Mozambican technicians. As one of its professionals reported, however: 'There were no professionals in Mozambique trained in social sciences ... so staff with secondary level education only had to be hired, and this posed a challenge and a problem' (Pedro, 2011). Those of the company's Mozambican technicians who were interviewed invariably referred to their own lack of training as one of the elements hindering the resettlement process. The biggest consequence of this fact was that the key decisions were essentially taken by Brazilian technicians without any prior experience in Mozambique.

While it is true that the company has a vast and reputable experience in this area – which can, indeed, be observed in the exemplary form in which, logistically speaking, the resettlement took place – there does seem to have been a mismatch between how the people had lived previously and the new reality created for them.

As Vale is also a Brazilian company, other social projects implemented in parallel with the resettlement, which should function as a lever for the development of the resettled population (such as the Knowledge Station), ended up being carbon copies of projects existing in Brazil, a situation not different with many other Brazilian 'successful' projects which are being replicated throughout Mozambique.

This can be seen, for example, in the fact that the Knowledge Station was fitted with an oven to toast manioc flour[178] – in Mozambique, and especially in the area under study, manioc flour comprises an important food staple, but is cooked rather than toasted as in Brazil. Another example was the initial purchases of horses to be used in herding cattle, as practised in some regions of Brazil: in Mozambique horses are not employed for this purpose and the population, essentially out of fear, did not want to use these animals.

The Knowledge Station, now called Fazenda Modelo, should now be responding to concerns about the over-generalised education and the very low number of people with technical training (Austral and Impacto, 2006). However, the gap between the programme and the real situation seems to have provoked the opposite: on the one hand, not a feeling of learning but a feeling of inferiority, and, on the other, an indifference to the material being taught, with which the population fails to identify.

While actors like the Banco Mundial (2012) correctly argue that Brazil's economic growth, its success in reducing social inequality and its experience in development offer important lessons to African countries, it is also imperative to stress that the success of development and resettlement measures depends largely on their adaptation to the specific culture and reality of each place. Hence, when trying to reproduce models applied in real-life Brazilian contexts, it is important that these are adapted, avoiding the temptation to imagine, given the numerous similarities between the two countries, that the problems and potential solutions are also the same.

Will there be more 'January the 11ths'?

'So, if there's money, Cateme can recover and grow well' (inhabitant of Cateme, interviewed in June 2012).

This chapter has explored the topic of 'development refugees' through a case

---

178 Toasted manioc flour is a very important part of the Brazilian diet.

study of the resettlement programme implemented by the Brazilian company Vale in Moatize, in the northwest of Mozambique, to see how this change affected their lives.

Analysing the resettlement, advances can be registered both in the level of basic conditions such as health, education and access to drinking water and energy, and in environmental conditions, which depend to a large extent on the construction of infrastructural works. In relation to more immaterial questions, there was a clear setback due to the incapacity to invest in the population's cultural identity and in the restructuring of their everyday lives and survival strategies. This incapacity is reflected now in the impoverishment of some people and in the population's general feeling of living as a guest in new districts that do not pertain to them.

This failure results, in part, from the population's lack of participation. Resettlement is primarily a top-down process in which people are forced to leave their family territory without taking any part in decision-making. In this case, contact with the inhabitants was essentially at an informative level: the population was told about the project and how the company was planning the resettlement, without being given any part to play in the process. One example of this situation was the population's consultation about the houses: people were asked to express their opinion during visits to the model homes, but during a phase when the project was almost complete, without much room for major alterations. Likewise, the resettlement committee did not contain a single representative from the community, meaning that its voice never formed part of the decisions set to define their future lives.

This situation led to the population treating the project as Vale's entire responsibility, evident in the responses to contemporary problems in the district, with people turning constantly to the company to resolve these. The population's appropriation of the space would have been easier had it been involved from the outset and been allowed an active part in the different stages of the process. This would have included the choice of the site for the settlement (using its empirical knowledge, both in terms of agricultural potential and spiritual questions); the design and choice of house construction materials (adapted to the population's own techniques); the choice of the organisational pattern of the housing development (respecting everyday life practices and social aspects); and also the construction of the houses and the district's infrastructure (something that forms reference points for the population, which had constructed its own habitations for generations).

On the other hand, this failure could also result from an attempt to apply a development model for resettlement identical to models already implemented in Brazil. The fact that the resettlement was managed by Brazilian technicians without any experience in Mozambique, rather than Mozambican technicians, or technicians with experience in the country, may have contributed to the population remaining distant from the process.

However, the population is adapting to the new reality and the resettlement work is not yet concluded. An improvement in life quality is still possible, but this requires constant work with the community and an investment in mitigating the risks of resettlement, which have not yet been minimised and have already become a reality. This is the case particularly with respect to the loss of land for *machambas* among the local population, who have nowhere to grow crops and have thus lost their productive system and some of their everyday practices; the loss of jobs and marginalisation, essentially because of the large distance from Moatize town and the mining project, which are leading to the population's impoverishment; the food insecurity caused largely by the poor agricultural potential of the *machambas* in Cateme, their complete absence in 25 de Setembro, and the impoverishment of the resettled population; and the loss of access to collective resources, which were never accounted for during the process.

This study also concludes that, for the population's quality of life to improve, people need to appropriate the space in which they live and recreate their own survival strategies — an effort that should receive the support of the project responsible for the population's destructuring. At the same time, the resettled population, as the group of people most affected by the mining project, should be the first to enjoy its benefits.

The social officers assisting the resettlement process need to keep in mind the communities' self-sustainability, ensuring that their quality of life continues to improve, even after the team has left the area. To ensure these actions develop as well as possible, a monitoring and evaluation system is needed, based on socio-economic indicators that can inform technicians about the results of their actions at various moments.

In the medium- to long-term, the apparent absence of sustainable strategies for resolving the current situation could translate into a growing discontent among the population and a worsening of the economic base of survival, leading to the eruption of social conflicts.

In January 2012, the population of Cateme showed that it knows how to be heard, disrupting the transportation of the mine's coal output. If concrete strategies are not defined, in the next few years we may witness a repetition of January 2012, not just in Cateme, but in all the resettlements currently being conducted in Mozambique.

The Mozambican state has the fundamental duty not to ignore the problem or the discussion, which it seems to have been doing over the recent period, but to assume responsibility for these resettlements, admitting the mistakes made in the near past and using this project as a source of lessons for the various other planned projects. As the body responsible for bringing together diverse enterprises, it is important that it defines shared development strategies that benefit Mozambicans and the country, so that it can effectively take advantage of the knowledge and experiences existing in other countries, like Brazil, for its own benefit. The recent approval of the law relating to resettlements, though subjected to diverse criticisms, may be an important step in marking a fresh stance from the government.

As a country from the Global South, belonging to the group of countries with a colonial past and a climate like Mozambique's, Brazil, over the last few years, has emerged as an ideal potential partner for Mozambique. However, it is up to the Mozambican government to define its policies and assume responsibility for the development that it desires for the country.

References

Allafrica (2012) Mozambique: Government urged to defend resettled communities. Available at: http://allafrica.com/stories/201201171222.html (accessed March 2013).

Almeida, E and Kraychete, ES (2012) *O Discurso Brasileiro para a Cooperação em Moçambique: Existe ajuda desinteressada?* Comunicação apresentada na III Conferência Internacional do IESE, Maputo.

Andræ, G (1992) Urban workers as Farmers: Agro-links of Nigerian textile workers in the crisis of the 1980s. *The Rural–Urban Interface in África: Expansion and adaptation,* Seminar Proceedings, 27.

Angola Press (2012) Moçambicanos bloqueiam ferrovia para protestar contra Vale. Available at: http://www.portalangop.co.ao/motix/pt_pt/noticias/africa/2012/0/2/Mocambicanos-bloqueiam-ferrovia-para-protestar-contra-Vale,7d682a7b-be6a-4cf0-8a19-3fff4bdecb05.html (accessed March 2013).

Austral and Impacto (2006) Pesquisa qualitativa de subsídio ao desenvolvimento do PAR, Maputo.

Aurecon (2010) Projecto do Corredor de Nacala. Estudo de Impacto Ambiental da linha férrea Moatize-Malawi, *Relatório*, Vol. 3, Maputo (December).

Banco Mundial (2012) Ponte sobre o Atlântico Brasil e África Subsaariana: parceria Sul-Sul para o crescimento. Available at: http://siteresources.worldbank.org/AFRICAEXT/Resources/africa-brazil-bridging-final-PORT.pdf (accessed March 2013).

Bénard da Costa, A (1994) Estudo de Famílias Deslocadas na Cidade de Maputo: Análise das relações e comportamentos sócio económicos. Dissertation for MA in African Studies, Lisbon, Instituto Superior de Ciência do Trabalho e da Empresa.

Campbell, K. (2013). Vale seeks peace with potters, continues training Mozambicans, Mining Weekly, 3 May. Available at: http://www.miningweekly.com/article/vale-seeks-peace-with-potters-continues-training-mozambicans-2013-05-03 (accessed 30 May 2017).

Cernea, M (1996) Understanding and preventing Impoverishment from displacement: Reflections on the state of knowledge. *Understanding Impoverishment: The consequence of development-induced displacement,* Refugees and Forced Migration Studies, 2.

Cernea, M (1997) *African Involuntary Population Resettlement in a Global Context.* S.l. Washington, DC: World Bank, Environment Department Papers.

Clark, D (2000) *Resettlement: The World Bank's assault on the poor.* Washington, DC: Center for

International Environmental Law.

Cernea, M (1999) *The Economics of Involuntary Resettlement: Questions and challenges.* Washington, DC: World Bank.

Colson, E (1994) *Development Refugees: Indians, Africans and the big dams.* Oxford, University of Montana, the Refugee Studies Programme.

Diagonal Urbana (2006) Plano de Acção para Reassentamento do projecto de carvão de Moatize, Maputo.

Downing, T (1996) Mitigation social impoverishment when people are involuntary displaced. *Understanding impoverishment: The consequence of development-induced displacement,* Refugees and Forced Migration Studies, No. 2 Oxford University.

Geffray, C (1991) *A Causa das Armas: Antropologia da guerra contemporânea.* Porto: Afrontamento.

Gefu, J (1992) Pastoralist perspectives in Nigeria: The Fulbe of Udubo grazing reserve, *The Rural–Urban Interface in Africa: Expansion and adaptation,* Seminar Proceedings, No. 27.

Human Rights Watch (2013) 'What is a house without food?' Mozambique's coal mining boom and resettlements. Available at: https://www.hrw.org/report/2013/05/23/what-house-without-food/mozambiques-coal-mining-boom-and-resettlements (accessed 30 May 2017).

Liga dos Direitos Humanos et al (2012) *Sua excelência presidente da República Armando Guebuza. Assunto: Solicitação para o respeito e realização dos direitos e dignidade humanas das famílias reassentadas no contexto do megaprojecto de exploração do carvão de Moatize.* Available at: http://www.wlsa.org.mz/wp-content/uploads/2012/10/Cateme.pdf (accessed 30 May 2017).

Jornal do Brasil (2012) Moçambicanos bloqueiam ferrovia para protestar contra a Vale. Available at: http://www.jb.com.br/internacional/noticias/2012/01/12/mocambicanos-bloqueiam-ferrovia-para-protestar-contra-a-vale/ (accessed March 2013).

Mlozi, M (1992) *Inequitable agricultural extension services in the urban context: The* case of Tanzania. *The Rural–Urban Interface in Africa: Expansion and adaptation,* Seminar Proceedings, No. 27.

Pantie, J (2012) Comunidades reassentadas paralisam actividades da Vale Moçambique: Os manifestantes impediram a saída de Comboio para a Beira, FIR está no terreno a reprimir os manifestantes com o uso de força excessiva. CanalMoz, Year 4, No. 621.

Pedro, J (2011) Reassentamentos Forçados: Dos impactos às oportunidades. MA dissertation in African Studies, Instituto Superior de Ciência do Trabalho e da Empresa, Lisbon.

Polgreen, L (2012) As coal boosts Mozambique, the rural poor are left behind, *New York Times.* Available at: http://www.nytimes.com/2012/11/11/world/africa/as-coal-boosts-mozambique-the-rural-poor-are-left-behind.html?pagewanted=all&_r=0 (accessed March 2013).

Raposo I (1999) Urbaniser villages et maisons. Projets poltiques et réalités sociales. Manica (Mozambique) et Alte (Portugal). PhD dissertation, Institut d'Urbanisme de Paris, Université de Paris XII, Val de Marne.

Rio Doce Moçambique (2006a) Projecto Carvão Moatize: Diagnóstico Ambiental da Mina de Carvão de Moatize.

Rio Doce Moçambique (2006b) Caracterização Urbanístico-Ambiental.

Rio Doce Moçambique (2006c) Relatório Técnico De Estudo Das Alternativas Para Definição Da Área Anfitriã.

Santos, BS (2012) Moçambique: A maldição da abundância? Coluna escrita para Carta Maior. Available at: http://cartamaior.com.br/?/Coluna/Mocambique-a-maldicao-da-abundancia-/26864 (accessed March 2013).

The Economist (2012) Brazil in Africa: A new Atlantic alliance: Brazilian companies are heading for Africa, laden with capital and expertise. Available at: http://www.economist.com/news/21566019-brazilian-companies-are-heading-africa-laden-capital-and-expertise-new-atlantic-alliance (accessed March 2013).

Windsor JE (2005) Annihilation of both place and sense of place: The experience of the

Cheslatta T'En Canadian First Nation within the context of large-scale environmental projects, Canada, *The Geographical Journal*, **171** (2), pp 146–65.

World Bank Operations Evaluation Department (2000) *Involuntary Resettlement: The Large Dam Experience. Precis*, No. 194. Washington, DC: World Bank.

Yunus, M (2006) O banqueiro dos pobres. Lisbon: Difel.

Chapter 12

Cultural exchange between Brazil and Mozambique: The positive impact of the activities of the Maputo Theatre of the Oppressed Group

Elizabete Sanches Rocha

One of the main functions of our art is to make conscious these spectacles of everyday life in which the actors are the spectators themselves, the stage is the audience, and the audience the stage. We are all artists: by making theatre, we learn to see what leaps before our eyes, but which we are incapable of seeing by being so accustomed to just looking. What is familiar to us becomes invisible: making theatre, by contrast, lights up the stage of our everyday life (Boal, 2009).[179]

The Maputo Theatre of the Oppressed Group comprises one of the best examples of cultural exchange between Brazil and Mozambique over recent years. GTO-Maputo, to use its popular name, has engaged in artistic–cultural and social work with the most vulnerable communities in Mozambique for 12 years, taking as its methodology the theatrical techniques created by the Brazilian dramatist Augusto Boal in the 1970s. Today the international training courses offered by the Theatre of the Oppressed Centre (*Centro de Teatro do Oprimido*: CTO) in Rio de Janeiro are responsible for the diffusion of the Theatre of the Oppressed's practices worldwide. Indeed, it was this apprenticeship that gave GTO-Maputo the first impulse that eventually turned it into a concrete and fundamental element in the expansion of politico–social and educational awareness in the regions in which it has worked in Mozambique since 2001. Receiving financial aid – unfortunately, still insufficient – from the United Nations Children's Fund (UNICEF) and other international agencies, and theoretical, methodological and conceptual support from CTO-Rio de Janeiro, GTO-Maputo works in various regions of Mozambique using the language of theatre. Its primary aim is to raise the awareness of the poorer and more vulnerable population about a series of crucial problems faced by Mozambican

---

179 An excerpt from the speech given by Augusto Boal in March 2009, at an official ceremony in Paris to celebrate his appointment as UNESCO World Theatre Ambassador.

society. One of the main challenges is the search to reduce the HIV/AIDS infection and mortality rates.

In 1993, the first seeds of what would later develop into the Maputo Theatre of the Oppressed Group were planted in Mozambique in the 'Gota de Lume' cultural collective, one of whose participants was Alvim Cossa – the main spokesperson for GTO-Maputo today. It was in this space of creation and cultural promotion that the collective could show its work, for example, at the Amateur Theatre Festival of the City of Maputo, where it won second place in the festival competition. In 1999, stimulated by the new possibilities for expanding its theatre activities and by a robust proposal for social transformation, Alvim Cossa applied for a United Nations Educational, Scientific and Cultural Organization (UNESCO) grant to receive training in Brazil at the Rio de Janeiro Theatre of the Oppressed Centre. In 2000, having completed his training period in Rio de Janeiro, Alvim Cossa returned to Mozambique filled with ideas and hopes derived from his experiences at CTO-Rio, where he had also maintained direct contact with the ever-enthusiastic Augusto Boal. In 2001, in Maputo, what would become one of the most successful experiences in the internationalisation of the Theatre of the Oppressed began with the creation of GTO-Maputo.

Since then there have been many achievements – and many struggles. GTO-Maputo has gained national visibility in Mozambique and recognition internationally. However, the difficulties of keeping the project running are numerous, exacerbated by the absence of domestic funding – from the Mozambican state agencies – and the difficulties inherent in a society in which the democratic system remains very fragile. In other words, the creation and continuance of GTO-Maputo provide an extremely important boost to the democratic dialogue in the country, an indispensable element in any society, but especially in nations like Mozambique with a very recent history of civil war and colonial exploitation. Discussing this question, Alvim Cossa (2013) made the following observation in an interview:

> Unfortunately, we still face a considerable shortfall in terms of democratic debate in this country. I don't know why this happens. We lack the anthropological and sociological knowledge for an evaluation at this level. But it's true that we have a huge gap in democratic debate in every sphere of our society. We don't discuss the relations between husband and wife, the family home, between neighbours, parents and children, work colleagues. Moreover, this lack of freedom – for people to express themselves – extends to positions of governance and leadership where people feel challenged and disrespected whenever they are questioned. This is why the opening up of spaces for democratic debate is, I think,

one of the huge advances that the Theatre of the Oppressed can provide to the country. We encourage people to look at reality and – rebelling against it when necessary – refuse to live passively. People need to be helped to think about why their lives follow certain paths.

Today the group comprises five people who work out of the GTO office in Maputo. No rigid hierarchical structure exists since the methodology and concept of the Theatre of the Oppressed are based on the principles of dialogue and horizontality. All the participants are coordinators, therefore, able to debate any kind of problem that surfaces and to take decisions in conjunction with one another. Although GTO-Maputo's main base is in Mozambique's capital, its work extends across the whole country, where there are other centres with their own local coordinators. This group faces major challenges daily: travelling to the interior of the country and seeking to use theatre to dialogue in the context of the cultural and social specificities of each of Mozambique's distinct regions. However, this work has proved highly successful, despite all the difficulties hurled in its path; for example, in January 2013, GTO-Maputo saw all its precious material archive – including detailed reports, internal and external assessments, collective experiences and training courses recorded on different media, official documents and other important records – simply swept away in yet another flood that swamped the city. In sum, GTO-Maputo comprises a group of artists – but above all citizens – with the soul of a phoenix and the potential to inspire a continual and endless rebirth. Undoubtedly the perseverance and determination to obtain good results help make GTO-Maputo an organisation that positively affects everyone with whom it has contact.

And it is in this spirit that this chapter examines some of the topics relating to Brazil's presence in Mozambique. This includes examining the techniques used by the Theatre of the Oppressed and its ideological motivations within a historical perspective; comprehending GTO-Maputo's work through the meanings of oppression attributed to and lived by the Mozambican population reached by the group; and, finally, describing some of the positive outcomes set out in the Evaluation Report on Community Theatre Activities, a study commissioned by UNICEF and published on 24 February 2009, which provides clear data on the work of GTO-Maputo in various regions of Mozambique.

The Theatre of the Oppressed as a cultural, social and political manifestation
Born from the political circumstances of a Brazil in which cultural expression, including its manifestation in the theatre, suffered bitterly during the repressive military dictatorship, the Arena Theatre was conceived as a privileged space for dramatic creation and experimentation within the wider political struggles in

São Paulo in the 1960s. A laboratory of artistic ideas and ideological effusion, the Arena Theatre is remembered here as the seminal space for what would later develop into the Theatre of the Oppressed: the Arena played a hugely important role in uniting the best minds around a project of theatrical creation in a context that demanded very clear political positions in response to the absence of democracy in the country.

The theatrical experiences of the Arena Group, in which Augusto Boal was one of the leading figures, gave birth to a series of drama productions, which today form a vital part of the history of the modern Brazilian theatre, evincing the creative energy of those years. They also opened possibilities for aesthetic and political reflections, which, little by little, generated new conceptions of and in Brazilian theatre practice. This was how, for example, the concept of the Joker emerged, which is central to understanding the Theatre of the Oppressed's main proposals. The Arena was a key locus for debates and the emergence of new ideas, contradictions and positionings, not only theatrical but also political and cultural in a wider sense. As Nunes (2004:39) argues, it was not enough, especially for Boal, to 'raise the awareness' of society through a critical and engaged form of theatre. The aesthetic–dramatic experience itself, the making of theatre, had to move closer to real life. It is also worth noting that the Arena and its creators drew huge inspiration from the Epic Theatre of Berthold Brecht: it adopted the Brechtian aesthetic both through its innovations in set design, which helped problematise the theatrical illusion, and, of course, through its critical nature and its proposal for social transformation via art. For Boal, there was a clear need to bridge the distance between theatre and life. Whereas Brecht saw his Epic Theatre as a way to rupture the cathartic illusion conjured by bourgeois theatre, seeking to awaken the audience's awareness of the structural contradictions of the social system, Boal proposes a theatrical aesthetic capable of questioning the very idea of any distance between life and art, society and theatre, actors and everyday people. Thus, it was decided to draw the population into the actual theatre production itself, thereby enabling the audience to seek their own solutions, setting out from their own contexts and their own realities. This led to the creation of the Curinga System of the Theatre of the Oppressed.

Dramaturgically, the Curinga – at first written with an *o*, as Nunes (2004:38) informs us, referred to the playing card, the *coringa* or joker, which can assume different positions – is responsible for linking stage and audience, theatre and life. The person who assumes this function in the performance mediates between the interventions of the audience and the actors on stage. In other words, the joker is located on the tenuous line that simultaneously divides and unites the theatre show and the desires of society. The Curinga/Joker System is a decisive step in what would later transform into the Theatre of the Oppressed.

In this sense, the stage opens up to society, provoking the spectator to become the author and actor of the play/life. This is the concept of the *spect-actor*. This flexibility inherent in this idea provides the conceptual bedrock of the Theatre of the Oppressed and is one of the factors explaining its spread across the five continents, enabling it to adjust constantly to local social demands.

The Theatre of the Oppressed is based on the idea that theatre needs to adapt to local problems but without losing sight of the most important aim of the work: humanising humanity (Boal, 2005:25). As we can see, the debate informing the basis and foundations of the practice of the Theatre of the Oppressed is determined by a relativist viewpoint (Geertz, 2001). In other words, there is an appreciation of the need to absorb local cultures to put the dramaturgical techniques into practice and attain the objective of emancipation from any kind of oppression chosen by the groups as the focus of their work. At the same time, though, it needs to be emphasised that this vision does not imply any lack of definition or cohesion in its objectives. On the contrary, the Theatre of the Oppressed is resolutely convinced of the need to work with those people who find themselves in a situation of vulnerability, in all kinds of circumstances. In other words, it involves a relativism of form and method with a clear conviction of content: assuming the side of the oppressed is essential. One of the main functions of the Theatre of the Oppressed practice is to lend a voice to those who usually lack one. The theatre becomes a mirror, a magnifying glass, a privileged platform capable of providing the necessary focus on these socially, culturally, politically and/or historically muted voices.

To attain its main objective, the Theatre of the Oppressed has developed various drama techniques, though the most well-known and widespread at global level is the Forum Theatre. Boal writes:

> The Forum Theatre … uses or can use all the resources of all known theatrical forms, but adding to these an essential feature: the spectators – who we call *spect-actors* – are invited to come on stage and, by performing theatrically, not just enunciating words, reveal their thoughts, desires and strategies. The latter in turn can suggest to the group to whom they belong a range of possible life alternatives invented by themselves: the theatre should be a rehearsal for action in real life, not an end in itself (Boal, 2005:19).

The main objective Theatre of the Oppressed as a dramaturgy is to raise awareness about the forms of oppression, allowing everyday men and women to assume the 'theatrical' role which is art but also life; it thus reveals, in ontological terms, a problematisation of concepts like art, theatre, culture and actor at the very base of their existence. For Boal (2005:11), 'all theatre is necessarily political, since all man's activities are political, and theatre is one of them'.

Shortly before his death, Augusto Boal completed his book, *A Estética do Oprimido* (The Aesthetic of the Oppressed), published first in French and, in 2009, in Portuguese. In his work, Boal provides a detailed explanation of the aesthetic and political discussions that he had continually explored in earlier works, like *Teatro do Oprimido e outras Poéticas Políticas* (Theatre of the Oppressed and other Political Poetics), first published in 1973. In his final work, Boal discusses what he understands as theatre and the aesthetic of the oppressed, leaving no doubt about the vision and the social consciousness that always oriented his creative output as a dramatist and director. Explaining the foundations to his thought, Boal observes that:

> As there are so many cultures and so many truths that emanate from them, so many divisions in the heart of societies, and so many disparate values, Aesthetics and Beauty do not possess universal and eternal values. One cannot speak of a single and unique Aesthetic that would belong to a unique thought, a weapon in the exploitation of the oppressed and in the opulence of the oppressors (Boal, 2009:35).

Boal makes it clear that his intention here is not to annul the historically legitimised forms of aesthetic manifestation. These retain their intrinsic value. What the dramatist is emphasising here, instead, is the existence of diverse ways of comprehending aesthetics, depending on the lens through which we see the world – in other words, depending on our specific cultural outlook. For Boal, then, what we consider to be aesthetic cannot be valorised universally; on the contrary, it corresponds to the social, political, cultural, historical and even geographical contingencies of each social group. Along these lines, Boal argues:

> We don't want to offer the people *access to culture* – as is usually said, as though the people lacked their own culture or were incapable of making one. In dialogue with all cultures, we wish to stimulate the existing culture of the oppressed sectors of each people (Boal, 2009:46).

For Boal, aesthetics is intrinsically connected to ethics. The political, social and aesthetic merge; indeed, they are indissociable. The dramatist advocates a primordial theatre that should be born and grow from the people. This is a proposal for theatre not *for* the people, but made *by* the people. In this sense, it retains a capacity for aesthetic signification in accordance with the desire of the group performing it. It should be liberating and emancipating, insofar as, aesthetically, it reveals paths and potential solutions to social problems.

It should also be noted that Boal insists on the aesthetic nature of the spectacle, which can be realised by transforming the street, the union, the prison, the school or the public square into stages. In the dramatist's view, however, the main factor is the transformation effected by the theatre: Boal shows a deep concern for the tenuous limit between the social and the aesthetic. For him, the Theatre of the Oppressed can achieve its objectives only by working hard to develop people's senses. This he calls Sensible Thought (Boal, 2009:27). For him, 'the Aesthetic Space is a Magnifying Mirror that reveals disguised, unconscious or hidden behaviour' (Boal, 2005:31).

As we can see, the philosophical idea behind the Theatre of the Oppressed – irrespective of its diverse dramaturgical techniques – takes human life to be an inalienable wealth and all its actions are directed towards achieving better living conditions – and not just survival – in whatever part of the world it finds itself. For Boal (2003:152), the notion of culture reflects the perception that it is through cultural phenomena that humans reveal themselves to be truly human. The expansion from humankind to nature, of which it forms part, to the arts and to the other is enabled by culture. Obviously, the right to aesthetic enjoyment lies at the core of all the Theatre of the Oppressed's projects: in fact, it defines it. The question is not one of working to mechanically resolve the problems that affect social groups and individuals. In fact, it is a way of raising awareness, humanising those involved to confront both the external monsters and those created by each one of us. Very often people discover that the oppressor is not the external other, but the one internalised within ourselves, which is why art performs such an important role: it is through art that we can discern what lies beyond the stereotypes and the socially created and sustained images. Revelation is not only found in what is said by others: the emancipation process occurs when each person discovers him- or herself and manages to see the context better through their own experience. It is precisely this lived experience that is enabled by the various dramatic techniques used by the Aesthetics of the Theatre of the Oppressed. Discussing this point, Boal (2003:108) explains the decisive role played by art:

> Art transcribes the real – whose familiarity renders it invisible to our eyes – so that this real can be comprehended in its human dimension, which makes it meaningful and rational. As well as everyday appearances, Art helps us discover the hidden meaning of the real, accustomed as we are to not seeing it, such is the horror it evokes in us. Art unveils the Truth.

Ultimately, then, what the Aesthetics of the Theatre of the Oppressed proposes is a change in the way in which people think about themselves and about the other. Its various techniques provide the possibility of materialising this aim to understand our own being in the world. This involves an encounter with diverse perceptions, which forms a new paradigm for thinking about the human, an endeavour that requires overcoming past and present forms of oppression:

> Human beings, since the moment of conception, need to expand both inwards and outwards. Outwards, in search of a territory that is larger than the volume of our body: the house, the garden. Inwards, in search of poetry. All forms of poetry. Outwards, dry land, bread and flowers; inwards, wisdom (Boal, 2003:155).

Given this observation, it is curious to ponder the process involved in the internationalisation of the Theatre of the Oppressed itself. It emerged in a context in which the most important debates reflected ideological struggles that were very clearly embedded in a bipolarised political landscape: the historical environment of the 1960s and 1970s, both inside and outside Brazil. The fact is, then, that this aesthetic was created within a dialogical perception of the world, enabling it to respond to the demands of contemporary societies in which cultural exchange is a necessity and a challenge.

The Theatre of the Oppressed in Mozambique

The development of closer ties between Brazil and African countries has been a constant theme of recent Brazilian governments, which have looked to strengthen the political and cultural relations of countries sharing many common characteristics. Brazilian foreign policy has emphasised this approximation through numerous geopolitical and economic, as well as cultural, interests. For Visentini:

> It is also worth highlighting the continuity in the assistance given by Brazil to African States through technical cooperation programs and the sending of trained personnel; this is evident, for example, in the biofuel production viability study in Senegal, in the Brazil–EU–Mozambique partnership for the sustainable development of bioenergy, and in the support for victims of sexual violence in the Democratic Republic of Congo through personnel and funding (Visentini, 2013:124).

In relation to cultural policies, Brazil's Ministry of Culture launched the Living Culture Programme in 2004. This marked another paradigm in the formulation of cultural public policies in Brazil (Santos, 2011:155), especially because of its democratic, inclusive and dialogical character. Its implantation, in official terms,

> anticipates a continuous and dynamic process; its development is similar to a living organism, which connects with pre-existing actors. Rather than determining (or imposing) actions and local behaviours, the program stimulates creativity, empowering desires and creating situations of social enchantment (Ministry of Culture, 2005:18).

Since Mozambique already had a significant track record in hosting the Theatre of the Oppressed's work in different parts of the country since 2001, the Brazilian government announced its choice of the Maputo Theatre of the Oppressed Group to establish a Culture Point abroad, along the same lines as the Living Culture Programme. According to the Ministry of Culture:

> As an integral part of the foreign policy developed by the Presidency of the Republic and by the Ministry of Foreign Affairs, founded on international cooperation and the country's status as a sovereign Nation, *Living Culture* plans to locate *Culture Points* in the communities of Brazilians living abroad, in the countries of Mercosur and in the Community of Portuguese-speaking Countries (Portugal, Africa and Asia) … These Points, connected to the Points in Brazil itself, will form an international network of shared production and exchange of symbolic products, strengthening the south/south relation, working to develop more horizontal south/north relations and collaborating towards the construction of a solidary and counter-hegemonic current (Ministry of Culture, 2005:22).

With the implementation of this programme as part of the Living Culture Programme, run by the Ministry of Culture in partnership with Brazil's Ministry of Foreign Affairs, the selection of the Maputo Theatre of the Oppressed Group acquired considerable significance: it amounted to an important form of recognition for both the Rio de Janeiro Centre of the Theatre of the Oppressed and for GTO-Maputo itself. Unfortunately, though, apart from the institutional gesture and the importance of the symbolism, no actual funds – the main practical element – were ever released. Nonetheless, in political terms, it demonstrated Brazil's interest over the last 10 years in intensifying its cultural exchanges with countries from the African continent.

In the research on international relations, much has been said about the role played by agents and structures, and the ontology and epistemology that these concepts involve; also on the pragmatic scope of the possibilities for analyses and interventions in support of the theories developed in the context of this debate, including the Constructivist Theory of International Relations (Klotz and Lynch, 2007). One of the central topics examined in this literature is the frequent inefficiency of the projects and proposals that are not materialised through public policies or actions run directly by state or government institutions. Here other social agents, not necessarily linked to governments or official state organisms, can assume an important role in their international orchestration. This applies to the Theatre of the Oppressed: with CTO-Rio de Janeiro acting as its base for training both national and international leaders, it is a clear example of how social webs spread out along a variety of paths, very often independently of the official proposals of the public authorities. But it also needs to be said that – especially during the two consecutive mandates of President Luis Inácio Lula da Silva, 2003–2010, and principally due to the design of cultural policies like the Living Culture Programme by the Minister of Culture, Gilberto Gil – there was an effort to strengthen ties between the actions of the Theatre of the Oppressed Groups in Brazil and the concretisation of proposals like Living Culture and the Culture Points in Brazil and abroad. This energy gave a fresh impetus to the work of these cultural and social fronts, valorising their actions and placing them at the centre of the debates and decisions on cultural public policies. The work already achieved by leading social actors like the Theatre of the Oppressed Centre (CTO-Rio) in Brazil and GTO-Maputo in Mozambique acquired an even stronger capacity for diffusion and legitimisation under cultural policies with the kind of visibility provided by the Living Culture Programme, promoted too by a foreign policy committed to closer cooperation with African countries. For Visentini:

> The relations between Brazil and Africa continued to develop under the Dilma government through technical cooperation projects in areas like agriculture and tropical medicine, professional training, energy and social protection. Along these lines, in April agreements were signed with Ethiopia in the agricultural area and with Mozambique. On a visit to Brazil, the Prime Minister of Mozambique, Aires Bonifácio Baptista Ali, signed trade agreements and discussed the presence of Brazilian companies in the country. The cooperation between the two countries covers areas like health, education, agriculture, food security and energy. According to the MDIC [Ministry of Overseas Development, Industry and Trade], in 2011 the trade between them amounted to US$85.3 million (a 101.2% increase compared to 2010) (Visentini, 2013:131).

With the primary objective of exploring the positive advances achieved by GTO-Maputo over more than 10 years of continuous work in Mozambique, it is worth pointing out that the group gained prominence by using theatre to try to minimise the impact of a history of exploitation in a country as richly diverse as Mozambique. As mentioned earlier, the Theatre of the Oppressed's proposal stresses the importance of learning about the environment in which the work will be developed, prior to any intervention. This includes becoming familiar with its historical and political context and, of course, perceiving and defining – always collectively – the main forms of oppression found in the surrounding social environment. This process by itself brings to light a series of latent questions, frequently hidden among the components of the social groups involved. In the case of Mozambique, this dialogical technique enabled one of the most important forms of oppression to be identified and confronted: the lack of information and access to basic knowledge on both the prevention and treatment of HIV/AIDS. Therefore, together with groups from the provinces of Zambézia, Tete, Nampula, Maputo, Sofala, Manica, Gaza and Cabo Delgado, GTO-Maputo – through the project Social Mobilisation via the Community Theatre Network, developed in partnership with UNICEF – undertook work so important that the project became cited as an exemplary case. It is worth recalling here that the First International Conference of the Theatre of the Oppressed was organised in Rio de Janeiro in July 2009, where GTO-Maputo was present. The objective, of this conference, besides celebrating the life and work of Boal, who had died that year, was to bring together the different groups located in diverse countries and this contributed prominently to the exchange of experiences and practices among these groups. The video, *My Husband is in Denial*, directed by Rogério Manjate, was shown, which provided other participants with a sensitive and clear depiction of how GTO-Maputo's work is carried out and its encouraging results.

That same year, 2009, saw the publication of the Evaluation Report on Community Theatre Activities, a study commissioned by UNICEF from the company Ernst & Young. The report presents an assessment of the results obtained through the actions of the Theatre of the Oppressed Group in Mozambique. I turn now to examine some of the observations contained in this document, which help shed light on the kind of intervention undertaken by GTO-Maputo's methodology and its cultural and social impacts.

Firstly, it should be noted that the report is very extensive and includes many variables important to its final conclusions. The document is based on interviews conducted in various localities in Mozambique where GTO-Maputo had worked extensively. There is an assessment by age group and gender: children and adults, and men and women were interviewed, including the members of GTO-Maputo. Questions included: 'Do you think the messages presented in the GTO theatre plays are acceptable and appropriate, or are they bad? Explain.' 'What did you learn in the GTO theatre sessions that you watched? Do you think the transmitted message changed your habits in relation to preventing HIV/AIDS, cholera and malaria and the promotion of children's and women's rights? If so, why?' There were also questions designed to evaluate how the population perceived and experienced the theatre in communicational and aesthetic terms, and what the impact of the theatre plays was on these family households: 'Name three things that you most liked about how the actors performed and transmitted the messages in the plays that you watched. And three things that you least liked about how the public participates in the plays that you watched. How can the audience's participations be improved?' (UNICEF, 2009; Appendix 2). The interviews also emphasised the theme developed by GTO-Maputo and the percentage of people capable of responding positively to what the researchers identified as key questions. Obviously, all the criteria used both in the research methodology and sample selection, and in the analysis of the results, are clearly set out and explained at the very beginning of the report. Owing to space constraints, I decided not to explore these aspects here: I focus instead on some of the topics that help shed light on the emancipatory space created by GTO-Maputo within the social context of the groups that took part in their theatre activities.

The conclusions presented in the report are divided into general and specific aspects. In relation to the former, the document explicitly states that:

> The program retains its relevance, therefore, since the current national context of combating HIV/AIDS as well as a set of diseases like malaria and cholera, on one hand, and questions of gender equality and the testimony of representatives from the communities contacted in the focus group discussions, on the other, show that the program is highly useful. Indeed, the belief is that it is gradually changing the population's behaviour and way of life (UNICEF, 2009:90).

The document contains various recommendations based on the results obtained, delimiting the suggestions concerning the general and specific aspects. One of the items suggests, for example, that GTO-Maputo should devote more time and resources to discussing other urgent themes in Mozambican society, such as gender equality, violence against children, and preventing violence and abuse against women. This point is particularly worth noting since the main form of oppression highlighted by the participants in the plays themselves is AIDS prevention. Obviously, since the Theatre of the Oppressed's methodology is based on collective work and a process that allows the needs to emerge from the population itself, encouraging people to participate actively in the creative process and the debate on what oppresses them, other urgent problems are not directly considered. The report's recommendation clearly states that, 'Forms of making other areas besides HIV/AIDS more attractive should be found, highlighting topics that have not received much attention from the communities' (UNICEF, 2009:98). A direct relation is identified, therefore, between GTO-Maputo's work and some of the key issues, the results of which are highly encouraging since the population's increased awareness of HIV/AIDS is emphasised throughout the report. Analysed from another angle, though, there is a need to widen the range of actions to address problems that have yet to be covered by the current initiatives. For a better understanding of the demands expressed and reported in the official document in question, it is important to stress that this is a feature of GTO-Maputo's methodology and not a limitation of the work carried out by it per se. By working collectively, seeking to construct an awareness of real local needs, the choices made determine the continuation of the theatre work via the creation of the play with its central figures, as well as shaping the forms of questioning that will allow the audience to participate in solving the problem being addressed. Elsewhere, the report gives positive emphasis precisely to the group's method of working in a participatory form, allowing the demands of the society itself to determine the themes to be explored and the creation of the theatre play that will tackle the problem set by the group. This, in my view, demonstrates the pre-eminent need, recognised by GTO-Maputo itself, to value the voices of the people involved – the basic principle underlying the Theatre of the Oppressed – in the knowledge that this approach will strengthen the projection that people will make when watching the play and participating as actors and spectators simultaneously (*spect-actors*). Along these lines, the report observes that: 'Recognizing the value of the ideas of the communities and transforming these into a reinforcement of the plays seems to assume a key role in terms of improving performance' (UNICEF, 2009:95). As demonstrated earlier, the participation of the community is not presented as an additional element; it is the generative concept of the Theatre of the Oppressed. There is little doubt, though, on the need to widen the thematic areas on which GTO-Maputo works without losing the essence of the proposal: to raise the consciousness of those who are oppressed and those who oppress, and the social place occupied by the actors of this oppression, to empower local forms of emancipation. And this consciousness needs to originate and develop from the populations living in vulnerable situations. I believe that the pre-eminence and importance of this type of external evaluation, as in the case of the report commissioned by UNICEF, effectively reside in the document's capacity to illuminate the different aspects and nuances of a work as rich as it is complex, as in the case of GTO-Maputo.

In this sense, taking another example from a topic explored in depth by the report, the researchers observe the population's positive response to the methodology used by GTO-Maputo, namely the theatre plays. It is curious to note that the population feels recognised by this language and the participatory way in which it is constructed. This undoubtedly demonstrates the communicative strength of theatre, as Boal always argued. Textually, the perception of the interviewees is explained in the report as follows:

> Interviewees liked the educational and constructive form in which the messages were transmitted. Moreover, the fact that the messages had been transmitted through theatre plays has been a determining factor in visualizing what they were trying to transmit (UNICEF, 2009:91).

Next, there is a substantial account of the expectations of the participating public – the *spect-actors* – concerning the performed plays. In some regions of the country, the interviewees particularly emphasised the need to separate the plays made and performed by children with topics aimed directly at them – such as raising awareness of children's rights – from the shows produced by adults and involving subjects understood by the population as primarily addressed to adults, such as the discussion of the use of condoms in HIV/AIDS prevention. This question is described as follows in the official report:

> However, certain sensitive topics, such as the use of condoms, should be explored in depth in forums that differentiate between children and older people. The clothes used by the presenters, particularly the women, with short skirts and exposure of intimate parts of the body during performance of the plays, and the fact that the plays were highly condensed, were also identified as aspects that needed to be improved (UNICEF, 2009:92).

These data seem to show the sensitivity and subtlety with which the work of the Theatre of the Oppressed is undertaken – and all over the world, not just in Mozambique – since there are always cultural and social particularities that need to be considered. Indeed, these certainly are considered by GTO-Maputo, as we can assume from the good results obtained in general. Precisely through his comprehension of the profundity of what Boal, in his last book, called Sensible Thought, he expressed the indissolubility of both aesthetics and ethics, art and politics. In other words, were the practices of the Theatre of the Oppressed to be conceived in merely technical or mechanical terms, without the intensive work of enhancing the aesthetic sensibility of everyone involved, the objectives of emancipation and humanisation would undoubtedly not be achieved. After all, the Theatre of the Oppressed's strength resides in the symbiosis of aesthetic sensibility and political attitude. Hence, form cannot be detached from content in its dramatic creations. And this demands intense preparation from those leading the creative process, especially the *curingas* (jokers). This, indeed, is one of the biggest challenges faced by members of GTO-Maputo: the distances, the different languages and ethnic groups, the constant struggle for funding and other factors intrinsic to work that is as ambitious as it is urgent, in a country as diverse as Mozambique. Clearly the report shows that, despite all of this, the actions of GTO-Maputo have been predominantly successful.

The question, 'What do you do when your children do something wrong at home?' also reflects an urgent need to explore the issue more deeply so that violence is not taken to be natural and acceptable. The report we read said:

> Intensive awareness-raising should be developed to reduce the acts of violence that still persist, such as beating children, imprisoning them or tying them up inside the home, prohibiting them from playing, punishing them as a corrective measure, practised by around a fifth of those we interviewed ... Unfortunately, cases were cited in which children were imprisoned inside the home: the people treating them like this urgently need to be made aware that they should not do this ... this could be a priority for GTO's theatre plays (UNICEF, 2009:102).

Here it is worth noting an observation that extends from the question concerning the working methods used by the Theatre of the Oppressed and its legitimacy vis-à-vis the participating groups. The above recommendation is crucial, of course, since domestic violence is widespread in many regions. When Boal states that art is a mirror through which we can see and understand ourselves better, it becomes clear that opportunities need to be provided not only for the person who suffers from violence, but also those who commit violent acts, to see and recognise themselves on stage/in life. This theme, which involves the relation between adults and children, is one of the most sensitive for the theatre practice described in the report, which, as cited earlier, recommends separating the adult themes and children's themes into different play performances. In some cases, this is impossible since the adults and youngsters – very often parents and their children – need to see themselves together on stage for them to recognise the violence existing in the local social environment and the roles assumed by oppressors and oppressed. If beating children is naturalised by some of the population, enacting a situation based on the family's everyday life with the involvement of an audience directly implicated in this kind of social context is a precondition for the success of GTO-Maputo's work. In other words, there are moments when children and adults need to be together to create and debate the problems/theatre play and to enable the vital recognition of the situations involving parents and children, men and women, children and adults, the young and the old – however difficult and sensitive the issues presented. This is a major challenge that needs to be resolved: knowing the cultural limits acceptable to the groups involved and, at the same time, proposing the changes needed to address everyday problems that cannot be taken as taboo, since they materialise the oppression suffered by the participants. Therefore, the form in which the plays are staged and their dramatic proposal become so important. Through artistic means, messages can be translated that would be difficult to treat effectively through any other kind of communication. If these premises are not observed, there is a risk of working with artificial narratives and dialogues, which fail to reflect what really happens in the everyday life of the family households. In sum, the simple separation of the plays/debates by age group and themes is not easy to implement: it can generate considerable limitations to the scope of GTO-Maputo's objectives.

In February 2009, I was fortunate to have the chance to get to know the work conducted by GTO-Maputo during a short stay in Mozambique. One of the main aims of my investigative trip was to see the work and organisation of those involved in the initiatives in situ. I could observe that there is a real engagement with and commitment to Boal's ideas and, above all, a strong endeavour to transform the Mozambican social context with all its numerous challenges. Hence, when the report went into detail on the results obtained by the project, I could compare them with my own conclusions – already duly published and divulged in the academic environment through my scientific articles. These matched the observation that, despite all the difficulties and limitations involved, significant and undeniable changes have already occurred and others are under way, as a direct result of GTO-Maputo's presence in various regions of the country. The report makes explicit several factors that help us visualise the positive impact of the dramatic interventions – for example, when the document signals what it calls good practices, or when it provides the following appraisal of the project design:

> The project design could not have been better, since it is based on a tested methodology recognised as effective in achieving the proposed objectives. Additionally, it anticipates the involvement of the main

beneficiaries of the project during its implementation, allowing them to assume an active and determinant role in the transmission of the project's messages (UNICEF, 2009:88).

Furthermore, specifically in relation to the project's implementation, the report emphasises that:

> its implementation integrates people from the community itself, who speak the local languages. In accordance with the methodology of the Theatre of the Oppressed, this allows the communities to experience, identify, believe and above all resolve their problems. More importantly, the actors chosen from the community act out situations from the everyday reality of the communities themselves. This performance results from the prior effort of the GTO staff to identify the best local tales and stories so that, as mentioned earlier, the people can identify with the material and above all become aware of the need to change behaviours relating to their personal hygiene, their health, prevention of HIV/AIDS, child rights and other relevant issues (UNICEF, 2009:88–9).

In another section of the document, discussing a variable that explains a change in the behaviour of inhabitants of the regions where GTO-Maputo intervened, the report's authors observe that:

> Nearly four-fifths of the interviewees affirmed that the theatre had changed habits considerably, with people starting to protect themselves more against HIV/AIDS, cholera and malaria. This allowed us to conclude that the program is having an impact on the way of life of the communities and, above all, that the latter have started to accept that, thanks to the project, they are better prepared to confront a series of life challenges (UNICEF, 2009:94).

In exploring this data, these favourable outcomes become clear, demonstrated in detail in this evaluative report, consolidate the recognition of GTO-Maputo as one of the main groups outside of Brazil disseminating the Theatre of the Oppressed and its capacity to provoke profound and promising social transformations. Reaching this conclusion does not, of course, mean overlooking the weaknesses that the research itself has also shown in GTO-Maputo's work.

As an example, another item that can be highlighted concerns the following question: 'Where do you take your children when they are sick?' The researchers asked this question in the family households in which the interviews were conducted and, of course, where GTO-Maputo had implemented its drama initiatives. On this point, the report highlights the need for GTO to broaden its activities, especially in the provinces of Zambézia and Tete, where people make fewer hospital visits, still preferring to look for help from a traditional doctor. The report recommends, therefore, that the GTO sessions are extended to these traditional doctors:

> The awareness-raising sessions must be extended to the healers as a form of controlling the propagation of diseases like HIV/AIDS, given that going to healers rather than hospital remains an option for the family households; indeed, there are still some cases in the interior where the healers are the main providers of medical care to the families. These should be a target for project capacitation, therefore, given the impact and influence of their activities in the zone (UNICEF, 2009:100).

I emphasise this section of the report since it provides a clear example of the Theatre of the Oppressed's capacity to transform, merely through the presence of GTO-Maputo in certain regions of the country. As the report recommends, there are other campaigns that could be implemented, since when it comes to evaluating the discourses of authority found in the communities, the traditional doctors – called healers in the report – occupy a very important position of power and persuasion, possessing a huge influence over much of the population. The role played by GTO-Maputo, then, is fundamental insofar as it can dialogue with all kinds of social agents, who can combine to form a force that is culturally recognised by the population. Hence a network of influence and solidary emancipation needs to be created, which includes everyone. GTO-Maputo can achieve this amplification since its methodology is built around working together without hierarchies or the simple overlapping of social voices. Founded on this dialogical approach, GTO-Maputo has already acquired, and continues to delimit, its own legitimising discourse, respected by different social actors involved in the process. This validation constitutes the root without which the work would be unsuccessful, since its own execution would become impossible. This is the meaning contained in the ontology and epistemology of the Theatre of the Oppressed, already described at the start of this chapter.

In the section 'Identification of good practices', the report also presents several items that reflect the advances achieved by GTO-Maputo and discusses the importance of this methodology/dramaturgy being implemented in a dialogical form, attentive to the local demands of those living in the most vulnerable situations. On one hand, attention is drawn to the appeal made for more actions on issues besides HIV/AIDS, as indicated in other parts of the report. Simultaneously, emphasis is given to the importance of the amplification achieved in addressing themes relating to the sustainability of the implemented actions:

> Once people's awareness has been raised, the GTO members have helped the populations to build better houses and latrines (Corredor da Beira, for example), open up new roads and distribute food, in coordination with the provincial directorates of public works. As a way of ensuring the sustainability of these activities, so that they are permanent and can expand, the groups have been encouraged to implement income-generating activities. This revenue is intended to sustain the group. In the case of Manica, for example, the group is paying wages to around 25 people, has a driver and its own means of transport, facilities and a guard, making it to some extent self-sustainable (UNICEF, 2009:89).

This shows that, through a central thematic focus, it is possible to widen the scope of the debate and the theatrical creation itself, helping the group touch on various topics through the same theatrical intervention. In other words, through awareness-raising linked to the creation and performance of the theatre plays, many other actions of considerable importance to the communities can emerge and be implemented. Indeed, it becomes apparent to those involved that problems and their potential solutions are always interwoven. A correlation exists between them, just as an interdependence exists between all the people who form the groups involved in the process. On this point, the report emphasises the importance of:

> [an] involvement of the stakeholders in the communities where the activities are implemented, so as to ensure the alignment of the messages disseminated by the program to the surrounding environment ... in order to guarantee continuity and a better insertion of the lessons being taught (UNICEF, 2009:95)

On the one hand, setting out from this suggestion, the research shows the clear need for the communities and GTO-Maputo agents to work in conjunction, along with more direct involvement of other similar networks, as is the case – also highlighted positively in the research – of the joint actions involving GTO-Maputo and the Institute of Social Communication.

On the other hand, a subsection of the document explaining behavioural changes, along with specific aspects concerning the analysis of the research samples, shows that basic questions of hygiene and disease prevention, such as washing hands, are still not being fully incorporated by the populations, especially in the Sofala and Manica regions (UNICEF, 2009:94). The report also recommends that GTO-Maputo extends its presence to more remote rural areas in order to reach a larger number of people, as yet unfamiliar with the group's work. These data lend support to the recommendations made for GTO to intensify and broaden its approach to certain themes. At the same time, it is a clear signal of the immensity of the work untaken by the group, since it occupies strategic social spaces where scarcities and vulnerability are manifested in diverse ways and with multiple meanings. Without doubt, this reveals the sheer scale of the work undertaken; but in some respects, the group itself also lacks more support. GTO-Maputo recently had to deal with the consequences of a flood, which led to the loss of much of what had been constructed over these years in material terms. The impact is, indeed, still ongoing. Problems exist, therefore, in relation to infrastructure, financial support, recognition of the amplitude of the challenge untaken and the benefits already achieved through the work carried out over the 12 years of its existence.

In the face of these facts, can theatre respond to such basic and urgent problems? Boal believed so, as his works and life demonstrated. GTO-Maputo, for its part, has also been showing the urgency of assuming control of the course of history through dialogical and emancipatory actions. In 2008, reflecting the international impact and socio-cultural results obtained by his work, Augusto Boal was nominated for the Noble Peace Prize. In March 2009, he was named World Theatre Ambassador by UNESCO. The contribution of the Theatre of the Oppressed was duly recognised, therefore, and its presence around the planet has helped consolidate the libertarian ideals of its creator, who has become eternalised in the process. Brazil as a nation should be proud to have been the birthplace of Augusto Boal. The reality is, though, that the benefits of his aesthetics/politics extend far beyond the borders artificially imposed by nation states. The penetration of the Theatre of the Oppressed in countries of the five continents, using languages in tune with each locality, without failing to maintain the proposal to defend the rights of the most vulnerable populations, shows the greatness of a dramaturgy that aims to go far beyond the limits between art and life, actor and spectator. Mozambique welcomed Theatre of the Oppressed with open arms and added the strength and courage needed to implement the initiatives. Its continuity over so many years reveals the dedication inherent in the process. It provides an example of how culture can be a path to union and approximation between different peoples. What apparently divides us can also unite us. And it is in this sense, too, that, beyond the institutional initiatives of governments (although they are also essential), exchanges of culture and knowledge can be created and fomented that are capable of transforming realities, creating spaces where theatre translates these messages into hope and into concrete improvements in social conditions. In February 2009, during my field research, I asked one of the members of GTO-Maputo how she dealt with the inevitable despondency that sometimes affected her in the face of so many challenges, all of them so persistent. She replied with a comment that sheds light on the process of the whole group. Here I merely recall the gist of her words, but the strength of her conviction remains intact in the meaning that can be drawn from her affirmation: 'If you are aware, you simply cannot stop acting. It's inevitable that you'll continue working, it's simply a question of being aware.'

References

Boal, A (2003) *O Teatro como Arte Marcial*. Rio de Janeiro: Garamond.
Boal, A (2005) *Teatro do Oprimido e Outras Poéticas Políticas*. Rio de Janeiro: Civilização Brasileira.
Boal, A (2009) *A Estética do Oprimido*. Rio de Janeiro: Garamond.
Cossa, A (2013) Há um grande medo de financiar as actividades que colocam o povo a pensar. [Depoimento a Inocêncio Albino]. *A Verdade,* Maputo, 7 February. Available at: http://www.verdade.co.mz/tema-de-fundo/35-themadefundo/34335-ha-um-grande-medo-de-financiar-as-actividades-que-colocam-o-povo-a-pensar (accessed 28 October 2013).
Geertz, C (2001) *Nova Luz Sobre a Antropologia*. Rio de Janeiro: Jorge Zahar.
Klotz, A and Lynch, C (2007). *Strategies for Research in Constructivism International Relations*. Armonk, NY/London: ME Sharpe.
Ministério da Cultura (2005) *Cultura Viva: Programa Nacional de Arte, Educação, Cidadania e Economia Solidária*, 3rd edition. Brasilia: Ministério da Cultura.
Nunes, SB (2004) *Boal e Bene: Contaminações para um teatro menor*. PhD Thesis, Postgraduate Programme in Clinical Psychology, Pontifical Catholic University of São Paulo.
Santos, EG (2011) Formulação de políticas culturais: As leis de incentivo e o Programa Cultura Viva. In F Barbosa and L Calabre (eds) *Pontos de Cultura*: *Olhares sobre o Programa Cultura Viva*. Brasilia: IPEA, pp 155-178.
United Nations Children's Fund (UNICEF) (2009) *Relatório Final,* Mozambique. New York: UNICEF.
Visentini, PF (2013) *A Projeção Internacional do Brasil*: 1930–2012. Porto Alegre: Elsevier.

Chapter 13
The culture politics of Brazilian Christianity in Mozambique

Linda van de Kamp

Brazilian churches are a relatively new phenomenon in southern Africa and have gained most prominence in Mozambique, Angola and South Africa (Corten, Dozen and Oro, 2003; Freston, 2005). The increasing political, economic and cultural interaction between Brazil and Africa has run parallel to Brazilian missionaries travelling across the Atlantic. While discussions take place about the extent to which Brazil as a *mestizo* country may play a different role in Africa compared to Western countries and China (see, for example, Visentini, 2012), Brazilian pastors and African converts have established unique and remarkable South–South connections, as will be demonstrated in the case of Mozambique. Most of the Brazilian (evangelical) missionaries went to Mozambique (Freston, 2005:55) and today, Brazilian churches are integrated and prominent in its (peri-) urban landscapes.

The Brazilian churches that are featuring most prominently in Mozambique belong to the new global brand of neo-Pentecostal Christianity[180] that thrives in Africa, Latin America and Asia, and stresses the importance of a direct personal experience with God through the embodiment of the Holy Spirit by followers of Jesus Christ (Freston, 2001; Jenkins, 2002; Anderson, 2004; Asamoah-Gyaduh, 2013). They place special emphasis on the gifts of the Holy Spirit, such as speaking in tongues, prophecy, dreams and visions, prayer healing, and deliverance from evil spirits. Pentecostals view the world as the site of a spiritual battle between demonic and heavenly forces, a view that supports a Pentecostal global mission to spread the gospel among all nations. Most Pentecostal churches operate in global networks of exchange, whereby public media as well as the circulation of charismatic leaders, films, books and all sorts of other materials are crucial in targeting localities around the world as

---

180 Often also called Pentecostal-Charismatic Christianity or the third wave within Pentecostalism. In this chapter, I use as a shorthand the term Pentecostalism while being aware of the variety of Pentecostalisms (for Africa, see Asamoah-Gyadu, 2013; for Brazil see Freston, 1995). I do not include the African Independent Churches, such as the Zionist Churches in Mozambique, in this category, because of their different histories and different approaches to issues of cultural (dis)continuity (Meyer, 2004; for a discussion see Engelke, 2010).

part of the faith's project to transform nations, communities and personal lives through the power of the Holy Spirit (Coleman, 2000; Gifford, 2004; Meyer, 2010).

While this form of Christianity often serves as the exemplar of cultural globalisation in modern times – i.e. in the way that it appears to foster a homogenising of the Pentecostal born-again identity around the world – the precise way in which the faith relates to local cultural traditions and national circumstances appears to result in myriad diverse engagements and cross-cultural exchanges (Corten and Marshall-Fratani, 2001; Freston, 2001). In this respect, the faith's South–South links offer an interesting and different perspective to the standard discussion of the linkage between globalisation and Pentecostalism that focuses on North–South connections (Velho, 2007; Van de Kamp and Van Dijk, 2010). As I will show in this chapter, what renders the Pentecostal faith relevant to its followers is not only the global aspects of the religion, but also its position regarding the nation-state and (national) cultural projects combined with the particularly cross-cultural approach of the missionaries. The specific way in which Brazilian Pentecostalism in Mozambique is fostering identities that transcend national cultural projects highlight the role of southern Pentecostals in raising critical awareness vis-à-vis certain local cultural practices and national politics, especially in the domain of family and marriage, and of economic enterprise.

Methodologically, this chapter is based on ethnographic research carried out mainly in Maputo, the capital of Mozambique, over a period of 26 months between 2005 and 2011 (Van de Kamp, 2011a). The research concentrated on the process of conversion to Brazilian Pentecostalism by urban Mozambicans in which the Brazilian Pentecostal culture politics, especially regarding family, marriage, gender and work, turned out to be crucial.[181] I focused on the South–South transnational connection of Brazilian Pentecostalism in Mozambique from the Mozambican perspective. While I interviewed several Brazilian Pentecostal pastors, the churches and their organisation were not the principal focus of my fieldwork but rather the converts themselves. By following people instead of churches, I gained better insight into the role of Pentecostal religion in converts' lives. Because I had not chosen pastors and leaders as gate persons, people felt freer to share their lives with me, also when it was not congruent with the churches' ideology.

---

181 In October 2006, I did fieldwork in the city of Beira, in central Mozambique, where I found the same concerns among converts of Brazilian Pentecostal churches about family, gender and marriage as in Maputo.

Brazilian Pentecostalism in urban Mozambique

Since the early 1990s, Christianity has started to boom in Mozambique (see, for example, Agadjanian, 1999; Morier-Genoud, 2000; Seibert, 2005; Cruz e Silva, 2008; Schuetze, 2010), shortly after the end of the civil war.[182] The end of the war also marked the end of the socialist era and the start of the democratisation and liberalisation of the economic and political domains,[183] including a relaxing of regulations concerning religious expression. Since the colonial period, the Roman Catholic Church had been the country's biggest Christian church followed by various Protestant churches and African Independent Churches (AICs). The results of the 2007 Census (INE, 2010) show, however, that in the southern provinces of Maputo and Gaza, Catholicism is no longer the most important religion, but that Zionism has become one of the country's main African Independent Christian movements. Moreover, for the first time, Evangelicals and Pentecostals were counted together as one separate category, showing their growing importance, representing 11 per cent of the total population.[184] In the capital, Maputo, their share is 21 per cent (INE, 2009).[185]

The most prominent Pentecostal churches come from Brazil (Cruz e Silva, 2003; Freston, 2005). Shortly after the signing of the peace treaty between FRELIMO and RENAMO in October 1992, the Brazilian Universal Church of the Kingdom of God opened its doors in Maputo. Brazilian pastors started to hold church services in empty cinemas in Maputo and their performances rapidly gained popularity. Some people initially attended services just out of curiosity, having heard that the Brazilians were entertaining, exorcised spirits, cured diseases, presented solutions for problems and could make one rich. Services used to be a good option for an evening out as no films were screened at cinemas in the early 1990s.[186] After the long period of civil war,

---

182 The total number of churches officially registered at the government's Religious Affairs Department in Maputo was 110 in 1992, the year the civil war officially ended. Some 18 years later, in September 2010, this was 758 (DNAR, 2010). However, the real number can be assumed to be even higher since not all churches, especially the smaller ones, have been able to register (Seibert, 2005:133).

183 For more on the type of socialism in Mozambique and the transition to privatisation, see Pitcher (2002).

184 According to the Census, Catholicism represents 28 per cent of the total population and Islam 18 per cent.

185 It should be noted here that the classifications used in the 2007 Census are debatable (Cruz e Silva, 2008:168–72). Most of the AICs, for instance, have been classified as Zionist, even if in the strictest sense they were not Zionists. Moreover, many of the people classified as not having any religion, in reality adhere to forms of traditional religion which does not have a specific category in the Census.

186 After a gradual decline, the national cinema collapsed in the early 1990s after the liberalisation of the media and the introduction of structural adjustment programmes (Power, 2004). In other African countries and elsewhere, Pentecostal churches have taken over cinemas too, making their engagement with the public sphere very visible (Meyer, 2002).

when everything, including entertainment, had been scarce, new activities and diversions were welcomed and embraced. Others, however, accused the church of being a sect and a money machine, and of preventing films from being shown in the cinemas. People wrote letters to the national newspapers in which they complained that the church and its Brazilian pastors, television and radio programmes were invading the country.[187] However, a growing number of people became active followers of the church and other Brazilian Pentecostal churches and missionaries arrived. Today, Brazilian Pentecostal churches are integrated and prominent in the (peri-) urban landscape, particularly in the capital, Maputo.

The Brazilian Pentecostal church *Igreja Universal do Reino de Deus* (Universal Church of the Kingdom of God, known as the Universal Church) is by far the largest and most aggressive in terms of recruiting strategies, as well as in its critiques of the local cultures. In his article on the manifestation of the Universal Church in southern Africa (Angola, South Africa and Mozambique), Freston (2005:1) claimed that this church is an important player in the growth and spread of 'Third World evangel religion'[188] as it is the 'first major example in the region of a new phenomenon: a successful church which is neither of First World nor African origin'. Another prominent Brazilian Pentecostal church in Mozambique, which competes heavily with the Universal Church, is the *Igreja Mundial do Poder de Deus* (World Church of the Power of God, known as World Church). It is led by a former bishop of the Universal Church and is expanding rapidly. A smaller one is the *Igreja Pentecostal Deus é Amor* (Pentecostal Church God is Love, known as God is Love) – this church was at the start of the neo-Pentecostal era in Brazil (Chesnut, 1997), and since its arrival has also been using cinemas for its services. In the past years, other well-known Brazilian Pentecostal churches were established, such as the *Igreja Internacional da Graça de Deus* (International Church of God's Grace), and Brazilian missionaries have been arriving and creating their own independent

---

187   Some of the critique was also related to suspicions that the Universal Church would have made a deal with the FRELIMO government before the first multi-party elections, which allowed the church to set up its radio and TV stations and to rent a part of the FRELIMO Central Committee building in Maputo (see also Freston, 2005:56, 57). The possible links between the Brazilian Pentecostal leaders and the government are not the focus of this chapter, partly because this was not an important issue for converts, but the government's politics of culture (see later). Generally, engaging themselves in politics or even speaking about it meant they would be dealing with mundane, evil powers (Burchardt, 2013:253–5). During my last fieldwork in 2011, I noticed that the number of politicians participating in Brazilian Pentecostal churches had increased, which in my view could be related to the growing influence of the so-called prosperity theology, see the section 'Prosperity and taking ownership'.

188   Evangelicals emphasise a personal conversion experience and Pentecostal Evangelicals stress the importance of the additional reception of the Holy Spirit, such as speaking in tongues (Shibley, 1998:77).

churches. Brazilian evangelists also work in the classical Pentecostal Assemblies of God Church, which is generally acknowledged to be the biggest Pentecostal (and maybe even Protestant and Evangelical) church in Mozambique. It was founded in the country at the beginning of the 20th century (Upton, 1980). In addition, Mozambique hosts the Brazilian *Igreja Baptista Renovada* (Renewed/ Charismatic Baptist Church), which also has some neo-Pentecostal features.

Non-Brazilian transnational Pentecostal churches mostly originate from South Africa or Zimbabwe and sometimes also from Malawi or Tanzania (see Van Koevering, 1992).[189] Other churches come from outside the southern African region, such as the Redeemed Christian Church of God, which has its roots in Nigeria. Many of these non-Brazilian churches attract expats but few Mozambicans, because English is the prevailing language used. More importantly, these non-Brazilian neo-Pentecostal churches lack the cultural imagery that has developed in the transnational setting of the Brazilian churches. As a result, the transnational neo-Pentecostal churches in Mozambique remain predominantly of Brazilian origin, and even if they did not originate in Brazil, they have close ties with Brazil. For example, the prominent Pentecostal *Igreja Evangélica Cristã Maná* (Christian Evangelical Church Maná, known locally as Maná) originated in Portugal, but many Mozambicans consider it to be Brazilian because it is also active there, and probably because people label this type of Christianity as coming from Brazil. The situation is often similar in transnational churches set up by Mozambicans. For example, the fast-growing *Evangelho em Acção* (Gospel in Action) maintains close ties with Brazil. Almost all the transnational neo-Pentecostal churches in Mozambique have been run by foreign pastors who are predominantly from Brazil, and to a lesser extent from Angola, and in the case of Maná, from Portugal too.[190] The Portuguese language and the countries' shared history because of colonialism have facilitated the connection between Brazilians, Angolans and Mozambicans. Consequently, the international network enjoyed by these churches in Mozambique is primarily Lusophone, with Brazil playing a key role.

Since Pentecostal churches do not keep records of members and they also attract temporary visitors, it is difficult to say exactly how many people attend

---

189   The transnational connections of the non-Brazilian Pentecostal churches relate to a longer history of migration in the southern African region. For example, most of the Protestant mission churches and African Independent churches (AICs) in southern Mozambique were initiated by returning migrants (Helgesson, 1994:131–6; Harries, 2007), particularly Mozambican mine workers returning from South Africa, who had come into contact with mission posts and AICs on the mines. The Zimbabwe Assemblies of God, Africa is an example of a classical African Pentecostal church that started in Zimbabwe and spread in southern Africa (Maxwell, 2006).

190   This seems to be changing as, among other reasons, the Mozambican government is pressurising foreign churches to employ local pastors.

Brazilian Pentecostal churches but they attract substantial numbers. The Universal Church has about 250 similar-looking church buildings in Mozambique, of which 100 are in Maputo (at least one in every neighbourhood),[191] mostly at strategic locations like a central market or on a main road (Figure 13.1). Huge cathedrals (*catedrais*) have also been built. The new main cathedral of the Universal Church at the *Avenida 24 de Julho* (Avenue 24th of July), which was inaugurated in March 2011, is the largest modern church building in Mozambique and is also called *Cenáculo da Fé* (Cenacle of Faith). It contains a main auditorium with several thousand seats, a few smaller auditoriums, offices, a bookshop and a cash machine. This visible and public presence of church buildings is an important element in their strategy. With their television and radio broadcasting activities, the Universal Church has a prominent position in Mozambican urban society. All the Brazilian Pentecostal churches organise three to six services every day in each of their buildings and all the churches are packed with both temporary and permanent visitors, especially at the early-morning and evening services just before and after work hours (Figure 13.2). Between 100 and 2 000 people attend the different churches, depending on the size of the building. Increasingly, the World Church is taking a similar position in urban society as the Universal Church. Based on interviews and observations, I estimated that both Maná and God is Love have about 50 places of worship in Mozambique. Maná has become particularly prominent due to its radio activities and their radio station, *Viva* (Lively or Hurray!), is the preferred channel in many *chapas* (public transport, mini-buses) as it features popular (secular) songs and offers listeners the chance to send messages to friends (Figure 13.3). Alongside the international TV channel ManaSat, Maná has also been running a local television channel for several years. God is Love also uses (radio) air time like most bigger Brazilian Pentecostal churches that can afford it, and they also (try to) feature on television, such as the World Church. The Universal Church has its own television channel, *Miramar*, belonging to TV Record.

---

191 These numbers are based on personal observation and interviews with church leaders in the period 2005–2008 and were updated in 2011.

Figure 13.1: Universal Church at the start of the highway EN-1 in Maputo, April 2006. © Rufus de Vries

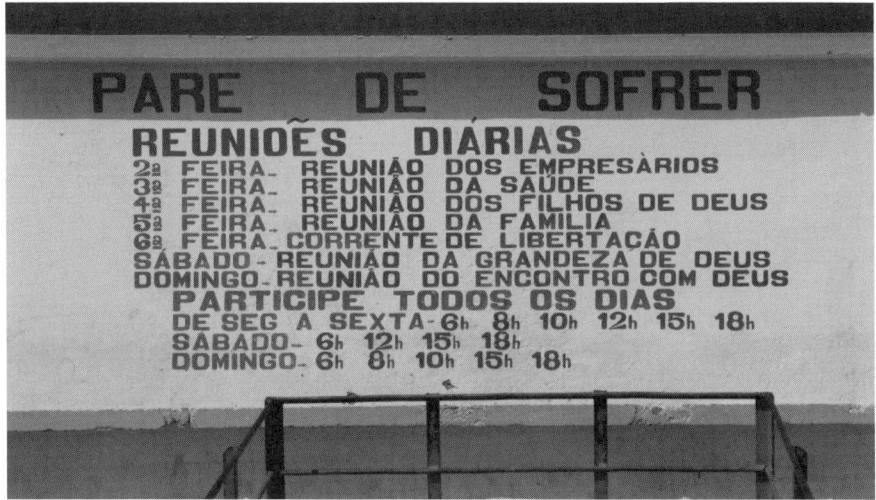

Figure 13.2: Programme of services, Universal Church: 'Stop Suffering'; Daily reunions; Monday: reunion of entrepreneurs; Tuesday: reunion of health; Wednesday: reunion of God's children; Thursday: reunion of the family; Friday: chain of liberation; Saturday: reunion of the greatness of God; Sunday: reunion of the encounter with God.
Participate every day; from Monday to Friday – 6 hours: 6 h, 8 h, 10 h, 12 h, 15 h, 18 h;
Saturday 6 h, 12 h, 15 h, 18 h;
Sunday 6 h, 8 h, 10 h, 15 h, 18 h.
© Rufus de Vries

Figure 13.3: Radio mast, Maná Church
© Rufus de Vries

Pentecostalism in Mozambique flourishes particularly among upwardly mobile women in urban areas. Nearly 75 per cent of the visitors and converts at Pentecostal churches in Maputo are women of differing ages, who generally earn some money, and many of them are relatively well-educated.[192] In general, women outnumber men in Christian churches (Woodhead, 2001:73) but when compared to Mozambique's Catholic and Protestant mission churches, Pentecostalism is a very female-oriented religion. Worldwide, Pentecostalism attracts high numbers of women, with similar percentages to those found in Mozambique (Chesnut, 1997:22; Martin, 2002:56). During church services,

---

192   Normally the women had at least followed some years of primary-school education and, thus, spoke Portuguese, the official language, which is also spoken in the Brazilian churches. In many other churches, such as in the African Independent Churches, local languages were used. Some of the women were studying at university and at institutes of higher education. In principle, they all earned their own (informal) salary, even though the amounts could differ from the minimum wage to 10 times the minimal wage. In the case of the Universal Church, Gaspar (2006) also found that most of the visitors are women but, different to my findings, he found that many of them had not followed any education. It appears that at an earlier stage of the Brazilian Pentecostal presence in the country, the church attracted people from different socio-economic groups (see also Cruz e Silva, 2003:111–12). Yet, we both found that most converts have some form of income, and this is crucial because of the strong emphasis on tithing and offerings in these churches (discussed later).

Brazilian pastors address the new social challenges that the upwardly mobile women in their congregations are encountering. For example, pastors organise church services around how to find a faithful husband and how to build a successful marriage and family. They have also developed business courses to improve women's economic skills.

The introduction of a neo-liberal market economy, because of the Structural Adjustment Programmes at the end of the 1980s, the implementation of more democratic social structures and the influx and rise of non-governmental organisations focusing on women's rights and emancipation have been stimulating women's access to education and professional careers (Casimiro, 2004:146; Sheldon, 2002:229–66). The enhanced economic position of these women has put them in new socio-cultural domains. In contrast to former generations of women in the cities, more and more urban women are no longer dependent on marriage for their economic survival (Penvenne, 1997). And their role in biological reproduction is no longer decisive in establishing their position and identity either. They are exploring new lifestyles and cultural positions by living on their own, choosing their partner without the interference of kin or deciding to stay single, going on vacation, getting a driving licence and constructing their own houses. In addition to new opportunities, these new social circumstances are raising questions, conflicts and uncertainties. Despite or precisely because of their increasing socio-economic independence, many younger women are not able to find a 'good', 'faithful' partner. Men are afraid that the women (can) earn more than they do and that they will lose their position of influence (Manuel, 2011). Families-in-law are not sure whether these women will be good housewives. In short, these women are benefitting from the new economic and socio-cultural possibilities available to them but, like their partners and in-laws, are uncertain about how exactly to fulfil their new role as they lack the appropriate role models in their families because they are often the first generation running a company or following higher education (Van de Kamp, 2012). These women constitute a large part of the followers of Brazilian Pentecostal churches. Yet, even if the Brazilian pastors address the issues that keep these women busy, this does not automatically mean that they develop successful marriages and professional careers, as I shall show later.

From socialist to Pentecostal modernisation: The politics of culture
Mozambicans who attended the first Brazilian Pentecostal services in the early 1990s emphasised how they were amazed to hear the Brazilians talk openly about ancestor spirits and evil spirits. The urban centre of Mozambique had been dominated by policies focused on abandoning 'backward beliefs',

starting with the Portuguese colonisers who labelled local cultural customs and worldviews as 'uncivilised'. After Independence in 1975, the FRELIMO government continued working on the abandonment of 'superstitious beliefs' and 'backward cultural habits' by proclaiming the socialist modernisation as the new faith (Mazula, 1995; Honwana, 2002; Lundin, 2007). People were subsequently forbidden to engage in rituals dedicated to the ancestors or with local customs such as initiation rituals and local marriage ceremonies (such as *lobolo*). In Maputo, the most nationalised place of the country (Abrahamsson and Nilsson, 1995:83; Sumich, 2010:2–5), these policies have been especially influential. Here, Mozambicans distanced themselves from 'tradition' or learnt to act as if they were not involved in practices related to ancestor spirits (Lundin, 2007:105–08; 147–9; 168–73). For example, the local languages were strongly discouraged. Pentecostals and non-Pentecostals who grew up during that time told me that at home their parents thought it better for their future to speak the official language, Portuguese. They could often understand the local language but it was not theirs and they could not or did not speak it. They experienced difficulties communicating with their grandparents and other kin, who were not used to speaking Portuguese and who used to teach the younger generations their cultural traditions. They internalised a certain distance to a cultural past (Sumich, 2010; Cipriano, 2011).

Although the introduction of neo-liberal economic and democratic policies since the end of the 1980s brought a new openness to Mozambique's cultural traditions, the role of spirits in daily life still cannot easily be discussed (see also Honwana, 2003). Discussing spirits is not common and can fill people with fear, in part because this could provoke them to act. However, the Brazilian missionaries did not seem to be impressed by the politics of silencing and openly talked about influences of ancestor spirits and evil forces caused by witchcraft. For example, the pastors brought the material used by local healers into the church, such as the divination tools they got from healers who had converted. By touching such things without any consequences, they could show that these things had no power over them. The pastors demonstrated that they knew the sources of local spiritual powers and could overrule them.

The Brazilian Pentecostal churches are well known for their demonisation of 'traditional culture' (see, for example, Almeida, 2009). They fulminate against any *macumba* by pointing at its occult powers. In Brazil, *macumba* is a pejorative term used to denominate those Afro-Brazilian practices and ritual objects that are held to involve witchcraft or black magic. Despite the variety of Afro-Brazilian religions and the differences with respect to African religions, many Brazilian pastors claim that in all these cases they are dealing with the same demonic powers. Since the religions of the African slaves shipped to Brazil during the transatlantic past forms the basis for a variety of Afro-Brazilian religions in Brazil, the Brazilian pastors believe the heart of evil lies in Africa (Macedo, 2000; compare Birman, 2006:65) and it is this evil that they have come to Africa to fight.[193] The *orixás*, the spiritual entities worshiped in Afro-Brazilian religions, originating from West Africa, as well as the spirits active in Mozambique are all declared demonic. According to the Brazilian pastors, Mozambicans are to be made aware of the real nature of their cultural past, as they are not necessarily familiar with it. To lead successful lives, people must be aware of generational curses and break them (Meyer, 1998; Van Dijk, 1998). The Afro-Brazilian Pentecostal imagery of *macumba* is presented as a mirror to the Mozambicans to generate a reflection on cultural issues (Van de Kamp, 2013).

By raising a critical awareness about cultural issues, the Pentecostals take a certain position in a public, urban domain in which 'Mozambican culture' is a topic of debate and concern. Since the FRELIMO government has departed from its socialist ideals, a process of revaluing 'traditional Mozambican culture' has started. Today the message of FRELIMO is that awareness and knowledge of Mozambique's cultural past will enrich all Mozambicans; it is an important instrument to prosper and for the nation to develop further. Consequently, changes occurred, for example, in the way in which the position of traditional healing is now perceived as being part of the nation state project, including through the establishment of the government-supported National Association of Traditional Healers (AMETRAMO). Moreover, state officials participate in local rituals dedicated to the ancestors when they officially open a new building or a bridge, or when they pay a visit to a local community.

At the same time, especially in the city, many contradictory and ambivalent visions exist about what being Mozambican really means and which aspects of 'tradition' should be captured. This is reflected in discussions on the use of local languages at schools, on how customary law and civil law should be integrated (Sousa Santos and Trindade, 2003), and in debates about how 'African' women should dress. Importantly, members of the upper and middle classes – mostly those people and families who most actively participated in the former socialist project – rarely speak openly about their visits to *curandeiros* (traditional healers) and they warn each other of the disastrous influences of *feiticeiros* (sorcerers) everywhere, fearing that their material wellbeing will be the subject of witchcraft practices. Numerous stories circulate of suspicious medicines put

---

193 A Mozambican pastor at the Universal Church explained that there are many more demons in Brazil than in Mozambique 'but they came to Brazil because of the slaves, thus their origin is in Africa' (conversation, 12 March 2007).

under people's chairs at work, in newly purchased cars or at the doors of luxury houses. Women share their anxieties about the *feitiços* (spells) used by other women to win over the hearts of their husbands. These discussions and anxieties are being influenced by the Pentecostal churches, whose spiritual leaders keep the imagery and fears of good and evil forces alive.

Yet, many Mozambican Pentecostals stressed how they felt that the Brazilian missionaries are particularly capable of dealing with evil powers, more than African or Western missionaries and healers, because these Brazilians are both insiders and outsiders to the spiritual world in Africa. Brazilian missionaries' simultaneous knowledge of and break with the Afro-Brazilian spirits demonstrates their experience with the real nature of 'evil' spiritual beings and their power to overrule them. Bringing the instruments with which *curandeiros* work into the church and ridiculing them is proof of the special power Brazilian Pentecostal pastors have for Mozambican Pentecostals.[194] One example of this Brazilian Pentecostal supremacy is the case of the spirit spouse or the spirit of *pombagira*.

Marriage, family and love

During special church services for the family and during 'therapies of love', Pentecostal pastors confront women with evil forces that influence their relationships negatively (Van de Kamp, 2011b). The pastors stress that many women are unsuccessful in their love relations and marriages because of the spirit of *pombagira* or the spirit husband. In Afro-Brazilian imagery, *pombagira* is a female spirit that personifies the ambiguities of femininity and female sexuality (Hayes, 2008). Mozambican women recognised their own experiences when hearing the pastors' stories about *pombagira* in Brazil. Pentecostal women told me how their sexual and marital relations were frustrated by so-called spirit husbands or spirit spouses. According to these women or their kin, they were related to a spirit – with whom they could experience sexual intercourse – who would not allow the women to engage in another relationship. I encountered various explanations for this phenomenon. One claimed that the spirit was a war spirit made up of the spirit of a murdered person who seeks revenge and attacks the murderer's family with illness and misfortune (Honwana 2002: 62–8; 2003:71–4; Igreja, Dias-Lambranca and Richters, 2008). To calm the spirit, compensation for his death and his reintegration into society is needed, which could happen through marriage to a virgin girl in the murderer's family. In this

---

194 More generally, *curandeiros* in Mozambican society stress in their advertisements, their experiences in other countries: using 'foreign' knowledge seemed to prove the efficacy of their healing techniques and medicines. Popular healers, pastors and prophets often appear to come from the other side of a border (Luedke and West, 2006).

way, the spirit becomes the girl's spouse, but the girl cannot later marry another man or special procedures must be followed. *Curandeiros* identified these spirits as belonging to persons who were murdered during wars in the colonial era.[195] In addition to the ongoing impact of these historical spirits, worries about a new wave of spirits seeking vengeance because of the latest post-independence civil war (until 1992) have increased (Igreja, Dias-Lambranca and Richters, 2008). The spirits of persons killed in the civil war are expected to seek revenge in the coming years. Now that soldiers who underwent cleansing rituals (Granjo, 2007) are getting old and dying, spirits that were temporarily calmed by these rituals are expected to become active again because they are still seeking revenge. According to both *curandeiros* and Pentecostal pastors, there are active avenging spirits in every (extended) family.

Another account about the spirit spouse explains how, in the current neo-liberal economic order, (grand)parents are selling their children to spirits to become rich. The (grand)parents consult a *feitiçeiro* who, in return, is given a girl (because the spirit is male) to feed the strong spiritual powers the sorcerer uses to produce luck and wealth. In the southern African region, this spirit spouse that eats human flesh refers to the spirit of persons who have been appropriated or killed for the benefit of another person. This generally involves accumulating wealth at the cost of others, which points to witchcraft (see, for example, Niehaus, 1997; West, 2005:35–9).

Many women who attended Brazilian Pentecostal church services knew or suspected that they were involved in a spiritual relationship. Others, however, were hearing from Brazilian pastors that certain incidents with spirits in their family may have been behind their failure to stay with their partner or marry. These, mostly younger, women had grown up with no clear notion of possible relations with ancestral spirits and had learnt about spiritual influences in their lives for the first time through the Afro-Brazilian Pentecostal churches (Van de Kamp, 2012). Often, these young women were the daughters of parents who had actively participated in the socialist project of modernisation, which had banned or wanted to ban religion and spirits. The Pentecostal women

---

[195] The *curandeiros* I spoke to in southern Mozambique date this to a practice from the 19th century, when major social changes were taking place in southern Africa because of the migration of Nguni groups (*Mfecane*). A special role was played by King Ngungunyane, who was from one of the Nguni groups that established the Gaza Empire in southern Mozambique. King Ngungunyane (1884–1895) was known for the violent wars he fought against Portuguese colonial oppression and his attempts to incorporate groups from other parts of the country, like the Ndau of central Mozambique, into his kingdom (Liesegang, 1986). Since the Ndau were murdered and enslaved against their will, and some of the dead Ndau bodies were not properly buried, they came to get revenge in Nguni and Tsonga families by *mupfuka*; the spirit of the dead person could resuscitate and seek rehabilitation and reintegration (see also, Langa, 1992:29–32, 43–6; Honwana, 2002:62–4). Boys could also become engaged in a spiritual marriage (see Bagnol, 2006:185–202).

adopted the Afro-Brazilian Pentecostal spiritual discourse about spirit spouses and participated in specific prayer sessions in which these evil spirits were expelled from their bodies, followed by months and sometimes years of active participation in education programmes about family, marriage and love. Other women did not necessarily convert to Brazilian Pentecostalism but found it interesting to explore.

For example, 29-year-old university-student Patricia[196] initially attended the services of the Universal Church out of curiosity, having heard that the Brazilians were entertaining because they organised spectacles of exorcising demons and curing diseases. When I met Patricia in early 2006, she took the work of the Brazilian pastors more seriously than before because strange things were happening to her. She had strange dreams and was often sick. Patricia was afraid that she would have to follow in her grandmother's steps and work as a *curandeira*. Since her grandmother died, nobody had yet been appointed to live and work with her grandmother's spirits. As all Patricia's sisters and most of her cousins were married, she thought she would probably be forced to follow her grandmother's work. 'Does that mean that all my studying and working has been for nothing?' she asked me with fear.[197] Patricia hoped that her prayers in church would protect her from becoming part of the spiritual history of her family.

Patricia's kin considered her unmarried status at the age of 29 years as abnormal. To end suspicion about her and, therefore, her family, her kin organised sessions with a *curandeiro* to find out about the family spirits' wishes. But Patricia was not tuned into the views of her family. She asked the *curandeiro*, who started to put something on her feet, what it was all about, but her family told her she should not ask questions. The stories Patricia heard about women married to spirits and her own participation in a Pentecostal church put her kin's activities in a different light. Moreover, she wanted to stay in control of her own life. She studied, had a job and was constructing her own house. She could be independent of her kin, and of a possible husband. At the same time, she did not want to disassociate from her relatives and was also worried about the fact that she wanted to find the appropriate life partner and have children. She questioned why she was unsuccessful in doing this. Patricia did not immediately take a pro or contra position regarding the spirit to whom she could probably be related. Her relatedness to, as well as independence from, her kin and her interest in the history of the spirits in her family, parallel with the challenging views presented by the pastors, offered a space from which she

---

196 The names I use are not the converts' real names and the citations are my translations from Portuguese.
197 Conversation, 29 October 2006.

could reflect on her situation. Patricia continued to attend the family sessions with the *curandeiro* and the services in church. For some time, she frequented the therapies of love (known as therapy) organised by the Universal Church.

The therapy resembles a church service but is dedicated to the subjects of marriage, love and sexuality. Thousands of people participate every week and most of them are young (aged 15 to 35 years) and female. There is always a sermon on a topic such as how to find a good partner; how to trust each other; whether anal sex is allowed; what love is; or what marriage should be like. The Brazilian pastors feel that they should teach Mozambicans what real love is. At the end of most therapies, the pastor asks couples to come to the podium to apologise to each other for the mistakes they have committed towards each other. While romantic music plays, the pastor summons them to embrace and kiss each other and to say: 'I love you'. Even though this has been changing in urban settings, it is generally uncommon to show affection to your partner publicly in Mozambican society. The pastors highlight that, through marriage, a couple are starting a nuclear family by leaving their extended families to live their own lives. Practical tools are given: the couple should live as far away from their kin as possible and the wife should not follow the advice of her mother-in-law, but that of her husband. The pastors criticise local marriages for the dependence they create between the couple and the extended family, which, in their view, hinders the healthy establishment of a Christian family. The pastors are particularly disapproving of the important role of the ancestral spirits who must approve of the marriage during the *lobolo* ceremonies.[198] In addition, pastors underscore the importance of the role of sexuality in marriage and stress its pleasure – sexuality in marriage has not only reproductive goals but should be something both the man and the woman enjoy. Women are encouraged to play an active role during sex. In the teachings, the presence of love in a relationship is promoted and love means that both parties should try to understand each other and make each other happy. Husband and wife should spend time together, go to the cinema or on holiday.

Various converts compared the words and behaviour of the Brazilian pastors with that of the soap stars playing in the Brazilian *telenovelas* that feature prominently on Mozambican television. Convert and university-student Elena (aged 25 years) explained that she and other women were experiencing problems in their relationships because Mozambican men are cold, 'as the pastors say', she added. She continued: 'In Brazil you hold hands with your wife, like you

---

198 *Lobolo* is often translated as bride-price but is in fact a process of exchange between the family of the future bride and bridegroom (see, for example Granjo, 2005).

see in the *telenovelas*, he kisses her in the streets, men show affection. But, here, no, that isn't possible. If it occurs, it will only happen in the bedroom.'[199] For the Pentecostal women (and some men), both the Brazilian pastors and the soap stars are becoming icons of identification in the development of new conceptions of what courtship and marriage should be. They are analysing their own situations in relation to these role models.

Most of the participants in the therapy are single women. They prefer a Pentecostal partner because they would be trained to be faithful and caring towards their wives. Since there are more women at church than men, women complain that there are insufficient men with whom to engage. Consequently, their involvement in the therapy does not often result in a loving relationship. Even though being married is not the only ideal of women who attend the church, as professional success is equally important, the underlying idea behind most therapy sessions is that being married is better than being single and, for most women, marriage is an ultimate ideal. The effects of involvement in the therapy are that women feel uncomfortable if they remain single. Moreover, preoccupation with the activities of either the Holy Spirit or evil spirits in converts' lives appeared to disrupt various marriages and relationships (Van de Kamp, 2011b). The pastors preach that jealousy, domestic violence and infidelity are caused by evil spirits. To ensure a successful marriage, women are thus encouraged to confront the Devil for his control over their husband's behaviour (Soothill, 2007:209–18). As a result, some women enter into quite an ambivalent relationship with their husbands, who they see as being imbued with an evil spirit. Subsequently, they found it difficult to be intimate with their partner, which could increase the husband's distrust of his wife's intentions.

In several cases, converts' relationships with their kin become problematic, as in the case of Mariza. Mariza (aged 38 years) was an assistant (*obreira*) of the Brazilian pastors in the God is Love church. She had suffered from a spirit spouse herself and when she heard about the God is Love church on the radio in the early 1990s, she started to go to its services in the Charlot Cinema, where a 'tall black person, a Brazilian pastor, exorcised the spirit'.[200] It took a year or two before the spirit really left her and, finally, after much praying by her and the pastors, the spirit relented: 'One night I saw the Devil in my dream, he looked very ugly, and said that he would go away because he was tired of God. God had burned him too often.'[201] When Mariza began to organise her civil marriage, the Devil/spirit spouse returned to tell her that she would not

---

199 Interview, 28 June 2006.
200 I interviewed Mariza on 21 November 2006 and 9 March 2007.
201 Often, during the services in Brazilian Pentecostal churches, everybody was called on to burn the evil spirits in their bodies in the name of Jesus, by yelling 'burn, burn, burn' (*queima, queima, queima*).

marry. Right up until the day of her wedding, it was uncertain whether she and her husband would get married or not. But Mariza knew that this was part of a spiritual battle: her faith was being tested. She told me that on her wedding day, the documents were missing at the civil registration and as the pastor prayed, he saw the Devil with the papers. In the end, the documents were found and they got married. Her family was not present since they could not believe that it would be possible for Mariza to get married as she had been related to her spirit spouse since childhood. They were afraid that something terrible would happen. According to them, by challenging the spirit spouse, Mariza was risking that 'evil' would hit the whole extended family and, therefore, her kin preferred to stay disconnected from her. They continued to be suspicious as Mariza, despite her fervent praying, fasting and sacrificing money in church, had not yet conceived after several years of marriage.

Prosperity and 'taking ownership'

An important feature of neo-Pentecostalism is the focus on the so-called Prosperity Theology or Health and Wealth Gospel, underlining how a combative faith brings happiness, health and prosperity in all aspects of life (Coleman, 2000; Martin, 2002; Gifford, 2004). This includes the financial practice of 'sowing and reaping': converts' church-related investments in both spiritual and monetary terms will generate success for them in this world in the form of prosperous businesses and a happy life. The Pentecostal leaders in Mozambique teach that tithes and offerings are vital tools for the dissemination of the gospel. It was clear and logical to converts that their money was being used to pay the salaries of pastors, the church rent and to broadcast their message. Moreover, by giving tithes and offerings (Figure 13.4), converts become blessed and they have the right to collect their blessings according to Malachi 3: 10,[202] a Bible verse that was often used in services. Pastors always gave the example of persons who had shown their respect for God by paying tithes and had been transformed into millionaires. By showing similar faith, according to the pastors, converts would be surprised how their money would multiply and they would have everything they had always wanted, such as peace, happiness, health, love and food. Through the money one gives, God is pressed to offer abundance in return. Yet the spirit in which one gives is crucial. In principle, offerings are made by free and spontaneous will; and the most important thing is not the amount of money donated, but whether one gives wholeheartedly.

---

[202] 'Bring the full amount of your tithes to the Temple, so that there will be plenty of food there. Put me to the test and you will see that I will open the windows of heaven and pour out on you in abundance all kinds of good things' (*Good News Bible*, 1994).

Figure 13.4: Collecting offerings in the God is Love church
© *Rufus de Vries*

Every Monday evening there are special services in the branches of all the Brazilian Pentecostal churches for financial success that are directed mainly at (potential) entrepreneurs.[203] The central message is that seemingly negative circumstances, such as a lack of education and high unemployment rates, do not automatically mean one cannot develop a thriving business. If people take responsibility for their financial lives, and their lives more generally, and invest in their future, they will be successful. On the first evening of the course on doing business in the second half of 2005, the Brazilian pastor of the Universal Church clearly said: 'when you aren't rich, it is your own fault. It is your faith in God that will be rewarded.' He, like other pastors, stressed that Mozambicans should take more initiative in setting up businesses and he felt that Mozambicans should be more creative in their economic activities. The pastor of the course said in one session:

---

203 Compared to the other services where most of the visitors are female, these services attract more men.

> People here [in Mozambique], are afraid of starting a business. Mozambique is lacking many things. There are shops selling fashions, food and home appliances. But in various neighbourhoods there is a shortage of good bakeries and of bread deliveries. In addition, I discussed with the bishop how a lot could be done in the field of tourism. Foreigners are coming to invest in tourism. But you are here already. There are so many possibilities. Rent an office, take pictures all over the country and put them on a website!

At the end, he said: 'you should be optimistic and not give up' and 'don't forget that God doesn't want to look like a fool and thus will give you abundantly [in return]'.

Convert Paula (aged 37 years), who worked at a telecommunication company and was finishing her studies at the University Eduardo Mondlane, incorporated this faith. She explained the vital importance of changing one's life personally:[204]

> In Mozambique, we are talking about the fight against poverty [*luta contra a pobreza*] but we have to fight mental poverty; it is a question of mentality. People are just sitting the whole day selling bananas and waiting for a job, but they have to do something. It is important to look forward. I have a good job and a good salary but I want to earn more money so I'm always looking around for another job. You can't ask God and do nothing yourself.

The then Mozambican president, Guebuza, was known for his slogans to fight poverty, emphasising that people should work hard to escape poverty. While this seems to resemble the Pentecostal discourse, converts were very critical of their government because they felt that the leaders were not good role models and were involved with the wrong (spiritual) powers. However, the pastors knew how to fight for change: by giving tithes and offerings, fasting, praying, following chains of services and participating in specific spiritual and financial campaigns, converts have the right to collect their blessings. During every service, participants could offer money directed to one request, such as building a house. To excel, one should give banknotes, preferably in US dollars, the currency used by entrepreneurs, which is worth far more than the Mozambican currency. Competition in the amounts people give was encouraged, particularly in the World Church and in the Universal Church.

---

204 Interview, 21 June 2006.

First, the pastors called forward those who give US$500, then those who give US$300 and then US$100, etc.; thus, even though the Bible passage often cited by pastors said that the amount of money given is not important, the pastors declared that Mozambican coins were worthless (Maxwell, 1998). Converts who gave coins would receive coins in return. There were also special campaigns (*campanhas*) that allowed people to realise a specific dream (*meu sonho vai se realizar* – my dream will come true), such as finding a faithful husband. Jesus gave his life in sacrifice and so converts must make (financial) sacrifices as well: they should concentrate all their energy into one request by fasting, praying and giving money. In these campaigns, amounts of US$20 000 were no exception and meant that converts donated all the savings in their bank account or sold their car or their house.

I came to know many converts who went bankrupt in the process (Van de Kamp, 2010), but continued to participate in the churches and in financial offerings or moved to another Pentecostal church. However, converts do not necessarily perceive themselves as victims of Pentecostal financial practices. They must act and are acting through faith, so one day they will be rewarded. Particularly important in the reasons women gave to continue their participation was that they felt that they were learning from their 'mistakes'. They blamed themselves and not the pastors for having lost all their money as they had not used their faith intelligently.[205] One woman, Julia (a civil servant, aged 40 years) explained how she should give her money in church only if she really wanted to:[206] 'In the past I didn't use my brains, I gave what the pastor asked. Now, I give when I want to, when I feel that this is the pledge I want to participate in, otherwise it won't work.'

She and other converts stressed that born-again persons need to engage in self-responsibility, which is central to the Pentecostal faith. This demonstrates how these upwardly mobile women are attracted by the fact that the churches are not places where support and sociability are central, as has been argued many times, but where they are pressured to take care of themselves (Van Dijk, 2010). This is an attitude to which they aspire and through which they can learn and demonstrate their capacities to pioneer in the world and establish powerful positions. The appropriation of particular modes of 'taking ownership' (*tomar posse*) as the pastors call it, introduces mechanisms of self-pressure to effectuate blessings that will demonstrate converts' proven commitment and, thus, their entitlement to prosperity. This is also reflected in the fact that several Pentecostal

---

205 The Universal Church's bishop, Macedo, introduced the concept of intelligent faith (*fé inteligente*) to stress the necessity of knowing how to use faith (Macedo, 2004:81–3).
206 Conversation, 17 August 2011.

women I came to know regularly moved from one Brazilian Pentecostal church to another. As they were pressured to take care of themselves with little support from the church and, consequently, did not create a relationship of trust with the Brazilian pastors (Van Wyk, 2011), some of them left when they were disappointed with the effects of their prayers and sacrifices. Julia had been frequenting different Brazilian Pentecostal churches over a period of about 10 years and, during my fieldwork period, Paula moved from the Universal Church to the World Church.

This further demonstrates that these women's engagement with Pentecostalism is not so much a reaction to the neo-liberal capitalist economy in Maputo, but is entangled with it (Comaroff, 2009; Meyer, 2007), as these churches are, in many ways, operating as enterprises. Even stronger, in their interaction, Brazilian pastors and Mozambican converts appear to expand a neo-liberal economic order beyond its limits by pressurising each other to engage in opportunities and challenges with a minimum of support. The Pentecostal women are very keen to become part of a new socio-economic and cultural order in which it is possible to study and get a well-paid job. The Pentecostal business courses, for example, are perceived by these women as a place where they can gain some basic understandings of the economic market and how to become successful women in the economic as well as in the socio-cultural spheres. They feel that they must learn to make personal choices and take control of their lives, even if this is at a (literally) high price.

Conclusion

Transnational Pentecostalism, and especially its South–South links, are crucial to understanding upwardly mobile women's religious involvement in Brazilian Pentecostalism in urban Mozambique. Brazilian Pentecostalism in Mozambique contributes to a critical cultural awareness by stimulating people to break with local cultures, a fact that is strengthened by the specific interpretation of the historical connections between Africa and Brazil. Brazilian missionaries have come to combat the origins of *macumba*, which they perceive as African, and even though it is a Brazilian concept for Mozambican Pentecostals in Maputo, they have incorporated it to address the negative forces in their lives. Brazilian pastors have brought the spirits, which travelled to Brazil so long ago with the slaves, back to what is supposed to be their home, to remind Mozambicans of their roots. In the Pentecostal context, these roots are considered dangerous and evil, and the cause of problems in people's lives.

This Brazilian Pentecostal approach to 'African culture' has become especially relevant to upwardly mobile women in Maputo, who are seeking to direct and control their new social positions in a shifting and challenging urban environment. Uncertainties about new ways of living demand a critical cultural reflection, especially in the reproductive domain, such as relationships with kin, partners and spirits. By navigating Brazilian Pentecostalism, they are exploring new ideas and forms of relating, and creating alternative options of family life, courtship and marriage. How much various Pentecostal women are prepared to invest in an alternative life becomes visible in their participation in financial campaigns to realise success in the current neo-liberal urban society. Female converts feel attracted by the fact that Pentecostal pastors do not offer help but, instead, push them to help themselves. This is an attitude to which upwardly mobile women aspire and through which they can learn and demonstrate their capacities to pioneer a new socio-economic reality, even if the women sometimes lose everything they have.

This interaction between Mozambican and Brazilian Pentecostals has reinforced aspects of the struggle against evil forces and of the Prosperity Gospel. Mozambican Pentecostal women and Brazilian missionaries find and reinforce one another in their capacities to challenge and move frontiers in the national sphere, particularly regarding issues of family, gender and work. The foreign but Afro-Brazilian religious knowledge is allowing Brazilian missionaries to cross sensitive cultural boundaries and is making them important and attractive counsellors. Their transgression of socio-cultural boundaries connects with upwardly mobile women's desire to push relational and spiritual innovation, as well as economic prosperity. While the specific transnational religious connection in Mozambique is a form of generating change, it also carries the danger of shaping new barriers and problems because the willingness to destabilise the dominant cultural order by converts results in tensions between the Pentecostal women, their partners and other kin, or their businesses cannot flourish because they offer all their money to the church.

References

Abrahamsson, H and Nilsson, A (1995) *Mozambique, the Troubled Transition: From socialist construction to free market capitalism*. London: Zed Books.

Agadjanian, V (1999) As Igrejas Zione no Espaço Sóciocultural de Moçambique Urbano (anos 1980 e 1990), *Lusotopie*, **6** (1/2), pp 415–23.

Almeida, R de (2009) *A Igreja Universal e Seus Demônios: Um estudo etnográfico*. São Paulo: Terceiro Nome.

Anderson, A (2004) *An Introduction to Pentecostalism: Global Charismatic Christianity*. Cambridge: Cambridge University Press.

Asamoah-Gyadu, JK (2013) *Contemporary Pentecostal Christianity: Interpretations from an African context*. WIPF & STOCK, Regnum Studies in Global Christianity, Eugene, Oregon.

Bagnol, B (2006) Gender, self, multiple identities, violence and magical interpretations in Lovolo practices in southern Mozambique. PhD Thesis, University of Cape Town.

Birman, P (2006) Future in the mirror: The media, Evangelicals and politics in Rio de Janeiro. In B Meyer and A Moors (eds) *Religion, Media and the Public Sphere*. Bloomington, IN:

Indiana University Press, pp 52–72.

Burchardt, M (2013) Equals before the law? Public religion and queer activism in the age of judicial politics in South Africa, *Journal of Religion in Africa*, **43** (3), pp 237–60.

Casimiro, I (2004) *'Paz na Terra, Guerra em Casa': Feminismo e Organizações de Mulheres em Moçambique*. Maputo: Promédia.

Chesnut, A (1997) *Born Again in Brazil: The Pentecostal boom and the pathogens of poverty*. New Brunswick, NJ: Rutgers University Press.

Cipriano, A (2011) *Educação, Modernidade e Crise Ética em Moçambique*. Maputo: Dondza Editora.

Coleman, S (2000) *The Globalisation of Charismatic Christianity: Spreading the gospel of prosperity*. Cambridge, UK: Cambridge University Press.

Comaroff, J (2009) The politics of conviction: Faith on the neo-liberal frontier, *Social Analysis*, **53** (1), pp 17–38.

Corten, A, Dozon, JP and Oro, AP (eds) (2003) *Les Nouveaux Conquérants de la Foi. L'Église Universelle du Royaume de Dieu (Brésil)*. Paris: Karthala [Published in Portuguese by Paulinas, São Paulo, 2003.]

Corten, A and Marshall-Fratani, R (eds.) (2001) *Between Babel and Pentecost. Transnational Pentecostalism in Africa and Latin America*. London: Hurst & Company.

Cruz e Silva, T (2003) Mozambique. In A Corten, J-P Dozon and AP Oro (eds) *Les Nouveaux Conquérants de la Foi. L'Église Universelle du Royaume de Dieu (Brésil)*. Paris: Karthala, pp 109–17.

Cruz e Silva, T (2008) Evangelicals and democracy in Mozambique. In T Ranger (ed.) *Evangelical Christianity and Democracy in Africa*. Oxford: Oxford University Press, pp 161–89.

Direcção Nacional de Assuntos Religiosos (DNAR) (2010) *Lista das Confissões Religiosas Registadas*. Maputo, Ministério da Justiça, Direcção Nacional de Assuntos Religiosos.

Engelke, M (2010) Past Pentecostalism: Notes on rupture, realignment, and everyday life in Pentecostal and African independent churches, *Africa*, **80** (2): 177–99.

Freston, P (1995) Pentecostalism in Brazil: A brief history, *Religion*, **25**, pp 119–33.

Freston, P (2001) *Evangelicals and Politics in Asia, Africa and Latin America*. Cambridge: Cambridge University Press.

Freston, P (2005) The Universal Church of the Kingdom of God: A Brazilian church finds success in southern Africa, *Journal of Religion in Africa*, **35** (1), pp 33–65.

Gaspar, GD (2006) 'É Dando que se Recebe': A igreja universal do reino de Deus e o Negócio da fé em Moçambique. MA thesis, Departamento de História, Faculdade de Filosofia e Ciências Humanas, Salvador, Brasil.

Gifford, P (2004) *Ghana's New Christianity: Pentecostalism in a globalising African economy*. London: Hurst & Company.

Good News Bible (1994) *Good News Bible*. The United Bible Societies.

Granjo, P (2005) *Lobolo em Maputo: Um velho idioma para novas vivências conjugais*. Porto: Campo das Letras.

Granjo, P (2007) The homecomer: Postwar cleansing rituals in Mozambique, *Armed Forces & Society*, **33** (3), pp 382–95.

Harries, P (1994) *Work, Culture, and Identity: Migrant laborers in Mozambique and South Africa, c. 1860–1910*. Portsmouth, NH: Heinemann.

Harries, P (2007) *Junod e as Sociedades Africanas. Impacto dos Missionários Suíços na África Austral*. Maputo: Paulinas [English edn. *Butterflies and Barbarians: Swiss missionaries and systems of knowledge in south-east Africa*. Oxford: James Currey, Athens, OH: Ohio University Press, Johannesburg: Wits University Press.

Hayes, KE (2008) Wicked women and *femmes fatales*: Gender, power and Pomba Gira in Brazil, *History of Religions*, **48** (1), pp 1–21.

Helgesson, A (1994) Church, state and people in Mozambique: an historical study with special emphasis on Methodist developments in the Inhambane region, PhD dissertation, Unversity of Ghent. Available at: lib.urgent.be/en/catalog/rug01:000317918 131–6 (accessed 6 May 2013).

Honwana, AM (2002) *Espíritos Vivos, Tradições Modernas: Possessão de espíritos e reintegração social pós-guerra no sul de Moçambique*. Maputo: Promédia.

Honwana, AM (2003) Undying past: Spirit possession and the memory of war in southern Mozambique. In B Meyer and P Pels (eds) *Magic and Modernity: Interfaces of revelation and concealment*. Stanford: Stanford University Press, p 60–80.

Igreja, V, Dias-Lambranca, B and Richters, A (2008) Gamba spirits, gender relations and healing in post-civil war Gorongosa, Mozambique, *Journal of the Royal Anthropological Institute*, **14** (2), pp 353–71.

Instituto Nacional de Estatística (INE) (2009) *Sinopse dos Resultados Definitivos do 3º Recenseamento Geral da População e Habitação. Cidade de Maputo*. Maputo: Instituto Nacional de Estatística.

Instituto Nacional de Estatística (INE) (2010) *III Recenseamento Geral da População e Habitação, 2007: Resultados definitivos*. Maputo: Instituto Nacional de Estatística.

Jenkins, P (2002) *The Next Christendom: The coming of global Christianity*. New York: Oxford University Press.

Langa, A (1992) *Questões Cristãs à Religião Tradicional Africana, Moçambique*. Braga: Editorial Franciscana.

Liesegang, GJ (1986) *Ngungunyane: A Figura de Ngungunyane Nqumayo, Rei de Gaza 1884–1895 e o Desaparecimento do seu Estado*. Maputo, ARPAC: Colecção Embondeiro No. 8.

Luedke, T and West, H (2006) *Borders and Healers: brokering therapeutic resources in southeast Africa* Bloomington, Indiana: Indiana University Press.

Lundin, IB (2007) *Negotiating Transformation: Urban livelihoods in Maputo adapting to thirty years of political and economic changes*. Department of Human and Economic Geography, Göteborg University.

Macedo, E (2000) *Orixás, Caboclos & Guias: Deuses ou demônios?* Rio de Janeiro: Editora Gráfica Universal Ltda.

Macedo, E (2004) *Mensagens que Edificam*, Volume 1. Rio de Janeiro: Editora Gráfica Universal Ltda.

Manuel, S (2011) Maputo Has no Marriage Material: Sexual relationships in the politics of social affirmation and emotional stability in a cosmopolitan African city. PhD Thesis, School of Oriental and African Studies, University of London.

Martin, B (2001) The Pentecostal gender paradox: A cautionary tale for the sociology of religion. In R Fenn (ed.) *The Blackwell Companion to Sociology of Religion*. Oxford: Blackwell, pp 52–66.

Martin, D (2002) *Pentecostalism: The world their parish*. Oxford: Blackwell.

Maxwell, D (1998) 'Delivered from the spirit of poverty?': Pentecostalism, prosperity and modernity in Zimbabwe, *Journal of Religion in Africa*, **28** (3), pp 350–73.

Maxwell, D (2006) *African Gifts of the Spirit: Pentecostalism and the rise of a Zimbabwean transnational religious movement*. Oxford: James Currey.

Mazula, B (1995) *Educação, Cultura e Ideologia em Moçambique: 1975–1985*. Lisbon: Edições Afrontamento.

Meyer, B (1998) 'Make a complete break with the past': Memory and postcolonial modernity in Ghanaian Pentecostal discourse, *Journal of Religion in Africa*, **28** (3), pp 316–49.

Meyer, B (2002) Pentecostalism, prosperity and popular cinema in Ghana, *Culture and Religion*, **3** (1), pp 67–87.

Meyer, B (2004) Christianity in Africa: From African Independent to Pentecostal-Charismatic Churches, *Annual Review of Anthropology*, **33**, pp 447–74.

Meyer, B (2007) Pentecostalism and neoliberal capitalism: Faith, prosperity and vision in African

Pentecostal-Charismatic churches, *Journal for the Study of Religion*, **20** (2), pp 5–28.

Meyer, B (2010) Pentecostalism and globalization. In Allan Anderson, Michael Bergunder, AD and Van der Laan, C (eds.) *Studying Global Pentecostalism. Theories and Methods*. University of California Press, pp 113–29.

Morier-Genoud, E (2000) Archives, historiographie et églises Évangéliques au Mozambique'. *Lusotopie* 2000, pp 621–30.

Niehaus, I (1997) 'A witch has no horn': The subjective reality of witchcraft in the South African Lowveld, *African Studies*, **56** (2), pp 251–78.

Penvenne, JM (1997) Seeking the factory for women: Mozambican urbanization in the late colonial era, *Journal of Urban History*, **23** (3), pp 342–79.

Pitcher, A (2002) *Transforming Mozambique. The politics of privatisation, 1975–2000*. Cambridge: Cambridge University Press.

Power, M (2004) Post-colonial cinema and the reconfiguration of Moçambicanidade, *Lusotopie*, **11** (1/2), pp 261–78.

Schuetze, C. (2010) 'The world is upside down': Womens' participation in religious movements in Mozambique. Unpublished PhD dissertation, University of Pennsylvania, repository. Available at: upenn.edu/edissertations/101/ (accessed 10 May 2013).

Seibert, G (2005) But the manifestation of the spirit is given to every man to profit withal: Zion churches in Mozambique since the early 20th century, *Le Fait Missionnaire*, **17**, pp 125–50.

Sheldon, KE (2002) *Pounders of Grain: A history of women, work, and politics in Mozambique*. Portsmouth, NH: Heinemann.

Shibley, MA (1998) Contemporary Evangelicals: Born-again and world affirming, *Annals of the American Academy of Political and Social Science*, **558** (1), pp 67–87.

Soothill, JE (2007) *Gender, Social Change and Spiritual Power: Charismatic Christianity in Ghana*. Leiden: Brill.

Sousa Santos, B de and Trindade, JC (eds) (2003) *Conflito e Transformação Social: Uma paisagem das justiças em Moçambique*, Volumes 1 and 2. Porto: Ediçoes Afrontamento.

Sumich, J (2010) *Nationalism, Urban Poverty and Identity in Maputo, Mozambique*. London School of Economics, Crises States Research Centre, Working Paper No. 68.

Upton, GR (1980) *The Miracle of Mozambique. The Overseas Missions Department of the Pentecostal Assemblies of Canada*. Clearbrook, BC: A Olfert & Sons Ltd.

Van de Kamp, L (2010) Burying life: Pentecostal religion and development in urban Mozambique. In B Bompani and M Frahm-Arp (eds) *Development and Politics from Below: Exploring religious space in the African state*, London: Palgrave- MacMillan, pp 152–68.

Van de Kamp, L (2011a) *Violent Conversion. Brazilian Pentecostalism and the Urban Pioneering of Women in Mozambique*. PhD thesis, Vrije Universiteit, Amsterdam,

Van de Kamp, L (2011b) Converting the Spirit Spouse: The violent transformation of the Pentecostal female body in post-war urban Mozambique, *Ethnos* **76** (4), pp 510–33.

Van de Kamp, L (2012) Afro-Brazilian Pentecostal re-formations of relationships across two generations of Mozambican women, *Journal of Religion in Africa*, **42** (4), pp 433–52.

Van de Kamp, L (2013) South–South transnational spaces of conquest: Afro-Brazilian Pentecostalism, 'Feitiçaria' and the reproductive domain in urban Mozambique. *Exchange: A Journal of Missiological and Ecumenical Research*, **42** (4), pp 343–65.

Van de Kamp, L and Van Dijk, R (2010) Pentecostals moving South–South: Brazilian and Ghanaian transnationalism in southern Africa. In A Adogame and J Spickard (eds) *Religion Crossing Boundaries: Transnational dynamics in Africa and the new African diasporic religions*. Leiden: Brill, pp 123–42.

Van Dijk, R (1998) Pentecostalism, cultural memory and the state: Contested representations of time in postcolonial Malawi'. In R Werbner (ed.) *Memory and the Postcolony. African anthropology and the critique of power*. London: Zed Books, pp 155–81.

Van Dijk, R (2010) Social catapulting and the spirit of entrepreneurialism: Migrants, private initiative, and the pentecostal ethic in Botswana. In G Hüwelmeier and K Krause (eds.) *Traveling Spirits: Migrants, markets and mobilities*. London: Routledge, pp 101–17.

Van Koevering, H (1992) Recent developments in Mozambican Christianity. In P Gifford (ed.) *New Dimensions in African Christianity*. Nairobi: All Africa Conference of Churches, African Challenge Series No. 3, pp 103–34.

Velho, O (2007) Missionization in the post-colonial world: A view from Brazil and elsewhere. *Anthropological Theory* **7** (3), pp 273–93.

Visentini, PF (ed.) (2012) Brazilian foreign policy and South–South cooperation, *Brazilian Journal of Strategy & International Relations* 1/2 (2012), special issue, 9–272.

West, HG (2005) *Kupilikula. Governance and the Invisible Realm in Mozambique*. Chicago, IL: Chicago University Press.

WLSAMOÇ (2001) *Famílias em Contexto de Mudança em Moçambique*, 2nd edition. Maputo: Women and Law in Southern Africa.

Woodhead, L (2001) Feminism and the sociology of religion: From gender-blindness to gendered difference'. In R Fenn (ed.) *The Blackwell Companion to Sociology of Religion*. Oxford: Blackwell, pp 67–84.

Conclusion
Beyond partnership and dependency?

Sérgio Chichava, Ana Cristina Alves and Chris Alden

The purpose of this conclusion is to condense some implications of the present political and economic crisis that is shaking Brazil in relation to its cooperation with Africa, and particularly with Mozambique. We also seek to address key aspects of the Brazilian involvement in Africa that are perceived locally as a contradiction of the principles of equality, horizontal cooperation or solidarity expressed by that country, which are not only damaging its image but also leading to a certain degree of opposition and local resistance.

Brazilian political and economic crisis and implications for Africa

The current political and economic crisis affecting Brazil coincided with the arrival of Dilma Rousseff in the Brazilian presidency in 2011. Among other aspects, the crisis is expressed in the contraction of its overseas investments and its GDP, as well as increased inflation and unemployment. These factors have affected Brazil's relationship with Africa, and particularly with Mozambique, a key economic partner. Although the Latin American country announced the cancellation or rescheduling of almost US$900 million of African debt to Brazil in 2013, the budget for technical cooperation with Africa fell by 25 per cent in 2012 and, thereafter, investment in development cooperation programmes has stagnated. The Brazilian Cooperation Agency (ABC) reduced the number of its projects in Africa from 253 to 161. Brazil's exports to Africa fell from US$12.22 billion in 2011 to US$9.7 billion in 2014, while imports increased from US$15.4 billion to US$17.1 billion, resulting in a greater trade deficit for Brazil.[207] This situation also affected Brazilian companies, which, as a result, considerably reduced their investments in Africa (BBC, 2013; Chichava and Durán, 2015; Mello, 2015; Pedduzi, 2015).

The crisis also dictated the postponement *sine die* of the project to set up a Professional Training Centre by the National Industrial Apprenticeship Service (SENAI) in Maputo, in partnership with Mozambique's National Employment

---

207 It should be stressed that the trade balance was always favourable to Africa. Like the other great 'emerging economy', China, oil is the main product imported by Brazil from Africa, accounting for 88 per cent of all imports.

and Professional Training Institute (INEFP), which is still waiting for the release of funds by the ABC. The agreement to set up the centre was signed in 2009 during the second visit by President Lula da Silva to Maputo. Based on the model implemented in Brazil, the centre, aimed at training and building the capacity of workers in areas such as mechanics, civil construction, information technology, brickwork and electricity, among others, should have been operational by 2012. Likewise, Brazil's activities in ProSavana have practically ground to a halt. Most of ProSavana's continuing activities are in partnership with JICA (the Japanese International Cooperation Agency), since Brazil has withdrawn its ABC and Embrapa representatives from Maputo and the necessary resources have yet to be approved for the construction of the laboratory in Lichinga. Even the National Program on School Feeding (PRONAE), a trilateral programme between Mozambique (Ministry of Education), Brazil (ABC) and the World Food Programme (WFP) established in 2010 with the aim to replicate the Brazilian experience in Mozambique is facing tremendous difficulties in its efforts to expand across the country. At this stage, PRONAE is under implementation only thanks to support from WFP and USAID.

Even though bilateral economic relations have evolved positively, accusations of corruption, involving high-ranking political figures in both countries, are tending to darken the reputation of Brazil in Mozambican public opinion. These public figures include Lula da Silva and Dilma Rousseff on the Brazilian side, and Joaquim Chissano and Armando Guebuza on the Mozambican side, all of whom were seen in the previous period as catalysing the intensification of the relations between the two countries.

Lula da Silva and Dilma Rousseff have been accused systematically by the Brazilian media, particularly the media close to the right, and are under investigation by the Brazilian justice system for using their political influence to assist Brazilian companies, such as Odebrecht and Andrade Gutierrez, to win international contracts in exchange for bribes. In Mozambique, the awards of the construction of the Moamba-Major Dam and of Nacala International Airport to Andrade Gutierrez and to Odebrecht, respectively, are among the cases cited.[208] Because of this situation, the BNDES loan to the Moamba-Major Dam has been suspended and is among the 25 projects, all of which are citied in the '*Operação Lava Jato*' ('Operation Car Wash'), put on hold

---

208 In what is known in Brazil as 'Operação Lava Jato', the chairpersons of the companies Odebrecht and Andrade Gutierrez were arrested by the Brazilian federal police. Marcelo Odebrecht is still serving a sentence, while the chairperson of Andrade Gutierrez was released this year after a plea-bargaining agreement. Recently Marcelo Odebrecht also reached a plea-bargaining agreement with a judge. However, it is important to mention that, despite the various accusations, the Brazilian judiciary did not have sufficient evidence to open an inquiry into Rousseff or Lula linked directly to 'Operação Lava Jato'. Hence the impeachment of Rousseff in 2016 is not related to 'Lava Jato'

across the world by the Brazilian Bank. Regarding the Moamba-Major Dam, for example, Dilma Rousseff is accused of having received R$10 million after helping Andrade Gutierrez to win the construction contract. At the same time, it seems that the award of Maomba-Major Dam construction to Andrade Gutierrez was done in exchange of inclusion of Infra Engineering-Mozambique, a Mozambican company belongingto Frelimo top figures. The purchase of two BrazilianEmbraer aircrafts by Mozambique and construction of Nacala International Airport (BNDES loan) are also suspected of being linked to corruption. Three senior Mozambican State officials with ties to Frelimo are under investigation by Mozambique's Attorney General.

The repercussion of 'Operação Lava Jato' divides opinions of various bodies in Mozambique. Some actors, such as the Centre for Public Integrity (CIP), an independent organisation that advocates transparency and good governance, praise the independence of the Brazilian judicial system, and declare unequivocally that Mozambique should take it as an example to act against countless cases of corruption involving the local political elite (Fael and Cortez, 2016). Others, such as the prominent journalist Marcelo Mosse, regard as dangerous an 'Operação Lava Jato' in Mozambique, since it could lead to the disintegration of FRELIMO, the current ruling party (Mosse, 2016).[209] For their part, the two main opposition parties, RENAMO and the Mozambique Democratic Movement (MDM), favour a similar operation in the country and allege that, since there are Mozambicans involved in this scandal, they should be questioned under the legal system. For RENAMO and the MDM, the bench warrant against Lula da Silva shows that in Brazil, unlike Mozambique, nobody is above the law.[210] Partly because of the strong ties established between

---

or to any crime for which she was responsible. Her removal from office concerns the so-called 'pedaladasfiscais' (accounting tricks) which are financial practices frequently used in Brazil's federal, state and municipal spheres. Since the use of the *pedaladasfiscais* happens repeatedly in Brazil, the impeachment of Rousseff is regarded as a legal-parliamentary coup d'état, fomented by the PMDB, the party of the current interim president, Michel Temer, as a way of hindering the progress of 'Operação Lava Jato'. In the case of Lula da Silva, the accusations against him, referred to 'Operação Lava Jato', are unduly receiving resources for remodelling a triplex in Guarujá and of a site in Atibaia, paid for by contractors involved in diverting money in Petrobras. This is in addition to investigations into the grants made by the contractors to the Lula Institute and its lectures (BBC, 2016; Carta Capital, 2016). However, data recently published about the Odebrecht whistle-blowing indicate that Michel Temer, the current president, and José Serra, the current foreign minister, received kickbacks from the company (Pereira, 2016; Megale, 2016). On the role of the Brazilian media in Lava Jato, see Al-jazeera (2016).

209 In power since independence in 1975 and seen by some as indispensable for the stability and unity of the country.

210 It is important, however, to stress that the behaviour of the judiciary in ordering the bench warrant against Lula da Silva in March 2016 was illegal and unconstitutional. According to articles 218 and 260 of the Brazilian Penal Code, a bench warrant can be used only against a witness if they have not complied with a subpoena sent previously. For more information, see: *Folha de São Paulo* (2016).

the government of Lula da Silva and the Mozambican government, particularly during the presidency of Armando Guebuza, FRELIMO refuses to support 'Operação Lava Jato' and regards the bench warrant against Lula da Silva as an act of humiliation and a lack of recognition of a political figure who transformed Brazil into one of the major actors in international politics (O País, 2016).

This new political context has not only stained the image of the Brazilian ruling elite in the eyes of Mozambicans, but has also strengthened the criticisms that began to emerge in recent years of the more problematic and less positive aspects of Brazilian investment and cooperation. This seems to fall into a longstanding pattern of donor-inspired corruption in the Mozambican system while, perhaps paradoxically, demonstrating that even a weak civil society is capable of mobilising to challenge these practices.[211] This raises some troubling questions, however, as to the distinctive features presented by Brazilian engagement with Mozambique.

Brazil: A partner different from the others?

Brazil's intensification of its involvement in Mozambique happened in a context of the apparent convergence of interests at the turn of the 21st century, namely, Mozambique's fast economic growth rate and the thirst of Brazilian companies for internationalisation, and, on the other hand, the search for resources (capital, know-how and technology) by Maputo to promote its economic modernisation. This book shows that this apparent convergence of interests in fact hides countless weaknesses that distort the potential of this partnership and create serious problems in implementation. Among the most problematic aspects are the weak coordination of the architecture of Brazilian cooperation, insufficient resources to meet the growing demand, and the prevalence of corporate interests and predatory behaviour on the part of some Brazilian companies (such as Moatize and ProSavana). On the other hand, the greater weakness of the Mozambican institutional framework (political and economic) compared with Brazil not only facilitates this behaviour, but also makes it difficult, for example, to transpose social programmes (ProAlimentos), health projects (Fiocruz) and agricultural cooperation, largely due to the lack of financial sustainability in the long term.

Several Brazilian partnerships have aroused opposition and suspicion on the part of Mozambicans. For example, the negative impact on the communities affected by the resettlement of the population of Moatize, promoted by Vale in Tete to make way for its coal mining project, led to Vale's unpopularity

---

211 See Hanlon (2004:747–63); Manning (2010:151–65).

and the opposition to the Brazilian multinational by Mozambican civil society organisations and by the people affected. Vale was believed to exercise enormous influence over the then Mozambican president, Armando Guebuza, and the former chairperson of the company's board was regarded as his adviser in international matters (see Chapter 4 in this volume). Likewise, ProSavana has also been strongly opposed by Mozambican civil society, in the belief that, with agro-business as its focus and occupying a huge stretch of land, this project will expropriate peasant land in the Nacala Corridor in favour of large Brazilian and Japanese capital (see Chapter 9 in this volume). The less than clear relationship between the FRELIMO Party and the Universal Church of the Kingdom of God (IURD), a church with a dubious reputation, is also viewed with some suspicion in certain Mozambican circles. This Pentecostal church, which arrived in Mozambique in 1993, does, indeed, have close relations with FRELIMO. In their initial years, its radio and television stations operated out of FRELIMO's national headquarters in Maputo. The IURD has also publicly supported FRELIMO, particularly during election campaigns, calling on its believers to vote for this party.

Brazilian cooperation in the formal and informal cultural spaces with Lusophone Africa can, at times, seem to echo the cultural and identity claims that French apologists make regarding their country's ties with the continent.[212] From the campaign funds provided by self-styled Emperor Bokassa to then French president, Valerie Giscard d'Estaing, to the conviction of Francois Mitterrand's son, Jean-Christophe Mitterrand, and his former associate, Charles Pasqua, in the arms-for-energy deal in Angola, there is a history of scandal that permeates the high politics of relations.[213] There are deeply significant differences between France and Brazil, of course, with a colonial and neo-colonial legacy that underwrites France's enduring global ambitions, its involvement in security cooperation and its economic interests in Africa.[214] At the same time, one cannot help but reflect on how both Brazil and Mozambique have, like the Franco–African examples, experienced the long reach of deal-making and corruption in ways that shape their domestic politics.

Brazil is known in Mozambique particularly because of its television soap operas, as well as the IURD and many other Pentecostal churches. The image they paint of Brazilian society has also been viewed with suspicion.

---

212 Saraiva (2012); Manning (1998:178–80; 205–10).
213 Ce traffic legal des armes legeres, *Le Monde Diplomatique*, Janvier 2001. For more contemporary examples see Glaser (2014).
214 For instance, French economic interests in a set of key state-supported sectors, with sometimes subterranean links to the energy and arms trade, which have helped define the sensitive nature of ties between them. See Chafer (2005:9–14); also see Melly and Darracq (2013).

Paulina Chiziane, one of Mozambique's best-known writers, states that the Brazilian soap operas depict a society in which black people are discriminated against in favour of whites, in that they often appear in subordinate roles such as domestic servants, guards or porters. As for the Brazilian Pentecostal churches, they, in what Chiziane calls 'religious colonialism', are acting just as the Western churches did under colonial rule, expressing an image of the superiority of Brazilian culture, to the detriment of African culture, in denying or marginalising local traditions, religions and beliefs, claiming that they are outdated and should, thus, be abandoned (Rádio Moçambique, 2012).

The reading of the various chapters in this book leads to the general conclusion that, although the Brazilian development cooperation programmes and the cultural exchanges forge new partnerships and build local technical capacities, this is a relationship between unequal partners, which goes just one way – from Brazil to Mozambique, replicating Brazilian cultural experiences and realities, which are viewed as capable of leading to the socio-economic progress and modernisation of Mozambicans. In this relationship, Mozambique appears mainly as the 'pupil' and Brazil as the 'teacher', thus challenging the rhetoric of the principles of equality and of a horizontal relationship, which define South–South cooperation and, particularly, Brazilian cooperation. To a large extent, this replicates the top-down model of development of the colonial era, or the relation between Africa and the traditional donors. This volume at the same time illustrates the potential and the limitations of South–South cooperation, showing, on the one hand, disconnects between its rhetoric and practice and, on the other, the challenges raised in implementation (with responsibilities on both sides). The current context of the Brazil–Mozambique partnership thus constitutes a paradigmatic case, which calls for an urgent reassessment, not only of Brazilian cooperation in this country, but also of the general framework of South–South cooperation. In this context, the much touted cultural and political affinity, which would put Brazil in a privileged position in its relations with African countries, in comparison with the West and other emerging countries, seems difficult to sustain.

References

Al-Jazeera (2016) *Brazil's Petrobras scandal: Dilma Rousseff's Watergate?* Available at: http://www.aljazeera.com/programmes/listeningpost/2016/03/brazil-politics-protests-petrobras-scandal-160319092343730.html (accessed 14 August 2016).

BBC (2013) Brazil to write off almost $ 900 m of African debt. Available at: http://www.bbc.com/news/world-latin-america-22669331 (accessed 31 March 2016).

BBC (2016) *As 3 suspeitas do MPF sobre Lula e a defesa do ex-presidente.* Available at: http://www.bbc.com/portuguese/noticias/2016/03/160304_entenda_investigacao_lula_lgb (accessed 14 August 2016).

Carta Capital (2016) *Entenda as acusações contra Lula na Lava Jato.* Available at: http://www.

cartacapital.com.br/blogs/parlatorio/entenda-as-acusacoes-contra-lula-na-lava-jato (accessed 14 August 2016).

Chafer, T (2005) Chirac and 'la FrancAfrique': No longer a family affair, *Journal of Modern and Contemporary France*, **13** (1), pp 9–14.

Chichava, S and Durán, J (2015) Civil society organisations' political control over Brazil and Japan's development cooperation in Mozambique: More than a mere whim? *Working Paper*, 6/2015. London: LSE Global South Unit.

Colon, L, Talento, A, Nublat, J and Carvalho, MC (2016) Condução coercitiva de Lula foidecidida para evitartumulto, diz Moro, *Folha de São Paulo*. Available at: http://www1.folha.uol.com.br/poder/2016/03/1746437-conducao-coercitiva-de-lula-foi-decidida-para-evitar-tumulto-diz-moro.shtml (accessed 14 August 2016).

Fael, B and Cortez, E (2016) Os Exemplos das Operações 'Lava Jato' e 'Marquês' e a Inacção do Nosso Ministério Público, *CIP Newsletter*, 51/2016, Maputo.

Glaser, A (2014) *Africa France: Quand les dirigeants africains deviennent les maitres du jeu*. Paris: Fayard.

Hanlon, J (2004) Do donors promote corruption? *Third World Quarterly*, **25** (4), pp 747–63.

Manning, C (2010) Mozambique's slide into one party rule, *Journal of Democracy*, **21** (2), pp 151–65.

Manning, P (1998) *Francophone Sub-Saharan Africa, 1880–1995*, 2nd edition. Cambridge: Cambridge University Press, pp 178–80; 205–10.

Megale, B (2016) José Serra recebeu R$ 23 milhões via caixa dois, afirma Odebrecht, *Folha de São Paulo*. Available at: http://www1.folha.uol.com.br/poder/2016/08/1799887-jose-serra-recebeu-r-23-mi-via-caixa-2-afirma-odebrecht.shtml (accessed 14 August 2016).

Mello, P (2015) Brasil recua e reduz projetos de cooperação e doações à África, *Folha de São Paulo*, 23 March. Available at: http://www1.folha.uol.com.br/mundo/2015/03/1606466-brasil-recua-e-reduz-projetos-de-cooperacao-e-doacoes-para-a-africa.shtml (accessed 10 March 2016).

Melly, P and Darracq, V (2013) A new way to engage? French policy in Africa from Sarkozy to Hollande, *Africa 2013/01*, May. London: Chatham House.

Mosse, M (2016) Lava Jato do Brasil? Não obrigado, *Refletindo Moçambique*. Available at: http://comunidademocambicana.blogspot.com/2016/03/lava-jato-do-brasil-para-mocambique-nao.html (accessed 5 April 2016).

Pedduzi, P (2015) *Parcerias com África podem Ajudar Brasil a Amenizar Efeitos da Crise, diz Apex*, 24 October. Available at: http://agenciabrasil.ebc.com.br/economia/ noticia/2015-10/parcerias-com-africa-podem-ajudar-brasil-amenizar-efeitos-da-crise-diz-apex (accessed 10 March 2016).

O País (2016) *Partidos da Oposição diz* que 'Lava jato' revela independência da justiça Brasileira, 16 March. Available at: http://opais.sapo.mz/index.php/politica/63-politica/39962-partidos-da-oposicao-dizem-que-lava-jato-revela-independencia-da-justica-brasileira.html (accessed 10 April 2016).

Pereira, D (2016) Odebrecht cita Temer em negociação de delação premiada, *Veja*. Available at: http://veja.abril.com.br/brasil/odebrecht-cita-temer-em-negociacao-de-delacao-premiada/ (accessed 14 August 2016).

Rádio Moçambique (2012) Temos medo do Brasil, Paulina Chiziane, 14 April. Available at: http://www.rm.co.mz/index.php/component/k2/item/1451-temos-medo-do-brasil-paulina-chiziane (accessed 13 March 2016).

Saraiva, JFS (2012) África Parceira do Brasil Atlântico: Relações internacionais do Brasil e da África no início do século XXI. Belo Horizonte: Fino Traço, pp 427–33.

Index

A
Abdenur, A. 47
Abe, Shinzo 135
    visit to Mozambique (2014) 136
Abreu, Alcinda
    Mozambican Minister of Foreign Affairs and Cooperation 40
Academic Action for the Development of Rural Communities (Adecru) 77, 134, 137–8
Accra Agenda for Action 175
Africa Century Agriculture 95
Africa-Japan Forum (AJF) 135
African Development Bank 175
    infrastructure projects financed by 70
African Independent Churches (AICs) 237
Agricultural Development Fund (FDA) 75
Agricultural Mechanisation Programme 75
Agricultural Research and Technological Innovation Platform (Piait) 65, 73, 76
Agricultural Sector Development Strategic Plan (PEDSA) 68–9, 71
    reliance on Green Revolution Strategy 68
Agromix 124–5
Agromoz 95
Ahmed, F.Z. 49, 58
aid/foreign aid 55–6, 87
    donor influence 48–9, 56
    relationship with SSC 49–50, 60–1
    use for political support 49, 57–8
Aid Effectiveness Agenda 96
Alden, C. 82
Alencar, José 40
Algeria
    Algiers 10
Amorim, Celso
    Brazilian Foreign Minister 2, 18, 38–9
Andrade Gutierrez 4, 42
    Moamba-Major Dam project 262–3

Angola 14, 19, 26, 31, 37, 235, 265
    Brazilian recognition of independence of 32
    Luanda 32
    UN pacification programme in 17
Anseeuw, W. 67
Appadurai, A. 163
Aranha, Osvaldo
    Brazilian Foreign Minister 10
Arena Group 217
Arinos de Melo Franco, Afonso 1
Arvidsson, N. 149
Aso, Taro
    meeting with Luiz Inácio Lula da Silva (2009) 97
Association of Support and Legal Assistance to Communities (AAJC) 77
ATTAC Japan 135
Augustin, Carlos Ernesto
    President of Mato Grosso Association of Cotton Producers 56
Australia
    MOU with ABC (2010) 110
Azeredo da Silveira, Antônio 31

B
Baloi, Oldemiro
    Mozambican Foreign Minister 41
    visit to Brazil (2008) 41
Banco Mundial 208
Bauer, G. 26
Bénard da Coasta, A. 207
Benin 19
biofuels 51, 67
Boal, Augusto 214, 219–20, 227–9, 233
    A Estética do Oprimido (The Aesthetic of the Oppressed) (2009) 219, 221
    Teatro do Oprimido e outras Poéticas Políticas (Theatre of the Oppressed and other Political Poetics) (1973) 219

Borras, S. 79–80, 100
Branco, Marshal Humberto Castelo
 foreign policy of 29–30
Brazil 1–7, 9–10, 12, 15, 25, 27–8, 31, 34–7,
 42–3, 46, 54, 57, 65–6, 82, 88–9, 95, 99,
 107–8, 119, 131, 139, 141, 160, 162, 165,
 170–1, 181–2, 195, 209–11, 261, 265–6
 aid receipts 49–50
 Belo Horizonte 41
 Brasília 35, 41, 97, 121
 Brazilian Air Force 37–8
 civil society of 186
 Congress 180, 183–4
 Coup d'état (1964) 14
 debt relief activity in Africa 3–4, 39–40, 42, 51
 economy of 178
 Federal Constitution (1988) 179
 foreign aid activity of 56, 60–1
 GDP per capita 54
 government of 11, 34, 51, 60, 69, 71, 94, 134–5, 161, 166, 173, 176, 179–81, 187, 189, 222
 Imperial Law No. 3353 (*Lei Áuera*) 1
 Law 9313 180
 Living Culture Programme (2004) 221–3
 Maranhão 34
 Ministry of Agrarian Development (MDA) 102
 Ministry of Agriculture 50
 Ministry of Culture 221–2
 Ministry of Foreign Affairs (MRE/ Itamaraty) 1, 4, 14, 19, 31, 50, 71, 177–8, 186, 222
 Ministry of Health 50, 178, 186
 NAP 186
 National Health Service (*Sistema Único de Saúde* (SUS)) 179, 181
 National Health Surveillance Agency (ANVISA) 184
 National Petroleum Agency 24
 Operation Car Wash (*Operação Lava Jato*) 262–4
 Rio de Janeiro 41, 151, 214–15
 São Paulo 151, 161, 164, 217
 Seventh of September 40–1
Brazil-Mozambique José Aparecido de Oliveira Cultural Centre 41
 inauguration of 35
Brazil, Russia, India, China and South Africa group (BRICS) 47–8, 53
Brazilian Agribusiness Association
 personnel of 101–2
Brazilian Agricultural Research Corporation (Embrapa) 3, 23–4, 71–2, 90, 117–18, 123, 132–3, 167
 aid provided to 50
 criticisms of 73–4
 International Relations Office 123
 role in ProAlimentos project 117–18, 121
Brazilian Cooperation Agency (*Agência Brasileira de Cooperação* (ABC)) 17, 38, 41, 69, 96, 98, 103, 110, 117–20, 122, 161, 165, 177, 184, 186, 188, 261–2
 aid provided to 50
 budget of 177
 Memorandums of Understanding (MOUs) signed by 110
 personnel of 97, 132
 role in establishment of TCTP 111
 technical correction projects 43
 Trilateral Development Partnership Strategic Framework (2011) 111, 117
Brazilian Development Bank (BNDES) 262–3
Brazilian Expeditionary Force 10
Brazilian Programme for the Development of the Cerrado (Prodecer)
 influence of 72–3
Brazilian Social Democracy Party (PSDB)
 members of 36
Brazilian Universal Church of the Kingdom of God (*Igreja Universal do Reino de Deus* (IURD)) 240, 248–9, 252–3, 255, 265–6
 Miramar 240
 opening of (1992) 237
Brecht, Berthold
 Epic Theatre of 217
British Broadcasting Corporation (BBC) 55
Bueno de Mesquita, B. 49, 56
Buss, P.M.
 concept of health diplomacy 177

C
Cabral, L. 53–4
Caetano, Marcello
 removed from power (1974) 31

Camago Corrêa 4, 167
  Mphanda Nkuwa Hydroelectric Dam 164
Cape Verde 31
  government of 34
  Independence of (1975) 32
  public debt of 42
Cardoso, Fernando Henrique (FHC) 11, 180
  foreign policy of 16, 18–19, 22, 36–7
  visit to South Africa (1996) 17
Castro, Araújo
  foreign policy of 13
Catholic Church 139–40, 185, 237, 242
Centre for International Relations in Health (CRIS) 177–8
Centre for Public Integrity (CIP) 194, 263
Cepaluni, G. 108
Cernea, M.
  risks of resettlement identified by 204–6
Chang, H.J. 53
Chaves, G.C. 180
Chichava, S. 82, 101
China, People's Republic of 3, 11, 15, 18, 49, 107, 141, 175, 235
  economy of 52
Chissano, Joaquim Alberto 33, 37, 72, 182–3, 262
  visit to Brazil (1988) 35
  visit to Brazil (2004) 39
Chiziane, Paulina 265–6
Christian Evangelical Church Maná (*Igreja Evangélica Cristã Maná*) 239–40
  ManaSat 240
Christianity 235–6
  conversion to 254
  Evangelical 237, 239
  missionaries 235, 238–9, 242, 246
  neo-Pentecostal 235, 239, 251
  Pentecostal 4, 7, 56, 185, 236, 239–40, 242–8, 250, 252–6, 265
Cine Group 6, 144, 147, 151–5
  establishment of (1995) 151
Citizens Concerned with the Development of Mozambique (CCDM) 135
Civil Society Mechanism for the Development of the Nacala Corridor (MCSC) 139
  creation of (2016) 137
  personnel of 138–9

civil society organisations (CSOs) 5–6
Clark, D. 197
Clements, E.A. 57, 108
Cohen, C. 49, 58
Cold War 29
  end of 9, 14, 23
Collor de Mello, Fernando 11
  foreign policy of 15, 22, 36
  impeachment of (1992) 36
  visit to Mozambique (1991) 37
colonialism 30
  neo-colonialism 55, 170
  Portuguese 21
Colson, E. 196
Communidade de Sant'Egidio 185
communism 48
Community of Portuguese Language Countries (*Comunidade dos Países de Língua Portuguesa* (CPLP)) 14, 17, 34, 41, 181
  creation of (1996) 14, 16, 23, 37, 41
  Memorandum of Understanding with UNAIDS (2010) 181
  São Luís Meeting (1989) 14–15
Community Seed Bank Implantation Project 117
Comprehensive African Agriculture Development Programme (CAADP) 69–70
constructivism 53, 223
Correia, Celso
  Mozambican Minister of Land, Environment and Rural Development 199
Cossa, Alvim 215–16
da Costa e Silva, General Arthur
  foreign policy of 30
Countryside (Rural) Observatory (*Observatório do Mundo Rural* (OMR)) 137
Creuz, L.R.C. 162
Cultural Cooperation Agreement
  signing of (1989) 35
curandeiros 245–9

D
Dakar 14
Dantas, San Tiago 1
  foreign policy of 13
Dathein, R. 162

decolonisation 32
Denmark
    Danish International Development Agency (DANIDA) 175
Development Assistance Committee (DAC) 87
development refugees 196–7, 208
    concept of 196
    resettlement programmes targeting 197–200, 202–7, 209
    risks of resettlement 202–7
developmental integration
    concept of 161
Diagonal
    personnel of 207
Diogo, Luísa 40
Diplomacy of Prosperity 30
Do Rosário, D. 58
Downing, T. 196
Dunning, J.H. 144

E
Economic Reconstruction Programme (*Programa de Reabilitação Económica* (PRE)) 21
Economic Recovery Programme (*Programa de Reabilitação Económica* (PAE)) 34
Environmental Justice (Justiça Ambiental (JA)) 77, 133–4, 137
Equatorial Guinea 14, 19
d'Estaing, Valerie Giscard 265
European Union (EU) 175
Evaluation Report on Community Theatre Activities (2009) 224
Exim-Bank
    infrastructure projects financed by 70

F
famine
    efforts to combat 20
Farani, Marco
    agreement with Kenzo Oshima (2009) 97, 132
Federal Official Gazette 123
feitiçeiro 245, 247
Fernandes, B.M. 57, 108
Ferreira, Murilo
    President of Vale SA 167
Fifth Joint Commission of Brazil-Mozambique Cooperation (2010) 41
Figueiredo, João Batista
    foreign policy of 14, 30, 33
Folha de São Paulo 6
Food and Agricultural Organization (FAO) 100
Forum of Zambézia Non-Governmental Organisations (*Fórum das Organizações não Governamentais da Zambézia*, Fongza) 137–8
France 1
Franco, Itamar
    foreign policy of 15–16, 35–6
Franco, J. 100

G
Galli, R. 66–7
Geisel, Ernesto 14
    foreign policy of 29
General Cooperation Agreement (1981)
    Complementary Adjustment (1987) 34–5
    signing of 20–1, 33
George, G.
    definition of absorptive capacity 149
German Cooperation Agency (*Deutsche Gesellschaft für Internationale Zusammenarbeit* (GIZ)) 38
Germany
    Deutsche Gesellschaft für Internationale Zusammenarbeit (GTZ) 175, 178
    MOU with ABC (2010) 110
Getúlio Vargas Foundation (FGV Projectos) 90, 94, 161
    FGV Center for Agribusiness 102
    personnel of 95
Ghana 3
Gil, Gilberto
    Brazilian Minister of Culture 223
    role in development of Living Culture Programme 223
Global Fund 175
globalisation 53
    South–South 160
Gospel in Action (*Evangelho em Acção*) 239
Goulart, João 1
Grant, R.M. 148
Green Revolution Strategy
    provisions of 68
Grimm, S. 110
Group of 20 (G-20) 42, 53

Group of 7 (G7)
  influence on IMF 48
Group of 77 (G77) 12, 53
Group of 8 (G8)
  L'Aquila Summit 97
  New Alliance for Food and Nutritional
    Security 70
Grupo Américo Amorin
  partner in Agromoz 95
Grupo Pinesso
  partner in Agromoz 95
Guebuza, Armando 42–3, 194–5, 199, 253,
    262, 264
  inauguration of (2005) 40
  owner of Intelec Holdings 95
  visit to Brazil (2007) 40–1
Guinea-Bissau 31
  Brazilian recognition of (1974) 31–2
  government of 34

H
Hill, Christopher 27–8, 30
HIV/AIDS
  antiretroviral (ARV) drugs 3, 174–6, 179,
    182–5, 188–9
  efforts to prevent/treat 6, 17–18, 20, 24,
    51, 173–6, 179–80, 185–8, 224–6,
    232
  State Wide Approach (SWAp) 174–5
Hoyo Hoyo 95

I
Independent Foreign Policy (*Política Externa
  Independente* (PEI)) 13–14, 20, 29–30
  implementation of (1961–4) 11
India 18, 49, 107, 175
India, Brazil and South Africa (IBSA)
  Dialogue Forum (G-3) 48, 52–3, 110
  creation of 19
INSITEC Group 199
  CETA 199
Institute of Social Communication 232
Intelec Holdings 95
  partner in Agromoz 95
Inter-American Development Bank 178
International Agricultural Science Research
  Centre of Japan (JIRCAS) 133
International Center for Reproductive
  Health 185–6
International Centre for Technical

Cooperation (ICTC)
  founding of (2005) 178
International Church of God's Grace
  (*Internacional da Graça de Deus*) 238–9
international development cooperation
  (IDC) 107–8
International Fund for Agricultural
  Development 100
International Monetary Fund (IMF) 34, 53
  board of directors 48
  role in development of PRE 21
international political economy (IPE) 52
International Portuguese Language Institute
  (*Instuto Internacional da Língua Portuguesa*
  (IILP)) 34
international relations (IR) 46, 48, 53, 223
Investment Company Risk Capital (SICAR)
  95
Investment Cooperation and Facilitation
  Agreement (ACFI) 4
Israel 15
  MOU with ABC (2009) 110
Italy
  L'Aquila 97
  MOU with ABC (2007) 110
  Rome 36

J
Japan 3, 54, 70–1, 77, 82, 99, 131, 138–9
  government of 69, 134–5
  MOU with ABC (2000) 110
  Tokyo 97
Japan-Brazil Partnership Programme (JBPP)
  signing of (2000) 97
Japan International Volunteer Centre (JVC)
  135
Japanese International Cooperation Agency
  (JICA) 71, 117, 161, 165, 175, 262
  infrastructure projects financed by 70
  personnel of 97, 132
  role in establishment of TCTP 111
Jenkins-Smith, H. 65
Jesus Christ 235
Justiça Ambiental (Friends of the Earth
  Mozambique) 194
Justice and Peace Commission of the
  Nampula Archdiocese (CajuPaNa) 139

K
Kenya 19, 185

272

Kickbusch, I.
  concept of health diplomacy 177
Kilby, C. 48
Knowledge Station (Fazenda Modelo) 208
  opening of (2012) 203
knowledge transfer 148, 154–5
  absorptive capacity 149–50
  definitions of 144–6
  role of FDI in 147
  role of MNCs in 150–1, 155–6
  social integration mechanisms 146
  tacit knowledge 145, 148–9
Kogut, B. 148–9
Kubitschek, Juscelino 11

L

Leitão da Cunha, Vasco 10
Livaningo 137
Long, N. 108
Lula da Silva, Luiz Inácio 2, 4–5, 11–12, 97,
  164, 166, 170, 177, 180, 182, 223, 262–4
  foreign policy of 2, 9, 12, 18–20, 23,
    38–9, 42, 55, 177
  meeting with Taro Aso (2009) 97
  visit to Maputo (2003) 39
  visit to Mozambique (2010) 41, 184,
    195
  visit to Namibia (2003) 183
Lundan, S.M. 144
Lusaka Agreements (1974) 32–3
Luxembourg 95

M

Machel, Samora
  death of (1986) 34
Machlup, Fritz
  *History of Thought of Economic Integration,
    The* (1977) 162
Malabwé (ethnic group) 202
Malawi 70, 94, 239
Mandela, Nelson
  visit to Brazil (1998) 17
Manhenje, Almerino
  Mozambican Home Minister 37
  visit to Brasília (1998) 37
Manjate, Rogério
  My Husband is in Denial 224
Maputo Theatre of the Oppressed Group
  (GTO-Maputo) 214–16, 222–7, 229–32,
  234

establishment of (2001) 7
  members of 228
Marcelino, Jorge
  Mozambican General Inspector of
    Finance 37
  visit to Brasília (1998) 37
Marcuschi, L.A. 163
Mato Grosso Association of Cotton
  Producers
  personnel of 56
Mauritius 95
Médecins Sans Frontières (MSF) 180
mediascapes 165–6, 168
  press 160–1, 169–70
Médici, General Emílio Garrastazu 11
  foreign policy of 30
Memorandum of Understanding
  on Implementation of Technical
    Cooperation Activities in Third
    Countries (2010) 117
Mercosul
  creation of (1991) 12, 23
Mercosur 37
Michigan State University (MSU) 117–18,
  122–3, 125
MIPCOM 151
Mitterand, François 265
Mitterand, Jean-Christophe 265
More Food (*Mais Alimentos*) International
  Programme 65, 76, 83, 134–5
Morgenthau, H. 49
Mozambican Agricultural Research Institute
  (IIAM) 73–5, 81, 90, 99, 117–19, 121,
  123–6, 132–3, 186
  personnel of 73
Mozambican Aids Organization
  (MONASO) 185
Mozambican civil society organisations
  (OSCMs) 131–41
Mozambican Investment Promotion Centre
  (CPI) 81
Mozambican Pharmaceutical Association
  (*Sociedade Moçambicana de Medicamentos*
  (SMM)) 174, 184–6, 188
Mozambique 3, 5, 7, 9, 12, 14, 19, 23–7, 31,
  34–7, 40, 43, 46, 51, 54, 56, 58–9, 65–7,
  76, 78, 80, 82–3, 87, 89–90, 103–4, 108,
  139, 146, 148, 151–3, 160, 162, 164–5,
  170–1, 173, 181–2, 187–9, 195, 208,
  210–11, 214–16, 224, 229, 233, 235, 237,

240, 242, 244–5, 251, 261, 265–6
agricultural sector of 67–8, 70, 102, 201–2
Beira 194
Cabo Delgado 132, 134, 224
civil society in 76–8, 82, 91, 99, 130–1
Civil War (1977–92) 12, 21–2, 34, 36, 66, 144, 174, 237–8, 247
Cuamba 90, 136
Decree 31/2012 197
Democratic Constitutional State 36
economy of 66, 88, 103–4, 144, 154, 156
external debt of 22
FDI inflow in 144
floods (2000) 37–8
food crisis (2007–8) 67
Gaza 117, 224, 237
GDP per capita 51, 54, 66
government of 33–4, 69, 79, 82, 97, 111, 120, 134–5, 162, 166, 175–6, 185, 188
Independence of (1975) 20, 26, 29, 32, 244
Lichinga 70, 90, 262
Mandimba 90
Manica 224, 233
Maputo (Lourenço Marques) 26, 32–3, 40, 59, 77, 82, 98–9, 109, 117–18, 123, 134–7, 140, 168, 182, 224, 236, 240, 242, 244, 255, 261, 265
Ministry for the Coordination of Environmental Action 69
Ministry of Agriculture (MINAG) 70–2, 81, 96–7, 99, 109, 117, 120–1, 126, 133, 136, 165
Ministry of Education (MINED) 120–1, 186, 262
Ministry of Health (MISAU) 175, 182
Ministry of Land, Environment and Rural Development 69
Ministry of Mineral Resources and Energy 195
Moamba 118
Moatize 4, 6, 55, 69–70, 93, 164, 185, 194–5, 197–9, 201, 204–5, 210, 264
Monapo 94
Nampula 3, 70, 77, 79, 89–90, 98, 125, 132, 139, 224
Nampula Province 94, 136
National Health Institute (INS) 182

National Strategic Plan in Response to HIV/AIDS 175
Niassa 3, 77–9, 90, 134, 136
public debt of 39–40, 42
Sofala 224, 233
Special Economic Zones (ZEE) 66
Tete Province 4, 6, 77, 93, 132, 194–6, 224, 231, 264
Zambézia 3, 77, 90, 132, 134, 224, 231
Mozambique Democratic Movement (MDM) 263
Mozambique General Peace Agreement (1992)
signing of 36
Mozambique Liberation Front (FRELIMO) 22, 36, 58, 237, 244–5, 263–5
influence of 32
members of 21, 26
Third Congress (1977) 33–4
Mozambique National Resistance Movement (RENAMO) 21, 36, 237, 263
funding of 22
multinational corporations (MNCs) 144–8, 154, 157
role in knowledge transfer 150–1, 155–6
Mutuoa, António 138–9

N
Nacala Diocesan Justice and Peace Commission (CDJPN) 139
Nacala Fund 78, 94–5
Namibia 19, 183
Nampula Civil Society Platform (Plataforma Provincial des Organizações da Sociedade Civil de Nampula (PPOSC-N)) 77, 133–4, 137–8
National African Union for Independent Mozambique (UNAMI)
unification with UDENAMO 32
National Agricultural Sector Investment Plan (Pnisa) 68–9, 71, 75
provisions of 66
National AIDS Control Council (CNCS)
creation of (2000) 176
National Association of Tradtional Healers
National Democratic Union of Mozambique (UDENAMO)
unification with UNAMI 32
National Employment and Professional

Training Institute (INEFP)
Professional Training Centre 261–2
National HIV/AIDS Council 174
National Industrial Apprenticeship Service (SENAI)
Professional Training Centre 261–2
National Interest Diplomacy 30
National Program on School Feeding (PRONAE) 262
National Security Doctrine 30
National Union of Peasants (Unac) 77, 133–4, 137–9, 170
neoliberalism 22–3, 53
Netherlands 55
Network of Organisations for the Environment and Sustainable Development of Zambézia (*Rede de Organizações para Ambiente e Desenvolvimento Sustentável da Zambézia*, Radeza) 137
Neves, Tancredo 34
New Development Strategy (ENDE) (2015–35) 69
provisions of 66
New York Times 56
Niassa Forum of Non-Governmental Organisations (*Fórum das Organizações Não Governamentais do Niassa*, Fonagni) 137–8
Nigeria 17, 19
Nkomati Agreement (1984) 34
No to ProSavana 137–8
launch of (2014)135
Noberto Odebrecht 2
Nogueira, S.G. 163
Non-Aligned Movement (NAM) 53
non-governmental organisations (NGOs) 53, 58, 67, 73, 76, 79, 83, 131, 175, 179, 185, 194, 197
North–South Cooperation (NSC) 5, 46–7, 54, 88, 109
Norway 72

O

O Estado de São Paulo 6
Odebrecht 4, 14, 42, 144, 167, 262
Nacala International Airport project 262–3
personnel of 167
Official Development Assistance (ODA) 88
Oliveira, A. 52
Onuki, J. 52
Organisation for Economic Development (OECD) 175
aid receipts from 49–50
Development Assistance Committee (DAC) 110
donors in 55
Oriental Consulting 90
Oshima, Kenzo
agreement with Marco Farani (2009) 97, 132
visit to Brasília (2009) 97
Oswald Cruz Foundation (*Fundação Oswaldo Cruz* (Fiocruz)) 177–8, 184–7, 264
Institute of Drug Technology (Farmanguinhos) 183
National Public Health School 177
Oxfam International 77, 180
Oxfam Japan 135

P

PAA Africa Programme 76
Pacheco, José
Mozambican Minister of Agriculture 69
Pan American Operation 11
Paris Declaration on Aid Effectiveness (2005) 96, 175
Party of National Reconstruction (PRN)
members of 36
Pasqua, Charles 265
Pax Britannica 10
People's Movement for the Liberation of Angola (MPLA) 32
Pereira, A.D. 16, 19
Petrobrás 2, 17, 42
Braspetro 14
pombagira
concept of 246
Portugal 1, 14, 29, 95, 239
Carnation Revolution (1974) 26, 31
colonies of 31
government of 33–4
Portuguese (language) 2, 9, 11, 17, 35, 122, 137, 164, 202–3, 244
Principle of Responsible Agricultural Investment (PRAI) 100–1
ProAlimentos (Nutrition and Food Security Programme Technical Security Project) (ProFood) 5, 109, 117, 119, 122, 125–6
aims of 118

Cooperation Technical Project (*Projeto Técnico do Cooperação* (PCT)) 121–2
Evaluation Committee 118–19
Project Coordination Committee (*Comitê de Coordenação do Projeto* (CCP)) 118
Project Technical Committee (*Comitê Técnico do Projeto* (CTP)) 118
Nutrition and Food Security Programme 120
School Meals Project 120–1
World Food Programme 120
Prodecer 131, 140
  influence of 132, 134, 141
productive integration
  concept of 162
PROEX 40
Project to Stimulate Local Food Purchases 117
ProSavana 3, 5–6, 72–3, 76–8, 89–91, 99–100, 102–4, 111, 131–2, 135–7, 165, 171, 262, 264
  criticisms of 54, 74, 80–2, 95–8
  launch of (2009) 69, 72
  Master Plan 70–1, 74, 77, 90, 93, 95–103, 133
  opposition to 134–6, 140–1
  provisions of 70
  Quick Impact Projects (QIP) 71
  ProSavana-Extension and Models Project (ProSavana-PEM) 133
  ProSavana-PD 132–3, 136, 138
  ProSavana-PE 132
  ProSavana-PI 132–3
  strategies aligned with 96–7
Protocol of Intentions for Exchange and Technical Cooperation in the Area of Social Inclusion
  signing of (2006) 40
Protocol of Intentions in the Area of Fighting Discrimination and Promoting Racial Equality (2004)
  First Amendment 40

Q
Quadros, Jânio 1
Quick Impact Projects 93

R
Rei do Agro 95

Reis, R. 180
Renewed/Charismatic Baptist Church (*Igreja Baptista Renovada*) 239
Republic of Ireland
  aid programme of 55
Resettlement Action Plan (RAP) 197–8
Reynaud, J. 48
Ribeiro, C.O. 15, 19, 72
Ribeiro, G.L. 163
River, Save (Sabi River) 140
Rodrigues, José Honório 11
Rodrigues, Roberto 101–2
Rodrigues de Silva, Lélio Gonçalves
  Head of ONUMOZ 22
Rolim, C.F.C. 162
Rousseff, Dilma 4, 6, 51, 164, 166, 261
  foreign policy of 42–3, 178
  visit to Maputo (2011) 42
Rural Mutual Aid Association (ORAM) 77, 133–4
Russian Federation 18

S
Sá de Silva, M. 53
Sabatier, P.A. 65
Salazar, António de Oliveira 26
Sanahuja, J.A. 47
São Tomé and Príncipe
  government of 34
  Independence of (1975) 32
Sarney, José 11, 34
  foreign policy of 35
Second World War (1939–45) 10
Serra, José
  Brazilian Minister of Health 181
Shankland, A. 54
Silberschmidt, G.
  concept of health diplomacy 177
Simago, David
  Mozambican Minister of Youth and Sports 40
  visit to Brazil (2006) 40
Slaughter, M. 148
Smith, A. 49
Soares, Fernando 167
Soares de Lima, Maria Regina 12, 28, 37, 108
soft power 49
South Africa 2, 17, 19, 34, 42–3, 107, 124, 185, 235, 239

Apartheid 2
South Atlantic Peace and Cooperation Zone
 (ZOPACAS)
 approved by UN (1986) 14
 reactivation of (1993) 15, 37
South–South Cooperation (SSC) 5, 12, 20,
 24, 28–9, 33, 38, 46–7, 52, 54, 107–8,
 110, 125, 170, 173, 178–9, 189, 266
 concept of 47–8
 legitimisation of 42
 motivations in 52–3, 56–8
 relationship with aid 49–50, 60–1
South-South Development Cooperation
 (SSDC) 87–9, 96, 103
 concept of 92
Southern African Development Community
 (SADC) 22
de Souza, N.J. 162
Soviet Union (USSR) 11
Spain
 MOU with ABC (2009) 110
Stahl, A.K.
 definition of trilateral cooperation 110
Strategic Plan for Development of the
 Agrarian Sector (PEDSA)
 alignment with ProSavana 96–7
Structural Adjustment Programmes 243
Student Agreement Programme (*Programa
 Estudantes Convênio*) (PEC))
 expansion of 19–20
Sudan 19
Sweden 175–6

T
Tanzania 239
Taylor, S.D. 26
Technical Cooperation between Developing
 Countries (TCDC) 38
Tete-Nacala Corridor 3, 69, 89–91, 93, 103,
 131, 133, 140, 168
 agricultural development in 101
 Brazilian development projects in
  169–70
 land appropriation in 79, 91
 Vale investments in rehabilitation of 65,
  69–71, 93, 169
Tete-Nacala Development Hub 160–1, 163
Theatre of the Oppressed Centre of Rio
 de Janeiro (*Centro de Teatro do Oprimido*
 (CTO-Rio de Janeiro)) 7, 214–23,
 225–6, 230, 233–4
 Curinga System of 217–18
 First International Conference (2009)
  224
Third Countries Training Programme
 (TCTP) 111
Triangular Conference of the Peoples (2013)
 135–6
trilateral cooperation 109–10
Truman, Harry S. 53

U
Uganda 185
 government of 55
Umbeluzi Agricultural Station 124–5
 Collective Agrofood Processing Unit
  118
United Arab Emirates (UAE) 15
United Kingdom (UK) 1
 Department for International
  Development (DFID) 178
 London 95
United Nations (UN) 1, 14, 17, 36, 42, 110,
 180
 Children's Fund (UNICEF) 214, 216,
  224, 227
 Conference on Trade and Development
  (UNCTAD) 100
 Development Programme (UNDP) 19,
  123, 161, 175
 Economic and Social Council 110
 General Assembly (UNGA) 1, 30–2, 48,
  57–8
 Educational, Scientific and Cultural
  Organization (UNESCO) 215, 233
 Human Development Index 174
 Joint United Nations Programme on
  HIV/AIDS (UNAIDS) 181
 Millennium Development Goals
  (MDGs) 19, 175
 Operation in Mozambique
  (ONUMOZ) 22, 36
 Security Council (UNSC) 48, 179
 Security Council Resolution 792 (1992)
  36
 Trust Fund 22
 World Food Programme (WFP) 262
United States of America (USA) 1, 10–11,
 36, 119, 173–4
 Center for Diseases Control and

Prevention (CDC) 186
Memorandum of Understanding with ABC (2010) 110
President's Emergency Plan for AIDS Relief (PEPFAR) 186
US Agency for International Development (USAID) 73–4, 81, 109, 111, 117, 119, 122, 124, 175, 185–6, 262
Washington DC 186
University Eduardo Mondlane 253
University of Florida (UF) 117–18, 122
USAID-ABC Strategic Framework 120

V

Vale SA 4, 6, 42, 77, 81, 83, 90, 93–4, 144, 164, 166–7, 169, 194, 208, 264–5
  activity in health sector 185–6
  formerly Companhia Vale do Rio Doce 14, 24
  investment in rehabilitation of Tete-Nacala Corridor 65, 69–71, 93, 169
  mining operations of 55, 93, 164, 183, 195, 197
  personnel of 167
  protests against 55, 264–5
  resettlement process implemented by 194–5, 197, 207
Vauday, J. 48
Via Campesina 77
Vieira, M.F. 180
Vigevani, T. 17–18, 108
Visentini, P.F. 14, 19, 21–2, 221

W

War on Terror 48
Washington Consensus 36

Werker, E. 49, 58
Women's Forum 137
Workers' Party (PT)
  members of 38
World Bank 34, 60, 68, 100, 110, 176, 180
  development indicators of 60
  infrastructure projects financed by 70
  role in development of PRE 21
  US influence on 48
World Church of the Power of God (*Igreja Mundial do Poder de Deus*) 238, 240, 253, 255
World Health Organization (WHO) 175–6
World Wide Fund for Nature (WWF) 137, 194
World Trade Organization (WTO) 176, 181
  Agreement on Trade-Related Aspects of Intellectual Property Rights (TRIPS) 180

X

Xavier, A.C. 163

Y

Yunus, M. 203

Z

Zahra, S.
  definition of absorptive capacity 149
Zambezi, River 164
Zambezi Valley Development Planning Office (GPZ)
  personnel of 72
Zambia 70
Zander, U. 148
Zimbabwe 239